THE FRONTIER

in American Literature

PERSPECTIVES ON AMERICAN LITERATURE

Robert H. Woodward and James J. Clark
General Editors

THE
FRONTIER
in American Literature

———•———

EDITED BY

PHILIP DURHAM
EVERETT L. JONES

THE ODYSSEY PRESS

Bobbs-Merrill Educational Publishing
Indianapolis

The Bobbs-Merrill Company, Inc.
4300 West 62nd Street
Indianapolis, Indiana 46268

First Edition
Sixth Printing—1977
Library of Congress Catalog Card Number: 68–31708
ISBN 0–672–63040–0 (pbk.)

Acknowledgment is gratefully made for permission to reprint the following material:

Ashley Famous Agency. For "The Indian Well" by Walter Van Tilburg
Clark from *The Watchful Gods & Other Stories,* Random House, 1950,
Copyright 1943 by Walter Van Tilburg Clark. Reprinted by permission
of Ashley Famous Agency
Ballantine Books. For extract from "Flame on the Frontier." From *Indian
Country* by Dorothy Johnson, copyright © 1949, 1950, 1951, 1952, and
1953 by Dorothy M. Johnson, published by Ballantine Books, Inc. Re-
printed by permission of Ballantine Books, Inc.
Walter J. Black, Inc. For passages from *The History of Plymouth Colony*
by William Bradford, 1948. Reprinted by permission of Walter J. Black,
Inc.
John M. Cunningham. For "The Tin Star" by John M. Cunningham,
Collier's, December 6, 1947. Reprinted by permission of the author.
Curtis Brown, Ltd. For extract from *Lord Grizzly* by Frederick Feikama
Manfred, copyright 1954 by Frederick Feikama Manfred. Reprinted by
permission of Curtis Brown, Ltd.
Doubleday & Company, Inc. For extract from *Pemmican* by Vardis Fisher.
Copyright © 1956 by Vardis Fisher. Reprinted by permission of Double-
day & Company, Inc.
E. P. Dutton & Co., Inc. For extract from *Letters from an American Farmer*
by H. Hector St. John de Crèvecoeur. Dutton & Co., Inc.
Harcourt, Brace & World, Inc. For "Scanlon" from *The Field of Vision,*
© 1956, by Wright Morris. Reprinted by permission of Harcourt, Brace
& World, Inc.
Holt, Rinehart and Winston, Inc. For extract from *The Frontier in Amer-
ican History* by Frederick Jackson Turner. Copyright 1920 by Frederick
Jackson Turner. Copyright © 1948 by Caroline M. S. Turner. For "The
Gift Outright" from *The Complete Poems of Robert Frost.* Copyright
1942 by Robert Frost. For "The Ballad of William Sycamore" from
Ballads and Poems by Stephen Vincent Benét. Copyright 1931 by Stephen
Vincent Benét. Copyright © 1959 by Rosemary Carr Benét. All of these
selections reprinted by permission of Holt, Rinehart and Winston, Inc.
Houghton Mifflin Company. For selections from *My Ántonia* by Willa
Cather. Copyright 1918, 1926, and 1946 by Willa Sibert Cather. Copyright,
1954 by Edith Lewis. For selections from *The Way West* by A. B. Guthrie,
Jr. Copyright 1949 by A. B. Guthrie, Jr. For selection from *Shane* by Jack
Schaefer. Copyright 1949 by Jack Schaefer. Copyright, 1954 by John Mc-
Cormack. All of these selections reprinted by permission of the publishers,
Houghton Mifflin Company
Alfred A. Knopf, Inc. For "The Blue Hotel" from *Stephen Crane: An
Omnibus* edited by Robert Wooster Stallman, published 1930, 1952, and
the passage, "It Came a Tuesday" from *The Trees* by Conrad Richter,
copyright 1940 and renewed 1968 by Conrad Richter. Reprinted by per-
mission of Alfred A. Knopf, Inc.

Lenniger Literary Agency. For "The Trap" by Clay Fisher, taken from *The Oldest Maiden Lady of New Mexico and Other Stories*, published by The Macmillan Company, Copyright © 1962 by Clay Fisher. Reprinted by permission of the Author and Lenniger Literary Agency.

Marsha Lee Masters. For "Harry Wilmans" and "John Wasson" from *Spoon River Anthology* by Edgar Lee Masters, 1934, The Macmillan Company. Reprinted by permission of Marsha Lee Masters.

Scott Meredith Literary Agency. For "A Day in Town" by Ernest Haycox from *The Best Western Stories of Ernest Haycox* (Bantam, 1960). Copyright © 1960 by Ernest Haycox. Reprinted by permission of the author's agents, Scott Meredith Literary Agency, Inc., 580 Fifth Avenue, New York, N.Y. 10036.

William Morrow and Company, Inc. For selection from *Honey in the Horn* by H. L. Davis, copyright 1935 by H. L. Davis. For selection from *Grant of Kingdom* by Harvey Fergusson, copyright 1950 by Harvey Fergusson. These selections reprinted by permission of William Morrow and Company, Inc.

Harold Ober Associates Incorporated. For "The Buffalo Singer" by William E. Brandon, *The North American Review*, Summer 1964. Copyright © 1964 by William E. Brandon. Reprinted by permission of Harold Ober Associates Incorporated.

University of Texas Press. For passage from *The Great Frontier* by Walter Prescott Webb, University of Texas Press, 1952. Reprinted by permission of the publishers.

Vanguard Press, Inc. For passage from *Nick of the Woods* by Robert Montgomery Bird, Vanguard Press, 1928. Reprinted with the permission of the publisher.

The Viking Press. For "The Leader of the People" by John Steinbeck from *The Red Pony* by John Steinbeck. Copyright 1938, copyright © renewed 1966 by John Steinbeck. For "Departure" from *Winesburg, Ohio* by Sherwood Anderson. Copyright 1919 by B. W. Huebsch, Inc., 1947 by Eleanor Copenhaver Anderson. For excerpt from *The Great Meadow* by Elizabeth Madox Roberts. Copyright 1930 by The Viking Press, Inc., © 1958 by Ivor S. Roberts. All these selections reprinted by permission of The Viking Press, Inc.

PREFACE

THIS BOOK is a brief introduction to the great body of literature dealing with the moving American frontier. It is neither comprehensive nor systematic; it tries merely to sample the rich variety of fiction and poetry inspired by unique American experiences.

We have included a few brief passages from the writings of famous American historians and early settlers, selections that help to define and explain the peculiar nature and importance of the frontier in American history and culture. But everything else is fiction or poetry, work that best embodies special American feelings, loyalties, and self-images. We have tried to collect materials that are intrinsically interesting, diverse, and yet somehow representative of important themes or attitudes. In assembling this collection we have refused to be bound by a strict canon of accepted authors or literary reputations. We have preferred rather to provide entertainment, variety, and challenge. Consequently, we have reprinted not only established classics but also some of the best of American popular literature.

The resulting book can be used as a supplement for the study of either history or literature. It can also be used as a controlled research textbook, as a source for documented term papers. To facilitate such use, we have used standard texts and provided complete bibliographical data for each selection. And for many readers, certainly, this book can serve as an introduction to talented and fascinating authors.

We are delighted to be able to thank the National Endowment for Humanities for supporting us in a large research project of which this is one by-product.

We are indebted to our colleagues for suggestions and assistance, and we are particularly grateful to Alan Sandy and Kathleen Lindsay of UCLA. Our greatest indebtedness is to Miss Marjorie Griffin, who has been unfailingly efficient and indefatigable in helping us plan and prepare our manuscript.

PHILIP DURHAM
EVERETT L. JONES

University of California
Los Angeles

CONTENTS

1. ATTITUDES AND INTERPRETATIONS   1
WALTER PRESCOTT WEBB: *The American Frontier Concept*   3
FREDERICK JACKSON TURNER: *The Significance of the Frontier
   in American History*   9
MICHEL-GUILLAUME JEAN DE CRÈVECOEUR: *What Is an Amer-
   ican?*   20
OWEN WISTER: Preface to *The Virginian*   26
WALT WHITMAN: *Pioneers! O Pioneers!*   28
ROBERT FROST: *The Gift Outright*   29

2. THE FORESTS   30
WILLIAM BRADFORD: *The History of the Plymouth Plantation*   32
CHARLES BROCKDEN BROWN: *Escape from the Cave*   41
NATHANIEL HAWTHORNE: *Roger Malvin's Burial*   57
WASHINGTON IRVING: *The Legend of Sleepy Hollow*   74
JAMES FENIMORE COOPER: *The Death of the Trapper*   75
CONRAD RICHTER: *It Came a Tuesday*   86
ELIZABETH MADOX ROBERTS: *Diony's Vision*   95

3. THE MIDWESTERN FRONTIER   98
EDGAR LEE MASTERS: *Harry Wilmans* and *John Wasson*   100
HAMLIN GARLAND: *Under the Lion's Paw*   102
WRIGHT MORRIS: *Scanlon*   114
WILLA CATHER: *My Ántonia*   121
SHERWOOD ANDERSON: *Departure from Winesburg*   123

4. THE MOUNTAINS   126
VARDIS FISHER: *The Grizzly and the Buffalo*   128
FREDERICK F. MANFRED: *Survival*   133
A. B. GUTHRIE, JR.: *The Way West*   137
HARVEY FERGUSSON: *Virgin Earth*   142
EDWARD L. WHEELER: *Calamity Jane*   144

5. THE OLD SOUTHWEST   147
    ROBERT MONTGOMERY BIRD: *The Jibbenainosay*   149
    AUGUSTUS BALDWIN LONGSTREET: *The Fight*   156
    THOMAS BANGS THORPE: *The Big Bear of Arkansas*   165
    MARK TWAIN: *Life on the Mississippi*   176

6. THE FAR WEST   190
    JACK LONDON: *All Gold Canyon*   192
    WALTER VAN TILBURG CLARK: *The Indian Well*   209
    H. L. DAVIS: *Honey in the Horn*   224
    MARK TWAIN: *The Celebrated Jumping Frog of Calaveras County*   231
    BRET HARTE: *The Outcasts of Poker Flat*   237
    FRANK NORRIS: *Wheat*   246
    WALT WHITMAN: *Facing West from California's Shores*   252

7. THE CATTLEMAN'S FRONTIER   253
    DOROTHY JOHNSON: *The Girl Called Bluejay*   255
    STEPHEN CRANE: *The Blue Hotel*   258
    OWEN WISTER: *The Virginian*   283
    JACK SCHAEFER: *Shane*   300
    JOHN M. CUNNINGHAM: *The Tin Star*   304
    CLAY FISHER: *The Trap*   318
    ERNEST HAYCOX: *A Day in Town*   333

8. MEMORY   345
    STEPHEN VINCENT BENÉT: *The Ballad of William Sycamore (1790–1871)*   347
    JOHN STEINBECK: *The Leader of the People*   350
    WILLIAM BRANDON: *The Buffalo Singer*   363

QUESTIONS FOR STUDY, DISCUSSION, AND WRITING   374

SUGGESTIONS FOR FURTHER READING   384

NOTES ON THE AUTHORS   386

THE FRONTIER
in American Literature

1

Attitudes and Interpretations

MOST OF AMERICAN HISTORY and much of American literature have been conditioned or influenced by the existence of a changing frontier. In our homes and in our schools many of our greatest stories and legends are about men like Captain John Smith, Lewis and Clark, Daniel Boone, Davy Crockett, and Kit Carson. We celebrate not only Washington's achievements as our Revolutionary leader and first President, but also his exploits as an Indian fighter and surveyor of the wilderness. We remember Andrew Jackson as Old Hickory, a frontier figure. We honor Abraham Lincoln as a son of the prairie woodland, a rail-splitter who read the Bible by light from a fireplace.

Until recently, a politician who had not been born in a log cabin was handicapped in any election. Theodore Roosevelt gained glamor from his career as a cattleman and his fame as the organizer of the Rough Riders. Even a New Englander like Calvin Coolidge found it wise to visit the Black Hills of South Dakota and wear an Indian headdress for newspaper photographers. And in 1960 we elected as President another New Englander who promised us a "New Frontier."

For Americans, the frontier has always been an ambivalent symbol. It has been considered a source of freedom and a place of danger; an exciting challenge, but also a cause of hardship and exhaustion; a place for heroism, but also an excuse for racism, sadism, and brutality; an inexhaustible mine of humor, but humor too often tinged with cruelty or false sentimentality. It has been idealized as a source of health, vitality, and nobility; but it has been condemned as rude, ugly, and barbaric.

To be understood in all its complexity it must first be defined. The word *frontier* has a far different meaning for Americans than for Europeans, and it is this difference that Walter Prescott Webb defines in "The American Frontier Concept" and that Frederick Jackson Turner elaborates in a famous paper.

1

Michel-Guillaume Jean de Crèvecoeur and Owen Wister express two quite different attitudes toward the frontier and frontiersmen. Crèvecoeur, living when Ohio and Kentucky lay on the edge of civilization, described the near anarchy and dirty depravity of back-settlers, the first men to occupy a wilderness. Wister, on the other hand, writing twelve years after the U.S. Government declared that the frontier no longer existed, remembered the cowboy as the last frontiersman, a vanished but romantic figure. The tension between these two attitudes pervades much of American literature.

Another tension, or at least a difference of emphasis, exists between Whitman's apostrophe to the pioneers—to the strong men and women who could conquer a continent—and Robert Frost's more complicated "salvation in surrender" to the land "vaguely realizing westward." In these two poems the frontier finds two great but dissimilar literary celebrants.

WALTER PRESCOTT WEBB

The American Frontier Concept

THE WORD FRONTIER appears in similar form in nearly all the western European languages; and, as used in Europe, it means the boundary between two nations and is represented on maps by a thin line. It implies that the nations must not cross that line except by permission or at national peril; it is "the sharp edge of sovereignty," the door or bastion of a neighbor, friendly or hostile as the case may be. There protocol and diplomacy become important and a "frontier incident" may well become an international affair. In the United States the word *frontier* has an entirely different meaning, and carries a different set of implications and connotations. It becomes a concept with such wide ramifications and so many shades of meaning that it cannot be wrapped up in a neat definition like a word whose growth has ceased and whose meaning has become frozen. It is something that lives, moves geographically, and eventually dies.

In America the word is hardly used at all to indicate the nation's limits. No American would refer to the line separating the United States from Canada or that from Mexico as the frontier, and to apply it to them in this sense would lead to misunderstanding.[1] The American thinks of the frontier as lying *within,* and not at the edge of a country. It is not a line to stop at, but an *area* inviting entrance. Instead of having one dimension, length, as in Europe, the American frontier has two [2/3] dimensions, length and breadth. In Europe the frontier is stationary and presumably permanent; in America it *was* transient and temporal.[2]

[1] The line separating the United States from Canada is generally referred to as the boundary; that separating the country from Mexico is likely to be called the border. The distinction is a nice one, and probably comes from the historic fact that there has been more friction between the United States and Mexico than between it and Canada. There has also been more lawlessness on both sides along the southern line, and the word border suggests that.

[2] See Fulmer Mood, "Notes on the History of the Word *Frontier,*" *Agricultural History,* XXII (April, 1948), pp. 78–83. The evolution of the American meaning of the word is here traced from 1623 to recent times.

The concept of a moving frontier is applicable where a civilized people are advancing into a wilderness, an unsettled area, or one sparsely populated by primitive people. It was the sort of land into which the Boers moved in South Africa, the English in Australia, and the Americans and Canadians in their progress westward across North America. The frontier movement is an invasion of a land assumed to be vacant as distinguished from an invasion of an occupied or civilized country, an advance against nature rather than against men. On a frontier the invaders often have immediate and exclusive possession whereas in a nonfrontier the invaders have to contend with the original inhabitants whom they always find troublesome and frequently too much for them. Inherent in the American concept of a moving frontier is the idea of a body of free land which can be had for the taking.

This expanded concept of the frontier grew out of the American experience as the sole proprietor of an unsettled contiguous territory. Always, for three centuries, to the west of the settlements there stretched an empty country inviting settlement, luring the venturesome toward the sunset. Of this territory the United States came piece by piece into undisputed possession. No foreign power contended for it; it therefore did not present a problem in sovereignty, and movement into it was civilian, not military.[3] The territory was adjacent to the settled area, and the journey there did not involve a sea voyage, a long trek, or any considerable outlay of capital. The settlers who went there were not colonists, and the land to which they went was in no sense a colony. The settlers were citizens moving into territory owned by the nation. The only thing that distinguished these citizens and this territory from [3/4] the older region was the fact that the processes current were a step or two behind the processes of the older region, say in Virginia or Massachusetts.[4] It was understood on all sides that the status of the individual as a citi-

---

[3] I am ignoring the scattered Indian population who did present some resistance but were not a major problem except for the few people who were in contact with them on the farthest fringes of settlement. In the present area of the United States the Indian population was probably not more than 500,000, one Indian to about six square miles.

[4] The American method of expansion was simple and, for the people, highly impersonal. When new territory was acquired, it was understood that within a short time it would be cut up into states which would be admitted to the Union. The process was as follows:

1. Acquisition of an area by purchase, conquest, or treaty.
2. Government of the area as unorganized territory.
3. Territorial organization of prospective state or states.
4. Admission of organized territory into Union.

From the time of acquisition until admission, the territory, organized or unzen was unchanged, and that within a short time the new territory would become automatically a state in the Union whose status would not differ from that of the oldest member. The absence of the military, the proximity of the new land to the old, the ease of migration, and the absence of any attempt on the part of government to regulate or control the process made the whole American situation the last word in simplicity, so simple that it amounted to chaos. In these respects the movement of the American people into the frontier after independence was unlike the movement of people from European nations into their overseas colonial possessions.

American historians assume that the frontier process began with the English settlement at Jamestown, Virginia, in 1607. Since the process depended on the act of taking possession of new land, it would go on as long as there was new land to be taken. The year 1890 is usually accepted as marking the date when there was no more frontier available, when the new land was no longer new. Though there is some quibbling about the date, 1890 does approximate the end of the frontier process in the United States, an experience of almost three centuries.[5]

It is the magnitude and the unbroken continuity of the experience that makes the frontier of major importance in American development. It made no difference what other tasks the [4/5] Americans had on their hands at a given time, there was the additional, ever-present task of moving into and settling new country. They did it while they fought for independence, before and after; they did it while they hammered out the principles of a democratic government and that government was eventually shaped to the needs of frontier men; and they did not cease doing it in the period of civil strife. They rarely reached the limits of the vacancy they owned before they acquired another vacancy, the Louisiana territory by purchase, the Florida country by negotiation, Texas by treaty, and the southwestern quarter of the United States by conquest.[6] In every case the

---

organized, was governed by the United States Congress. After admission, state and local government was in the hands of the resident people. Any citizen of the United States could migrate to and become a legal resident of a territory without permit or formality of any sort. The land was never a colony nor the resident a colonist.

[5] The year 1890 is generally given as the date marking the close of the frontier. Actually the closing was gradual, covering the period from 1880 to 1910.

[6] The territorial expansion of the United States occurred in the following order: Louisiana territory, 1803; Florida, 1819; Teaxs, 1845; the Oregon country, 1846; the Southwestern territory, including all or part of seven present states, 1848. These acquisitions were all made in advance of the migratory horde that was moving west with the result that vacant land was available throughout the nineteenth century.

frontiersmen had infiltrated the country before the nation acquired it. Like locusts they swarmed, always to the west, and only the Pacific Ocean stopped them.

It would be strange indeed if such an experience as this should have had no effect on the people and the nation. Could people have as their main task for three centuries working with raw land without getting its dirt under their nails and deep under their skins? The effects were present everywhere, in democratic government, in boisterous politics, in exploitive agriculture, in mobility of population, in disregard for conventions, in rude manners, and in unbridled optimism. Though these effects were present everywhere, they were not understood anywhere by the people who felt and reflected them. The frontier lacked its philosopher, the thinker who could view the whole scene and the whole dramatic experience and tell what was its meaning. This philosopher arrived three years after the experience ended and told the American people that from the beginning the American frontier had been the dominant force, the determining influence in their history.

It was in 1893 that a young and unknown historian appeared before the American Historical Association and read a paper entitled "The Significance of the Frontier in American History." That paper made him a scholar with honor in his own [5/6] country, for, brief though his essay is, it is recognized as the most influential single piece of historical writing ever done in the United States. It altered the whole course of American historical scholarship. The young man was Frederick Jackson Turner of the University of Wisconsin. Following Turner's lead, there arose in the United States a whole school of frontier historians who have worked out in many directions the rich mine that Turner opened up. It is not necessary here to elaborate Turner's famous thesis except to reiterate that it expounded the overwhelming importance of the frontier as the dominant force in creating a democracy and making the individual free from Old World restrictions.[7]

[7] The essay appears in various places but is most accessible in Frederick Jackson Turner, *The Frontier in American History* (New York: Henry Holt and Co., Inc., 1920), pp. 1–38. For the pros and cons of the Turner thesis see George Rogers Taylor (ed.), *The Turner Thesis Concerning the Role of the Frontier in American History* (Boston: D. C. Heath and Co., 1949). A much quoted passage from the opening paragraph reads: "Up to our own day American history has been in a large degree the history of the colonization of the Great West. *The existence of an area of free land, its continuous recession, and the advance of American settlement westward, explain American development.*" (Italics supplied.)

Though Turner's interpretation has been challenged, it has continued to grow, and its influence has spread to literature, political science, philosophy, and even

What should be emphasized is that Turner confined his attention to *American* history. The frontier that he talked about was the new *American* land lying west of the *American* settlements. His disciples and followers have not greatly extended the scope of his investigation. Most of them have treated the frontier as if it were something exclusively American, as if the United States were the only nation that had felt the powerful influence of access to vacant land. As for historians in other countries,[8] in the New World or the Old World, they have with few exceptions ignored the frontier completely, have never become more than vaguely conscious of its existence. As stated above, the European scholars, excepting W. K. Hancock of Oxford (formerly of Australia), Eric A. Walker of Cambridge (formerly of South Africa), and Fred Alexander of Aus- [6/7] tralia,[9] have not even noticed the frontier concept, have not broadened the meaning of the term beyond its application to a boundary line.

I have often thought that each nation has something peculiar to itself that could be borrowed with advantage by its neighbors. If I could export one thing American to European scholars, something which, I believe, would help them to a better understanding of their troubled world, our troubled world, it would be an understanding of the frontier—not the American frontier, but their own—and its significance in their history and in their present lives. It is the American frontier concept that needs to be lifted out of its present national setting and applied on a much larger scale to all of Western civilization in modern times. This application will be of interest to European scholars only insofar as it helps them to a better understanding of their own history. The basic assumption for the discussion of the frontier as a factor in western European civilization is that Europe, too, had a frontier.

Europe had a frontier within the American concept more than a century before the United States was settled. Europe's frontier was much greater than that of the United States, included the present United States, and was the greatest frontier of world record. The frontier was almost if not quite as important in determining the life and institutions of modern Europe as it was in shaping the course of American history. Without its frontier modern Europe would be so

---

to psychiatry. It is today imbedded in the fabric of American thought, and is slowly invading other frontier societies.

[8] Canada is an exception. Its proximity to the United States has made it impossible for Canadian historians to escape the frontier hypothesis.

[9] Eric A. Walker, *The Frontier Tradition in South Africa* (London: Oxford University Press, 1930); W. K. Hancock, *Survey of British Commonwealth Affairs* (London: Oxford University Press, 1940), chap. I; Fred Alexander, *Moving Frontiers* (Melbourne: University Press, 1947).

different from what it is that it could hardly be considered modern at all. The close of Europe's frontier may mark the end of an epoch in Western civilization, and as a result of that close, many of the institutions designed to function in a society dominated by frontier forces should find themselves in strain and crisis.

The relation between Europe and its frontier must be surveyed from the date the relationship was established, say about the year 1500, down to the present year (1950), in the perspec- [7/8] tive of 450 years. But before examining this relationship it is necessary to define the terms mentioned earlier so that we may not be lost in the complexities of the long period of history. The nature of the subject makes it necessary for us to ignore the artificial subdivisions of the two reciprocal regions whose relationships are to be examined. To divide Europe as the politicians have done is to invite confusion, and to divide the frontier as the Europeans did is to confound the confusion. Our task is to discover and impose a unity on each one which is not superficially apparent, the unity of western Europe and the unity of its opposite, the frontier. Once we conceive of western Europe as a unified, densely populated small region with a common culture and civilization—which it has always had basically—and once we see the frontier also as a unit, as a vast and vacant land without culture, we are in position to view the interaction between the two as a simple but gigantic operation extending over more than four centuries, an operation which may well appear as the drama of modern civilization.[10] [8]

[10] Adam Smith was able to view Europe, the Metropolis, as a unit, and to see that the frontier (colonies) exerted an influence on the whole. He wrote:

"The general advantages which Europe, *considered as a great country*, has derived from the discovery and colonization of America, consist, first, in the increase of its enjoyments; and secondly, in the augmentation of its industry. [Italics supplied.]

"The surplus produce of America, imported into Europe, furnishes the inhabitants of this great continent with a variety of commodities which they could not otherwise have possessed. . . .

"The discovery and colonization of America . . . have contributed to augment the industry, first, of all the countries which trade to it directly . . . and, secondly, of all those which, without trading to it directly, send, through the medium of other countries, goods to it of their own produce."—Adam Smith, *An Inquiry into the Nature and Causes of the Wealth of Nations*, Edwin Cannan, ed. (London: Methuen and Co., 1904), vol. II, chap. VII, pt. III, p. 92.

He goes on to elaborate the indivisible influence of the new country on Europe.

FREDERICK JACKSON TURNER

The Significance of the Frontier in American History[1]

IN A RECENT BULLETIN of the Superintendent of the Census for 1890 appear these significant words: "Up to and including 1880 the country had a frontier of settlement, but at present the unsettled area has been so broken into by isolated bodies of settlement that there can hardly be said to be a frontier line. In the discussion of its extent, its westward movement, etc., it can not, therefore, any longer have a place in the census reports." This brief official statement marks the closing of a great historic movement. Up to our own day American history has been in a large degree the history of the colonization of the Great West. The existence of an area of free land, its continuous recession, and the advance of American settlement westward, explain American development. [1/2]

Behind institutions, behind constitutional forms and modifications, lie the vital forces that call these organs into life and shape them to meet changing conditions. The peculiarity of American in-

Only the introductory section of Turner's famous paper is reprinted here. [Ed. note]

[1] A paper read at the meeting of the American Historical Association in Chicago, July 12, 1893. It first appeared in the Proceedings of the State Historical Society of Wisconsin, December 14, 1893, with the following note: "The foundation of this paper is my article entitled 'Problems in American History,' which appeared in *The Ægis,* a publication of the students of the University of Wisconsin, November 2, 1892. . . . It is gratifying to find that Professor Woodrow Wilson—whose volume on 'Division and Reunion' in the Epochs of American History Series, has an appreciative estimate of the importance of the West as a factor in American History —accepts some of the views set forth in the papers above mentioned, and enhances their value by his lucid and suggestive treatment of them in his article in *The Forum,* December, 1893, reviewing Goldwin Smith's 'History of the United States.'" The present text is that of the *Report of the American Historical Association* for 1893, 199–227. It was printed with additions in the *Fifth Year Book of the National Herbart Society,* and in various other publications.

9

stitutions is the fact that they have been compelled to adapt themselves to the changes of an expanding people—to the changes involved in crossing a continent, in winning a wilderness, and in developing at each area of this progress out of the primitive economic
and political conditions of the frontier into the complexity of city
life. Said Calhoun in 1817, "We are great, and rapidly—I was about
to say fearfully—growing!"[2] So saying, he touched the distinguishing
feature of American life. All peoples show development; the germ
theory of politics has been sufficiently emphasized. In the case of
most nations, however, the development has occurred in a limited
area; and if the nation has expanded, it has met other growing peoples whom it has conquered. But in the case of the United States we
have a different phenomenon. Limiting our attention to the Atlantic
coast, we have the familiar phenomenon of the evolution of institutions in a limited area, such as the rise of representative government; the differentiation of simple colonial governments into complex organs; the progress from primitive industrial society, without
division of labor, up to manufacturing civilization. But we have in
addition to this a recurrence of the process of evolution in each western area reached in the process of expansion. Thus American development has exhibited not merely advance along a single line, but a
return to primitive conditions on a continually advancing frontier
line, and a new development for that area. American social development has been continually beginning over again on the frontier.
This perennial rebirth, this fluidity of American life, this expansion
westward with its new opportunities, its continuous touch with
[2/3] the simplicity of primitive society, furnish the forces dominating American character. The true point of view in the history of this
nation is not the Atlantic coast, it is the Great West. Even the slav-
ery struggle, which is made so exclusive an object of attention by
writers like Professor von Holst, occupies its important place in
American history because of its relation to westward expansion.

   In this advance, the frontier is the outer edge of the wave—the
meeting point between savagery and civilization. Much has been
written about the frontier from the point of view of border warfare
and the chase, but as a field for the serious study of the economist
and the historian it has been neglected.

   The American frontier is sharply distinguished from the European frontier—a fortified boundary line running through dense pop-
ulations. The most significant thing about the American frontier is,
that it lies at the hither edge of free land. In the census reports it is
treated as the margin of that settlement which has a density of two

[2] "Abridgment of Debates of Congress," v, p. 706.

or more to the square mile. The term is an elastic one, and for our purposes does not need sharp definition. We shall consider the whole frontier belt, including the Indian country and the outer margin of the "settled area" of the census reports. This paper will make no attempt to treat the subject exhaustively; its aim is simply to call attention to the frontier as a fertile field for investigation, and to suggest some of the problems which arise in connection with it.

In the settlement of America we have to observe how European life entered the continent, and how America modified and developed that life and reacted on Europe. Our early history is the study of European germs developing in an American environment. Too exclusive attention has been paid by institutional students to the Germanic origins, too little to the American factors. The frontier is the line of [3/4] most rapid and effective Americanization. The wilderness masters the colonist. It finds him a European in dress, industries, tools, modes of travel, and thought. It takes him from the railroad car and puts him in the birch canoe. It strips off the garments of civilization and arrays him in the hunting shirt and the moccasin. It puts him in the log cabin of the Cherokee and Iroquois and runs an Indian palisade around him. Before long he has gone to planting Indian corn and plowing with a sharp stick; he shouts the war cry and takes the scalp in orthodox Indian fashion. In short, at the frontier the environment is at first too strong for the man. He must accept the conditions which it furnishes, or perish, and so he fits himself into the Indian clearings and follows the Indian trails. Little by little he transforms the wilderness, but the outcome is not the old Europe, not simply the development of Germanic germs, any more than the first phenomenon was a case of reversion to the Germanic mark. The fact is, that here is a new product that is American. At first, the frontier was the Atlantic coast. It was the frontier of Europe in a very real sense. Moving westward, the frontier became more and more American. As successive terminal moraines result from successive glaciations, so each frontier leaves its traces behind it, and when it becomes a settled area the region still partakes of the frontier characteristics. Thus the advance of the frontier has meant a steady movement away from the influence of Europe, a steady growth of independence on American lines. And to study this advance, the men who grew up under these conditions, and the political, economic, and social results of it, is to study the really American part of our history.

In the course of the seventeenth century the frontier was advanced up the Atlantic river courses, just beyond the "fall line," and the tidewater region became the settled area. In [4/5] the first half of the eighteenth century another advance occurred. Traders followed the

Delaware and Shawnese Indians to the Ohio as early as the end of the first quarter of the century.[3] Gov. Spotswood, of Virginia, made an expedition in 1714 across the Blue Ridge. The end of the first quarter of the century saw the advance of the Scotch-Irish and the Palatine Germans up the Shenandoah Valley into the western part of Virginia, and along the Piedmont region of the Carolinas.[4] The Germans in New York pushed the frontier of settlement up the Mohawk to German Flats.[5] In Pennsylvania the town of Bedford indicates the line of settlement. Settlements soon began on the New River, or the Great Kanawha, and on the sources of the Yadkin and French Broad.[6] The King attempted to arrest the advance by his proclamation of 1763,[7] forbidding settlements beyond the sources of the rivers flowing into the Atlantic; but in vain. In the period of the Revolution the frontier crossed the Alleghanies into Kentucky and Tennessee, and the upper waters of the Ohio were settled.[8] When the first census was taken in 1790, the continuous settled area was bounded by a line which ran near the coast of Maine, and included New England except a portion of Vermont and New Hampshire, New York along the Hudson [5/6] and up the Mohawk about Schenectady, eastern and southern Pennsylvania, Virginia well across the Shenandoah Valley, and the Carolinas and eastern Georgia.[9] Beyond

---

[3] Bancroft (1860 ed.), iii, pp. 344, 345, citing Logan MSS.; [Mitchell] "Contest in America," etc. (1752), p. 237.

[4] Kercheval, "History of the Valley"; Bernheim, "German Settlements in the Carolinas"; Winsor, "Narrative and Critical History of America," v, p. 304; Colonial Records of North Carolina, iv, p. xx; Weston, "Documents Connected with the History of South Carolina," p. 82; Ellis and Evans, "History of Lancaster County, Pa.," chs. iii, xxvi.

[5] Parkman, "Pontiac," ii; Griffis, "Sir William Johnson," p. 6; Simms's "Frontiersmen of New York."

[6] Monette, "Mississippi Valley," i, p. 311.

[7] Wis. Hist. Cols., xi, p. 50; Hinsdale, "Old Northwest," p. 121; Burke, "Oration on Conciliation," Works (1872 ed.), i, p. 473.

[8] Roosevelt, "Winning of the West," and citations there given; Cutler's "Life of Cutler."

[9] Scribner's Statistical Atlas, xxxviii, pl. 13; McMaster, "Hist. of People of U.S.," i, pp. 4, 60, 61; Imlay and Filson, "Western Territory of America" (London, 1793); Rochefoucault-Liancourt, "Travels Through the United States of North America" (London, 1799); Michaux's "Journal," in *Proceedings American Philosophical Society*, xxvi, No. 129; Forman, "Narrative of a Journey Down the Ohio and Mississippi in 1780-'90" (Cincinnati, 1888); Bartram, "Travels Through North Carolina," etc. (London, 1792); Pope, "Tour Through the Southern and Western Territories," etc. (Richmond, 1792); Weld, "Travels Through the States of North America" (London, 1799); Baily, "Journal of a Tour in the Unsettled States of North America, 1796-'97" (London, 1856); Pennsylvania Magazine of History, July, 1886; Winsor, "Narrative and Critical History of America," vii, pp. 491, 492, citations.

this region of continuous settlement were the small settled areas of Kentucky and Tennessee, and the Ohio, with the mountains intervening between them and the Atlantic area, thus giving a new and important character to the frontier. The isolation of the region increased its peculiarly American tendencies, and the need of transportation facilities to connect it with the East called out important schemes of internal improvement, which will be noted farther on. The "West," as a self-conscious section, began to evolve.

From decade to decade distinct advances of the frontier occurred. By the census of 1820[10] the settled area included Ohio, southern Indiana and Illinois, southeastern Missouri, and about one-half of Louisiana. This settled area had surrounded Indian areas, and the management of these tribes became an object of political concern. The frontier region of the time lay along the Great Lakes, where Astor's American Fur Company operated in the Indian trade,[11] and beyond the Mississippi, [6/7] where Indian traders extended their activity even to the Rocky Mountains; Florida also furnished frontier conditions. The Mississippi River region was the scene of typical frontier settlements.[12]

The rising steam navigation[13] on western waters, the opening of the Erie Canal, and the westward extension of cotton[14] culture added five frontier states to the Union in this period. Grund, writing in 1836, declares: "It appears then that the universal disposition of Americans to emigrate to the western wilderness, in order to enlarge their dominion over inanimate nature, is the actual result of an expansive power which is inherent in them, and which by contin-

[10] Scribner's Statistical Atlas, xxxix.

[11] Turner, "Character and Influence of the Indian Trade in Wisconsin" (Johns Hopkins University Studies, Series ix), pp. 61 ff.

[12] Monette, "History of the Mississippi Valley," ii; Flint, "Travels and Residence in Mississippi," Flint, "Geography and History of the Western States," "Abridgment of Debates of Congress," vii, pp. 397, 398, 404; Holmes, "Account of the U.S."; Kingdom, "America and the British Colonies" (London, 1820); Grund, "Americans," ii, chs. i, iii, vi (although writing in 1836, he treats of conditions that grew out of western advance from the era of 1820 to that time); Peck, "Guide for Emigrants" (Boston, 1831); Darby, "Emigrants' Guide to Western and Southwestern States and Territories"; Dana, "Geographical Sketches in the Western Country"; Kinzie, "Waubun"; Keating, "Narrative of Long's Expedition"; Schoolcraft, "Discovery of the Sources of the Mississippi River," "Travels in the Central Portions of the Mississippi Valley," and "Lead Mines of the Missouri"; Andreas, "History of Illinois," i, 86–99; Hurlbut, "Chicago Antiquities"; McKenney, "Tour to the Lakes"; Thomas, "Travels Through the Western Country," etc. (Auburn, N.Y., 1819).

[13] Darby, "Emigrants' Guide," pp. 272 ff; Benton, "Abridgment of Debates," vii, p. 397.

[14] De Bow's *Review*, iv, p. 254; xvii, p. 428.

ually agitating all classes of society is constantly throwing a large
portion of the whole population on the extreme confines of the
State, in order to gain space for its development. Hardly is a new
State or Territory formed before the same principle manifests itself
again and gives rise to a further emigration; and so is it destined to
go on until a physical barrier must finally obstruct its progress."[15]
[7/8]

In the middle of this century the line indicated by the present
eastern boundary of Indian Territory, Nebraska, and Kansas
marked the frontier of the Indian country.[16] Minnesota and Wisconsin still exhibited frontier conditions,[17] but the distinctive frontier
of the period is found in California, where the gold discoveries had
sent a sudden tide of adventurous miners, and in Oregon, and the
settlements in Utah.[18] As the frontier had leaped over the Alleghanies, so now it skipped the Great Plains and the Rocky Mountains;
and in the same way that the advance of the frontiersmen beyond
the Alleghanies had caused the rise of important questions of transportation and internal improvement, so now the settlers beyond the
Rocky Mountains needed means of communication with the East,
and in the furnishing of these arose the settlement of the Great
Plains and the development of still another kind [8/9] of frontier
life. Railroads, fostered by land grants, sent an increasing tide of immigrants into the Far West. The United States Army fought a series
of Indian wars in Minnesota, Dakota, and the Indian Territory.

[15] Grund, "Americans," ii, p. 8.
[16] Peck, "New Guide to the West" (Cincinnati, 1848), ch. iv; Parkman, "Oregon
Trail"; Hall, "The West" (Cincinnati, 1848); Pierce, "Incidents of Western
Travel"; Murray, "Travels in North America"; Lloyd, "Steamboat Directory"
(Cincinnati, 1856); "Forty Days in a Western Hotel" (Chicago), in *Putnam's Maga-
zine,* December, 1894; Mackay, "The Western World," ii, ch. ii, iii; Meeker, "Life
in the West"; Bogen, "German in America" (Boston, 1851); Olmstead, "Texas
Journey"; Greeley, "Recollections of a Busy Life"; Schouler, "History of the
United States," v, 261–267; Peyton, "Over the Alleghanies and Across the Prairies"
(London, 1870); Loughborough, "The Pacific Telegraph and Railway" (St. Louis,
1849); Whitney, "Project for a Railroad to the Pacific" (New York, 1849); Peyton,
"Suggestions on Railroad Communication with the Pacific, and the Trade of
China and the Indian Islands"; Benton, "Highway to the Pacific" (a speech delivered in the U.S. Senate, December 16, 1850).
[17] A writer in *The Home Missionary* (1850), p. 239, reporting Wisconsin conditions, exclaims: "Think of this, people of the enlightened East. What an example,
to come from the very frontier of civilization!" But one of the missionaries writes:
"In a few years Wisconsin will no longer be considered as the West, or as an out-
post of civilization, any more than Western New York, or the Western Reserve."
[18] Bancroft (H. H.), "History of California," "History of Oregon," and "Popular
Tribunals"; Shinn, "Mining Camps."

By 1880 the settled area had been pushed into northern Michigan, Wisconsin, and Minnesota, along Dakota rivers, and in the Black Hills region, and was ascending the rivers of Kansas and Nebraska. The development of mines in Colorado had drawn isolated frontier settlements into that region, and Montana and Idaho were receiving settlers. The frontier was found in these mining camps and the ranches of the Great Plains. The superintendent of the census for 1890 reports, as previously stated, that the settlements of the West lie so scattered over the region that there can no longer be said to be a frontier line.

In these successive frontiers we find natural boundary lines which have served to mark and to affect the characteristics of the frontiers, namely: the "fall line;" the Alleghany Mountains; the Mississippi; the Missouri where its direction approximates north and south; the line of the arid lands, approximately the ninety-ninth meridian; and the Rocky Mountains. The fall line marked the frontier of the seventeenth century; the Alleghanies that of the eighteenth; the Mississippi that of the first quarter of the nineteenth; the Missouri that of the middle of this century (omitting the California movement); and the belt of the Rocky Mountains and the arid tract, the present frontier. Each was won by a series of Indian wars.

At the Atlantic frontier one can study the germs of processes repeated at each successive frontier. We have the complex European life sharply precipitated by the wilderness into the simplicity of primitive conditions. The first frontier had to meet its Indian question, its question of the disposition of the public domain, of the means of intercourse with older settlements, of the extension of political organization, of religious [9/10] and educational activity. And the settlement of these and similar questions for one frontier served as a guide for the next. The American student needs not to go to the "prim little townships of Sleswick" for illustrations of the law of continuity and development. For example, he may study the origin of our land policies in the colonial land policy; he may see how the system grew by adapting the statutes to the customs of the successive frontiers.[19] He may see how the mining experience in the lead regions of Wisconsin, Illinois, and Iowa was applied to the mining laws of the Sierras,[20] and how our Indian policy has been a series of experimentations on successive frontiers. Each tier of new States has found in the older ones material for its constitutions.[21] Each

[19] See the suggestive paper by Prof. Jesse Macy, "The Institutional Beginnings of a Western State."

[20] Shinn, "Mining Camps."

[21] Compare Thorpe, in *Annals American Academy of Political and Social Science,* September, 1891; Bryce, "American Commonwealth" (1888), ii, p. 689.

frontier has made similar contributions to American character, as
will be discussed farther on.

But with all these similarities there are essential differences, due
to the place element and the time element. It is evident that the
farming frontier of the Mississippi Valley presents different conditions from the mining frontier of the Rocky Mountains. The frontier reached by the Pacific Railroad, surveyed into rectangles,
guarded by the United States Army, and recruited by the daily im-
migrant ship, moves forward at a swifter pace and in a different way
than the frontier reached by the birch canoe or the pack horse. The
geologist traces patiently the shores of ancient seas, maps their areas,
and compares the older and the newer. It would be a work worth the
historian's labors to mark these various frontiers and in detail compare one with another. Not only would there result a [10/11] more
adequate conception of American development and characteristics,
but invaluable additions would be made to the history of society.

Loria,[22] the Italian economist, has urged the study of colonial life
as an aid in understanding the stages of European development, af-
firming that colonial settlement is for economic science what the
mountain is for geology, bringing to light primitive stratifications.
"America," he says, "has the key to the historical enigma which Europe has sought for centuries in vain, and the land which has no history reveals luminously the course of universal history." There is
much truth in this. The United States lies like a huge page in the
history of society. Line by line as we read this continental page from
West to East we find the record of social evolution. It begins with
the Indian and the hunter; it goes on to tell of the disintegration of
savagery by the entrance of the trader, the pathfinder of civilization;
we read the annals of the pastoral stage in ranch life; the exploitation of the soil by the raising of unrotated crops of corn and wheat
in sparsely settled farming communities; the intensive culture of the
denser farm settlement; and finally the manufacturing organization
with city and factory system.[23] This page is familiar to the student of
census statistics, but how little of it has been used by our historians.
Particularly in eastern States this page is a palimpsest. What is now a
manufacturing State was in an earlier decade an area of intensive
farming. Earlier yet it had been a wheat area, and still earlier the
"range" had attracted the cattleherder. Thus Wisconsin, now devel-

[22] Loria, Analisi della Proprieta Capitalista, ii, p. 15.
[23] Compare "Observations on the North American Land Company," London,
1796, pp. xv, 144; Logan, "History of Upper South Carolina," i, pp. 149–151;
Turner, "Character and Influence of Indian Trade in Wisconsin," p. 18; Peck,
"New Guide for Emigrants" (Boston, 1837), ch. iv; "Compendium Eleventh
Census," i, p. xl.

oping manufacture, is a [11/12] State with varied agricultural interests. But earlier it was given over to almost exclusive grain-raising, like North Dakota at the present time.

Each of these areas has had an influence in our economic and political history; the evolution of each into a higher stage has worked political transformations. But what constitutional historian has made any adequate attempt to interpret political facts by the light of these social areas and changes?[24]

The Atlantic frontier was compounded of fisherman, fur-trader, miner, cattle-raiser, and farmer. Excepting the fisherman, each type of industry was on the march toward the West, impelled by an irresistible attraction. Each passed in successive waves across the continent. Stand at Cumberland Gap and watch the procession of civilization, marching single file—the buffalo following the trail to the salt springs, the Indian, the fur-trader and hunter, the cattle-raiser, the pioneer farmer—and the frontier has passed by. Stand at South Pass in the Rockies a century later and see the same procession with wider intervals between. The unequal rate of advance compels us to distinguish the frontier into the trader's frontier, the rancher's frontier, or the miner's frontier, and the farmer's frontier. When the mines and the cow pens were still near the fall line the traders' pack trains were tinkling across the Alleghanies, and the French on the Great Lakes were fortifying their posts, alarmed by the British trader's birch canoe. When the trappers scaled the Rockies, the farmer was still near the mouth of the Missouri.

Why was it that the Indian trader passed so rapidly across the continent? What effects followed from the trader's frontier? The trade was coeval with American discovery. The Norsemen, Vespuccius, Verrazani, Hudson, John Smith, all [12/13] trafficked for furs. The Plymouth pilgrims settled in Indian cornfields, and their first return cargo was of beaver and lumber. The records of the various New England colonies show how steadily exploration was carried into the wilderness by this trade. What is true for New England is, as would be expected, even plainer for the rest of the colonies. All along the coast from Maine to Georgia the Indian trade opened up the river courses. Steadily the trader passed westward, utilizing the older lines of French trade. The Ohio, the Great Lakes, the Mississippi, the Missouri, and the Platte, the lines of western advance, were ascended by traders. They found the passes in the Rocky Mountains and guided Lewis and Clark,[25] Frémont, and Bidwell. The explanation

---

[24] See *post,* for illustrations of the political accompaniments of changed industrial conditions.

[25] But Lewis and Clark were the first to explore the route from the Missouri to the Columbia.

of the rapidity of this advance is connected with the effects of the trader on the Indian. The trading post left the unarmed tribes at the mercy of those that had purchased fire-arms—a truth which the Iroquois Indians wrote in blood, and so the remote and unvisited tribes gave eager welcome to the trader. "The savages," wrote La Salle, "take better care of us French than of their own children; from us only can they get guns and goods." This accounts for the trader's power and the rapidity of his advance. Thus the disintegrating forces of civilization entered the wilderness. Every river valley and Indian trail became a fissure in Indian society, and so that society became honeycombed. Long before the pioneer farmer appeared on the scene, primitive Indian life had passed away. The farmers met Indians armed with guns. The trading frontier, while steadily undermining Indian power by making the tribes ultimately dependent on the whites, yet, through its sale of guns, gave to the Indian increased power of resistance to the farming frontier. French colonization was dominated [13/14] by its trading frontier; English colonization by its farming frontier. There was an antagonism between the two frontiers as between the two nations. Said Duquesne to the Iroquois, "Are you ignorant of the difference between the king of England and the king of France? Go see the forts that our king has established and you will see that you can still hunt under their very walls. They have been placed for your advantage in places which you frequent. The English, on the contrary, are no sooner in possession of a place than the game is driven away. The forest falls before them as they advance, and the soil is laid bare so that you can scarce find the wherewithal to erect a shelter for the night."

And yet, in spite of this opposition of the interests of the trader and the farmer, the Indian trade pioneered the way for civilization. The buffalo trail became the Indian trail, and this became the trader's "trace;" the trails widened into roads, and the roads into turnpikes, and these in turn were transformed into railroads. The same origin can be shown for the railroads of the South, the Far West, and the Dominion of Canada.[26] The trading posts reached by these trails were on the sites of Indian villages which had been placed in positions suggested by nature; and these trading posts, situated so as to command the water systems of the country, have grown into such cities as Albany, Pittsburgh, Detroit, Chicago, St. Louis, Council Bluffs and Kansas City. Thus civilization in America has followed the arteries made by geology, pouring an ever richer tide through

[26] "Narrative and Critical History of America," viii, p. 10; Sparks' "Washington Works," ix, pp. 303, 327; Logan, "History of Upper South Carolina," i; McDonald, "Life of Kenton," p. 72; Cong. Record, xxiii, p. 57.

them, until at last the slender paths of aboriginal intercourse have been broadened and interwoven into the complex mazes of modern commercial lines; the wil- [14/15] derness has been interpenetrated by lines of civilization growing ever more numerous. It is like the steady growth of a complex nervous system for the originally simple, inert continent. If one would understand why we are to-day one nation, rather than a collection of isolated states, he must study this economic and social consolidation of the country. In this progress from savage conditions lie topics for the evolutionist.[27] [15]

[27] On the effect of the fur trade in opening the routes of migration, see the author's "Character and Influence of the Indian Trade in Wisconsin."

MICHEL-GUILLAUME JEAN
de CRÈVECOEUR

What Is an American?

I WISH I could be acquainted with the feelings and thoughts which must agitate the heart and present themselves to the mind of an enlightened Englishman, when he first lands on this continent. He must greatly rejoice that he lived at a time to see this fair country discovered and settled; he must necessarily feel a share of national pride, when he views the chain of settlements which embellishes these extended shores. When he says to himself, this is the work of my countrymen, who, when convulsed by factions, afflicted by a variety of miseries and wants, restless and impatient, took refuge here. They brought along with them their national genius, to which they principally owe what liberty they enjoy, and what substance they possess. Here he sees the industry of his native country displayed in a new manner, and traces in their works the embryos of all the arts, sciences, and ingenuity which flourish in Europe. Here he beholds fair cities, substantial villages, extensive fields, an immense country filled with decent houses, good roads, orchards, meadows, and bridges, where an hundred years ago all was wild, woody, and uncultivated! What a train of pleasing ideas this fair spectacle must suggest; it is a prospect which must inspire a good citizen with the most heartfelt pleasure. The difficulty consists in the manner of viewing so extensive a scene. He is arrived on a new continent; a modern society offers itself to his contemplation, different from what he had hitherto seen. It is not composed, as in Europe, of [39/40] great lords who possess everything, and of a herd of people who have nothing. Here are no aristocratical families, no courts, no kings, no bishops, no ecclesiastical dominion, no invisible power giving to a few a very visible one; no great manufacturers employing thousands, no great refinements of luxury. The rich and the poor are not so far removed from each other as they are in Europe. Some few towns excepted, we are all tillers of the earth, from Nova Scotia to West Florida. We are a people of cultivators, scattered over an immense territory, communicating with each other by means of good roads and navigable rivers, united by the silken bands of mild government, all respecting the laws, without dreading their power, because they are equitable. We are all animated with the spirit of an industry which is unfettered and unrestrained, because each person works for himself. If he travels through our rural districts he views not the hostile castle, and the haughty mansion, contrasted with the clay-built hut and miserable cabin, where cattle and men help to keep each other warm, and dwell in meanness, smoke, and indigence. A pleasing uniformity of decent competence appears throughout our habitations. The meanest of our log-houses is a dry and comfortable habitation. Lawyer or merchant are the fairest titles our towns afford; that of a farmer is the only appellation of the rural inhabitants of our country. It must take some time ere he can reconcile himself to our dictionary, which is but short in words of dignity, and names of honour. There, on a Sunday, he sees a congregation of respectable farmers and their wives, all clad in neat homespun, well mounted, or riding in their own humble waggons. There is not among them an esquire, saving the unlettered magistrate. There he sees a parson as simple as his flock, a farmer who does not riot on the labour of others. We have no princes, for whom we [40/41] toil, starve, and bleed: we are the most perfect society now existing in the world. Here man is free as he ought to be; nor is this pleasing equality so transitory as many others are. Many ages will not see the shores of our great lakes replenished with inland nations, nor the unknown bounds of North America entirely peopled. Who can tell how far it extends? Who can tell the millions of men whom it will feed and contain? for no European foot has as yet travelled half the extent of this mighty continent!

The next wish of this traveller will be to know whence came all these people? they are a mixture of English, Scotch, Irish, French, Dutch, Germans, and Swedes. From this promiscuous breed, that race now called Americans have arisen. The eastern provinces must indeed be excepted, as being the unmixed descendants of Englishmen. I have heard many wish that they had been more intermixed also: for my part, I am no wisher, and think it much better as it has happened. They exhibit a most conspicuous figure in this great and variegated picture; they too enter for a great share in the pleasing perspective displayed in these thirteen provinces. I know it is fashionable to reflect on them, but I respect them for what they have done; for the accuracy and wisdom with which they have settled their territory; for the decency of their manners; for their early love of letters; their ancient college, the first in this hemisphere; for their

industry; which to me who am but a farmer, is the criterion of everything. There never was a people, situated as they are, who with so
ungrateful a soil have done more in so short a time. Do you think
that the monarchical ingredients which are more prevalent in other
governments, have purged them from all foul stains? Their histories
assert the contrary.

In this great American asylum, the poor of Europe have by some
means met together, and in consequence of [41/42] various causes;
to what purpose should they ask one another what countrymen they
are? Alas, two thirds of them had no country. Can a wretch who
wanders about, who works and starves, whose life is a continual
scene of sore affliction or pinching penury; can that man call England or any other kingdom his country? A country that had no
bread for him, whose fields procured him no harvest, who met with
nothing but the frowns of the rich, the severity of the laws, with jails
and punishments; who owned not a single foot of the extensive surface of this planet? No! urged by a variety of motives, here they
came. Every thing has tended to regenerate them; new laws, a new
mode of living, a new social system; here they are become men: in
Europe they were as so many useless plants, wanting vegetative
mould, and refreshing showers; they withered, and were mowed
down by want, hunger, and war; but now by the power of transplan-
tation, like all other plants they have taken root and flourished! Formerly they were not numbered in any civil lists of their country, except in those of the poor; here they rank as citizens. By what invisible power has this surprising metamorphosis been performed? By
that of the laws and that of their industry. The laws, the indulgent
laws, protect them as they arrive, stamping on them the symbol of
adoption; they receive ample rewards for their labours; these accumulated rewards procure them lands; those lands confer on them
the title of freemen, and to that title every benefit is affixed which
men can possibly require. This is the great operation daily performed by our laws. From whence proceed these laws? From our government. Whence the government? It is derived from the original
genius and strong desire of the people ratified and confirmed by the
crown. This is the great chain which links us all, this is the picture
which every province exhibits, Nova Scotia excepted. [42/43] There
the crown has done all; either there were no people who had genius,
or it was not much attended to: the consequence is, that the province is very thinly inhabited indeed: the power of the crown in con-
junction with the musketos has prevented men from settling there.
Yet some parts of it flourished once, and it contained a mild harmless set of people. But for the fault of a few leaders, the whole were
banished. The greatest political error the crown ever committed in

America, was to cut off men from a country which wanted nothing but men!

What attachment can a poor European emigrant have for a country where he had nothing? The knowledge of the language, the love of a few kindred as poor as himself, were the only cords that tied him: his country is now that which gives him land, bread, protection, and consequence: *Ubi panis ibi patria,* is the motto of all emigrants. What then is the American, this new man? He is either an European, or the descendant of an European, hence that strange mixture of blood, which you will find in no other country. I could point out to you a family whose grandfather was an Englishman, whose wife was Dutch, whose son married a French woman, and whose present four sons have now four wives of different nations. *He* is an American, who, leaving behind him all his ancient prejudices and manners, receives new ones from the new mode of life he has embraced, the new government he obeys, and the new rank he holds. He becomes an American by being received in the broad lap of our great *Alma Mater.* Here individuals of all nations are melted into a new race of men, whose labours and posterity will one day cause great changes in the world. Americans are the western pilgrims, who are carrying along with them that great mass of arts, sciences, vigour, and industry which began long since in the east; they will finish the [43/44] great circle. The Americans were once scattered all over Europe; here they are incorporated into one of the finest systems of population which has ever appeared, and which will hereafter become distinct by the power of the different climates they inhabit. The American ought therefore to love this country much better than that wherein either he or his forefathers were born. Here the rewards of his industry follow with equal steps the progress of his labour; his labour is founded on the basis of nature, *self-interest;* can it want a stronger allurement? Wives and children, who before in vain demanded of him a morsel of bread, now, fat and frolicsome, gladly help their father to clear those fields whence exuberant crops are to arise to feed and to clothe them all; without any part being claimed, either by a despotic prince, a rich abbot, or a mighty lord. Here religion demands but little of him; a small voluntary salary to the minister, and gratitude to God; can he refuse these? The American is a new man, who acts upon new principles; he must therefore entertain new ideas, and form new opinions. From involuntary idleness, servile dependence, penury, and useless labour, he has passed to toils of a very different nature, rewarded by ample subsistence.—This is an American.

British America is divided into many provinces, forming a large association, scattered along a coast 1500 miles extent and about 200 wide. This society I would fain examine, at least such as it appears in the middle provinces; if it does not afford that variety of tinges and gradations which may be observed in Europe, we have colours peculiar to ourselves. For instance, it is natural to conceive that those who live near the sea, must be very different from those who live in the woods; the intermediate space will afford a separate and distinct class.

Men are like plants; the goodness and flavour of the [44/45] fruit proceeds from the peculiar soil and exposition in which they grow. We are nothing but what we derive from the air we breathe, the climate we inhabit, the government we obey, the system of religion we profess, and the nature of our employment. Here you will find but few crimes; these have acquired as yet no root among us. I wish I was able to trace all my ideas; if my ignorance prevents me from describing them properly, I hope I shall be able to delineate a few of the outlines, which are all I propose.

Those who live near the sea, feed more on fish than on flesh, and often encounter that boisterous element. This renders them more bold and enterprising; this leads them to neglect the confined occupations of the land. They see and converse with a variety of people; their intercourse with mankind becomes extensive. The sea inspires them with a love of traffic, a desire of transporting produce from one place to another; and leads them to a variety of resources which supply the place of labour. Those who inhabit the middle settlements, by far the most numerous, must be very different; the simple cultivation of the earth purifies them, but the indulgences of the government, the soft remonstrances of religion, the rank of independent freeholders, must necessarily inspire them with sentiments, very little known in Europe among people of the same class. What do I say? Europe has no such class of men; the early knowledge they acquire, the early bargains they make, give them a great degree of sagacity. As freemen they will be litigious; pride and obstinacy are often the cause of law suits; the nature of our laws and governments may be another. As citizens it is easy to imagine, that they will carefully read the newspapers, enter into every political disquisition, freely blame or censure governors and others. As farmers they will be careful and anxious to get as much as they can, because what they get is [45/46] their own. As northern men they will love the cheerful cup. As Christians, religion curbs them not in their opinions; the general indulgence leaves every one to think for themselves in spiritual matters; the laws inspect our actions, our thoughts are left to God. Industry, good living, selfishness, litigiousness, country politics, the pride of freemen, religious indifference, are their characteristics. If you recede still farther from the sea, you will come into more modern settlements; they exhibit the same strong lineaments, in a ruder appearance. Religion seems to have still less influence, and their manners are less improved.

Now we arrive near the great woods, near the last inhabited districts; there men seem to be placed still farther beyond the reach of government, which in some measure leaves them to themselves. How can it pervade every corner; as they were driven there by misfortunes, necessity of beginnings, desire of acquiring large tracts of land, idleness, frequent want of economy, ancient debts; the reunion of such people does not afford a very pleasing spectacle. When discord, want of unity and friendship; when either drunkenness or idleness prevail in such remote districts; contention, inactivity, and wretchedness must ensue. There are not the same remedies to these evils as in a long established community. The few magistrates they have, are in general little better than the rest; they are often in a perfect state of war; that of man against man, sometimes decided by blows, sometimes by means of the law; that of man against every wild inhabitant of these venerable woods, of which they are come to dispossess them. There men appear to be no better than carnivorous animals of a superior rank, living on the flesh of wild animals when they can catch them, and when they are not able, they subsist on grain. He who would wish to see America in its proper light, and have a true [46/47] idea of its feeble beginnings and barbarous rudiments, must visit our extended line of frontiers where the last settlers dwell, and where he may see the first labours of settlement, the mode of clearing the earth, in all their different appearances; where men are wholly left dependent on their native tempers, and on the spur of uncertain industry, which often fails when not sanctified by the efficacy of a few moral rules. There, remote from the power of example and check of shame, many families exhibit the most hideous parts of our society. They are a kind of forlorn hope, preceding by ten or twelve years the most respectable army of veterans which come after them. In that space, prosperity will polish some, vice and the law will drive off the rest, who uniting again with others like themselves will recede still farther; making room for more industrious people, who will finish their improvements, convert the loghouse into a convenient habitation, and rejoicing that the first heavy labours are finished, will change in a few years that hitherto barbarous country into a fine fertile, well regulated district. Such is our progress, such is the march of the Europeans toward the interior parts of this continent. In all societies there are off-casts; this impure part serves as our precursors or pioneers; my father himself was one of that class, but he came upon honest principles, and was therefore one of the few who held fast; by good conduct and temperance, he transmitted to me his fair inheritance, when not above one in fourteen of his contemporaries had the same good fortune. [47/48]

OWEN WISTER

———•———

Preface to The Virginian

HAD YOU LEFT NEW YORK or San Francisco at ten o'clock this morning, by noon the day after to-morrow you could step out at Cheyenne. There you would stand at the heart of the world that is the
subject of my picture, yet you would look around you in vain for the
reality. It is a vanished world. No journeys, save those which memory can take, will bring you to it now. The mountains are there, far
and shining, and the sunlight, and the infinite earth, and the air
that seems forever the true fountain of youth,—but where is the buffalo, and the wild antelope, and where the horseman with his pas-
turing thousands? So like its old self does the sage-brush seem when
revisited, that you wait for the horseman to appear.

But he will never come again. He rides in his historic yesterday.
You will no more see him gallop out of the unchanging silence than
you will see Columbus on the unchanging sea come sailing from
Palos with his caravels. [3/4]

And yet the horseman is still so near our day that in some chapters of this book, which were published separate at the close of the
nineteenth century, the present tense was used. It is true no longer.
In those chapters it has been changed, and verbs like "is" and
"have" now read "was" and "had." Time has flowed faster than my
ink.

What is become of the horseman, the cowpuncher, the last romantic figure upon our soil? For he was romantic. Whatever he did, he
did with his might. The bread that he earned was earned hard, the
wages that he squandered were squandered hard,—half a year's pay
sometimes gone in a night,—"blown in," as he expressed it, or
"blowed in," to be perfectly accurate. Well, he will be here among
us always, invisible, waiting his chance to live and play as he would
like. His wild kind has been among us always, since the beginning: a
young man with his temptations, a hero without wings.

The cow-puncher's ungoverned hours did not unman him. If he
gave his word, he kept it; Wall Street would have found him behind

26

the times. Nor did he talk lewdly to women; Newport would have thought him old-fashioned. He and his brief epoch make a complete picture, for in themselves they were as complete as the pioneers of the land or the explorers of the sea. A transition has followed the horseman of the plains; a shapeless state, a condition of men and manners as unlovely as is that moment in the year when winter is gone and spring not come, and the face of Nature is ugly. I shall not dwell upon it here. Those who have seen it know well what I mean. Such transition was inevitable. Let us give thanks that it is but a transition, and not a finality.

Sometimes readers inquire, Did I know the Virginian? As well, I hope, as a father should know his son. And sometimes it is asked, Was such and such a thing true? Now to this I have the best answer in the world. Once a cowpuncher listened patiently while I read him a manuscript. It concerned an event upon an Indian reservation. "Was that the Crow reservation?" he inquired at the finish. I told him that it was no real reservation and no real event; and his face expressed displeasure. "Why," he demanded, "do you waste your time writing what never happened, when you know so many things that did happen?"

And I could no more help telling him that this was the highest compliment ever paid me than I have been able to help telling you about it here! [4]

WALT WHITMAN

Pioneers! O Pioneers!

COME my tan-faced children,
Follow well in order, get your weapons ready,
Have you your pistols? have you your sharp-edged axes?
     Pioneers! O pioneers!

For we cannot tarry here,
We must march, my darlings, we must bear the brunt of danger,
We the youthful sinewy races, all the rest on us depend,
     Pioneers! O pioneers!

O you youths, Western youths,
So impatient, full of action, full of manly pride and friendship,
Plain I see you Western youths, see you tramping with the foremost,
     Pioneers! O pioneers!

Have the elder races halted?
Do they droop and end their lesson, wearied over there beyond the
       seas?
We take up the task eternal, and the burden and the lesson,
     Pioneers! O pioneers! [279/280]

All the past we leave behind,
We debouch upon a newer, mightier world, varied world,
Fresh and strong the world we seize, world of labor and the march,
     Pioneers! O pioneers!

We detachments steady throwing,
Down the edges, through the passes, up the mountains steep,
Conquering, holding, daring, venturing as we go the unknown ways,
     Pioneers! O pioneers!

ROBERT FROST

The Gift Outright

THE LAND was ours before we were the land's.
She was our land more than a hundred years
Before we were her people. She was ours
In Massachusetts, in Virginia,
But we were England's still, still colonials,
Possessing what we still were unpossessed by,
Possessed by what we now no more possessed.
Something we were withholding made us weak
Until we found out that it was ourselves
We were withholding from our land of living,
And forthwith found salvation in surrender.
Such as we were we gave ourselves outright
(The deed of gift was many deeds of war)
To the land vaguely realizing westward,
But still unstoried, artless, unenhanced,
Such as she was, such as she would become. [467]

2

The Forests

ONE OF THE FIRST FRONTIERS lay fifty yards up a Cape Cod beach and on the stony verge of the bay in Plymouth, Massachusetts. It was the New World, inhabited by "savages" and menaced by a winter colder and more cruel than any the first settlers had ever known. Here the Pilgrims had to develop the fundamental quality of the frontiersman—the ability to fight and survive.

Unlike some explorers of the wilderness, the members of the Plymouth colony landed with their wives, their children, and an organized community. They also arrived in a strange land, ignorant of the climate and the native inhabitants. Theirs was one of the first in a long series of accommodations in which Europeans conquered a New World, but in doing so also surrendered to the land and became a new people. William Bradford describes both the beginning of the conquest, as musket fire terrified Cape Cod Indians, and the beginning of the surrender, as the Pilgrims learned from Squanto how to plant their corn and catch their fish.

Their settlement survived and was eventually absorbed by the Puritan colony that settled in 1630 in Massachusetts Bay. The new communities were still essentially European, bound to the Old Country by language, culture, and government. In loyalties, as in literature, their values were those that they had brought with them. But slowly these loyalties and values were modified and changed by the demands of their new environment.

The earliest Colonial literature looked east, not west. Much of it echoed the literature of England, following tardily but faithfully the changes in the literary styles of the mother country. Almost none of it celebrated the peculiarly American experience of living between sea and forest, winning each slow acre with gun and axe.

In the work of Charles Brockden Brown, who has sometimes been called America's first professional writer, a European literary tradition acted upon the American scene. His hero turned west and ventured into the forest, but the wilderness was a picturesque and terrifying stage set, a threatening environment that owed more to the English Gothic novel than it did to realistic observation. And even Hawthorne, who was a greater artist and certainly a more careful student of American history, used the forest as an exotic setting, a mysterious threat, or as a rich, somber, and complex symbol.

The reality of the forest must certainly have been a simpler and coarser influence on the pioneer who experienced it. Perhaps Washington Irving drew the first portrait of the man it produced, a rustic who strongly resembled Fielding's Tom Jones, but also a man who was peculiarly American. With his "overbearing roughness," his "waggish good humor," and his distinguishing fur cap, Brom Bones entered American literature to contend against an archetypal effete Easterner, Ichabod Crane.

The classic picture of the frontiersman was created by Irving's contemporary, James Fenimore Cooper. When Cooper first described Natty Bumppo in *The Pioneers,* he created a character who was seemingly simple, yet unbelievably complex. Natty was a woodsman, a child, yet master of the forest, distrustful and resentful of civilization, but respectful of its social gradations and cultural values. He was the killer of certain Indians and the friend of others; he respected Indian customs and beliefs, yet was himself a proud white supremacist. A natural gentleman, he was attractive to women, but he also had a small boy's distrust of them. Better than any other character in American literature, in spite of all of Cooper's artistic short-comings, Natty Bumppo illustrated the richness and the complexity of the frontier hero in our culture.

Natty was a child of the forest, but his adventures in the *Leather-Stocking Tales* took him from the Eastern forests of the French and Indian wars to his death as an old man at the base of the Rocky Mountains. His death scene illustrates the contradictory and conflicting values in his code of life that made his character fascinating to Europeans and Americans alike.

Since Cooper wrote his novels, other writers have added to the complexity of the frontier character. Conrad Richter has grasped the cruelty, the grotesquerie, the ribaldry, and the inescapable pressure of necessity in the pioneer community. And Elizabeth Madox Roberts has captured the irony that has moved with our history and literature from the Atlantic to the Pacific Ocean: the frontiersman may love the wild forest, the fenceless plain, or the rugged mountain, but his whole life, intentionally or unintentionally, contributes to the destruction of what he loves. He is an instrument of change; he may hate the tamed, fenced, and settled East, but he and his woman work to tame, fence, and settle the West.

WILLIAM BRADFORD

The History of the Plymouth Plantation

THEY THUS ARRIVED at Cape Cod on the 11th of November, and necessity called on them to look out for a place of habitation. Having brought a large shallop with them from England, stowed in quarters in the ship, they now got her out, and set their carpenters to work to trim her up; but being much bruised and battered in the foul weather they saw she would be long mending. So a few of them volunteered to go by land and explore the neighboring parts, whilst the shallop was put in order; particularly since, as they entered the bay, there seemed to be an opening some two or three leagues off, which the captain thought was a river. It was conceived there might be some danger in the attempt; but seeing them resolute, sixteen of them, well-armed, were permitted to go, under charge of Captain Standish.

They set forth on the 15th of November, being landed by the ship's boat, and when they had marched about the space of a mile by the seaside, they espied five or six persons with a dog coming towards them. They were savages; but they fled back into the woods, followed by the English, who wished to see if they could speak with them, and to discover if there were more lying in ambush. But the Indians, seeing themselves followed, left the woods, and ran along the sands as hard as they could, so our men could not come up with them, but followed the track of their feet several miles. Night coming on, they made their rendezvous, and set sentinels, and rested in quiet.

Next morning they again pursued the Indians' tracks, till they came to a great creek, where they had left the sands and turned into the woods. But they continued to follow them by guess, hoping to find their dwellings; but soon they lost both the Indians and themselves, and fell into such thickets that their clothes and armor were injured severely; but they suffered most from want of water. At length they found some, and refreshed themselves with the first New England water they had drunk; and in their great thirst they found it as pleasant as wine or beer had been before. Afterwards they directed their course towards the other shore, for they knew it was only a neck of land they had to cross over. At length they got to the seaside, and marched to this supposed river, and by the way found a pond of fresh water, and shortly after a quantity of cleared ground where the Indians had formerly planted corn; and they found some of their graves.

Proceeding further, they saw stubble where corn had been grown the same year, and also found a place where a house had lately been, with some planks, and a great kettle and heaps of sand newly banked, under which they found several large baskets filled with corn, some in the ear of various colors, which was a very goodly sight, they having never seen any like it before. This was near the supposed river that they had come to seek. When they reached it, they found that it opened into two arms, with a high cliff of sand at the entrance, but more likely to be creeks of salt water than fresh, they thought. There was good harborage for their shallop, so they left it to be further explored when she was ready. The time allowed them having expired, they returned to the ship, lest the others should be anxious about their safety. They took part of the corn and buried the rest; and so, like the men from Eschol, carried with them of the fruits of the land, and showed their brethren; at which the rest were very glad, and greatly encouraged.

After this, the shallop being ready, they set out again for the better reconnoitering of the place. The captain of the ship desired to go himself, so there were some thirty men. However, they found it to be no harbor for ships, but only for boats..They also found two of the Indians' houses covered with mats, and some of their implements in them; but the people had run away and could not be seen. They also found more corn, and beans of various colors. These they brought away, intending to give them full satisfaction when they should meet with any of them,—as about six months afterwards they did.

And it is to be noted as a special providence of God, and a great mercy to this poor people, that they thus got seed to plant corn the next year, or they might have starved; for they had none, nor any likelihood of getting any, till too late for the planting season. Nor is it likely that they would have got it if this first voyage had not been made, for the ground was soon all covered with snow and frozen hard. But the Lord is never wanting unto His in their great need; let His holy name have all the praise.

The month of November being spent in these affairs, and foul weather coming on, on the sixth of December they sent out their shallop again with ten of their principal men and some sailors upon further discovery, intending to circumnavigate the deep bay of Cape Cod. The weather was very cold, and it froze so hard that the spray of the sea froze on their coats like glass. Early that night they got to the lower end of the bay, and as they drew near the shore they saw ten or twelve Indians very busy about something. They landed about a league or two from them; though they had much ado to put ashore anywhere, it was so full of flats. It was late when they landed, so they made themselves a barricade of logs and boughs as well as they could in the time, and set a sentinel and betook them to rest, and saw the smoke of the fire the savages made that night. When morning came they divided their party, some to coast along the shore in the boat, and the rest to march through the woods to see the land, and, if possible, to find a fit place for their settlement. They came to the place where they had seen the Indians the night before and found they had been cutting up a great fish like a grampus, covered with almost two inches of fat, like a hog. The shallop found two more of the same kind of fish dead on the sands, a usual thing after storms there, because of the great flats of sand.

They ranged up and down all that day, but found no people nor any place they liked. When the sun got low they hastened out of the woods to meet their shallop, making signs to it to come into a creek hard by, which it did at high water. They were very glad to meet, for they had not seen each other since the morning. They made a barricade, as they did every night with logs, stakes, and thick pine boughs, the height of a man, leaving it open to leeward; partly to shelter them from the cold wind, making their fire in the middle and lying around it; and, partly to defend them from any sudden assaults of the savages, if they should try to surround them. So being very weary, they betook them to rest. But about midnight they heard a hideous cry, and their sentinel called "Arm, arm!" So they bestirred themselves and took to their arms, and shot a couple of muskets and then the noise ceased. They concluded it was a pack of wolves, or some such wild beasts; for one of the sailors told them he had often heard such noises in Newfoundland. So they rested till about five o'clock in the morning.

After prayer they prepared for breakfast, and it being day dawning, it was thought best to be carrying things down to the boat. Some said it was not best to carry the guns down; others said they would be the readier, for they had wrapped them up in their coats to keep them from the dew. But some three or four would not carry their guns down to the boat till they went themselves. However, as the water was not high enough, the others laid theirs down on the bank of the creek, and came up to breakfast. But soon, all of a sudden, they heard a great and strange cry, which they knew to be the same as they had heard in the night, though with various notes. One of the company who was outside came running in and cried: "Men! Indians, Indians!" and at that their arrows came flying amongst them. The men ran down to the creek with all speed to recover their guns, which by the providence of God they succeeded in doing. In the meantime two of those who were still armed discharged their muskets at the Indians; and two more stood ready at the entrance of the rendezvous, but were commanded not to shoot till they could take fell aim at them; and the other two loaded again at full speed, there being only four guns there to defend the barricade when it was first assaulted.

The cry of the Indians was dreadful, especially when they saw the men run out of the rendezvous towards the shallop to recover their guns, the Indians wheeling about them. But some of the men, armed with coats of mail and with cutlasses in their hands, soon got their guns and let fly among them, which quickly stopped their violence. There was one big Indian, and no less valiant, who stood behind a tree, within half a musket-shot, and let his arrows fly at them. He was seen to shoot three arrows, which were all avoided. He stood three musket-shots, till one of them made the bark and splinters of the tree fly about his ears, at which he gave an extraordinary shriek, and away all of them went. The men left some of the party to guard the shallop, and followed the Indians about a quarter of a mile, shouting once or twice, and shooting off two or three guns, and then returned. They did this so that the natives might not think they were afraid of them.

Thus it pleased God to vanquish their enemies and give them deliverance; and by His special providence so to dispose that not one of them was hit, though the arrows came close to them, on every side, and some of their coats which were hung up in the barricade were shot through and through. Afterwards they gave God solemn thanks and praise for their deliverance, and gathered up a bundle of the arrows, and later sent them to England by the captain of the ship. They called the place "The First Encounter."

Then they left, and coasted all along, but discovered no likely place for a harbor. So they made all speed to a spot which their pilot —a Mr. Coppin, who had been in the country before—assured them was a good harbor, which he had been in, and which they might fetch before night. Of this they were glad, for the weather began to be foul.

After some hours' sailing, it began to snow and rain, and about the middle of the afternoon the wind increased, and the sea became very rough. They broke their rudder, and it was as much as two men could do to steer her with a couple of oars. But the pilot bade them be of good cheer, and said he saw the harbor; but the storm increasing and night drawing on, they carried all the sail they could to get in while they could see. Then their mast broke in three pieces, and the sail fell overboard in a very heavy sea, so that they were in danger of being wrecked; but by God's mercy they recovered themselves, and having the tide with them, struck in towards the harbor.

But when they came to, the pilot found he had mistaken the place, and said the Lord be merciful to them, for he had never seen the place before; and he and the mate were about to run her ashore, in a cove full of breakers, before the wind. But one of the seamen, who steered, bade the rowers, if they were men, about with her, or they would all be cast away; which they did with speed. So he bid them be of good cheer and row lustily for there was a fair sound before them, and he did not doubt but they would find a place where they could come to safely. Though it was very dark and rained hard, they ultimately got under the lee of a small island, and remained there safely all night; but they did not know it was an island till morning. They were divided in their mind; some wished to stay in the boat, for fear there would be more Indians; others were so weak and cold they could not endure it, but got ashore and with much ado made a fire—everything being wet—and then the rest were glad enough to join them; for after midnight the wind shifted to the northwest and it froze hard.

But though this had been a night of much hardship and danger, God gave them a morning of comfort and refreshment, as He usually doth to His children; for the next day was a fair sun-shining day, and they found they were on an island secure from the Indians, where they could dry their stuff, fix their arms, and rest themselves and give God thanks for His mercies in their manifold deliverances. This being the last day of the week they prepared to keep the Sabbath there. On Monday they sounded the harbor and found it fit for shipping; and marching inland they found several cornfields and little running brooks—a place, as they supposed, fit for a settlement; at least it was the best they could find, and considering the season of the year and their present necessity they were thankful for it. So they returned with this news to the rest of their people aboard the ship, which cheered them greatly.

On the 15th day of December they weighed anchor to go to the place they had discovered, and came within two leagues of it, but had to bear up again. On the 16th day the wind came fair, and they arrived safe in the habor. Afterwards they took a better view of the place, and resolved where to pitch their dwellings; and on the 25th day they began to erect the first house for common use, to receive them and their goods.

The rest of this work—if God give me life and opportunity—I shall, for brevity's sake, handle in the form of Annals, noting only the principal doings, chronologically.

First, I will turn back a little, and begin with a compact or deed drawn up by them before they went ashore to settle, constituting the first foundation of their government. This was occasioned partly by the discontented and mutinous speeches that some of the strangers amongst them had let fall: that when they got ashore they would use their liberty, that none had power to command them, the patent procured being for Virginia, and not for New England, which belonged to another company, with which the Virginia company had nothing to do. And, further, it was believed by the leading men among the settlers that such a deed, drawn up by themselves, considering their present condition, would be as effective as any patent, and in some respects more so.

The form of the deed was as follows:

> In the name of God, Amen. We whose names are underwritten, the loyal subjects of our dread sovereign lord, King James, by the grace of God, of Great Britain, France and Ireland, King, Defender of the Faith, etc., having undertaken for the glory of God, and advancement of the Christian faith, and honor of our king and country, a voyage to plant the first colony in the northern parts of Virginia, do by these presents solemnly and mutually in the presence of God and of one another, covenant and combine ourselves into a civil body politic, for our better ordering and preservation, and the furtherance of the ends aforesaid and by virtue hereof to enact, constitute, and frame, such just and equal laws, ordinances, acts, constitutions, and offices from time to time, as shall be thought most meet and convenient for the general use of the Colony, unto which we promise all due submission and obedience. In witness whereof we have here underscribed our names at Cape Cod, 11th of November, in the year of the reign of our sovereign lord, King James of England, France and Ireland the eighteenth, and of Scotland the fifty-fourth.
>
> A.D. 1620.

They then chose, or rather confirmed, Mr. John Carver, a godly man and highly approved among them, as their governor for that year. After they had provided a place for their goods and common stores, which they were long in unlading owing to want of boats, the severity of the winter weather and sickness, and had begun some small cottages for dwellings—as time would admit they met and consulted of law and order, both for civil and military government, as seemed suited to their conditions, adding to them from time to time as urgent need demanded. In these arduous and difficult beginnings, discontent and murmuring arose amongst some, and mutinous speech and bearing in others; but they were soon quelled and overcome by the wisdom, patience, and just and equal administration of things by the Governor and the better part, who held faithfully together in the main.

But soon a most lamentable blow fell upon them. In two or three months' time half of their company died, partly owing to the severity of the winter, especially during January and February, and the want of houses and other comforts; partly to scurvy and other diseases, which their long voyage and their incommodious quarters had brought upon them. Of all the hundred odd persons, scarcely fifty remained, and sometimes two or three persons died in a day. In the time of worst distress, there were but six or seven sound persons, who, to their great commendation be it spoken, spared no pains night or day, but with great toil and at the risk of their own health, fetched wood, made fires, prepared food for the sick, made their beds, washed their infected clothes, dressed and undressed them—in a word, did all the homely and necessary services for them which dainty and queasy stomachs cannot endure to hear mentioned; and all this they did willingly and cheerfully, without the least grudging, showing their love to the friends and brethren; a rare example, and worthy to be remembered.

Two of these seven were Mr. William Brewster, their reverend elder, and Myles Standish, their captain and military commander, to whom myself and many others were much beholden in our low and sick condition. And yet the Lord so upheld these men that in this general calamity they were not at all infected with sickness. And what I have said of these few, I should say of many others who died in this general visitation, and others yet living, that while they had health or strength, they forsook none that had need of them. I doubt not that their recompense is with the Lord.

But I must not pass by another remarkable and unforgettable occurrence. When this calamity fell among the passengers who were to be left here to settle, they were hurried ashore and made to drink water, so that the sailors might have the more beer, and when one sufferer in his sickness desired but a small can of beer, it was answered that if he were their own father he should have none. Then the disease began to seize the sailors also, so that almost half of the crew died before they went away, and many of their officers and strongest men, amongst them the boatswain, gunner, three quartermasters, the cook and others. At this the captain was somewhat struck, and sent to the sick ashore and told the Governor that he could send for beer for those that had need of it, even should he have to drink water on the homeward voyage.

But amongst the sailors there was quite a different bearing in their misery. Those who before, in the time of their health and welfare, had been boon companions in drinking and jollity, began now to desert one another, saying they would not risk their lives for the sick among them, lest they should be infected by coming to help them in their cabins; if they died, let them die! But the passengers who were still aboard showed them what pity they could, which made some of their hearts relent, such as the boatswain, who was an overbearing young man, and before would often curse and scoff at the passengers. But when he grew weak they had compassion on him and helped him. Then he confessed he did not deserve it at their hands, for he had abused them in word and deed. "Oh," said he, "I see now you show your love like Christians indeed to one another; but we let one another lie and die like dogs." Another lay cursing his wife, saying if it had not been for her he had never come on this unlucky voyage; and anon cursed his fellows, saying he had done this or that for some of them, he had spent so much and so much amongst them, and they were now weary of him, and did not help him in his need. Another made over to one of his mates all he had, when he should die, if he would but help him in his weakness. So his companion went and got a little spice and prepared some food once or twice; and when he did not die as soon as he expected, he went among his comrades and swore the rogue would cheat him of his inheritance; he would see him choke before he prepared him any more food; and so the poor fellow died before morning!

All this while the Indians came skulking about those who were ashore and would sometimes show themselves aloof, at a distance, but when any approached them, they would run away. Once they stole away the men's tools, where they had been at work and were gone to dinner. About the 16th of March a certain Indian came boldly among them, and spoke to them in broken English, which they could well understand, but were astonished at it. At length they understood by speaking with him that he was not of these parts, but belonged to the eastern country where some English ships came to fish; and with some of these English he was acquainted, and could name several of them. From them he had got his knowledge of the language.

He became useful to them in acquainting them with many things concerning the state of the country in the east parts where he lived, as also of the people there, their names and number, their situation and distance from this place, and who was chief among them. His name was Samoset. He told them also of another Indian whose name was Squanto, a native of this part, who had been in England and could speak English better than himself. After some time of entertainment, being dismissed with gifts, in a little while he returned with five more, and they brought back all the tools that had been

stolen, and made way for the coming of their great sachem, called
Massasoyt, who about four or five days after, came with the chief of
his friends and other attendants, and with Squanto. With him, after
friendly entertainment and some gifts, they made a peace which has
now continued for twenty-four years.

CHARLES BROCKDEN BROWN

Escape from the Cave

I HAVE SAID that I slept. My memory assures me of this: it informs me of the previous circumstances of my laying aside my clothes, of placing the light upon a chair within reach of my pillow, of throwing myself upon the bed, and of gazing on the rays of the moon reflected on the wall and almost obscured by those of the candle. I remember my occasional relapses into fits of incoherent fancies, the harbingers of sleep. I remember, as it were, the instant when my thoughts ceased to flow and my senses were arrested by the leaden wand of forgetfulness.

My return to sensation and to consciousness took place in no such tranquil scene. I emerged from oblivion by degrees so slow and so faint, that their succession cannot be marked. When enabled at length to attend to the information which my senses afforded, I was conscious for a time of nothing but existence. It was unaccompanied with lassitude or pain, but I felt disinclined to stretch my limbs or raise my eyelids. My thoughts were wildering and mazy, and, though consciousness was present, it was disconnected with the locomotive or voluntary power.

From this state a transition was speedily effected. I perceived that my posture was supine, and that I lay upon my back. I attempted to open my eyes. The weight that oppressed them was too great for a slight exertion to remove. The exertion which I made cost me a pang more acute than any which I ever experienced. My eyes, however, were opened; but the darkness that environed me was as intense as before.

I attempted to rise, but my limbs were cold, and my joints had almost lost their flexibility. My efforts were repeated, and at length I attained a sitting posture. I was now sensible of pain in my shoulders and back. I was universally in that state to which the frame is reduced by blows of a club, mercilessly and endlessly repeated; my temples throbbed, and my face was covered with clammy and cold drops: but that which threw me into deepest consternation was my

41

inability to see. I turned my head to different quarters; I stretched my eyelids, and exerted every visual energy, but in vain. I was wrapped in the murkiest and most impenetrable gloom.

The first effort of reflection was to suggest the belief that I was blind; that disease is known to assail us in a moment and without previous warning. This, surely, was the misfortune that had now befallen me. Some ray, however fleeting and uncertain, could not fail to be discerned, if the power of vision were not utterly extinguished. In what circumstances could I possibly be placed, from which every particle of light should, by other means, be excluded?

This led my thoughts into a new train. I endeavoured to recall the past; but the past was too much in contradiction to the present, and my intellect was too much shattered by external violence, to allow me accurately to review it.

Since my sight availed nothing to the knowledge of my condition, I betook myself to other instruments. The element which I breathed was stagnant and cold. The spot where I lay was rugged and hard. I was neither naked nor clothed: a shirt and trousers composed my dress, and the shoes and stockings, which always accompanied these, were now wanting. What could I infer from this scanty garb, this chilling atmosphere, this stony bed?

I had awakened as from sleep. What was my condition when I fell asleep? Surely it was different from the present. Then I inhabited a lightsome chamber and was stretched upon a down bed; now I was supine upon a rugged surface and immersed in palpable obscurity. Then I was in perfect health; now my frame was covered with bruises and every joint was racked with pain. What dungeon or den had received me, and by whose command was I transported hither?

After various efforts I stood upon my feet. At first I tottered and staggered. I stretched out my hands on all sides, but met only with vacuity. I advanced forward. At the third step my foot moved something which lay upon the ground: I stooped and took it up, and found, on examination, that it was an Indian tomahawk. This incident afforded me no hint from which I might conjecture my state.

Proceeding irresolutely and slowly forward, my hands at length touched a wall. This, like the flooring, was of stone, and was rugged and impenetrable. I followed this wall. An advancing angle occurred at a short distance, which was followed by similar angles. I continued to explore this clue, till the suspicion occurred that I was merely going round the walls of a vast and irregular apartment.

The utter darkness disabled me from comparing directions and distances. This discovery, therefore, was not made on a sudden, and was still entangled with some doubt. My blood recovered some warmth, and my muscles some elasticity, but in proportion as my sensibility returned, my pains augmented. Overpowered by my fears and my agonies, I desisted from my fruitless search, and sat down, supporting my back against the wall.

My excruciating sensations for a time occupied my attention. These, in combination with other causes, gradually produced a species of delirium. I existed, as it were, in a wakeful dream. With nothing to correct my erroneous perceptions, the images of the past occurred in capricious combinations and vivid hues. Methought I was the victim of some tyrant who had thrust me into a dungeon of his fortress, and left me no power to determine whether he intended I should perish with famine, or linger out a long life in hopeless imprisonment. Whether the day was shut out by insuperable walls, or the darkness that surrounded me was owing to the night and to the smallness of those crannies through which daylight was to be admitted, I conjectured in vain.

Sometimes I imagined myself buried alive. Methought I had fallen into seeming death, and my friends had consigned me to the tomb, from which a resurrection was impossible. That, in such a case, my limbs would have been confined to a coffin, and my coffin to a grave, and that I should instantly have been suffocated, did not occur to destroy my supposition. Neither did this supposition overwhelm me with terror or prompt my efforts at deliverance. My state was full of tumult and confusion, and my attention was incessantly divided between my painful sensations and my feverish dreams.

There is no standard by which time can be measured but the succession of our thoughts and the changes that take place in the external world. From the latter I was totally excluded. The former made the lapse of some hours appear like the tediousness of weeks and months. At length, a new sensation recalled my rambling meditations, and gave substance to my fears. I now felt the cravings of hunger, and perceived that, unless my deliverance were speedily effected, I must suffer a tedious and lingering death.

I once more tasked my understanding and my senses to discover the nature of my present situation and the means of escape. I listened to catch some sound. I heard an unequal and varying echo, sometimes near and sometimes distant, sometimes dying away and sometimes swelling into loudness. It was unlike any thing I had before heard, but it was evident that it arose from wind sweeping through spacious halls and winding passages. These tokens were incompatible with the result of the examination I had made. If my hands were true, I was immured between walls through which there was no avenue.

I now exerted my voice, and cried as loud as my wasted strength would admit. Its echoes were sent back to me in broken and confused sounds from above. This effort was casual, but some part of that uncertainty in which I was involved was instantly dispelled by it. In passing through the cavern on the former day, I have mentioned the verge of the pit at which I arrived. To acquaint me as far as was possible with the dimensions of the place, I had hallooed with all my force, knowing that sound is reflected according to the distance and relative positions of the substances from which it is repelled.

The effect produced by my voice on this occasion resembled, with remarkable exactness, the effect which was then produced. Was I, then, shut up in the same cavern? Had I reached the brink of the same precipice and been thrown headlong into that vacuity? Whence else could arise the bruises which I had received, but from my fall? Yet all remembrance of my journey hither was lost. I had determined to explore this cave on the ensuing day, but my memory informed me not that this intention had been carried into effect. Still, it was only possible to conclude that I had come hither on my intended expedition, and had been thrown by another, or had, by some ill chance, fallen, into the pit.

This opinion was conformable to what I had already observed. The pavement and walls were rugged like those of the footing and sides of the cave through which I had formerly passed.

But if this was true, what was the abhorred catastrophe to which I was now reserved? The sides of this pit were inaccessible; human footsteps would never wander into these recesses. My friends were unapprized of my forlorn state. Here I should continue till wasted by famine. In this grave should I linger out a few days in unspeakable agonies, and then perish forever.

The inroads of hunger were already experienced; and this knowledge of the desperateness of my calamity urged me to frenzy. I had none but capricious and unseen fate to condemn. The author of my distress, and the means he had taken to decoy me hither, were incomprehensible. Surely my senses were fettered or depraved by some spell. I was still asleep, and this was merely a tormenting vision; or madness had seized me, and the darkness that environed and the hunger that afflicted me existed only in my own distempered imagination.

The consolation of these doubts could not last long. Every hour added to the proof that my perceptions were real. My hunger speedily became ferocious. I tore the linen of my shirt between my teeth and swallowed the fragments. I felt a strong propensity to bite the flesh from my arm. My heart overflowed with cruelty, and I pondered on the delight I should experience in rending some living animal to pieces, and drinking its blood and grinding its quivering fibres between my teeth.

This agony had already passed beyond the limits of endurance. I saw that time, instead of bringing respite or relief, would only aggravate my wants, and that my only remaining hope was to die before I should be assaulted by the last extremes of famine. I now recollected that a tomahawk was at hand, and rejoiced in the possession of an instrument by which I could so effectually terminate my sufferings.

I took it in my hand, moved its edge over my fingers, and reflected on the force that was required to make it reach my heart. I investigated the spot where it should enter, and strove to fortify myself with resolution to repeat the stroke a second or third time, if the first should prove insufficient. I was sensible that I might fail to inflict a mortal wound, but delighted to consider that the blood which would be made to flow would finally release me, and that meanwhile my pains would be alleviated by swallowing this blood.

You will not wonder that I felt some reluctance to employ so fatal though indispensable a remedy. I once more ruminated on the possibility of rescuing myself by other means. I now reflected that the upper termination of the wall could not be at an immeasurable distance from the pavement. I had fallen from a height; but if that height had been considerable, instead of being merely bruised, should I not have been dashed into pieces?

Gleams of hope burst anew upon my soul. Was it not possible, I asked, to reach the top of this pit? The sides were rugged and uneven. Would not their projectures and abruptness serve me as steps by which I might ascend in safety? This expedient was to be tried without delay. Shortly my strength would fail, and my doom would be irrevocably sealed.

I will not enumerate my laborious efforts, my alternations of despondency and confidence, the eager and unwearied scrutiny with which I examined the surface, the attempts which I made, and the failures which, for a time, succeeded each other. A hundred times, when I had ascended some feet from the bottom, I was compelled to relinquish my undertaking by the *untenable* smoothness of the spaces which remained to be gone over. A hundred times I threw myself, exhausted by fatigue and my pains, on the ground. The consciousness was gradually restored that, till I had attempted every part of the wall, it was absurd to despair, and I again drew my tottering limbs and aching joints to that part of the wall which had not been surveyed.

At length, as I stretched my hand upward, I found somewhat that seemed like a recession in the wall. It was possible that this was the top of the cavity, and this might be the avenue to liberty. My heart leaped with joy, and I proceeded to climb the wall. No undertaking could be conceived more arduous than this. The space between this

verge and the floor was nearly smooth. The verge was higher from
the bottom than my head. The only means of ascending that were
offered me were by my hands, with which I could draw myself upward so as, at length, to maintain my hold with my feet.

My efforts were indefatigable, and at length I placed myself on the
verge. When this was accomplished, my strength was nearly gone.
Had I not found space enough beyond this brink to stretch myself at
length, I should unavoidably have fallen backward into the pit, and
all my pains had served no other end than to deepen my despair and
hasten my destruction.

What impediments and perils remained to be encountered I could
not judge. I was now inclined to forebode the worst. The interval of
repose which was necessary to be taken, in order to recruit my
strength, would accelerate the ravages of famine, and leave me without the power to proceed.

In this state, I once more consoled myself that an instrument of
death was at hand. I had drawn up with me the tomahawk, being
sensible that, should this impediment be overcome, others might remain that would prove insuperable. Before I employed it, however, I
cast my eyes wildly and languidly around. The darkness was no less
intense than in the pit below, and yet two objects were distinctly
seen.

They resembled a fixed and obscure flame. They were motionless.
Though lustrous themselves, they created no illumination around
them. This circumstance, added to others, which reminded me of
similar objects noted on former occasions, immediately explained
the nature of what I beheld. These were the eyes of a panther.

Thus had I struggled to obtain a post where a savage was lurking
and waited only till my efforts should place me within reach of his
fangs. The first impulse was to arm myself against this enemy. The
desperateness of my condition was, for a moment, forgotten. The
weapon which was so lately lifted against my own bosom was now
raised to defend my life against the assault of another.

There was no time for deliberation and delay. In a moment he
might spring from his station and tear me to pieces. My utmost
speed might not enable me to reach him where he sat, but merely to
encounter his assault. I did not reflect how far my strength was adequate to save me. All the force that remained was mustered up and
exerted in a throw.

No one knows the powers that are latent in his constitution.
Called forth by imminent dangers, our efforts frequently exceed our
most sanguine belief. Though tottering on the verge of dissolution,
and apparently unable to crawl from this spot, a force was exerted
in this throw, probably greater than I had ever before exerted. It

was resistless and unerring. I aimed at the middle space between those glowing orbs. It penetrated the skull, and the animal fell, struggling and shrieking, on the ground.

My ears quickly informed me when his pangs were at an end. His cries and his convulsions lasted for a moment and then ceased. The effect of his voice, in these subterranean abodes, was unspeakably rueful.

The abruptness of this incident, and the preternatural exertion of my strength, left me in a state of languor and sinking, from which slowly and with difficulty I recovered. The first suggestion that occurred was to feed upon the carcass of this animal. My hunger had arrived at that pitch where all fastidiousness and scruples are at an end. I crept to the spot. I will not shock you by relating the extremes to which dire necessity had driven me. I review this scene with loathing and horror. Now that it is past I look back upon it as on some hideous dream. The whole appears to be some freak of insanity. No alternative was offered, and hunger was capable of being appeased even by a banquet so detestable.

If this appetite has sometimes subdued the sentiments of nature, and compelled the mother to feed upon the flesh of her offspring, it will not excite amazement that I did not turn from the yet warm blood and reeking fibres of a brute.

One evil was now removed, only to give place to another. The first sensations of fulness had scarcely been felt when my stomach was seized by pangs, whose acuteness exceeded all that I ever before experienced. I bitterly lamented my inordinate avidity. The excruciations of famine were better than the agonies which this abhorred meal had produced.

Death was now impending with no less proximity and certainty, though in a different form. Death was a sweet relief for my present miseries, and I vehemently longed for its arrival. I stretched myself on the ground. I threw myself into every posture that promised some alleviation of this evil. I rolled along the pavement of the cavern, wholly inattentive to the dangers that environed me. That I did not fall into the pit whence I had just emerged must be ascribed to some miraculous chance.

How long my miseries endured, it is not possible to tell. I cannot even form a plausible conjecture. Judging by the lingering train of my sensations, I should conjecture that some days elapsed in this deplorable condition; but nature could not have so long sustained a conflict like this.

Gradually my pains subsided, and I fell into a deep sleep. I was visited by dreams of a thousand hues. They led me to flowing streams and plenteous banquets, which, though placed within my view, some power forbade me to approach. From this sleep I recovered to the fruition of solitude and darkness, but my frame was in a state less feeble than before. That which I had eaten had produced temporary distress, but on the whole had been of use. If this food had not been provided for me I should scarcely have avoided death. I had reason, therefore, to congratulate myself on the danger that had lately occurred.

I had acted without foresight, and yet no wisdom could have prescribed more salutary measures. The panther was slain, not from a view to the relief of my hunger, but from the self-preserving and involuntary impulse. Had I foreknown the pangs to which my ravenous and bloody meal would give birth, I should have carefully abstained; and yet these pangs were a useful effort of nature to subdue and convert to nourishment the matter I had swallowed.

I was now assailed by the torments of thirst. My invention and my courage were anew bent to obviate this pressing evil. I reflected that there was some recess from this cavern, even from the spot where I now stood. Before, I was doubtful whether in this direction from this pit any avenue could be found; but, since the panther had come hither, there was reason to suppose the existence of some such avenue.

I now likewise attended to a sound, which, from its invariable tenor, denoted somewhat different from the whistling of a gale. It seemed like a murmur of a running stream. I now prepared to go forward and endeavour to move along in that direction in which this sound apparently came.

On either side, and above my head, there was nothing but vacuity. My steps were to be guided by the pavement, which, though unequal and rugged, appeared, on the whole, to ascend. My safety required that I should employ both hands and feet in exploring my way.

I went on thus for a considerable period. The murmur, instead of becoming more distinct, gradually died away. My progress was arrested by fatigue, and I began once more to despond. My exertions produced a perspiration, which, while it augmented my thirst, happily supplied me with imperfect means of appeasing it.

This expedient would, perhaps, have been accidentally suggested; but my ingenuity was assisted by remembering the history of certain English prisoners in Bengal, whom their merciless enemy imprisoned in a small room, and some of whom preserved themselves alive merely by swallowing the moisture that flowed from their bodies. This experiment I now performed with no less success.

This was slender and transitory consolation. I knew that, wandering at random, I might never reach the outlet of this cavern, or might be disabled, by hunger and fatigue, from going farther than the outlet. The cravings which had lately been satiated would speedily return, and my negligence had cut me off from the resource which had recently been furnished. I thought not till now that a second meal might be indispensable.

To return upon my footsteps to the spot where the dead animal lay was a heartless project. I might thus be placing myself at a hopeless distance from liberty. Besides, my track could not be retraced. I had frequently deviated from a straight direction for the sake of avoiding impediments. All of which I was sensible was, that I was travelling up an irregular acclivity. I hoped some time to reach the summit, but had no reason for adhering to one line of ascent in preference to another.

To remain where I was was manifestly absurd. Whether I mounted or descended, a change of place was most likely to benefit me. I resolved to vary my direction, and, instead of ascending, keep along the side of what I accounted a hill. I had gone some hundred feet when the murmur, before described, once more saluted my ear.

This sound, being imagined to proceed from a running stream, could not but light up joy in the heart of one nearly perishing with thirst. I proceeded with new courage. The sound approached no nearer, nor became more distinct; but, as long as it died not away, I was satisfied to listen and to hope.

I was eagerly observant if any the least glimmering of light should visit this recess. At length, on the right hand, a gleam, infinitely faint, caught my attention. It was wavering and unequal. I directed my steps toward it. It became more vivid and permanent. It was of that kind, however, which proceeded from a fire, kindled with dry sticks, and not from the sun. I now heard the crackling of flames.

This sound made me pause, or, at least, to proceed with circumspection. At length the scene opened, and I found myself at the entrance of a cave. I quickly reached a station, when I saw a fire burning. At first no other object was noted, but it was easy to infer that the fire was kindled by men, and that they who kindled it could be at no great distance.

Thus was I delivered from my prison, and restored to the enjoyment of the air and the light. Perhaps the chance was almost miraculous that led me to this opening. In any other direction, I might have involved myself in an inextricable maze and rendered my destruction sure; but what now remained to place me in absolute security? Beyond the fire I could see nothing; but, since the smoke rolled rapidly away, it was plain that on the opposite side the cavern was open to the air.

I went forward, but my eyes were fixed upon the fire; presently, in consequence of changing my station, I perceived several feet, and the skirts of blankets. I was somewhat startled at these appearances. The legs were naked, and scored into uncouth figures. The *moccasins* which lay beside them, and which were adorned in a grotesque manner, in addition to other incidents, immediately suggested the suspicion that they were Indians. No spectacle was more adapted than this to excite wonder and alarm. Had some mysterious power snatched me from the earth, and cast me, in a moment, into the heart of the wilderness? Was I still in the vicinity of my parental habitation, or was I thousands of miles distant?

Were these the permanent inhabitants of this region, or were they wanderers and robbers? While in the heart of the mountains, I had entertained a vague belief that I was still within the precincts of Norwalk. This opinion was shaken for a moment by the objects which I now beheld, but it insensibly returned; yet how was this opinion to be reconciled to appearances so strange and uncouth, and what measure did a due regard to my safety enjoin me to take?

I now gained a view of four brawny and terrific figures, stretched upon the ground. They lay parallel to each other, on their left sides; in consequence of which their faces were turned from me. Between each was an interval where lay a musket. Their right hands seemed placed upon the stocks of their guns, as if to seize them on the first moment of alarm.

The aperture through which these objects were seen was at the back of the cave, and some feet from the ground. It was merely large enough to suffer a human body to pass. It was involved in profound darkness, and there was no danger of being suspected or discovered as long as I maintained silence and kept out of view.

It was easily imagined that these guests would make but a short sojourn in this spot. There was reason to suppose that it was now night, and that, after a short repose, they would start up and resume their journey. It was my first design to remain shrouded in this covert till their departure, and I prepared to endure imprisonment and thirst somewhat longer.

Meanwhile my thoughts were busy in accounting for this spectacle. I need not tell that Norwalk is the termination of a sterile and narrow tract which begins in the Indian country. It forms a sort of rugged and rocky vein, and continues upwards of fifty miles. It is crossed in a few places by narrow and intricate paths, by which a communication is maintained between the farms and settlements on the opposite sides of the ridge.

During former Indian wars, this rude surface was sometimes traversed by the Red-men, and they made, by means of it, frequent and destructive inroads into the heart of the English settlements. During the last war, notwithstanding the progress of population, and the multiplied perils of such an expedition, a band of them had once penetrated into Norwalk, and lingered long enough to pillage and murder some of the neighbouring inhabitants.

I have reason to remember that event. My father's house was placed on the verge of this solitude. Eight of these assassins assailed it at the dead of night. My parents and an infant child were murdered in their beds; the house was pillaged, and then burnt to the ground. Happily, myself and my two sisters were abroad upon a visit. The preceding day had been fixed for our return to our father's house; but a storm occurred, which made it dangerous to cross the river, and, by obliging us to defer our journey, rescued us from captivity or death.

Most men are haunted by some species of terror or antipathy, which they are, for the most part, able to trace to some incident which befell them in their early years. You will not be surprised that the fate of my parents, and the sight of the body of one of this savage band, who, in the pursuit that was made after them, was overtaken and killed, should produce lasting and terrific images in my fancy. I never looked upon or called up the image of a savage without shuddering.

I knew that, at this time, some hostilities had been committed on the frontier; that a long course of injuries and encroachments had lately exasperated the Indian tribes; that an implacable and exterminating war was generally expected. We imagined ourselves at an inaccessible distance from the danger, but I could not but remember that this persuasion was formerly as strong as at present, and that an expedition which had once succeeded might possibly be attempted again. Here was every token of enmity and bloodshed. Each prostrate figure was furnished with a rifled musket, and a leathern bag tied round his waist, which was, probably, stored with powder and ball.

From these reflections, the sense of my own danger was revived and enforced, but I likewise ruminated on the evils which might impend over others. I should, no doubt, be safe by remaining in this nook; but might not some means be pursued to warn others of their danger? Should they leave this spot without notice of their approach being given to the fearless and pacific tenants of the neighbouring district, they might commit, in a few hours, the most horrid and irreparable devastation.

The alarm could only be diffused in one way. Could I not escape, unperceived, and without alarming the sleepers, from this cavern? The slumber of an Indian is broken by the slightest noise; but, if all noise be precluded, it is commonly profound. It was possible, I conceived, to leave my present post, to descend into the cave, and issue forth without the smallest signal. Their supine posture assured me that they were asleep. Sleep usually comes at their bidding, and, if perchance, they should be wakeful at an unseasonable moment, they always sit upon their haunches, and, leaning their elbows on their knees, consume the tedious hours in smoking. My peril would be great. Accidents which I could not foresee, and over which I had no command, might occur to awaken some one at the moment I was passing the fire. Should I pass in safety, I might issue forth into a wilderness, of which I had no knowledge, where I might wander till I perished with famine, or where my footsteps might be noted and pursued and overtaken by these implacable foes. These perils were enormous and imminent; but I likewise considered that I might be at no great distance from the habitations of men, and that my escape might rescue them from the most dreadful calamities. I determined to make this dangerous experiment without delay.

I came nearer to the aperture, and had, consequently, a larger view of this recess. To my unspeakable dismay, I now caught a glimpse of one seated at the fire. His back was turned towards me, so that I could distinctly survey his gigantic form and fantastic ornaments.

My project was frustrated. This one was probably commissioned to watch and to awaken his companions when a due portion of sleep had been taken. That he would not be unfaithful or remiss in the performance of the part assigned to him was easily predicted. To pass him without exciting his notice (and the entrance could not otherwise be reached) was impossible. Once more I shrunk back, and revolved with hopelessness and anguish the necessity to which I was reduced.

This interval of dreary foreboding did not last long. Some motion in him that was seated by the fire attracted my notice. I looked, and beheld him rise from his place and go forth from the cavern. This unexpected incident led my thoughts into a new channel. Could not some advantage be taken of his absence? Could not this opportunity be seized for making my escape? He had left his gun and hatchet on the ground. It was likely, therefore, that he had not gone far, and would speedily return. Might not these weapons be seized, and some provision be thus made against the danger of meeting him without, or of being pursued?

Before a resolution could be formed, a new sound saluted my ear. It was a deep groan, succeeded by sobs that seemed struggling for utterance but were vehemently counteracted by the sufferer. This low and bitter lamentation apparently proceeded from some one within the cave. It could not be from one of this swarthy band. It must, then, proceed from a captive, whom they had reserved for torment or servitude, and who had seized the opportunity afforded by the absence of him that watched to give vent to his despair.

I again thrust my head forward, and beheld, lying on the ground, apart from the rest, and bound hand and foot, a young girl. Her dress was the coarse russet garb of the country, and bespoke her to be some farmer's daughter. Her features denoted the last degree of fear and anguish, and she moved her limbs in such a manner as showed that the ligatures by which she was confined produced, by their tightness, the utmost degree of pain.

My wishes were now bent not only to preserve myself and to frustrate the future attempts of these savages, but likewise to relieve this miserable victim. This could only be done by escaping from the cavern and returning with seasonable aid. The sobs of the girl were likely to rouse the sleepers. My appearance before her would prompt her to testify her surprise by some exclamation or shriek. What could hence be predicted but that the band would start on their feet and level their unerring pieces at my head!

I know not why I was insensible to these dangers. My thirst was rendered by these delays intolerable. It took from me, in some degree, the power of deliberation. The murmurs which had drawn me hither continued still to be heard. Some torrent or cascade could not be far distant from the entrance of the cavern, and it seemed as if one draught of clear water was a luxury cheaply purchased by death itself. This, in addition to considerations more disinterested, and which I have already mentioned, impelled me forward.

The girl's cheek rested on the hard rock, and her eyes were dim with tears. As they were turned towards me, however, I hoped that my movements would be noticed by her gradually and without abruptness. This expectation was fulfilled. I had not advanced many steps before she discovered me. This moment was critical beyond all others in the course of my existence. My life was suspended, as it were, by a spider's thread. All rested on the effect which this discovery should make upon this feeble victim.

I was watchful of the first movement of her eye which should indicate a consciousness of my presence. I laboured, by gestures and looks, to deter her from betraying her emotion. My attention was, at the same time, fixed upon the sleepers, and an anxious glance was cast towards the quarter whence the watchful savage might appear.

I stooped and seized the musket and hatchet. The space beyond the fire was, as I expected, open to the air. I issued forth with trembling steps. The sensations inspired by the dangers which environed me, added to my recent horrors, and the influence of the moon, which had now gained the zenith, and whose lustre dazzled my long-benighted senses, cannot be adequately described.

For a minute, I was unable to distinguish objects. This confusion was speedily corrected, and I found myself on the verge of a steep. Craggy eminences arose on all sides. On the left hand was a space that offered some footing, and hither I turned. A torrent was below me, and this path appeared to lead to it. It quickly appeared in sight, and all foreign cares were, for a time, suspended.

This water fell from the upper regions of the hill, upon a flat projecture which was continued on either side, and on part of which I was now standing. The path was bounded on the left by an inaccessible wall, and on the right terminated at the distance of two or three feet from the wall in a precipice. The water was eight or ten paces distant, and no impediment seemed likely to rise between us. I rushed forward with speed.

My progress was quickly checked. Close to the falling water, seated on the edge, his back supported by the rock, and his legs hanging over the precipice, I now beheld the savage who left the cave before me. The noise of the cascade and the improbability of interruption, at least from this quarter, had made him inattentive to my motions.

I paused. Along this verge lay the only road by which I could reach the water, and by which I could escape. The passage was completely occupied by this antagonist. To advance towards him, or to remain where I was, would produce the same effect. I should, in either case, be detected. He was unarmed; but his outcries would instantly summon his companions to his aid. I could not hope to overpower him, and pass him in defiance of his opposition. But, if this were effected, pursuit would be instantly commenced. I was unacquainted with the way. The way was unquestionably difficult. My strength was nearly annihilated; I should be overtaken in a moment, or their deficiency in speed would be supplied by the accuracy of their aim. Their bullets, at least, would reach me.

There was one method of removing this impediment. The piece which I held in my hand was cocked. There could be no doubt that it was loaded. A precaution of this kind would never be omitted by a warrior of this hue. At a greater distance than this, I should not fear to reach the mark. Should I not discharge it, and, at the same moment, rush forward to secure the road which my adversary's death would open to me?

Perhaps you will conceive a purpose like this to have argued a sanguinary and murderous disposition. Let it be remembered, however, that I entertained no doubts about the hostile designs of these men.

This was sufficiently indicated by their arms, their guise, and the captive who attended them. Let the fate of my parents be, likewise, remembered. I was not certain but that these very men were the assassins of my family, and were those who had reduced me and my sisters to the condition of orphans and dependants. No words can describe the torments of my thirst. Relief to these torments, and safety to my life, were within view. How could I hesitate?

Yet I did hesitate. My aversion to bloodshed was not to be subdued but by the direst necessity. I knew, indeed, that the discharge of a musket would only alarm the enemies who remained behind; but I had another and better weapon in my grasp. I could rive the head of my adversary, and cast him headlong, without any noise which should be heard, into the cavern.

Still I was willing to withdraw, to re-enter the cave, and take shelter in the darksome recesses from which I had emerged. Here I might remain, unsuspected, till these detested guests should depart. The hazards attending my re-entrance were to be boldly encountered, and the torments of unsatisfied thirst were to be patiently endured, rather than imbrue my hands in the blood of my fellowmen. But this expedient would be ineffectual if my retreat should be observed by this savage. Of that I was bound to be incontestably assured. I retreated, therefore, but kept my eye fixed at the same time upon the enemy.

Some ill fate decreed that I should not retreat unobserved. Scarcely had I withdrawn three paces when he started from his seat, and, turning towards me, walked with a quick pace. The shadow of the rock, and the improbability of meeting an enemy here, concealed me for a moment from his observation. I stood still. The slightest motion would have attracted his notice. At present, the narrow space engaged all his vigilance. Cautious footsteps, and attention to the path, were indispensable to his safety. The respite was momentary, and I employed it in my own defence.

How otherwise could I act? The danger that impended aimed at nothing less than my life. To take the life of another was the only method of averting it. The means were in my hand, and they were used. In an extremity like this, my muscles would have acted almost in defiance of my will.

The stroke was quick as lightning, and the wound mortal and deep. He had not time to descry the author of his fate, but, sinking on the path, expired without a groan. The hatchet buried itself in his breast, and rolled with him to the bottom of the precipice.

Never before had I taken the life of a human creature. On this head I had, indeed, entertained somewhat of religious scruples. These scruples did not forbid me to defend myself, but they made me cautious and reluctant to decide. Though they could not with-hold my hand when urged by a necessity like this, they were suffi-cient to make me look back upon the deed with remorse and dismay.

I did not escape all compunction in the present instance, but the tumult of my feelings was quickly allayed. To quench my thirst was a consideration by which all others were supplanted. I approached the torrent, and not only drank copiously, but laved my head, neck, and arms, in this delicious element.

NATHANIEL HAWTHORNE

Roger Malvin's Burial

ONE OF THE FEW INCIDENTS of Indian warfare naturally susceptible of the moonlight of romance was that expedition undertaken for the defence of the frontiers in the year 1725, which resulted in the well-remembered "Lovell's Fight." Imagination, by casting certain circumstances judicially into the shade, may see much to admire in the heroism of a little band who gave battle to twice their number in the heart of the enemy's country. The open bravery displayed by both parties was in accordance with civilized ideas of valor; and chivalry itself might not blush to record the deeds of one or two individuals. The battle, though so fatal to those who fought, was not unfortunate in its consequences to the country; for it broke the strength of a tribe and conduced to the peace which subsisted during several ensuing years. History and tradition are unusually minute in their memorials of this affair; and the captain of a scouting party of frontier men has acquired as actual a military renown as many a victorious leader of thousands. Some of the incidents contained in the following pages will be recognized, notwithstanding the substitution of fictitious names, by such as have heard, from old men's lips, the fate of the few combatants who were in a condition to retreat after "Lovell's Fight."

The early sunbeams hovered cheerfully upon the tree-tops, beneath which two weary and wounded men had stretched their limbs the night before. Their bed of withered oak leaves was strewn upon the small level space at the foot of a rock, situated near the summit of one of the gentle swells by which the face of the country is there diversified. The mass of granite, rearing its smooth, flat surface fifteen or twenty feet above their heads, was not unlike a gigantic gravestone, upon which the veins seemed to form an inscription in forgotten characters. On a tract of several acres around this rock, oaks and other hard-wood trees had supplied the place of the pines which were the usual growth of the land; and a young and vigorous sapling stood close beside the travellers.

The severe wound of the elder man had probably deprived him of sleep; for, so soon as the first ray of sunshine rested on the top of the highest tree, he reared himself painfully from his recumbent posture and sat erect. The deep lines of his countenance and the scattered gray of his hair marked him as past the middle age; but his muscular frame would, but for the effects of his wound, have been as capable of sustaining fatigue as in the early vigor of life. Languor and exhaustion now sat upon his haggard features; and the despairing glance which he sent forward through the depths of the forest proved his own conviction that his pilgrimage was at an end. He next turned his eyes to the companion who reclined by his side. The youth—for he had scarcely attained the years of manhood—lay, with his head upon his arm, in the embrace of an unquiet sleep, which a thrill of pain from his wounds seemed each moment on the point of breaking. His right hand grasped a musket; and, to judge from the violent action of his features, his slumbers were bringing back a vision of the conflict of which he was one of the few survivors. A shout —deep and loud in his dreaming fancy—found its way in an imperfect murmur to his lips; and, starting even at the slight sound of his own voice, he suddenly awoke. The first act of reviving recollection was to make anxious inquiries respecting the condition of his wounded fellow traveller. The latter shook his head.

"Reuben, my boy," said he, "this rock beneath which we sit will serve for an old hunter's gravestone. There is many and many a long mile of howling wilderness before us yet; nor would it avail me anything if the smoke of my own chimney were but on the other side of that swell of land. The Indian bullet was deadlier than I thought."

"You are weary with our three days' travel," replied the youth, "and a little longer rest will recruit you. Sit you here while I search the woods for the herbs and roots that must be our sustenance; and, having eaten, you shall lean on me, and we will turn our faces homeward. I doubt not that, with my help, you can attain to some one of the frontier garrisons."

"There is not two days' life in me, Reuben," said the other calmly, "and I will no longer burden you with my useless body, when you can scarcely support your own. Your wounds are deep and your strength is failing fast; yet, if you hasten onward alone, you may be preserved. For me there is no hope, and I will await death here."

"If it must be so, I will remain and watch by you," said Reuben resolutely.

"No, my son, no," rejoined his companion. "Let the wish of a dying man have weight with you; give me one grasp of your hand, and get you hence. Think you that my last moments will be eased by the thought that I leave you to die a more lingering death? I have loved you like a father, Reuben; and at a time like this I should have something of a father's authority. I charge you to be gone, that I may die in peace."

"And because you have been a father to me, should I therefore leave you to perish and to lie unburied in the wilderness?" exclaimed the youth. "No; if your end be in truth approaching, I will watch by you and receive your parting words. I will dig a grave here by the rock, in which, if my weakness overcome me, we will rest together; or, if Heaven gives me strength, I will seek my way home."

"In the cities and wherever men dwell," replied the other, "they bury their dead in the earth; they hide them from the sight of the living; but here, where no step may pass perhaps for a hundred years, wherefore should I not rest beneath the open sky, covered only by the oak leaves when the autumn winds shall strew them? And for a monument, here is this gray rock, on which my dying hand shall carve the name of Roger Malvin; and the traveller in days to come will know that here sleeps a hunter and a warrior. Tarry not, then, for a folly like this, but hasten away, if not for your own sake, for hers who will else be desolate."

Malvin spoke the last few words in a faltering voice, and their effect upon his companion was strongly visible. They reminded him that there were other and less questionable duties than that of sharing the fate of a man whom his death could not benefit. Nor can it be affirmed that no selfish feeling strove to enter Reuben's heart, though the consciousness made him more earnestly resist his companion's entreaties.

"How terrible to wait the slow approach of death in this solitude!" exclaimed he. "A brave man does not shrink in the battle; and, when friends stand round the bed, even women may die composedly; but here"—

"I shall not shrink even here, Reuben Bourne," interrupted Malvin. "I am a man of no weak heart, and, if I were, there is a surer support than that of earthly friends. You are young, and life is dear to you. Your last moments will need comfort far more than mine; and when you have laid me in the earth, and are alone, and night is settling on the forest, you will feel all the bitterness of the death that may now be escaped. But I will urge no selfish motive to your generous nature. Leave me for my sake, that, having said a prayer for your safety, I may have space to settle my account undisturbed by worldly sorrows."

"And your daughter,—how shall I dare to meet her eye?" exclaimed Reuben. "She will ask the fate of her father, whose life I vowed to defend with my own. Must I tell her that he travelled three days' march with me from the field of battle and that then I

left him to perish in the wilderness? Were it not better to lie down
and die by your side than to return safe and say this to Dorcas?"

"Tell my daughter," said Roger Malvin, "that, though yourself
sore wounded, and weak, and weary, you led my tottering footsteps
for many a mile, and left me only at my earnest entreaty, because I
would not have your blood upon my soul. Tell her that through
pain and danger you were faithful,—and that, if your life-blood
could have saved me, it would have flowed to its last drop; and tell
her that you will be something dearer than a father, and that my
blessing is with you both, and that my dying eyes can see a long
and pleasant path in which you will journey together."

As Malvin spoke he almost raised himself from the ground, and
the energy of his concluding words seemed to fill the wild and lonely
forest with a vision of happiness; but, when he sank exhausted upon
his bed of oak leaves, the light which had kindled in Reuben's eyes
was quenched. He felt as it if were both sin and folly to think of
happiness at such a moment. His companion watched his changing
countenance, and sought with generous art to wile him to his own
good.

"Perhaps I deceive myself in regard to the time I have to live," he
resumed. "It may be that, with speedy assistance, I might recover of
my wound. The foremost fugitives must, ere this, have carried tid-
ings of our fatal battle to the frontiers, and parties will be out to
succor those in like condition with ourselves. Should you meet one
of these and guide them hither, who can tell but that I may sit by
my own fireside again?"

A mournful smile strayed across the features of the dying man as
he insinuated that unfounded hope,—which, however, was not without its effect on Reuben. No merely selfish motive, nor even the desolate condition of Dorcas, could have induced him to desert his companion at such a moment—but his wishes seized on the thought that
Malvin's life might be preserved, and his sanguine nature height-
ened almost to certainty the remote possibility of procuring human
aid.

"Surely there is reason, weighty reason, to hope that friends are
not far distant," he said half aloud. "There fled one coward, un-
wounded, in the beginning of the fight, and most probably he made
good speed. Every true man on the frontier would shoulder his musket at the news; and, though no party may range so far into the
woods as this, I shall perhaps encounter them in one day's march.
Counsel me faithfully," he added, turning to Malvin, in distrust of
his own motives. "Were your situation mine, would you desert me
while life remained?"

"It is now twenty years," replied Roger Malvin,—sighing, however, as he secretly acknowledged the wide dissimilarity between the two cases,—"it is now twenty years since I escaped with one dear friend from Indian captivity near Montreal. We journeyed many days through the woods, till at length, overcome with hunger and weariness, my friend lay down and besought me to leave him; for he knew that, if I remained, we both must perish; and, with but little hope of obtaining succor, I heaped a pillow of dry leaves beneath his head and hastened on."

"And did you return in time to save him?" asked Reuben, hanging on Malvin's words as if they were to be prophetic of his own success.

"I did," answered the other. "I came upon the camp of a hunting-party before sunset of the same day. I guided them to the spot where my comrade was expecting death; and he is now a hale and hearty man upon his own farm, far within the frontiers, while I lie wounded here in the depths of the wilderness."

This example, powerful in affecting Reuben's decision, was aided, unconsciously to himself, by the hidden strength of many another motive. Roger Malvin perceived that the victory was nearly won.

"Now, go, my son, and Heaven prosper you!" he said. "Turn not back with your friends when you meet them, lest your wounds and weariness overcome you; but send hitherward two or three, that may be spared, to search for me; and believe me, Reuben, my heart will be lighter with every step you take towards home." Yet there was, perhaps, a change both in his countenance and voice as he spoke thus; for, after all, it was a ghastly fate to be left expiring in the wilderness.

Reuben Bourne, but half convinced that he was acting rightly, at length raised himself from the ground and prepared himself for his departure. And first, though contrary to Malvin's wishes, he collected a stock of roots and herbs, which had been their only food during the last two days. This useless supply he placed within reach of the dying man, for whom, also, he swept together a bed of dry oak leaves. Then climbing to the summit of the rock, which on one side was rough and broken, he bent the oak sapling downward, and bound his handkerchief to the topmost branch. This precaution was not unnecessary to direct any who might come in search of Malvin; for every part of the rock, except its broad, smooth front, was concealed at a little distance by the dense undergrowth of the forest. The handkerchief had been the bandage of a wound upon Reuben's arm; and, as he bound it to the tree, he vowed by the blood that stained it that he would return, either to save his companion's life or to lay his body in the grave. He then descended, and stood, with downcast eyes, to receive Roger Malvin's parting words.

The experience of the latter suggested much and minute advice respecting the youth's journey through the trackless forest. Upon this subject he spoke with calm earnestness, as if he were sending Reuben to the battle or the chase while he himself remained secure at home, and not as if the human countenance that was about to leave him were the last he would ever behold. But his firmness was shaken before he concluded.

"Carry my blessing to Dorcas, and say that my last prayer shall be for her and you. Bid her to have no hard thoughts because you left me here,"—Reuben's heart smote him,—"for that your life would not have weighed with you if its sacrifice could have done me good. She will marry you after she has mourned a little while for her father; and Heaven grant you long and happy days, and may your children's children stand round your death-bed! And, Reuben," added he, as the weakness of mortality made its way at last, "return, when your wounds are healed and your weariness refreshed,—return to this wild rock, and lay my bones in the grave, and say a prayer over them."

An almost superstitious regard, arising perhaps from the customs of the Indians, whose war was with the dead as well as the living, was paid by the frontier inhabitants to the rites of sepulture; and there are many instances of the sacrifice of life in the attempt to bury those who had fallen by the "sword of the wilderness." Reuben, therefore, felt the full importance of the promise which he most solemnly made to return and perform Roger Malvin's obsequies. It was remarkable that the latter, speaking his whole heart in his parting words, no longer endeavored to persuade the youth that even the speediest succor might avail to the preservation of his life. Reuben was internally convinced that he should see Malvin's living face no more. His generous nature would fain have delayed him, at whatever risk, till the dying scene were past; but the desire of existence and the hope of happiness had strengthened in his heart, and he was unable to resist them.

"It is enough," said Roger Malvin, having listed to Reuben's promise. "Go, and God speed you!"

The youth pressed his hand in silence, turned, and was departing. His slow and faltering steps, however, had borne him but a little way before Malvin's voice recalled him.

"Reuben, Reuben," said he faintly; and Reuben returned and knelt down by the dying man.

"Raise me, and let me lean against the rock," was his last request. "My face will be turned towards home, and I shall see you a moment longer as you pass among the trees."

Reuben, having made the desired alteration in his companion's posture, again began his solitary pilgrimage. He walked more hastily at first than was consistent with his strength; for a sort of guilty feeling, which sometimes torments men in their most justifiable acts, caused him to seek concealment from Malvin's eyes; but after he had trodden far upon the rustling forest leaves he crept back, impelled by a wild and painful curiosity, and, sheltered by the earthy roots of an uptorn tree, gazed earnestly at the desolate man. The morning sun was unclouded, and the trees and shrubs imbibed the sweet air of the month of May; yet there seemed a gloom on Nature's face, as if she sympathized with mortal pain and sorrow. Roger Malvin's hands were uplifted in a fervent prayer, some of the words of which stole through the stillness of the woods and entered Reuben's heart, torturing it with unutterable pang. They were the broken accents of a petition for his own happiness and that of Dorcas; and, as the youth listened, conscience, or something in its similitude, pleaded strongly with him to return and lie down again by the rock. He felt how hard was the doom of the kind and generous being whom he had deserted in his extremity. Death would come like the slow approach of a corpse, stealing gradually towards him through the forest, and showing its ghastly and motionless features from behind a nearer and yet a nearer tree. But such must have been Reuben's own fate had he tarried another sunset; and who shall impute blame to him if he shrink from so useless a sacrifice? As he gave a parting look, a breeze waved the little banner upon the sapling oak and reminded Reuben of his vow. . . .

Many circumstances combined to retard the wounded traveller in his way to the frontiers. On the second day the clouds, gathering densely over the sky, precluded the possibility of regulating his course by the position of the sun; and he knew not but that every effort of his almost exhausted strength was removing him farther from the home he sought. His scanty sustenance was supplied by the berries and other spontaneous products of the forest. Herds of deer, it is true, sometimes bounded past him, and partridges frequently whirred up before his footsteps; but his ammunition had been expended in the fight, and he had no means of slaying them. His wounds, irritated by the constant exertion in which lay the only hope of life, wore away his strength, and at intervals confused his reason. But, even in the wanderings of intellect, Reuben's young heart clung strongly to existence; and it was only through absolute incapacity of motion that he at last sank down beneath a tree, compelled there to await death.

In this situation he was discovered by a party who, upon the first intelligence of the fight, had been despatched to the relief of the survivors. They conveyed him to the nearest settlement, which chanced to be that of his own residence.

Dorcas, in the simplicity of the olden time, watched by the bedside of her wounded lover, and administered all those comforts that are in the sole gift of woman's heart and hand. During several days Reuben's recollection strayed drowsily among the perils and hardships through which he had passed, and he was incapable of returning definite answers to the inquiries with which many were eager to harass him. No authentic particulars of the battle had yet been circulated; nor could mothers, wives, and children tell whether their loved ones were detained by captivity or by the stronger chain of death. Dorcas nourished her apprehensions in silence till one afternoon when Reuben awoke from an unquiet sleep, and seemed to recognize her more perfectly than at any previous time. She saw that his intellect had become composed, and she could no longer restrain her filial anxiety.

"My father, Reuben?" she began; but the change in her lover's countenance made her pause.

The youth shrank as if with a bitter pain, and the blood gushed vividly into his wan and hollow cheeks. His first impulse was to cover his face; but, apparently with a desperate effort, he half raised himself and spoke vehemently, defending himself against an imaginary accusation.

"Your father was sore wounded in the battle, Dorcas; and he bade me not burden myself with him, but only to lead him to the lakeside, that he might quench his thirst and die. But I would not desert the old man in his extremity; and, though bleeding myself, I supported him; I gave him half my strength, and led him away with me. For three days we journeyed on together, and your father was sustained beyond my hopes, but, awaking at sunrise on the fourth day, I found him faint and exhausted; he was unable to proceed; his life had ebbed away fast; and"—

"He died!" exclaimed Dorcas faintly.

Reuben felt it impossible to acknowledge that his selfish love of life had hurried him away before her father's fate was decided. He spoke not; he only bowed his head; and, between shame and exhaustion, sank back and hid his face in the pillow. Dorcas wept when her fears were thus confirmed; but the shock, as it had been long anticipated, was on that account the less violent.

"You dug a grave for my poor father in the wilderness, Reuben?" was the question by which her filial piety manifested itself.

"My hands were weak; but I did what I could," replied the youth in a smothered tone. "There stands a noble tombstone above his head; and I would to Heaven I slept as soundly as he!"

Dorcas, perceiving the wildness of his latter words, inquired no further at the time; but her heart found ease in the thought that Roger Malvin had not lacked such funeral rites as it was possible to bestow. The tale of Reuben's courage and fidelity lost nothing when she communicated it to her friends; and the poor youth, tottering from his sick-chamber to breathe the sunny air, experienced from every tongue the miserable and humiliating torture of unmerited praise. All acknowledged that he might worthily demand the hand of the fair maiden to whose father he had been "faithful unto death;" and, as my tale is not of love, it shall suffice to say that in the space of a few months Reuben became the husband of Dorcas Malvin. During the marriage ceremony the bride was covered with blushes, but the bridegroom's face was pale.

There was now in the breast of Reuben Bourne an uncommunicable thought—something which he was to conceal most heedfully from her whom he most loved and trusted. He regretted, deeply and bitterly, the moral cowardice that had restrained his words when he was about to disclose the truth to Dorcas; but pride, the fear of losing her affection, the dread of universal scorn, forbade him to rectify this falsehood. He felt that for leaving Roger Malvin he deserved no censure. His presence, the gratuitous sacrifice of his own life, would have added only another and a needless agony to the last moments of the dying man; but concealment had imparted to a justifiable act much of the secret effect of guilt; and Reuben, while reason told him that he had done right, experienced in no small degree the mental horrors which punish the perpetrator of undiscovered crime. By a certain association of ideas, he at times almost imagined himself a murderer. For years, also, a thought would occasionally recur, which, though he perceived all its folly and extravagance, he had not power to banish from his mind. It was a haunting and torturing fancy that his father-in-law was yet sitting at the foot of the rock, on the withered forest leaves, alive, and awaiting his pledged assistance. These mental deceptions, however, came and went, nor did he ever mistake them for realities; but in the calmest and clearest moods of his mind he was conscious that he had a deep vow unredeemed, and that an unburied corpse was calling to him out of the wilderness. Yet such was the consequence of his prevarication that he could not obey the call. It was now too late to require the assistance of Roger Malvin's friends in performing his long-deferred sepulture,—and superstitious fears, of which none were more susceptible than the people of the outward settlements, forbade Reuben to go alone. Neither did he know where in the pathless and illimitable forest to seek that smooth and lettered rock at the base of which the body lay: his remembrance of every portion of his travel thence was indistinct, and the latter part had left no impression upon his mind. There was, however, a continual impulse, a voice audible only to himself, commanding him to go forth and redeem his vow; and he had a strange impression that, were he to make the trial, he would be led straight to Malvin's bones. But year after year that summons, unheard but felt, was disobeyed. His one secret thought became like a chain binding down his spirit and like a serpent gnawing into his heart; and he was transformed into a sad and downcast yet irritable man.

In the course of a few years after their marriage changes began to be visible in the external prosperity of Reuben and Dorcas. The only riches of the former had been his stout heart and strong arm; but the latter, her father's sole heiress, had made her husband master of a farm, under older cultivation, larger, and better stocked than most of the frontier establishments. Reuben Bourne, however, was a neglectful husbandman; and, while the lands of the other settlers became annually more fruitful, his deteriorated in the same proportion. The discouragements to agriculture were greatly lessened by the cessation of Indian war, during which men held the plough in one hand and the musket in the other, and were fortunate if the products of their dangerous labor were not destroyed, either in the field or in the barn, by the savage enemy. But Reuben did not profit by the altered condition of the country; nor can it be denied that his intervals of industrious attention to his affairs were but scantily rewarded with success. The irritability by which he had recently become distinguished was another cause of his declining prosperity, as it occasioned frequent quarrels in his unavoidable intercourse with the neighboring settlers. The results of these were innumerable lawsuits; for the people of New England, in the earliest stages and wildest circumstances of the country, adopted, whenever attainable, the legal mode of deciding their differences. To be brief, the world did not go well with Reuben Bourne; and, though not till many years after his marriage, he was finally a ruined man, with but one remaining expedient against the evil fate that had pursued him. He was to throw sunlight into some deep recess of the forest, and seek subsistence from the virgin bosom of the wilderness.

The only child of Reuben and Dorcas was a son, now arrived at the age of fifteen years, beautiful in youth and giving promise of a glorious manhood. He was peculiarly qualified for, and already began to excel in, the wild accomplishments of frontier life. His foot was fleet, his aim true, his apprehension quick, his heart glad and high; and all who anticipated the return of Indian war spoke of Cyrus Bourne as a future leader in the land. The boy was loved by his father with a deep and silent strength, as if whatever was good and happy in his own nature had been transferred to his child, carrying his affections with it. Even Dorcas, though loving and beloved, was far less dear to him,—for Reuben's secret thoughts and insulated emotions had gradually made him a selfish man, and he could no longer love deeply except where he saw or imagined some reflection or likeness of his own mind. In Cyrus he recognized what he had himself been in other days; and at intervals he seemed to partake of the boy's spirit, and to be revived with a fresh and happy life. Reuben was accompanied by his son in the expedition, for the purpose of selecting a tract of land and felling and burning the timber, which necessarily preceded the removal of the household gods. Two months of autumn were thus occupied, after which Reuben Bourne and his young hunter returned to spend their last winter in the settlements. . . .

It was early in the month of May that the little family snapped asunder whatever tendrils of affection had clung to inanimate objects, and bade farewell to the few who, in the blight of fortune, called themselves their friends. The sadness of the parting moment had, to each of the pilgrims, its peculiar alleviations. Reuben, a moody man, and misanthropic because unhappy, strode onward with his usual stern brow and downcast eye, feeling few regrets and disdaining to acknowledge any. Dorcas, while she wept abundantly over the broken ties by which her simple and affectionate nature had bound itself to everything, felt that the inhabitants of her inmost heart moved on with her, and that all else would be supplied wherever she might go. And the boy dashed one teardrop from his eye, and thought of the adventurous pleasures of the untrodden forest.

O, who, in the enthusiasm of a day-dream, has not wished that he were a wanderer in a world of summer wilderness, with one fair and gentle being hanging lightly on his arm? In youth his free and exulting step would know no barrier but the rolling ocean or the snow-topped mountains; calmer manhood would choose a home where Nature had strewn a double wealth in the vale of some transparent stream; and when hoary age, after long, long years of that pure life, stole on and found him there, it would find him the father of a race, the patriarch of a people,—the founder of a mighty nation yet to be. When death, like the sweet sleep which we welcome after a day of happiness, came over him, his far descendants would mourn over the venerated dust. Enveloped by tradition in mysterious attributes, the men of future generations would call him godlike; and remote posterity would see him standing, dimly glorious, far up the valley of a hundred centuries.

The tangled and gloomy forest through which the personages of my tale were wandering differed widely from the dreamer's land of fantasy; yet there was something in their way of life that Nature asserted as her own, and the gnawing cares which went with them from the world were all that now obstructed their happiness. One stout and shaggy steed, the bearer of all their wealth, did not shrink from the added weight of Dorcas; although her hardy breeding sustained her, during the latter part of each day's journey, by her husband's side. Reuben and his son, their muskets on their shoulders and their axes slung behind them, kept an unwearied pace, each watching with a hunter's eye for the game that supplied their food. When hunger bade, they halted and prepared their meal on the bank of some unpolluted forest brook, which, as they knelt down with thirsty lips to drink, murmured a sweet unwillingness, like a maiden at love's first kiss. They slept beneath a hut of branches, and awoke at peep of light refreshed for the toils of another day. Dorcas and the boy went on joyously, and even Reuben's spirit shone at intervals with an outward gladness; but inwardly there was a cold, cold sorrow, which he compared to the snowdrifts lying deep in the glens and hollows of the rivulets while the leaves were brightly green above.

Cyrus Bourne was sufficiently skilled in the travel of the woods to observe that his father did not adhere to the course they had pursued in their expedition of the preceding autumn. They were now keeping farther to the north, striking out directly from the settlements, and into a region of which savage beasts and savage men were as yet the sole possessors. The boy sometimes hinted his opinions upon the subject, and Reuben listened attentively, and once or twice altered the direction of their march in accordance with his son's counsel; but, having so done, he seemed ill at ease. His quick and wandering glances were sent forward, apparently in search of enemies lurking behind the tree-trunks; and, seeing nothing there, he would cast his eyes backwards as if in fear of some pursuer. Cyrus, perceiving that his father gradually resumed the old direction, forbore to interfere; nor, though something began to weigh upon his heart, did his adventurous nature permit him to regret the increased length and the mystery of their way.

On the afternoon of the fifth day they halted, and made their simple encampment nearly an hour before sunset. The face of the country, for the last few miles, had been diversified by swells of land resembling huge waves of a petrified sea; and in one of the corresponding hollows, a wild and romantic spot, had the family reared their hut and kindled their fire. There is something chilling, and yet heartwarming in the thought of these three, united by strong bands of love and insulated from all that breathe beside. The dark and gloomy pines looked down upon them, and, as the wind swept through their tops, a pitying sound was heard in the forest; or did those old trees groan in fear that men were come to lay the axe to their roots at last? Reuben and his son, while Dorcas made ready their meal, proposed to wander out in search of game, of which that day's march had afforded no supply. The boy, promising not to quit the vicinity of the encampment, bounded off with a step as light and elastic as that of the deer he hoped to slay; while his father, feeling a transient happiness as he gazed after him, was about to pursue an opposite direction. Dorcas, in the meanwhile, had seated herself near their fire of fallen branches, upon the mossgrown and mouldering trunk of a tree uprooted years before. Her employment, diversified by an occasional glance at the pot, now beginning to simmer over the blaze, was the perusal of the current year's Massachusetts Almanac, which, with the exception of an old black-lettered Bible, comprised all the literary wealth of the family. None pay a greater regard to arbitrary divisions of time than those who are excluded from society; and Dorcas mentioned, as if the information were of importance, that it was now the twelfth of May. Her husband started.

"The twelfth of May! I should remember it well," muttered he, while many thoughts occasioned a momentary confusion in his mind. "Where am I? Whither am I wandering? Where did I leave him?"

Dorcas, too well accustomed to her husband's wayward moods to note any peculiarity of demeanor, now laid aside the almanac and addressed him in that mournful tone which the tender-hearted appropriate to griefs long cold and dead.

"It was near this time of the month, eighteen years ago, that my poor father left this world for a better. He had a kind arm to hold his head and a kind voice to cheer him, Reuben, in his last moments; and the thought of the faithful care you took of him has comforted me many a time since. O, death would have been awful to a solitary man in a wild place like this!"

"Pray Heaven, Dorcas," said Reuben, in a broken voice,—"pray Heaven that neither of us three dies solitary and lies unburied in this howling wilderness!" And he hastened away, leaving her to watch the fire beneath the gloomy pines.

Reuben Bourne's rapid pace gradually slackened as the pang, unintentionally inflicted by the words of Dorcas, became less acute. Many strange reflections, however, thronged upon him; and, straying onward rather like a sleepwalker than a hunter, it was attributable to no care of his own that his devious course kept him in the vicinity of the encampment. His steps were imperceptibly led almost in a circle; nor did he observe that he was on the verge of a tract of land heavily timbered, but not with pine-trees. The place of the latter was here supplied by oaks and other of the harder woods; and around their roots clustered a dense and bushy undergrowth,—leaving, however, barren spaces between the trees, thick strewn with withered leaves. Whenever the rustling of the branches or the creaking of the trunks made a sound, as if the forest were waking from slumber, Reuben instinctively raised the musket that rested on his arm, and cast a quick, sharp glance on every side; but, convinced by a partial observation that no animal was near, he would again give himself up to his thoughts. He was musing on the strange influence that had led him away from his premeditated course, and so far into the depths of the wilderness. Unable to penetrate to the secret place of his soul where his motives lay hidden, he believed that a supernatural voice had called him onward, and that a supernatural power had obstructed his retreat. He trusted that it was Heaven's intent to afford him an opportunity of expiating his sin; he hoped that he might find the bones so long unburied; and that, having laid the earth over them, peace would throw its sunlight into the sepulchre of his heart. From these thoughts he was aroused by a rustling in the forest at some distance from the spot to which he had wandered. Perceiving the motion of some object behind a thick veil of undergrowth, he fired, with the instinct of a hunter and the aim of a practised marksman. A low moan, which told his success, and by which even animals can express their dying agony, was unheeded by Reuben Bourne. What were the recollections now breaking upon him?

The thicket into which Reuben had fired was near the summit of a swell of land, and was clustered around the base of a rock, which, in the shape and smoothness of one of its surfaces, was not unlike a gigantic gravestone. As if reflected in a mirror, its likeness was in Reuben's memory. He even recognized the veins which seemed to form an inscription in forgotten characters: everything remained the same, except that a thick covert of bushes shrouded the lower part of the rock, and would have hidden Roger Malvin had he still been sitting there. Yet in the next moment Reuben's eye was caught by another change that time had effected since he last stood where he was now standing again behind the earthy roots of the uptorn tree. The sapling to which he had bound the blood-stained symbol of his vow had increased and strengthened into an oak, far indeed from its maturity, but with no mean spread of shadowy branches. There was one singularity observable in this tree which made Reuben tremble. The middle and lower branches were in luxuriant life, and an excess of vegetation had fringed the trunk almost to the ground; but a blight had apparently stricken the upper part of the oak, and the very topmost bough was withered, sapless, and utterly dead. Reuben remembered how the little banner had fluttered on that topmost bough, when it was green and lovely, eighteen years before. Whose guilt had blasted it? . . .

Dorcas, after the departure of the two hunters, continued her preparations for their evening repast. Her sylvan table was the moss-covered trunk of a large fallen tree, on the broadest part of which she had spread a snow-white cloth and arranged what were left of the bright pewter vessels that had been her pride in the settlements. It had a strange aspect, that one little spot of homely comfort in the desolate heart of Nature. The sunshine yet lingered upon the higher branches of the trees that grew on rising ground; but the shadows of evening had deepened into the hollow where the encampment was made, and the firelight began to redden as it gleamed up the tall trunks of the pines or hovered on the dense and obscure mass of foliage that circled round the spot. The heart of Dorcas was not sad; for she felt that it was better to journey in the wilderness with two whom she loved than to be a lonely woman in a crowd that cared not for her. As she busied herself in arranging seats of mouldering wood, covered with leaves, for Reuben and her son, her voice danced through the gloomy forest in the measure of a song that she had learned in youth. The rude melody, the production of a bard who won no name, was descriptive of a winter evening in a frontier cottage, when, secured from savage inroad by the high-piled snowdrifts, the family rejoiced by their own fireside. The whole song possessed the nameless charm peculiar to unborrowed thought, but four continually recurring lines shone out from the rest like the blaze of the hearth whose joys they celebrated. Into them, working magic with a few simple words, the poet had instilled the very essence of domestic love and household happiness, and they were poetry and picture joined in one. As Dorcas sang, the walls of her forsaken home seemed to encircle her; she no longer saw the gloomy pines, nor heard the wind which still, as she began each verse, sent a heavy breath through the branches, and died away in a hollow moan from the burden of the song. She was aroused by the report of a gun in the vicinity of the encampment; and either the sudden sound, or her loneliness by the glowing fire, caused her to tremble violently. The next moment she laughed in the pride of a mother's heart.

"My beautiful young hunter! My boy has slain a deer!" she exclaimed, recollecting that in the direction whence the shot proceeded Cyrus had gone to the chase.

She waited a reasonable time to hear her son's light step bounding over the rustling leaves to tell of his success. But he did not immediately appear; and she sent her cheerful voice among the trees in search of him.

"Cyrus! Cyrus!"

His coming was still delayed; and she determined, as the report had apparently been very near, to seek for him in person. Her assistance, also, might be necessary in bringing home the venison which she flattered herself he had obtained. She therefore set forward, directing her steps by the long-past sound, and singing as she went, in order that the boy might be aware of her approach and run to meet her. From behind the trunk of every tree, and from every hiding-place in the thick foliage of the undergrowth, she hoped to discover the countenance of her son, laughing with the sportive mischief that is born of affection. The sun was now beneath the horizon, and the light that came down among the leaves was sufficiently dim to create many illusions in her expecting fancy. Several times she seemed indistinctly to see his face gazing out from among the leaves; and once she imagined that he stood beckoning to her at the base of a craggy rock. Keeping her eyes on this object, however, it proved to be no more than the trunk of an oak fringed to the very ground with little branches, one of which, thrust out farther than the rest, was shaken by the breeze. Making her way round the foot of the rock, she suddenly found herself close to her husband, who had approached in another direction. Leaning upon the butt of his gun, the muzzle of which rested upon the withered leaves, he was apparently absorbed in the contemplation of some object at his feet.

"How is this, Reuben? Have you slain the deer and fallen asleep over him?" exclaimed Dorcas, laughing cheerfully, on her first slight observation of his posture and appearance.

He stirred not, neither did he turn his eyes towards her; and a cold, shuddering fear, indefinite in its source and object, began to creep into her blood. She now perceived that her husband's face was ghastly pale, and his features were rigid, as if incapable of assuming any other expression than the strong despair which had hardened upon them. He gave not the slightest evidence that he was aware of her approach.

"For the love of Heaven, Reuben, speak to me!" cried Dorcas; and the strange sound of her own voice affrighted her even more than the dead silence.

Her husband started, stared into her face, drew her to the front of the rock, and pointed with his finger.

O, there lay the boy, asleep, but dreamless, upon the fallen forest leaves! His cheek rested upon his arm—his curled locks were thrown back from his brow—his limbs were slightly relaxed. Had a sudden weariness overcome the youthful hunter? Would his mother's voice arouse him? She knew that it was death.

"This broad rock is the gravestone of your near kindred, Dorcas," said her husband. "Your tears will fall at once over your father and your son."

She heard him not. With one wild shriek, that seemed to force its way from the sufferer's inmost soul, she sank insensible by the side of her dead boy. At that moment the withered topmost bough of the oak loosened itself in the stilly air, and fell in soft, light fragments upon the rock, upon the leaves, upon Reuben, upon his wife and child, and upon Roger Malvin's bones. Then Reuben's heart was stricken, and the tears gushed out like water from a rock. The vow that the wounded youth had made the blighted man had come to redeem. His sin was expiated,—the curse was gone from him; and in the hour when he had shed blood dearer to him than his own, a prayer, the first for years, went up to Heaven from the lips of Reuben Bourne.

WASHINGTON IRVING

The Legend of Sleepy Hollow

AMONG THESE the most formidable was a burly, roaring, roystering blade, of the name of Abraham, or, according to the Dutch abbreviation, Brom Van Brunt, the hero of the country round, which rang with his feats of strength and hardihood. He was broad-shouldered and double-jointed, with short curly black hair, and a bluff, but not unpleasant countenance, having a mingled air of fun and arrogance. From his Herculean frame and great powers of limb, he had received the nickname of BROM BONES, by which he was universally known. He was famed for great knowledge and skill in horsemanship, being as dexterous on horseback as a tartar. He was foremost at all races and cock-fights; and, with the ascendency which bodily strength acquires in rustic life, was the umpire in all disputes, setting his hat on one side, and giving his decisions with an air and tone admitting of no gainsay or appeal. He was always ready for either a fight or a frolic; but had more mischief than ill-will in his composition; and, with all his overbearing roughness, there was a strong dash of waggish good humor at bottom. He had three or four boon companions, who regarded him as their model, and at the head of whom he scoured the country, attending every scene of feud or merriment for miles round. In cold weather he was distinguished by a fur cap, surmounted with a flaunting fox's tail; and when the folks at a country gathering descried this well-known crest at a distance, whisking about among a squad of hard riders, they always stood by for a squall. Sometimes his crew would be heard dashing along past the farmhouses at midnight, with whoop and halloo, like a troop of Don Cossacks; and the old dames, startled out of their sleep, would listen for a moment till the hurry-scurry had clattered by, and then exclaim, "Ay, there goes Brom Bones and his gang!" The neighbors looked upon with a mixture of awe, admiration, and good will; and when any madcap prank, or rustic brawl, occurred in the vicinity, always shook their heads, and warranted Brom Bones was at the bottom of it.

This one descriptive paragraph is reprinted here because it is probably the first fictional presentation of a frontier hero. [Ed. note]

JAMES FENIMORE COOPER

The Death of the Trapper

THE WATER-COURSES were at their height, and the boat went down the swift current like a bird. The passage proved prosperous and speedy. In less than a third of the time that would have been necessary for the same journey by land, it was accomplished by the favor of those rapid rivers. Issuing from one stream into another, as the veins of the human body communicate with the larger channels of life, they soon entered the grand artery of the western waters, and landed safely at the very door of the father of Inez.

The joy of Don Augustin, and the embarrassment of the worthy Father Ignatius, may be imagined. The former wept and returned thanks to heaven; the latter returned thanks, and did not weep. The mild provincials were too happy to raise any questions on the character of so joyful a restoration; and, by a sort of general consent, it soon came to be an admitted opinion that the bride of Middleton had been kidnapped by a villain, and that she was restored to her friends by human agency. There were, as respects this belief, certainly a few skeptics, but then they enjoyed their doubts in private, with that species of sublimated and solitary gratification that a miser finds in gazing at his growing but useless hoards.

In order to give the worthy priest something to employ his mind, Middleton made him the instrument of uniting Paul and Ellen. The former consented to the ceremony because he found that all his friends laid great stress on the matter; but shortly after he led his bride into the plains of Kentucky, under the pretense of paying certain customary visits to sundry members of the family of Hover. While there, he took occasion to have the marriage properly solemnized by a justice of the peace of his acquaintance, in whose ability to forge the nuptial chain he had much more faith than in that of

This passage from *The Prairie* describes the death of Cooper's most famous hero, who was known in the different novels of the Leatherstocking Tales as Natty Bumppo, Deerslayer, Hawkeye, Pathfinder, Leatherstocking, or simply "the trapper." [Ed. note]

all the gownsmen within the pale of Rome. Ellen, who appeared conscious that some extraordinary preventives might prove necessary to keep one of so erratic a temper as her husband within the proper matrimonial boundaries, raised no objections to these double knots, and all parties were contented.

The local importance Middleton had acquired by his union with the daughter of so affluent a proprietor as Don Augustin, united to his personal merit, attracted the attention of the government. He was soon employed in various situations of responsibility and confidence, which both served to elevate his character in the public estimation and to afford the means of patronage. The bee-hunter was among the first of those to whom he saw fit to extend his favor. It was far from difficult to find situations suited to the abilities of Paul, in the state of society that existed three-and-twenty years ago in those regions. The efforts of Middleton and Inez in behalf of her husband were warmly and sagaciously seconded by Ellen, and they succeeded, in process of time, in working a great and beneficial change in his character. He soon became a landholder, then a prosperous cultivator of the soil, and shortly after a town officer. By that progressive change in fortunes which in the republic is often seen to be as singularly accompanied by a corresponding improvement in knowledge and self-respect, he went on from step to step, until his wife enjoyed the maternal delight of seeing her children placed far beyond the dangers of returning to that state from which both their parents had issued.

Paul is actually at this moment a member of the lower branch of the Legislature of the State where he has long resided; and he is even notorious for making speeches that have a tendency to put that deliberative body in good-humor, and which, as they are based on great practical knowledge suited to the condition of the country, possess a merit that is much wanted in many more subtle and fine-spun theories that are daily heard, in similar assemblies, to issue from the lips of certain instinctive politicians. But all these happy fruits were the results of much care, and of a long period of time. Middleton, who fills, with a credit better suited to the difference in their educations, a seat in a far higher branch of legislative authority, is the source from which we have derived most of the intelligence necessary to compose our legend. In addition to what he has related of Paul, and of his own continued happiness, he has added a short narrative of what took place on a subsequent visit to the prairies, with which, as we conceive it a suitable termination to what has gone before, we shall judge it wise to conclude our labors.

In the autumn of the year that succeeded the season in which the preceding events occurred, the young man, still in the military service, found himself on the waters of the Missouri, at a point not far remote from the Pawnee towns. Released from any immediate calls of duty, and strongly urged to the measure by Paul, who was in his company, he determined to take horse, and cross the country to visit the partisan, and to inquire into the fate of his friend the trapper. As his train was suited to his functions and rank, the journey was effected with privations and hardships that are the accompaniments of all traveling in a wild, but without any of those dangers and alarms that marked his former passage through the same regions. When within a proper distance, he dispatched an Indian runner, belonging to a friendly tribe, to announce the approach of himself and party, continuing his route at a deliberate pace, in order that the intelligence might, as was customary, precede his arrival. To the surprise of the travelers, their message was unanswered. Hour succeeded hour, and mile after mile was passed, without bringing either the signs of an honorable reception or the more simple assurances of a friendly welcome. At length the cavalcade, at whose head rode Middleton and Paul, descended from the elevated plain, on which they had long been journeying, to a luxuriant bottom, that brought them to the level of the village of the Loups. The sun was beginning to fall, and a sheet of golden light was spread over the placid plain, lending to its even surface those glorious tints and hues that the human imagination is apt to conceive form the embellishment of still more imposing scenes. The verdure of the year yet remained, and herds of horses and mules were grazing peacefully in the vast natural pasture, under the keeping of vigilant Pawnee boys. Paul pointed out among them the well-known form of Asinus, sleek, fat, and luxuriating in the fullness of content, as he stood with reclining ears and closed eyelids, seemingly musing on the exquisite nature of his present indolent enjoyment.

The route of the party led them on at great distance from one of those watchful youths who was charged with a trust heavy as the principal wealth of his tribe. He heard the trampling of the horses, and cast his eye aside, but, instead of manifesting curiosity or alarm, his look instantly returned whence it had been withdrawn, to the spot where the village was known to stand.

"There is something remarkable in all this," muttered Middleton, half offended at what he conceived to be not only a slight to his rank, but offensive to himself personally; "yonder boy has heard of our approach, or he would not fail to notify his tribe; and yet he scarcely deigns to favor us with a glance. Look to your arms, men; it may be necessary to let these savages feel our strength."

"Therein, captain, I think you're in an error," returned Paul; "if honesty is to be met on the prairies at all, you will find it in our old friend, Hard-Heart; neither is an Indian to be judged of by the rules of a white. See! we are not altogether slighted, for here comes a party at last to meet us, though it is a little pitiful as to show and numbers."

Paul was right in both particulars. A group of horsemen were at length seen wheeling around a little copse and advancing across the plain directly towards them. The advance of this party was slow and dignified. As it drew nigh, the partisan of the Loups was seen at its head, followed by a dozen younger warriors of his tribe. They were all unarmed, nor did they even wear any of those ornaments or feathers which are considered testimonials of respect to the guest an Indian receives, as well as evidence of his own importance.

The meeting was friendly, though a little restrained on both sides. Middleton, jealous of his own consideration, no less than of the authority of his government, suspected some undue influence on the part of the agents of the Canadas; and, as he was determined to maintain the authority of which he was the representative, he felt himself constrained to manifest a *hauteur* that he was far from feeling. It was not so easy to penetrate the motives of the Pawnees. Calm, dignified, and yet far from repulsive, they set an example of courtesy, blended with reserve, that many a diplomatist of the most polished court might have striven in vain to imitate.

In this manner the two parties continued their course to the town. Middleton had time, during the remainder of the ride, to revolve in his mind all the probable reasons which his ingenuity could suggest for this strange reception. Although he was accompanied by a regular interpreter, the chiefs made their salutations in a manner that dispensed with his services. Twenty times the captain turned his glance on his former friend, endeavoring to read the expression of his rigid features. But every effort and all conjectures proved equally futile. The eye of Hard-Heart was fixed, composed, and a little anxious; but, as to every other emotion, impenetrable. He neither spoke himself, nor seemed willing to invite discourse in his visitors; it was therefore necessary for Middleton to adopt the patient manners of his companions, and to await the issue for the explanation.

When they entered the town, its inhabitants were seen collected in an open space, where they were arranged with the customary deference to age and rank. The whole formed a large circle, in the center of which were perhaps a dozen of the principal chiefs. Hard-Heart waved his hand as he approached, and, as the mass of bodies opened, he rode through, followed by his companions. Here they dismounted; and, as the beasts were led apart, the strangers found themselves environed by a thousand grave, composed, but solicitous faces.

Middleton gazed about him in growing concern, for no cry, no song, no shout welcomed him among a people from whom he had so lately parted with regret. His uneasiness, not to say apprehension, was shared by all his followers. Determination and stern resolution began to assume the place of anxiety in every eye, as each man silently felt for his arms and assured himself that his several weapons were in a state for service. But there was no answering symptom of hostility on the part of their hosts. Hard-Heart beckoned for Middleton and Paul to follow, leading the way toward the cluster of forms that occupied the center of the circle. Here the visitors found a solution of all the movements which had given them so much reason for apprehension.

The trapper was placed on a rude seat, which had been made, with studied care, to support his frame in an upright and easy attitude. The first glance of the eye told his former friends that the old man was at length called upon to pay the last tribute of Nature. His eye was glazed, and apparently as devoid of sight as of expression. His features were a little more sunken and strongly marked than formerly; but there all change, so far as exterior was concerned, might be said to have ceased. His approaching end was not to be ascribed to any positive disease, but had been a gradual and mild decay of the physical powers. Life, it is true, still lingered in his system; but it was as if at times entirely ready to depart, and then it would appear to reanimate the sinking form, reluctant to give up the possession of a tenement that had never been corrupted by vice or undermined by disease. It would have been no violent fancy to have imagined that the spirit fluttered about the placid lips of the old woodsman, reluctant to depart from a shell that had so long given it an honest and honorable shelter.

His body was placed so as to let the light of the setting sun fall full upon the solemn features. His head was bare, the long, thin locks of gray fluttering lightly in the evening breeze. His rifle lay upon his knee, and the other accouterments of the chase were placed at his side, within reach of his hand. Between his feet lay the figure of a hound, with its head crouching to the earth, as if it slumbered; and so perfectly easy and natural was its position, that a second glance was necessary to tell Middleton he saw only the skin of Hector, stuffed, by Indian tenderness and ingenuity, in a manner to represent the living animal. His own dog was playing at a distance with the child of Tachechana and Mahtoree. The mother herself stood at hand, holding in her arms a second offspring, that might boast of a parentage no less honorable than that which belonged to the son of Hard-Heart. Le Balafré was seated nigh the dying trapper, with every mark about his person that the hour of his own departure was not far distant. The rest of those immediately in the center were aged men, who had apparently drawn near in order to observe the manner in which a just and fearless warrior would depart on the greatest of his journeys.

The old man was reaping the rewards of a life remarkable for temperance and activity, in a tranquil and placid death. His vigor in a manner endured to the very last. Decay, when it did occur, was rapid but free from pain. He had hunted with the tribe in the spring, and even throughout most of the summer; when his limbs suddenly refused to perform their customary offices. A sympathizing weakness took possession of all his faculties; and the Pawnees believed that they were going to lose, in this unexpected manner, a sage and counselor whom they had begun both to love and respect. But, as we have already said, the immortal occupant seemed unwilling to desert its tenement. The lamp of life flickered, without becoming extinguished. On the morning of the day on which Middleton arrived there was a general reviving of the powers of the whole man. His tongue was again heard in wholesome maxims, and his eye from time to time recognized the persons of his friends. It merely proved to be a brief and final intercourse with the world, on the part of one who had already been considered, as to mental communion, to have taken his leave of it forever.

When he had placed his guests in front of the dying man, Hard-Heart, after a pause, that proceeded as much from sorrow as decorum, leaned a little forward, and demanded:

"Does my father hear the words of his son?"

"Speak," returned the trapper, in tones that issued from his chest, but which were rendered awfully distinct by the stillness that reigned in the place. "I am about to depart from the village of the Loups, and shortly shall be beyond the reach of your voice."

"Let the wise chief have no cares for his journey," continued Hard-Heart, with an earnest solicitude that led him to forget for the moment that others were waiting to address his adopted parent; "a hundred Loups shall clear his path from briers."

"Pawnee, I die as I have lived, a Christian man!" resumed the trapper, with a force of voice that had the same startling effect on his hearers as is produced by the trumpet, when its blast rises suddenly and freely on the air, after its obstructed sounds have been heard struggling in the distance; "as I came into life so will I leave it. Horses and arms are not needed to stand in the presence of the Great Spirit of my people. He knows my color, and according to my gifts will he judge my deeds."

"My father will tell my young men how many Mingoes he has struck, and what acts of valor and justice he has done, that they may know how to imitate him."

"A boastful tongue is not heard in the heaven of a white man!"

solemnly returned the old man. "What I have done he has seen. His eyes are always open. That which has been well done will he remember; wherein I have been wrong will he not forget to chastise, though he will do the same in mercy. No, my son; a pale-face may not sing his own praises, and hope to have them acceptable before his God!"

A little disappointed, the young partisan stepped modestly back, making way for the recent comers to approach. Middleton took one of the meager hands of the trapper, and, struggling to command his voice, he succeeded in announcing his presence.

The old man listened like one whose thoughts were dwelling on a very different subject; but, when the other had succeeded in making him understand that he was present, an expression of joyful recognition passed over his faded features.

"I hope you have not so soon forgotten those whom you so materially served!" Middleton concluded. "It would pain me to think my hold on your memory was so light."

"Little that I have ever seen is forgotten," returned the trapper: "I am at the close of many weary days, but there is not one among them all that I could wish to overlook. I remember you with the whole of your company; ay, and your gran'ther, that went before you. I am glad that you have come back upon these plains, for I had need of one who speaks English, since little faith can be put in the traders of these regions. Will you do a favor to an old and dying man?"

"Name it," said Middleton; "it shall be done."

"It is a far journey to send such trifles," resumed the old man, who spoke at short intervals, as strength and breath permitted, "a far and weary journey is the same, but kindnesses and friendships are things not to be forgotten. There is a settlement among the Otsego hills—"

"I know the place," interrupted Middleton, observing that he spoke with increasing difficulty; "proceed to tell me what you would have done."

"Take this rifle, pouch, and horn, and send them to the person whose name is graven on the plates of the stock—a trader cut the letters with his knife—for it is long that I have intended to send him such a token of my love."

"It shall be so. Is there more that you could wish?"

"Little else have I to bestow. My traps I give to my Indian son; for honestly and kindly has he kept his faith. Let him stand before me."

Middleton explained to the chief what the trapper had said, and relinquished his own place to the other.

"Pawnee," continued the old man, always changing his language to suit the person he addressed, and not unfrequently according to the ideas he expressed, "it is a custom of my people for the father to leave his blessing with the son before he shuts his eyes forever. This blessing I give to you; take it; for the prayers of a Christian man will never make the path of a just warrior to the blessed prairies either longer or more tangled! May the God of a white man look on your deeds with friendly eyes, and may you never commit an act that shall cause him to darken his face. I know not whether we shall ever meet again. There are many traditions concerning the place of Good Spirits. It is not for one like me, old and experienced though I am, to set up my opinions against a nation's. You believe in the blessed prairies, and I have faith in the sayings of my fathers. If both are true our parting will be final; but, if it should prove that the same meaning is hid under different words, we shall yet stand together, Pawnee, before the face of your Wahcondah, who will then be no other than my God. There is much to be said in favor of both religions, for each seems suited to its own people, and no doubt it was so intended. I fear I have not altogether followed the gifts of my color, inasmuch as I find it a little painful to give up forever the use of the rifle and the comforts of the chase. But then the fault has been my own, seeing that it could not have been his. Ay, Hector," he continued, leaning forward a little, and feeling for the ears of the hound, "our parting has come at last, dog, and it will be a long hunt. You have been an honest, and a bold, and a faithful hound. Pawnee, you cannot slay the pup on my grave, for where a Christian dog falls, there he lies forever; but you must be kind to him after I am gone, for the love you bear his master."

"The words of my father are in my ears," returned the young partisan, making a grave and respectful gesture of assent.

"Do you hear what the chief has promised, dog?" demanded the trapper, making an effort to attract the notice of the insensible effigy of his hound. Receiving no answering look, nor hearing any friendly whine, the old man felt for the mouth, and endeavored to force his hand between the cold lips. The truth then flashed upon him, although he was far from perceiving the whole extent of the deception. Falling back in his seat, he hung his head, like one who felt a severe and unexpected shock. Profiting by this momentary forgetfulness, two young Indians removed the skin with the same delicacy of feeling that had induced them to attempt the pious fraud.

"The dog is dead!" muttered the trapper, after a pause of many minutes; "a hound has his time as well as a man; and well has he filled his days!—Captain," he added, making an effort to wave his hand to Middleton, "I am glad you have come, for though kind and well-meaning according to the gifts of their color, these Indians are not the men to lay the head of a white man in his grave. I have been thinking, too, of this dog at my feet; it will not do to set forth the opinion that a Christian can expect to meet his hound again; still there can be little harm in placing what is left of so faithful a servant nigh the bones of his master."

"It shall be as you desire."

"I am glad you think with me in this matter. In order, then, to save labor, lay the pup at my feet; or, for that matter, put him side by side. A hunter need never be ashamed to be found in company with his dog!"

"I charge myself with your wish."

The old man made a long and apparently a musing pause. At times he raised his eyes wistfully, as if he would again address Middleton, but some innate feeling appeared always to suppress his words. The other, who observed his hesitation, inquired, in a way most likely to encourage him to proceed, whether there was aught else that he could wish to have done.

"I am without kith or kin in the wide world!" the trapper answered; "when I am gone there will be an end of my race. We have never been chiefs; but honest and useful in our way I hope it cannot be denied we have always proved ourselves. My father lies buried near the sea, and the bones of his son will whiten on the prairies——"

"Name the spot, and your remains shall be placed by the side of your father," interrupted Middleton.

"Not so, not so, captain. Let me sleep where I have lived—beyond the din of the settlements! Still I see no need why the grave of an honest man should be hid, like a red-skin in his ambushment. I paid a man in the settlements to make and put a graven stone at the head of my father's resting-place. It was of the value of twelve beaver-skins, and cunningly and curiously was it carved! Then it told to all comers that the body of such a Christian lay beneath; and it spoke of his manner of life, of his years, and of his honesty. When we had done with the Frenchers in the old war, I made a journey to the spot, in order to see that all was rightly performed, and glad I am to say, the workman had not forgotten his faith."

"And such a stone you would have at your grave?"

"I! no, no; I have no son but Hard-Heart, and it is little that an Indian knows of white fashions and usages. Besides, I am his debtor already, seeing it is so little I have done since I have lived in his tribe. The rifle might bring the value of such a thing—but then I know it will give the boy pleasure to hang the piece in his hall, for many is the deer and the bird that he has seen it destroy. No, no, the gun must be sent to him whose name is graven on the lock."

"But there is one who would gladly prove his affection in the way you wish; he who owes you not only his own deliverance from so many dangers, but who inherits a heavy debt of gratitude from his ancestors. The stone shall be put at the head of your grave."

The old man extended his emaciated hand and gave the other a squeeze of thanks.

"I thought you might be willing to do it, but I was backward in asking the favor," he said, "seeing that you are not of my kin. Put no boastful words on the same, but just the name, the age, and the time of the death, with something from the holy book; no more, no more. My name will then not be altogether lost on 'arth; I need no more."

Middleton intimated his assent, and then followed a pause that was only broken by distant and broken sentences from the dying man. He appeared now to have closed his accounts with the world and to await merely for the final summons to quit it. Middleton and Hard-Heart placed themselves on the opposite sides of his seat, and watched with melancholy solicitude the variations of his countenance. For two hours there was no very sensible alteration. The expression of his faded and time-worn features was that of a calm and dignified repose. From time to time he spoke, uttering some brief sentence in the way of advice, or asking some simple questions concerning those in whose fortunes he still took a friendly interest. During the whole of that solemn and anxious period each individual of the tribe kept his place, in the most self-restrained patience. When the old man spoke all bent their heads to listen; and when his words were uttered, they seemed to ponder on their wisdom and usefulness.

As the flame drew nigher to the socket his voice was hushed, and there were moments when his attendants doubted whether he still belonged to the living. Middleton, who watched each wavering expression of his weather-beaten visage with the interest of a keen observer of human nature, softened by the tenderness of personal regard, fancied he could read the workings of the old man's soul in the strong lineaments of his countenance. Perhaps what the enlightened soldier took for the delusion of mistaken opinion did actually occur —for who has returned from that unknown world to explain by what forms, and in what manner he was introduced into its awful precincts? Without pretending to explain what must ever be a mystery to the quick, we shall simply relate facts as they occurred.

The trapper had remained nearly motionless for an hour. His eyes alone had occasionally opened and shut. When opened his gaze seemed fastened on the clouds which hung around the western horizon, reflecting the bright colors, and giving form and loveliness to the glorious tints of an American sunset. The hour—the calm beauty of the season—the occasion—all conspired to fill the spectators with solemn awe. Suddenly while musing on the remarkable position in which he was placed, Middleton felt the hand which he held grasp his own with incredible power, and the old man, supported on either side by his friends, rose upright to his feet. For a moment he looked about him, as if to invite all in presence to listen (the lingering remnant of human frailty), and then, with a fine military elevation of the head, and with a voice that might be heard in every part of that numerous assembly, he pronounced the word:

"Here!"

A movement so entirely unexpected, and the air of grandeur and humility which were so remarkably united in the mien of the trapper, together with the clear and uncommon force of his utterance, produced a short period of confusion in the faculties of all present. When Middleton and Hard-Heart, each of whom had involuntarily extended a hand to support the form of the old man, turned to him again they found that the subject of their interests was removed forever beyond the necessity of their care. They mournfully placed the body in its seat, and Le Balafré arose to announce the termination of the scene to the tribe. The voice of the old Indian seemed a sort of echo from that invisible world to which the meek spirit of the trapper had just departed.

"A valiant, a just and a wise warrior, has gone on the path which will lead him to the blessed grounds of his people!" he said. "When the voice of the Wahcondah called him, he was ready to answer. Go, my children; remember the just chief of the pale-faces, and clear your own tracks from briers!"

The grave was made beneath the shade of some noble oaks. It has been carefully watched to the present hour by the Pawnees of the Loups, and is often shown to the traveler and the trader as a spot where a just white man sleeps. In due time the stone was placed at its head, with the simple inscription which the trapper had himself requested. The only liberty taken by Middleton was to add—"*May no wanton hand ever disturb his remains!*"

CONRAD RICHTER

It Came a Tuesday

SAYWARD didn't reckon this notion of Jake Tench's such a sin and a shame. If he could talk the Solitary into coming out of the woods and taking a woman, the Solitary couldn't be much worse and he might be a good ways better off.

When Sayward came back in the cabin, Idy Tull was still carrying on. Oh, she had the chance for attention now and wouldn't give up telling how she'd never take the Solitary. Sayward listened, drawing down the corners of her mouth. Idy might be stuck-up and bighead, but she was an old maid. She wouldn't let any man slip through her fingers at this date, let alone a Bay State lawyer. No, she'd jump out of her shortgown for a man who could read and write like herself. And the Solitary would have nothing to say once Jake Tench and his pack had him in tow and skinful of grog.

Now Sayward reckoned she had heard Idy enough. She moved up where the men hemmed in that pretty white and red staved cedar keg.

"You kin fetch him to my cabin, Jake," she said strong and knowing her own mind. "I'll marry with him if he's a willin."

Oh, Sayward needed no one to talk for her. She could fend for herself. Genny and Mrs. Covenhoven hurried after as she went firm and stout-willed out the front door. Mrs. Covenhoven looked sober when they caught up outside a ways and Genny had a scared look on her face.

"Now don't you fret, Genny," Sayward calmed her as she stooped to take off her shoepacks and make herself comfortable in her strong, bare feet on the path home. "I ain't afeard a this. I had my mind on him this long time."

"I only hope, Saird," Genny murmured, "the full moon ain't got you."

This passage from the novel *The Trees* describes the marriage of Sayward Luckett, a heroine whose story is continued in two other novels, *The Fields* and *The Town*. Before her death in the last volume of the trilogy, the wilderness has been replaced by civilization. [Ed. note]

Sayward turned her face to the east as she stooped. Here in the open hill patches Linus Greer had cleared, she could see a blob of yellow moon rising from the woods, and it was round and full. That gave her pause, for the moon can bend humans to strange ways. You could always tell on Jake when the moon was full or near it, for then he'd act the fool the worst, bellowing crazy jokes to folks half a mile off through the woods.

Could the moon have worked on her tonight? In her mind drifted something the bound boy said once of the time he heard a voice in the woods near the Fallen Timbers. He was picking blackberries and crept through the bush till he saw the Solitary sitting alone at the open door of his hut. He had a book in his hand and was reading it out loud in that lonesome place. The words at the end of every line made rhyme, but the bound boy couldn't make out a lick of it. When he got back to the post, George Roebuck told him that Portius Wheeler had books in Latin and Greek that nobody but himself could read, and it must be the bound boy had been listening to one of those.

Sayward straightened up with her shoepacks in her hand. She wouldn't take it to heart if the moon worked on her or not. She had set her triggers for Portius Wheeler and freely would she be his wife, for no man with such fine booklearning should bury himself out in the bush.

Jake must have talked to Squire Chew, for the squire came in good time though you could see he didn't think much of it.

"You certain you want to go on with this, Saird?" he asked her.

Oh, she might be sinful and out of her head, Sayward told herself, but she would go on with it. And when she saw the bridegroom that Jake and his cronies fetched to the door, she felt she had done right, for it made her mad some wilful body hadn't the sense to do this long ago. His ruffled linen shirt was pied with doeskin patches. His home-seamed buckskin britches had got wet and stretched some time or other till he had cut the legs down to suit. Then they had shrank and dried hard as iron, and now they clapped like clapboards when he moved. Oh, you would never have told this bushnipple for a master hand to read out of a Latin book or climb a stump and give speeches to a crowd or jury.

There he stood shaggy as a bear that for a short while would mind most anything Jake Tench told him. His high forehead was held gentle and tender to one side, but his eyes could still flash young and gray-green out of his briery beard.

"Don't crowd him so close!" Sayward told them angrily. "He ain't a greased hog. He kin come in without you a helpin'."

They fetched him in near the chimney corner and had him stand where the bridegroom ought to be. Squire Chew gave a kind of hard-put look around, then fixed himself so the firelight fell on his pages, for Sayward had no candles. Jake kept close. You might have reckoned he was the one getting married. Portius stood there taking no more notice of her than that York State bride and bridegroom took of each other, the ones Mrs. Covenhoven told about, who as soon as they were man and wife walked one out of one door and the other out of the other, and never did they see each other again except mayhap on the far side of the earth where they were still trying to get farther off from the other.

From where she stood, Sayward couldn't see the wedding company, for they were behind her. All she could lay eyes on were Genny and Mrs. Covenhoven tending the meat at the fire so it wouldn't burn on them. But she could feel that a good many waited uneasy for the time when the Solitary would have to speak out. Hardly a word had he said since they got him here. Would he make his vows when the time came or would he get balky as an ox and shame her? Or might the grog thicken his tongue and cause him to say some untoward thing that folks would always laugh and say behind her back?

Well, she told herself, they would mighty soon find out, for the Solitary's speaking-out place wasn't far off now. Squire Chew was lifting his book higher to the firelight.

"Portius Wheeler," he read, "do you take this woman, Saird Luckett, as your lawful married wife? Will you live with her in holy wedlock, protect and guide her, forsaking all others so long as you may live?" He looked over the temple spectacles he got with the book. "The answer is, 'I do, so help me God.'"

You could tell the squire hadn't done this but once before. He hemmed and hawed as he said it and mixed up some hims for hers. But never for a lick did Sayward wish it could have been different. The minute he stumbled and got a word wrong, she saw Portius cock his head as if something had caught in the back of his Bay State lawyer mind. From then on he listened close and when the squire got done, the bridegroom looked around in the master way he had that day on the log and his voice came out deep and schooled as a lawyer at the bar.

"I, Portius Wheeler," he said, and everybody turned so quiet that between words you could hear the death ticks in the logs, "a citizen of this territory, do take Miss Luckett as my lawfully married wife, vowing to protect and assuage her, to guide and direct her, and, living with her in the state of holy wedlock, to forsake all others so long as the twain of us may live or take our breath, so help me God." No, he hadn't taken the easy way of the book. All the squire's words he had kept in his head and added more to them, making it still more solemn and majestic than the book, and all rolling out sure and easy as breathing till he came to the end.

It was still the grog greasing him, Sayward knew, for this was the way he had held them spellbound for a while that Independence Day. And yet a feeling ran up her spine and over her limbs that she couldn't recollect before. It seemed she stood high above the trees where she could look out over a vasty sea of leaves. She heard the squire ask would she cleave to Portius, serve and obey him, comfort and help him through sickness and trouble till death did them part? And away down in the cabin she heard her voice firm and knowing her own mind say she would, so help her God.

The squire closed his book and said that by the power given him by the governor of Northwest Territory, Portius Wheeler and Sayward Luckett were now man and wife. Sayward saw Wyitt looking at her like she was somebody he had never had a good look at before. Through her cruelly triumphant mind ran that whoever that Bay State woman was and whatever she was like with her store scents, her fine rings and her whalebone stays, it was too late for her to sharpen a quill and write Portius Wheeler his letter now.

Before the wedding supper was ready right, the younger women came to whisper in Sayward's ear and drag her up the ladder. Everybody looked on, laughing and calling after. Genny fetched Sayward's bedgown from its peg behind the door. Up in the loft they offed with her shortgown, pinching at her bare skin and making screeches and giggles at what they saw in the half-light. Then they pulled on the bedgown and put her in Achsa's, Wyitt's and Sulie's old bed which she had laid over with two clean-washed yarn blankets. In most of this Genny took the lead. When the others went laughing and whispering down, it was Genny who stayed up a bit to give her some married woman's talk. Oh, you would reckon Genny was the older sister and Sayward the baby of the family being married off the way Genny busied herself about and the knowing airs she gave herself.

Warm air lifted through the loft hole again after they all were down. But the loft shutter was open and a skift of cool air flowed across the bed. The roof shelved close and comfortable over Sayward's head. It was a mighty peaceful place up here beside all the gabbing and taking on down in the cabin.

You could tell they were pulling Portius for the ladder now. Everybody called out good will words to him. The men said plenty to make the women blush. The women called he might as well get used to climbing that ladder, for many's the time he would have to, but Sayward told herself that she and him would make their bed down in the cabin after tonight. The only ones that would sleep up here would be their young ones, if God Almighty was good to her and him and sent them a loftful.

They were pushing Portius up first. She pulled the blanket up over her breasts. It was just as good, she told herself, they hadn't candles like the Tulls and Covenhovens. The firelight from the loft hole would make it plain enough for those men's sharp eyes to see by. She would close hers all but the lashes so as not to shame her man while they pulled his clothes off, all save his buckskin patched linen shirt. That would be his bed shirt.

Now the rungs of the old ladder were creaking. And now Portius stood with his head and shoulders up in the loft. And now the gray-green eyes in that tangled brier of beard were staring at her cold sober, as whose eyes wouldn't be to find his woman lying softly waiting for him in their bridal bed.

So far he had come easy enough. Further, no man could fetch him. One minute he was here and the next he was gone. She could hear the women and young ones pile out after him under her loft shutter and Jake Tench curse like a grenadier while the men beat the dark bushes.

Now who would have looked for a thing like this when all had been going so good! Sayward lay still as could be, studying up at the roof. Well, that's what she got for reckoning she could get a Bay State lawyer man who never courted her. It would have to be faced now and put up with.

When the women came back in the cabin, they found Sayward down and dressed, taking the meat off the fire.

"No use me a sayin' anything," she passed it off, hands and feet moving fast with her chore. "Every time the sheep baas, it loses a mouthful. Lucky he didn't run off with our supper."

Jake Tench came in, the devil raging out of his black beard.

"I'll learn that tarnal dolt he's a married man now!" he swore.

"You don't need to call him no names," Sayward said shortly. "He didn't call none at you."

The others tried to put a better face on it for her sake.

"You know how men are, Saird," Mary Harbison told her. "They never know where they'll roost from one night to the other."

"Don't you mind, Saird," Mrs. McFall said kindly. "I heerd a rhyme once. No goose so gray and none so late that at last she gits an honest gander for a mate."

Genny looked sick. Wyitt sneaked off shamed to his half-faced cabin. But Sayward laughed and talked that wedding supper like nothing had gone wrong. Never had they heard her raise such a sight of fun and chatter.

Had the bridegroom not run off, the wedding frolic would have run till morning. The company would have danced and made high jack all night and gone home by daylight. Now already some said they hated to run off so soon but they had to. Others waited around while Jake and his cronies wiped the supper grease from their lips and went out with torches to the Solitary's hut to see if he had come home. When they did not come back, the rest took light and reckoned they had to go, too. Genny told Sayward she'd stay with her this night, but Sayward said aside to Mrs. Covenhoven it would be easier on her mind and Genny's, too, if Genny were off in her bed at the Covenhovens' away from all this.

When the last party took off, Sayward stood at the door and watched them down the path till all you could see were their lights floating through the woods like corpse candles over some boggy place fetching bad luck to them that saw it. Truth to tell, they hardly needed a light tonight for the full moon almost let you see the path.

Could that full moon, Sayward pondered, be why they had all acted tonight like they were touched in the head? You hadn't dare wash and warp wool in a waning moon or it would shrink, like it would stretch if the moon were waxing. You hadn't dare lay roof boards when the moon was tipped up at one end or it would turn up those solid oak clapboards easy as the toe of a boot. But a moon blown up full of air as a bladder raised the most mischief of all for it made you lightheaded as itself. You couldn't see it here by the cabin. Yet you knew that somewhere up yonder above the trees it must be and all the heavy-raftered, leaf-thatched roof of the woods couldn't keep it out. No, if it hadn't places for it to shine down whole, it would come down in fine pieces and drift like spook smoke under the dark trees. It turned all night things false as a gypsy. Plain leaves looked like they were fine calico quilt patches and many-pointed stars.

Quietly she turned back indoors and redd up the cabin. Her splint broom scraped and hackled the bones, gristle, bed leaves and black boot dirt off the hard clay floor. The hearth she swept clean with a turkey wing. Her old buckskin rag wiped dust off logs and chinking. The clean-washed blankets she lugged down from the marriage bed and spread them over the everyday place she slept. Last she fetched out a choice slice of roast venison she had saved back for her man if he came home, and set a place at the trencher.

The moon was down somewhere in the black forest when she heard them come. Yes, the moon was down now and so were their didoes. When she went to the door, there was Portius limping between them. Oh, anybody could tell he was sober now. His green-gray eyes blazed out of his briery beard. His face and hands were raw from thorns and his shirt ripped till a woman would be hard put to mend it. A couple hounds slunk in the shadows behind them. So they had gone and tried to track him with Billy Harbison's dogs, like he was a bear that had robbed some body's hog pen!

Jake gave him a shove in the cabin.

"Leave him alone!" Sayward flared at him. "Don't you reckon you dogged him enough tonight?"

Jake stared at her in surprise, then at his cronies. His look said, "That's what we git for all we done for her!"

"You kin be glad we didn't shoot and skin him," he said.

Sayward's eyes told him he better not say any more right now.

"Keep tab on him, Saird," Billy Harbison spoke out. "First time you turn your back, he'll off from you like a gadd."

"Then he kin light off right now!" Sayward said. "I ain't a holdin' him."

She swung the door wide and stood there in her bare legs and feet, a strong figure dependent on no one or nothing. Out that door was the forest, cold, black and still. Around him inside, Portius Wheeler could see the firelight dancing cheerfully over the rubbed logs and scrubbed trencher set for one body to eat. A stool had been pulled up to it. On the poplar chip was a plump piece of brown-roasted meat. Beside it lay a cabin knife to eat it with, and a noggin stood for tea. The mint flavor of the steeped dittany filled the room.

She waited, but the only move Portius Wheeler made was to shiver, for he was soaked to the skin from runs and wet places.

When Jake and his cronies had gone, Sayward closed the door. She did not trouble to lay the stout hickory bar across.

"Set up to the trencher—if you're a hungry, Portius," she told him, filling his noggin with tea.

Oh, she didn't sit up with him or lean behind his stool asking him how it tasted or could she get him anything more he wanted. No, she let him eat and went about mixing a sponge of sour dough to rise till morning. Should he take a notion to jump up from the trencher and run, he could go. She wouldn't hold him. It might be she stole a look at him once in a while. for it did her good to see how hearty he ate her rations. But never did she let him know. When he was done, he waited for her to pester him and when she kept about her business, he threw her a sharp look under his heavy young eyebrows. And when she paid him no more attention than before, he came over and warmed himself at the fire.

His teeth still chattered, and she walked over to a peg and took down her father's old linsey hunting frock that had hung there since he went off looking for Sulie and never came home.

"I expect you better put this on till you dry your shirt and britches," she told him.

She turned her back on him now and went on mixing her dough. Oh, she could tell he didn't know for a good while whether he would do this thing or no. But when she set the dough by the fire to rise, his patched shirt and wet buckskin britches were laying on a stool and he was standing there with Worth's hunting frock down over him till it nigh onto touched his knees.

She gave those knees and the shanks below a sharp look.

"When was it you washed all over last?" she put to him, and before he could answer. "Is that how they learned you back in the Bay State?"

She fetched the wash trough Worth had hollowed out of a poplar log up to the fire and dipped hot water from the big kettle, using the gourd with the long handle. Then she laid out a sop rag and a gourd of soft soap.

"Don't you reckon you better wash that dirt off before you git in your bed?" she said shortly.

She had his wet britches over her shoulder. His eyes flashed her a hard look out of his briery young beard but she went on redding off her table and making a long ado of washing his knife and noggin. Once or twice she couldn't help looking after she heard him splash, and found him gaunt as a gutted deer. His haunches were all ham bone.

He had done with washing and stood drying himself with his front side to the fire when she took her bedgown from its pin and went to the door.

"Now I want to tell you something, Portius," she said. "You don't need to run off from me. Any time you want to go, just you say so. I'll see your clothes are mended and your belly full of fresh cooked meat for you to travel on."

Then she went out and when she came in, she saw he had pulled on Worth's frock again and crawled between the blankets of the bed she had made. She didn't know as she liked this so much, his going ahead and getting in first. For her to get in now would be the bride running after the bridegroom. He should have waited and let the bride in first. Then if he had enough grit to come after, that would be no more than befitting a bridegroom.

She made to fix the fire for the night but what she was doing was making up her mind. No, he had left her no other way now but to lay a pallet for herself where her and Genny's old bed used to be. Never, since he ran off from her, would she run a foot after him.

Then she saw he was holding back the top blanket so she could get in, and his eyes had a gentle look toward her as to a lady. She had heard how sometimes men of the gentry did mortal polite things such as this or helping their woman over a log like she was a helpless young one.

"Sayward," he spoke in his deep Bay State voice, " 'let's not to the marriage of true minds admit impediment.' "

Now what, Sayward thought, did he mean by that jawbreaking mouthful? Then he smiled and she judged it must be fine words out of one of his books, and it pleased her. She didn't know for sure whether or not she liked the way he spoke her name, Say-ward. Making two words of it like that seemed too high-toned and big-sounding for her. But if he wanted to say it that way, she expected he could. Like as not she'd get used to it in time, should he stay that long.

ELIZABETH MADOX ROBERTS

Diony's Vision

SHE WOULD SIT in the cabin at twilight, resting on a stiff little chair she had bought from a wood-workman of the fort. The supper waited on the hearth, ready backed before the fire, and her few wooden vessels were ready to contain it. She would prolong her reverie until it fell into a clearly defined desire.

This was a new world, the beginning before the beginning. Sitting thus alone in the cabin, while Berk looked for the cow on the snowy creekside and brought her safely to the fort, while he, with the other men of the stockade, dragged fodder inside the wall, getting the wood, closing the gates—sitting thus she would see a vision of fields turned up by the plow. A moist loam rolls up to take the seeds and the rain into itself. Over the field some birds would go swiftly, darting here and there, calling now one and now all together, plovers tossing over a made field to go to the creekside beyond a low rising shoulder of turned loam. A field! This would be a great happiness.

Or again: A vision of sheep sprinkled over a pasture or turned in on a hillside to crop the stubble and glean a fine rich eatage for themselves. On their backs would grow round fat fleeces of fine wool to be sheared away in the spring, to be spun into yarn and woven. The sheep stand in a strange stillness, each one bent to the earth, or they lift their heads and look off toward the south, all looking together. Their small thin faces are pointed toward some invisible thing, which they discern as if they examined it carefully, their small feet sunk into the low herbs, the wool put over their backs in a soft round coat. The odor of wool floats lightly about them as a more subtle coat they wear over their fleeces. To make them run forward to obey some command the farmer would cry out a musical "houee," and "sheep-ah, sheep-ah!" It was a vision. She saw thus in the embers in her cabin within Fort Harrod in the cold season of the early year, 1778, wolves howling on the hill beyond the burying place.

A vision of stone walls and rail fences setting bounds to the land, making contentment and limitations for the mind to ease itself upon. The wearying infinitives of the wilderness come to an end. The land stands now, in vision, as owned, this man's farm beside that man's, all contained now, bounded, divided, and shared, and one sinks into the security and lies down to rest himself. Through the farms run lanes and well-pounded roads, making a further happiness, ways to go to meet a neighbor at his own house.

A vision of neighbors, a man living to the right, a man to the left, each in his own land, their children meeting together to walk down the road to a schoolhouse or a church. Or the women learn of one another, each one using the best of her skill to make the food or the clothing a little better than they were before, each one wishing to do as well as the others, and some, those with skillful hands, excelling the rest.

A vision of places to sell the growth of the farms, there being farms now, a vision of some market place off in some town beyond the fields, where iron and glass could be had for the surplus of the harvest, where could be had books and journals and tools, clocks and vessels of earthenware, pewter spoons and vessels of brass, steel knives and smooth shoes for their feet, needles for their fingers . . . . It was a happiness to think of.

Berk delayed coming and she knew that the cows must be lost. The little children in the next cabin were crying for milk, being unable to eat the harsh corn pones and the jerked meats. She heard bobcats screaming in the stony places toward the west, and Gyp, her dog, whined at the door, wanting to be let in. Men at Harrod's cabin fired a rifle, a signal to those outside. There were more than a hundred men in the fort now, and some of them being wary hunters, there was always wild meat enough, but the turnips and pumpkins were gone. The children would gather into the mother's cabin at nightfall, and the sounds of the fort were then subdued under cabin rafters. Tears gathered through her entire being to hear the little children cry for their supper, wanting milk.

A vision of bridges over streams so that their horses or oxen need not be imperiled in flood waters and their goods lost, so that they might cross easily over and take no thought of the matter, so that they need not lash logs together to make a raft. The road runs smoothly down through settled fields and comes at last to a river where it runs lightly over a structure of smooth logs neatly trimmed and jointed, placed on stone pillars that stand well out of the flood. It was a wonder to dream on in the mind.

A vision of fine cattle in the pastures giving a rich yield of milk and cream, well-chosen beasts that stand secure in good barns, not the wiry little scrub sort that run on the open range and live in constant fear of wild creatures and savages. In the pastures too are good horses, graceful riding beasts, easy in hand, smooth carriers, strong and sound.

Bees, then, in hives set in neat rows near a dwelling. They gather sweet from the wild growth in the uncleared places and from the pollen of the corn, from the white clover. It would be a civil picture, the hives cut out of well-sawed logs and left to their own devices until the honey made a rich, sweet fatness within. Then a man, Berk Jarvis perhaps, goes among the hives and robs the bees of their harvest, and a woman, herself, Diony, stores the honey in earthen jars of which there would be a-plenty.

A dream of letters written between one and another, of messages sent freely through long miles of travel. A courier waits at the door, his horse pawing the earth, ready to go hence. One folds the pages together and writes a name on the outer page, writing "Mister Thomas Hall," writing "Mistress Polly Hall," writing "Mistress Betty Hall." . . . The courier takes the letter into his hand and goes swiftly, carrying the letter to the one named. The vision grew dim because of the long, scarcely broken tangles of trees and stones that reared themselves in the way, but it cleared itself and was renewed to become a vision of messages received, of word sent to her. A letter comes to her hands that are now folded in her lap. She feels the crisp edges of the paper and reads eagerly what is inscribed within, messages from a man, Thomas Hall, telling her how all fared in Albemarle. It was a vision: there were no letters; no word had ever come to her.

A dream of knowledge, of wisdom brought under beautiful or awful sayings and remembered, kept stored among written pages and brought together then as books. Books stand in a row on a shelf where a narrow beam of light falls through a high casement over a desk where one might rest a volume, where one might sit for an hour and search the terrible pages, looking for beauty, looking for some final true way of life. In them, the books, Man walks slowly down through the centuries, walking on the stairs of the years. . . .

Berk came at last, white with new-fallen frost. The children had become quiet, their cries now soft and full of content. Her vision went with the flare of a fresh stick among the embers. She set the supper on the board and their hungers were satisfied.

3

The Midwestern Frontier

AFTER HUNTERS, trappers, and soldiers have tamed a wilderness, they move on. What has been a scene of hunt and war becomes a farmer's frontier, the scene of conflict against soil and climate, urban markets and moneylenders.

So it was with what we now call the Middle West. Once it was three separate frontiers. One was the old Northwest Territory, stretching from Ohio to Minnesota, a land of streams and forests fought over by English and French, defended by Algonquin, Chippewa, Shawnee, and other Indians, subdued by men like George Rogers Clark. Another was the Middle Border, a plain that stretched from Minnesota to the Black Hills and from the Canadian border south to Nebraska. And a third was the buffer country of Missouri and Kansas, curiously unresolved states that were neither North nor South, neither all sodbusters nor all cattlemen.

Yet after the Civil War, this great heartland began to have one history with many common struggles against climate, rural isolation, emotional and intellectual poverty, and social injustice. As all America has now discovered, it is hard to build a community in a wilderness, but harder still to make that community hospitable to culture or even common humanity.

Disillusionment with the small community and with its constraints and prejudices pervades almost all of the epitaphs in Edgar Lee Masters' *Spoon River Anthology*. Even John Wasson, the frontier character who occupies what must surely be one of the oldest graves in the Spoon River cemetery, speaks with a kind of latter day bitterness. Disillusion with the small town marketplace and its mortgage lenders also infuses much of Hamlin Garland's work, particularly a classic story like "Under the Lion's Paw." And in Lone Tree, Nebraska, Wright Morris's Tom Scanlon discovers that what the world has been coming to has arrived. There is nothing to do but put off dying, and there is nothing left to say but "Clippers in the back, Eddie."

98

Much of the literature of the farmer's frontier is about poor and weary men and women like those of Hamlin Garland's *Main-travelled Roads*. But there are also joyous celebrations of the land and the seasons, frequently penned in nostalgia by writers who have left them both. As Willa Cather does, these writers talk "about what it is like to spend one's childhood in little towns . . . buried in wheat and corn . . . fairly stifled in vegetation." They remember the dramatic bleakness of winter and the long warm summer twilight. They prize the constant relationship and the special closeness—however constraining they may sometimes be—between the people in small Midwestern towns.

Like George Willard, who remembers little things as he sits in a railroad car about to leave Winesburg, Ohio, our writers have tried to recreate our past. They have known that even our small towns, like the frontier before them, are being destroyed. All America is rushing into an urban future, a time of great cities that will extend along whole seacoasts. Yet almost every American must share George Willard's sense of loss: "When he aroused himself and again looked out of the car window the town of Winesburg had disappeared and his life there had become but a background on which to paint the dreams of his manhood."

EDGAR LEE MASTERS

Harry Wilmans

I WAS just turned twenty-one,
And Henry Phipps, the Sunday-school superintendent,
Made a speech in Bindle's Opera House.
"The honor of the flag must be upheld," he said,
"Whether it be assailed by a barbarous tribe of Tagalogs
Or the greatest power in Europe."
And we cheered and cheered the speech and the flag he waved
As he spoke.
And I went to the war in spite of my father,
And followed the flag till I saw it raised
By our camp in a rice field near Manila,
And all of us cheered and cheered it.
But there were flies and poisonous things;
And there was the deadly water,
And the cruel heat,
And the sickening, putrid food;
And the smell of the trench just back of the tents
Where the soldiers went to empty themselves;
And there were the whores who followed us, full of syphilis;
And beastly acts between ourselves or alone,
With bullying, hatred, degradation among us,
And days of loathing and nights of fear
To the hour of the charge through the steaming swamp,
Following the flag,
Till I fell with a scream, shot through the guts.
Now there's a flag over me in Spoon River!
A flag! A flag!

John Wasson

Oh! the dew-wet grass of the meadow in North Carolina
Through which Rebecca followed me wailing, wailing,
One child in her arms, and three that ran along wailing,
Lengthening out the farewell to me off to the war with the British,
And then the long, hard years down to the day of Yorktown.
And then my search for Rebecca,
Finding her at last in Virginia,
Two children dead in the meanwhile.
We went by oxen to Tennessee,
Thence after years to Illinois,
At last to Spoon River.
We cut the buffalo grass,
We felled the forests,
We built the school houses, built the bridges,
Leveled the roads and tilled the fields
Alone with poverty, scourges, death—
If Harry Wilmans who fought the Filipinos
Is to have a flag on his grave
Take it from mine!

HAMLIN GARLAND

Under the Lion's Paw

I

Along this main-travelled road trailed an endless line of prairie-schooners, coming into sight at the east, and passing out of sight over the swell to the west. We children used to wonder where they were going and why they went.

IT WAS THE LAST of autumn and first day of winter coming together. All day long the ploughmen on their prairie farms had moved to and fro on their wide level field through the falling snow, which melted as it fell, wetting them to the skin—all day, notwithstanding the frequent squalls of snow, the dripping, desolate clouds, and the muck of the furrows, black and tenacious as tar.

Under their dripping harness the horses swung to and fro silently, with that marvellous uncomplaining patience which marks the horse. All day the wild geese, honking wildly, as they sprawled sidewise down the wind, seemed to be fleeing from an enemy behind, and with neck outthrust and wings extended, sailed down the wind, soon lost to sight.

Yet the ploughman behind his plough, though the snow lay on his ragged great-coat, and the cold clinging mud rose on his heavy boots, fettering him like gyves, whistled in the very beard of the gale. As day passed, the snow, ceasing to melt, lay along the ploughed land, and lodged in the depth of the stubble, till on each slow round the last furrow stood out black and shining as jet between the ploughed land and the gray stubble.

When night began to fall, and the geese, flying low, began to alight invisibly in the near cornfield, Stephen Council was still at work "finishing a land." He rode on his sulky-plough when going with the wind, but walked when facing it. Sitting bent and cold but cheery under his slouch hat, he talked encouragingly to his four-in-hand.

"Come round there, boys!—round agin! We got t' finish this land.

Come in there, Dan! *Stiddy,* Kate!—stiddy! None o' y'r tantrums, Kittie. It's purty tuff, but got a be did. *Tchk! tchk!* Step along, Pete! Don't let Kate git y'r single-tree on the wheel. *Once* more !"

They seemed to know what he meant, and that this was the last round, for they worked with greater vigor than before.

"Once more, boys, an' sez I oats an' a nice warm stall, an' sleep f'r all."

By the time the last furrow was turned on the land it was too dark to see the house, and the snow changing to rain again. The tired and hungry man could see the light from the kitchen shining through the leafless hedge, and lifting a great shout, he yelled, "Sup*per* f'r a half a dozen!"

It was nearly eight o'clock by the time he had finshed his chores and started for supper. He was picking his way carefully through the mud, when the tall form of a man loomed up before him with a pre-monitory cough.

"Waddy ye want?" was the rather startled question of the farmer.

"Well, ye see," began the stranger, in a deprecating tone, "we'd like t' git in f'r the night. We've tried every house f'r the last two miles, but they hadn't any room f'r us. My wife's just about sick, 'n' the children are cold and hungry—"

"Oh, y' want a stay all night, eh?"

"Yes, sir; it 'ud be a great accom—"

"Waal, I don't make it a practice t' turn anybuddy away hungry, not on sech nights as this. Drive right in. We ain't got much, but sech as it is—"

But the stranger had disappeared. And soon his steaming, weary team, with drooping heads and swinging single-trees, moved past the well to the block beside the path. Council stood at the side of the "schooner" and helped the children out—two little half-sleeping chil-dren—and then a small woman with a babe in her arms.

"There ye go!" he shouted, jovially, to the children. *"Now* we're all right. Run right along to the house there, an' tell Mam' Council you wants sumpthin' t' eat. Right this way, Mis'—keep right off t' the right there. I'll go an' git a lantern. Come," he said to the dazed and silent group at his side.

"Mother," he shouted, as he neared the fragrant and warmly-lighted kitchen, "here are some wayfarers and' folks who need sumpthin' t' eat an' a place t' snooze." He ended by pushing them all in.

Mrs. Council, a large, jolly, rather coarse-looking woman, took the children in her arms. "Come right in, you little rabbits. 'Most asleep, hay? Now here's a drink o' milk f'r each o' ye. I'll have s'm tea in a minute. Take off y'r things and set up t' the fire."

While she set the children to drinking milk, Council got out his lantern and went out to the barn to help the stranger about his team, where his loud, hearty voice could be heard as it came and went between the hay-mow and the stalls.

The woman came to light as a small, timid, and discouraged-looking woman, but still pretty, in a thin and sorrowful way.

"Land sakes! An' you've travelled all the way from Cleark Lake t'-day in this mud! Waal! waal! No wonder you're all tired out. Don't wait f'r the men, Mis'—" She hesitated, waiting for the name.

"Haskins."

"Mis' Haskins, set right up to the table an' take a good swig o' tea, whilst I make y' s'm toast. It's green tea, an' it's good. I tell Council as I git older I don't seem t' enjoy Young Hyson n'r Gunpowder. I want the reel green tea, jest as it comes off'n the vines. Seems t' have more heart in it some way. Don't s'pose it has. Council says it's all in m' eye."

Going on in this easy way, she soon had the children filled with bread and milk and the woman thoroughly at home, eating some toast and sweet-melon pickles, and sipping the tea.

"See the little rats!" she laughed at the children. "They're full as they can stick now, and they want to go to bed. Now don't git up, Mis' Haskins; set right where you are an' let me look after 'em. I know all about young ones, though I am all alone now. Jane went an' married last fall. But, as I tell Council, it's lucky we keep our health. Set right there, Mis' Haskins; I won't have you stir a finger."

It was an unmeasured pleasure to sit there in the warm, homely kitchen, the jovial chatter of the housewife driving out and holding at bay the growl of the impotent, cheated wind.

The little woman's eyes filled with tears which fell down upon the sleeping baby in her arms. The world was not so desolate and cold and hopeless, after all.

"Now I hope Council won't stop out there and talk politics all night. He's the greatest man to talk politics an' read the *Tribune.* How old is it?"

She broke off and peered down at the face of the babe.

"Two months 'n' five days," said the mother, with a mother's exactness.

"Ye don't say! I want t' know! The dear little pudzy-wudzy!" she went on, stirring it up in the neighborhood of the ribs with her fat forefinger.

"Pooty tough on 'oo to go gallivant'n' 'cross lots this way."

"Yes, that's so; a man can't lift a mountain," said Council, entering the door. "Sarah, this is Mr. Haskins from Kansas. He's been eat up 'n' drove out by grasshoppers."

"Glad t' see yeh! Pa, empty that wash-basin 'n' give him a chance t' wash."

Haskins was a tall man, with a thin, gloomy face. His hair was a reddish brown, like his coat, and seemed equally faded by the wind and sun. And his sallow face, though hard and set, was pathetic somehow. You would have felt that he had suffered much by the line of his mouth showing under his thin, yellow mustache.

"Hain't Ike got home yet, Sairy?"

"Hain't seen 'im."

"W-a-a-l, set right up, Mr. Haskins; wade right into what we've got; 'tain't much, but we manage to live on it—she gits fat on it," laughed Council, pointing his thumb at his wife.

After supper, while the women put the children to bed, Haskins and Council talked on, seated near the huge cooking-stove, the steam rising from their wet clothing. In the Western fashion, Council told as much of his own life as he drew from his guest. He asked but few questions; but by and by the story of Haskins's struggles and defeat came out. The story was a terrible one, but he told it quietly, seated with his elbows on his knees, gazing most of the time at the hearth.

"I didn't like the looks of the country, anyhow," Haskins said, partly rising and glancing at his wife. "I was ust t' northern Ingyannie, where we have lots a timber 'n' lots o' rain, 'n' I didn't like the looks o' that dry prairie. What galled me the worst was goin' s' far away acrosst so much fine land layin' all through here vacant."

"And the 'hoppers eat ye four years hand running, did they?"

"Eat! They wiped us out. They chawed everything that was green. They jest set around waitin' f'r us to die t' eat us too. My God! I ust t' dream of 'em sitt'n' 'round on the bedpost, six feet long, workin' their jaws. They eet the fork-handles. They got worse 'n' worse till they jest rolled on one another, piled up like snow in winter. Well, it ain't no use; if I was t' talk all winter I couldn't tell nawthin'. But all the while I couldn't help thinkin' of all that land back here that nobuddy was usin', that I ought a had 'stead o' bein' out there in that cussed country."

"Waal, why didn't ye stop an' settle here?" asked Ike, who had come in and was eating his supper.

"Fer the simple reason that you fellers wantid ten 'r fifteen dollars an acre fer the bare land and I hadn't no money fer that kind o' thing."

"Yes, I do my own work," Mrs. Council was heard to say in the pause which followed. "I'm a-gettin' purty heavy t' be on m' laigs all day, but we can't afford t' hire so I keep rackin' around somehow, like a foundered horse. S' lame—I tell Council he can't tell how lame I am f'r I'm jest as lame in one laig as t'other." And the good soul

laughed at the joke on herself as she took a handful of flour and
dusted the biscuit-board to keep the dough from sticking.

"Well, I hain't *never* been very strong," said Mrs. Haskins. "Our
folks was Canadians an' small-boned, and then since my last child I
hain't got up again fairly. I don't like t' complain—Tim has about
all he can bear now—but they was days this week when I jest wanted
to lay right down an' die."

"Waal, now, I'll tell ye," said Council from his side of the stove,
silencing everybody with his good-natured roar, "I'd go down and
see Butler, *anyway*, if I was you. I guess he'd let you have his place
purty cheap; the farm's all run down. He's ben anxious t' let t' some-
buddy next year. It 'ud be a good chance fer you. Anyhow, you go to
bed and sleep like a babe. I've got some ploughin' t' do anyhow, an'
we'll see if somethin' can't be done about your case. Ike, you go out
an' see if the horses is all right, an' I'll show the folks t' bed."

When the tired husband and wife were lying under the generous
quilts of the spare bed, Haskins listened a moment to the wind in
the eaves, and then said, with a slow and solemn tone:

"There are people in this world who are good enough t' be angels,
an' only haff t' die to *be* angels."

II

Jim Butler was one of those men called in the west "land poor."
Early in the history of Rock River he had come into the town, and
started in the grocery business in a small way, occupying a small
building in a mean part of the town. At this period of his life he
earned all he got, and was up early and late, sorting beans, working
over butter, and carting his goods to and from the station. But a
change came over him at the end of the second year, when he sold a
lot of land for four times what he paid for it. From that time forward he believed in land speculation as the surest way of getting
rich. Every cent he could save or spare from his trade he put into
land at forced sale, or mortgages on land, which were "just as good
as the wheat," he was accustomed to say.

Farm after farm fell into his hands, until he was recognized as one
of the leading land-owners of the county. His mortgages were scattered all over Cedar County, and as they slowly but surely fell in he
sought usually to retain the former owner as tenant.

He was not ready to foreclose; indeed, he had the name of being
one of the "easiest" men in the town. He let the debtor off again and
again, extending the time whenever possible.

"I don't want y'r land," he said. "All I'm after is the int'rest on
my money—that's all. Now if y' want 'o stay on the farm, why, I'll

give y' a good chance. I can't have the land layin' vacant." And in many cases the owner remained as tenant.

In the mean time he had sold his store; he couldn't spend time in it; he was mainly occupied now with sitting around town on rainy days, smoking and "gassin' with the boys," or in riding to and from his farms. In fishing time he fished a good deal. Doc Grimes, Ben Ashley, and Cal Cheatham were his cronies on these fishing excursions or hunting trips in the time of chickens or partridges. In winter they went to northern Wisconsin to shoot deer.

In spite of all these signs of easy life, Butler persisted in saying he "hadn't money enough to pay taxes on his land," and was careful to convey the impression that he was poor in spite of his twenty farms. At one time he was said to be worth fifty thousand dollars, but land had been a little slow of sale of late, so that he was not worth so much. A fine farm, known as the Higley place, had fallen into his hands in the usual way the previous year, and he had not been able to find a tenant for it. Poor Higley, after working himself nearly to death on it, in the attempt to lift the mortgage, had gone off to Dakota, leaving the farm and his curse to Butler.

This was the farm which Council advised Haskins to apply for; and the next day Council hitched up his team and drove down town to see Butler.

"You jest lem *me* do the talkin'," he said. "We'll find him wearin' out his pants on some salt-barrel somewe'rs; and if he thought you *wanted* a place, he'd sock it to you hot and heavy. You jest keep quiet; I'll fix 'im."

Butler was seated in Ben Ashley's store, telling "fish yarns," when Council sauntered in casually.

"Hello, But; lyin' agin, hay?"

"Hellow, Steve! how goes it?"

"Oh, so-so. Too dang much rain these days. I thought it was goin' t' freeze f'r good last night. Tight squeak if I git m' ploughin' done. How's farmin' with *you* these days?"

"Bad. Ploughin' ain't half done."

"It 'ud be a religious idee f'r you t' go out an' take a hand y'rself."

"I don't haff to," said Butler, with a wink.

"Got anybody on the Higley place?"

"No. Know of anybody?"

"Waal, no; not eggsackly. I've got a relation back t' Michigan who's ben hot an' cold on the idee o' comin' West f'r some time. *Might* come if he could get a good lay-out. What do you talk on the farm?"

"Well, I d' know. I'll rent it on shares or I'll rent it money rent."

"Waal, how much money, say?"

"Well, say ten per cent on the price—two-fifty."

"Waal, that ain't bad. Wait on 'im til 'e thrashes?"

Haskins listened eagerly to his important question, but Council was coolly eating a dried apple which he had speared out of a barrel with his knife. Butler studied him carefully.

"Well, knocks me out of twenty-five dollars interest."

"My relation 'll need all he's got t' git his crops in," said Council, in the same indifferent way.

"Well, all right; *say* wait," concluded Butler.

"All right; this is the man. Haskins, this is Mr. Butler—no relation to Ben—the hardest working man in Cedar county."

On the way home Haskins said: "I ain't much better off. I'd like that farm; it's a good farm, but it's all run down, an' so'm I. I could make a good farm of it if I had half a show. But I can't stock it n'r seed it."

"Waal, now, don't you worry," roared Council in his ear. "We'll pull y' through somehow till next harvest. He's agreed t' hire it ploughed, an' you can earn a hundred dollars ploughin' an' y' c'n git the seed o' me, an' pay me back when y' can."

Haskins was silent with emotion, but at last he said, "I ain't got nothin' t' live on."

"Now don't you worry 'bout that. You jest make your headquarters at ol' Steve Council's. Mother'll take a pile o' comfort in havin' y'r wife an children 'round. Y' see Jane's married off lately, an' Ike's away a good 'eal, so we'll be darn glad t' have ye stop with us this winter. Nex' spring we'll see if y' can't git a start agin;" and he chirruped to the team, which sprang forward with the rumbling, clattering wagon.

"Say, looky here, Council, you can't do this. I never saw—" shouted Haskins in his neighbor's ear.

Council moved about uneasily in his seat, and stopped his stammering gratitude by saying: "Hold on, now; don't make such a fuss over a little thing. When I see a man down, an' things all on top of 'm, I jest like t' kick em off an' help 'm up. That's the kind of religion I got, an' it's about the *only* kind."

They rode the rest of the way home in silence. And when the red light of the lamp shone out into the darkness of the cold and windy night, and he thought of this refuge for his children and wife, Haskins could have put his arm around the neck of his burly companion and squeezed him like a lover; but he contented himself with saying: "Steve Council, you'll git y'r pay f'r this some day."

"Don't want any pay. My religion ain't run on such business principles."

The wind was growing colder, and the ground was covered with a white frost, as they turned into the gate of the Council farm, and the children came rushing out, shouting "Papa's come!" They hardly looked like the same children who had sat at the table the night before. Their torpidity under the influence of sunshine and Mother Council had given way to a sort of spasmodic cheerfulness, as insects in winter revive when laid on the earth.

III

Haskins worked like a fiend, and his wife, like the heroic woman that she was, bore also uncomplainingly the most terrible burdens. They rose early and toiled without intermission till the darkness fell on the plain, then tumbled into bed, every bone and muscle aching with fatigue, to rise with the sun next morning to the same round of the same ferocity of labor.

The eldest boy, now nine years old, drove a team all through the spring, ploughing and seeding, milked the cows, and did chores innumerable, in most ways taking the place of a man; an infinitely pathetic but common figure—this boy—on the American farm, where there is no law against child labor. To see him in his coarse clothing, his huge boots, and his ragged cap, as he staggered with a pail of water from the well, or trudged in the cold and cheerless dawn out into the frosty field behind his team, gave the city-bred visitor a sharp pang of sympathetic pain. Yet Haskins loved his boy, and would have saved him from this if he could, but he could not.

By June the first year the result of such Herculean toil began to show on the farm. The yard was cleaned up and sown to grass, the garden ploughed and planted, and the house mended. Council had given them four of his cows.

"Take 'em an' run 'em on shares. I don't want a milk s' many. Ike's away s' much now, Sat'd'ys an' Sund'ys, I can't stand the bother anyhow."

Other men, seeing the confidence of Council in the new-comer, had sold him tools on time; and as he was really an able farmer, he soon had round him many evidences of his care and thrift. At the advice of Council he had taken the farm for three years, with the privilege of re-renting or buying at the end of the term.

"It's a good bargain, an' y' want 'o nail it," said Council. "If you have any kind ov a crop, you can pay y'r debts, an' keep seed an' bread."

The new hope which now sprang up in the heart of Haskins and his wife grew great almost as a pain by the time the wide field of wheat began to wave and rustle and swirl in the winds of July. Day after day he would snatch a few moments after supper to go and look at it.

"Have ye seen the wheat t'-day, Nettie?" he asked one night as he rose from supper.

"No, Tim, I ain't had time."

"Well, take time now. Le's go look at it."

She threw an old hat on her head—Tommy's hat—and looking almost pretty in her thin sad way, went out with her husband to the hedge.

"Ain't it grand, Nettie? Just look at it."

It was grand. Level, russet here and there, heavy-headed, wide as a lake, and full of multitudinous whispers and gleams of wealth, it stretched away before the gazers like the fabled field of the cloth of gold.

"Oh, I think—I *hope* we'll have a good crop, Tim; and oh, how good the people have been to us!"

"Yes; I don't know where we'd be t'-day if it hadn't ben f'r Council and his wife."

"They're the best people in the world," said the little woman. with a great sob of gratitude.

"We'll be in the field on Monday, sure," said Haskins, griping the rail on the fence as if already at the work of the harvest.

The harvest came, bounteous, glorious, but the winds came and blew it into tangles, and the rain matted it here and there close to the ground, increasing the work of gathering it threefold.

Oh, how they toiled in those glorious days! Clothing dripping with sweat, arms aching, filled with briers, fingers raw and bleeding, backs broken with the weight of heavy bundles, Haskins and his man toiled on. Tommy drove the harvester while his father and a hired man bound on the machine. In this way they cut ten acres every day, and almost every night after supper, when the hand went to bed, Haskins returned to the field, shocking the bound grain in the light of the moon. Many a night he worked till his anxious wife came out to call him in to rest and lunch.

At the same time she cooked for the men, took care of the children, washed and ironed, milked the cows at night, made the butter, and sometimes fed the horses and watered them while her husband kept at the shocking. No slave in the Roman galleys could have toiled so frightfully and lived, for this man thought himself a free man, and that he was working for his wife and babes.

When he sank into his bed with a deep groan of relief, too tired to change his grimy, dripping clothing, he felt that he was getting nearer and nearer to a home of his own, and pushing the wolf of want a little farther from his door.

There is no despair so deep as the despair of a homeless man or woman. To roam the roads of the country or the streets of the city, to feel there is no rood of ground on which the feet can rest, to halt weary and hungry outside lighted windows and hear laughter and song within—these are the hungers and rebellions that drive men to crime and women to shame.

It was the memory of this homelessness, and the fear of its coming again, that spurred Timothy Haskins and Nettie, his wife, to such ferocious labor during that first year.

IV

" 'M, yes; 'm, yes; first-rate," said Butler, as his eye took in the neat garden, the pigpen, and the well-filled barn-yard. "You're git'n' quite a stock around yer. Done well, eh?"

Haskins was showing Butler around the place. He had not seen it for a year, having spent the year in Washington and Boston with Ashley, his brother-in-law, who had been elected to Congress.

"Yes, I've laid out a good deal of money during the last three years. I've paid out three hundred dollars f'r fencin'."

"Um—h'm! I see, I see," said Butler, while Haskins went on.

"The kitchen there cost two hundred; the barn ain't cost much in money, but I've put o lot o' time on it. I've dug a new well, and I—"

"Yes, yes. I see! You've done well. Stock worth a thousand dollars," said Butler, picking his teeth with a straw.

"About that," said Haskins, modestly. "We begin to feel 's if we wuz git'n' a home f'r ourselves; but we've worked hard. I tell ye we begin to feel it, Mr. Butler, and were goin't' begin t' ease up purty soon. We've been kind o' plannin' a trip back t' *her* folks after the fall ploughin's done."

"*Eggs*-actly!" said Butler, who was evidently thinking of something else. "I suppose you've kine o' kalklated on stayin' here three years more?"

"Well, yes. Fact is I think I c'n buy the farm this fall, if you'll give me a reasonable show."

"Um—m! What do you call a reasonable show?"

"Waal; say a quarter down and three years' time."

Butler looked at the huge stacks of wheat which filled the yard, over which the chickens were fluttering and crawling, catching grasshoppers, and out of which the crickets were singing innumerably. He smiled in a peculiar way as he said, "Oh, I won't be hard on yer. But what did you expect to pay f'r the place?"

"Why, about what you offered it for before, two thousand five hundred, or *possibly* the three thousand dollars," he added quickly, as he saw the owner shake his head.

"This farm is worth five thousand and five hundred dollars," said Butler, in a careless but decided voice.

"*What!*" almost shrieked the astounded Haskins. "What's that? Five thousand? Why that's double what you offered it for three years ago."

"Of course; and it's worth it. It was all run down then; now it's in good shape. You've laid out fifteen hundred dollars in improvements, according to your own story."

"But *you* had nothin' t' do about that. It's my work an' my money."

"You bet it was; but it's my land."

"But what's to pay me for all my—"

"Ain't you had the use of 'em?" replied Butler, smiling calmly into his face.

Haskins was like a man struck on the head with a sand-bag; he couldn't think; he stammered as he tried to say: "But—I never'd git the use— You'd rob me. More'n that: you agreed—you promised that I could buy or rent at the end of three years at—"

"That's all right. But I didn't say I'd let you carry off the improvements, nor that I'd go on renting the farm at two-fifty. The land is doubled in value, it don't matter how; it don't enter into the question; an' now you can pay me five hundred dollars a year rent, or take it on your own terms at fifty-five hundred, or—git out."

He was turning away when Haskins, the sweat pouring from his face, fronted him, saying again:

"But *you've* done nothing to make it so. You hain't added a cent. I put it all there myself, expectin' to buy. I worked an' sweat to improve it. I was workin' f'r myself an' babes—"

"Well, why didn't you buy when I offered to sell? What y' kickin' about?"

"I'm kickin' about payin' you twice f'r my own things—my own fences, my own kitchen, my own garden."

Butler laughed. "You're too green t' eat, young feller. *Your* improvements! The law will sing another tune."

"But I trusted your word."

"Never trust anybody, my friend. Besides, I didn't promise not to do this thing. Why, man, don't look at me like that. Don't take me for a thief. It's the law. The reg'lar thing. Everybody does it."

"I don't care if they do. It's stealin' jest the same. You take three thousand dollars of my money. The work o' my hands and my wife's." He broke down at this point. He was not a strong man mentally. He could face hardship, ceaseless toil, but he could not face the cold and sneering face of Butler.

"But I don't take it," said Butler, coolly. "All you've got to do is to go on jest as you've been a-doin', or give me a thousand dollars down, and a mortage at ten per cent on the rest."

Haskins sat down blindly on a bundle of oats near by, and with staring eyes and drooping head went over the situation. He was under the lion's paw. He felt a horrible numbness in his heart and limbs. He was hid in a mist, and there was no path out.

Butler walked about, looking at the huge stacks of grain, and pulling now and again a few handfuls out, shelling the heads in his hands and blowing the chaff away. He hummed a little tune as he did so. He had an accommodating air of waiting.

Haskins was in the midst of the terrible toil of the last year. He was walking again in the rain and the mud behind his plough, he felt the dust and dirt of the threshing. The ferocious husking time, with its cutting wind and biting, clinging snows, lay hard upon him. Then he thought of his wife, how she had cheerfully cooked and baked, without holiday and without rest.

"Well, what do you think of it?" inquired the cool, mocking, insinuating voice of Butler.

"I think you're a thief and a liar!" shouted Haskins, leaping up. "A black-hearted houn'!" Butler's smile maddened him; with a sudden leap he caught a fork in his hands, and whirled it in the air. "You'll never rob another man, damn ye!" he grated through his teeth, a look of pitiless ferocity in his accusing eyes.

Butler shrank and quivered, expecting the blow; stood, held hypnotized by the eyes of the man he had a moment before despised—a man transformed into an avenging demon. But in the deadly hush between the lift of the weapon and its fall there came a gush of faint, childish laughter, and then across the range of his vision, far away and dim, he saw the sun-bright head of his baby girl, as, with the pretty tottering run of a two-year-old, she moved across the grass of the door-yard. His hands relaxed; the fork fell to the ground; his head lowered.

"Make out y'r deed an' morgige, an' git off'n my land, an' don't ye never cross my line agin; if ye do, I'll kill ye."

Butler backed away from the man in wild haste, and climbing into his buggy with trembling limbs, drove off down the road, leaving Haskins seated dumbly on the sunny pile of sheaves, his head sunk into his hands.

WRIGHT MORRIS

Scanlon

THE OLD MAN couldn't believe his eyes—the ones he had—but his ears told him the worst. He could hear the crowd yell and the fizzing squirt of the pop. If anybody had told him he would live to see the day a grown man would stand up and squirt pop at someone—but of course, he didn't. Live to see the day, that is. He'd had sense enough to go blind before he lived to see something like that. But one thing he didn't have sense enough to do was just stay put. Where he belonged, that is. He hadn't had sense enough to live, then die, back in Lone Tree.

When they told Tom Scanlon that his wife had died—his daughter, Lois, was the one to tell him—he had taken a kitchen match from his hat band, bit down on it. He let his daughter wait, then after a while he said, "Loey, what'll the hens do?"

She had replied, "Uncle Roy and Agnes are taking them."

It didn't mean that Scanlon didn't feel death any, or not care about people, or other things they said about him. What it meant was that he seldom felt *much,* so any feeling threw him off. When he thought about the chickens he knew what it was he felt, and that the chickens would feel it even more than he did. But being chickens they might not grasp it. So they would need help. They would miss her. That was what he meant.

Scanlon and his wife had been married forty years, but they had not lived more than half of them together, since she had decided, as she said, to go along with the century. So she went. Tom Scanlon didn't. He stayed right on in Lone Tree. Lone Tree was where—the way Scanlon would put it—the century he didn't care for turned on its axis, looked up and down the tracks just the way he did, then went east. But Lone Tree, along with Tom Scanlon, stayed put.

"Scanlon" is one of the twenty-four sections in the novel *Field of Vision,* which won the National Book Award for Morris. The scene is at a bullfight in Mexico, but this is only a device that allows a virtually blind man to remember life in a small Western town during the nineteenth century. [Ed. note]

For fifty years, closer now to sixty, he had worn a drayman's hat with brown cane sides, a license at the front, and a soft crown that shaped to his head. When he hung it on a nail, you could still see his head in it. But when they took a picture of him the week he nearly froze they wanted one without the hat, which he gave them, then he put it down somewhere and couldn't find it when they were gone. This coonskin hat he wore to please the boy. Not a hair of it was coon hair, as he told him, and the top got hot when the sun was on it, but still he wore it. Anything to please the boy.

This coat he was wearing—mohair they called it, from the horse-hairs in it—was all he had left, all they would let him wear of the outfit he had worn since his wife had left him, dating from the fall Herbert Hoover had defeated a man named Smith. A brown derby pin, stamped I'M FOR AL, was there in the frayed lapel of the coat. Scanlon had not been for Al, or anybody else, but a traveling salesman known to be a Catholic had stuck the pin there and Scanlon had let it stick. The pin was part of the coat, and the coat was part of the man.

Tom Scanlon was a plainsman, but he had a seaman's creased eyes in his face. The view from his window—the one in Lone Tree, where he had the bed pulled over to the window—was every bit as wide and as empty as a view of the sea. In the early morning, with just the sky light, that was how it looked. The faded sky was like the sky at sea, the everlasting wind like the wind at sea, and the plain rolled and swelled quite a bit like the sea itself. Like the sea it was lonely, and there was no place to hide. Scanlon had never been to sea, of course, but that was beside the point.

He looked to be a man in the neighborhood of ninety, and his passing, as people referred to it, had been expected from year to year, for the last thirty years. His wife, in good health when she left him, had had that understanding with his children, and the necessary arrangements had all been made. An undertaker in Cozad, the nearest town that had one, would meet the members of the family in Seward, where they would have a simple service, then drive back to Lone Tree and bury him. His father, his mother, and such life as he had lived were buried there. But he did not die. His death was prepared, but he put it off. With little or nothing to live for, he continued to live. He had renounced his children the moment it was clear that they intended to face the future, or even worse, like his daughter Lois, make a success of it. Tom Scanlon lived—if that was the word—only in the past. When the century turned and faced the east, he stood his ground. He faced the west. He made an interesting case, as Boyd had once observed, being a man who found more to live for, in looking backward, than those who died all around him, looking ahead.

The last of nine children, his mother dying within the year she had borne him, Tom Scanlon grew up waiting on his father, who was mad as a coot. Timothy Scanlon might have been mad all of his life, but only his wife would have known that, since it was only in his later years that he talked. Bedridden, that is, he tried to talk himself out of it. He ran this hotel—that is, his wife did—and when he could no longer get up and downstairs, he crawled into the bed in the room at the back of it. The single window looked down the railroad tracks to the west. His son, Tom Scanlon, would go up with his meals, sit there on the bed while the old man ate, then listen to him talk while he smoked his daily cigar. He was an odd one. Even the boy knew that. He slept in his clothes, lying out on top of the bed. If it got cold he might throw a comfort over his feet. One reason for that might be the fact that he wore cavalry boots, with tinkling silver spurs, that he found it harder and harder to get off. The spurs were made of iron, and even rusty, but little silver drops were attached to the rowels, and when he tapped the boot on the foot of the bed they made a tinkling sound. He also wore a leather jerkin, so dirty on the front that it looked like a piece of greasy oilcloth, and on a cord from his neck was suspended a powder horn and a firing wire. Also an awl, with a cherry wood handle, a bottle he had carved from an antelope's horn, and a small piece of leather with nipples on it for caps. They were the clothes he had worn, and the things he had used, as a young man. He saw less and less reason, as he told the boy, for taking them off.

But he was not full of yarns, as people said, but just one long yarn, told over and over, so long and drawnout that only the boy had heard the end of it. He had heard it many times. He never seemed to tire of it. The reason was his age—as his daughter pointed out—he was going on seven or eight at the time, and that same age group were Davy Crockett crazy at the present time. But her grandchild, just as crazy as the rest, would grow out of it. Her father didn't. He had been Davy Crockett crazy all his life. Nor was it hard to see why, according to his daughter, if you knew Lone Tree, where he was born. In growing up there when he did he felt no need to get out of it. *His* father had opened the West, his brothers had closed it, and his children had gone East. Everything had been done. Everything , that is, but just stay put.

If you knew Lone Tree—if you knew it, that is, right around the turn of the century, you might get an inkling as to why Tom Scanlon stayed. What was it like? A photograph had been taken of it. From a balloon, at an estimated height of two hundred thirty feet. Dated on the back July 4th, 1901. The century had just turned. The locomotive in the picture was headed East. It had come from the East—as a matter of fact, it had *backed* in from the East since there was no local roundhouse—and the balloon was due in Omaha later that night.

The town itself, the lone cottonwood tree, the row of tin-roofed buildings and the railroad tracks, seemed to dangle like toys at the far end of a string. On the roof of the hotel were the men who had gathered to watch the balloon rise. William Jennings Bryan, the man who might have been President, was one of them. Around the cottonwood tree, in its shade, were the ladies fanning themselves, and a water sprinkler that had dripped a dark trail in the dust. Down the tracks to the west, like a headless bird with the bloody neck still bleeding, the new tublike water tank sat high on stilts. A bunch of long-stemmed grass grew where the spout dripped on the tracks. To the east, beyond the new hotel, stood the lone cottonwood tree, dead at the top but with clumps of leaves near the bottom, like a man stripped for action. Out of the clumps the dead branches curved like cattle horns. The Western Hotel, a three story structure faced with sandstone blocks and red brick, sat where the caboose of the westbound trains came to a stop. The hotel faced the plain, once called a square, where a mixture of hardy grass had been planted, and it was believed that the town would appear like the orchards in the seed catalogues. A man with time on his hands, like young Tom Scanlon, could watch it grow. The picture had been taken to impress Eastern men that there was a future in Lone Tree, and a copy of it hung in the hotel lobby, with the calendars. Tom Scanlon, his shoeless feet propped on the desk top, used to sit and look at it.

Across the street stood the bank, with its marble front, a door to go in and one to come out, but turned into a movie palace before the money arrived from Omaha. In the empty lot adjoining were the rubber tired wheels of a fire hose cart, without the hose, and a strip of wooden sidewalk, like a fence blown over on its side. A city hall, to house the hose cart and the Sheriff, was planned, but never put up. At the back of the Feed Store, under the racks of harness, was the covered wagon that belonged to Tim Scanlon, in which he had traveled West, and in which five of his sons were born. Later known as the Dead Wagon, it had been used for funerals. Still later, it was used in parades in nearby towns. In the photograph it looked like a caterpillar put on wheels, to please the kiddies, and bore a legend that had been painted on both sides.

LONE TREE

THE BIGGEST LITTLE TOWN IN THE WORLD

Timothy Scanlon's wife, an Ohio girl who had made the trip to California with him, had given the town, just a tree then, its name.

In her opinion that was how it looked. A lonely tree in the midst of a lonely plain. Not much had changed—in so far as you could tell from the photograph.

Before the old man finally died (as of course he did) his son, Tom Scanlon, may have thought him immortal, his mind full of his deathless deeds. Because of the timeless life the old man had lived when young, something died in them both—as the doctor put it—leaving one you could bury, and one you couldn't, but in any sense that mattered just about as dead.

But a lifetime later, almost several of them, after being as good as dead for four generations, Tom Scanlon had suddenly turned up alive. Almost. One of the brakemen on the eastbound freight—one of the few who stopped for water—had found him in the kitchen of the Western Hotel almost frozen to death. The coal fire in the kitchen range had long burned out. He had been found sitting there, his feet in the oven, wrapped up in blankets and buffalo hides, a cold cigar in his mouth as if waiting for spring. Some of the brakemen were accustomed, summer and winter, to see the glow of his cigar in the curtainless window, since he had moved to his father's old room at the rear of the hotel. Men working on the tracks, or those hired to burn the ditch grass, might see, both morning and evening, the matches he struck on the sill of the window, or the rim of his pot. He was in bed, but he usually slept in it sitting up. He claimed that it made his wheezy breathing easier. There was some truth in that, but of course the thing that made his breathing hard in the first place was the open window, and the asthma he got from the burning grass.

But he was free—as he told his children—to do as he liked. To sleep in his clothes, or to just lie there and not sleep. He owned the bed. He slept in it alone. In the summer he liked the window open, in the winter he liked it closed, but summer and winter he liked to lie there looking out. There was nothing to see, but perhaps that was what he liked about it.

But the winter he froze—that is, almost—something had to be done about it, and his youngest daughter, Lois McKee, had the largest house; almost empty, since her own children had grown up and moved out. Those children, naturally, had seldom seen him; he was the ghost in the family closet, and there was nothing to be gained—they understood—in bringing him out. Since he put off dying it had not been necessary to bury him. He was still there, that is, when another generation made its appearance—oddly enough, at the same time he did, and in the same house. Gordon Scanlon McKee, the old man's great-grandson, wearing a coonskin hat and sporting two six-shooters, had been the first member of the family, so to speak, to speak to him. It had been love—as the family feared—at first shot.

Tom Scanlon never cared for his own children, but he hardly knew why until they grew up and had children of their own. Then he saw it. What the world had been coming to, had arrived. What could you expect of the younger generation if they had fathers like McKee, a hot shooter? Nothing. Which was pretty much what they got.

For twenty years—no, it was more like thirty—Scanlon hadn't said more than "Clippers in the back, Eddie," which he said to the barber over in Cozad about every six weeks. When the boy came along he had to learn to talk all over again. Not so much at first, since the boy did the talking, but when they got in the back seat of the car, way back where they put them, why, then he was free to talk a little more. The country they were in, which was south of El Paso, was dry and open the way his father had described it—country where there was nothing for the wind to blow on but himself. When a man died out there, which was often, they had to bury him deep, pile some big rocks on him, then run the wagons over him if they wanted to keep him dead. Otherwise the Indians or the coyotes would dig him up. Once his father saw an Indian with a hat he'd made from a wagon lantern, like a sort of helmet, the lantern door like a visor he could wear up, or down. He told the boy. The boy liked to hear stories like that. Just the telling of it led him to think of another one. One of the old squaws with a big family used to follow the wagons and live off the garbage, but the trouble was she had more little shavers than she could get on her horse. So what'd she do? Different than most squaws, she was smart. She rigged up a sort of sled, using saplings for runners, which she could trail along behind her little pony, and back on the sled, just as pretty as you please, were all her kids. Might not have been hers at all, but she'd adopted them.

The boy couldn't hear enough stories like that, and when they both got sick, on the little wild bananas, they had to sleep in the car, which got him to remembering more of them. That place where the flowers bloomed only at night, and this girl in the wagon, whose name was Samantha, kept fireflies in a bottle so when they buzzed their lanterns she could look at them. The flowers, that is. And while she looked at the flowers, Timothy Scanlon could look at her face. Well as he could see it, he couldn't tell you what it was like. He (his father, that is) said her hair was black as it was where the harness scuffed the hair off a mule's hide, but when he looked at her eyes he looked right through them without seeing anything. He couldn't tell you, he said, what color they were. All he could tell you was they weren't like his own eyes much, since she only saw different things with them—from the seat of the wagon she would see a flower, where he only saw a track. Even when she pointed and they looked at it together, they never saw the same thing.

That was something for the boy, so Scanlon told him that; the more he talked the more he remembered, and the more he remembered the nearer all of it seemed. He couldn't see more than the light out there in the bullring, but let him close his eyes, and just remember, and he could see from the fork of the Platte to Chimney Rock. The buffalo like an island with a brown furze on it, the wind blowing, the wagons strung out in a line like so many caterpillars with their fuzz burned off.

The truth was, he didn't know he was so blind until they came for him. In Lone Tree, where nothing had changed, he saw things in their places without the need to look at them. They were there, in case he wanted to see them, in his mind's eye. All he had to do was close his eyes and look at them. That was how it was with this remembering business, and one reason he talked so much, once he got started, was that the more he talked the clearer it all became. Back around El Paso, where he began to get started, he would say, "I tell you how they shot the Mormon?" but the boy couldn't seem to get it straight through his head who he meant by *they*. He seemed to think Scanlon did it. He always said *you* when Scanlon meant *they*. Since he couldn't seem to get it straight in his head, and since it simplified the story to tell it that way, Scanlon found it easier to go along with it, and just say we. And the more he told it that way, the truer it seemed.

"I tell you how *we* put in the time?" he would say, and it seemed that he had. He had put more of it in back there than anywhere else. Anyhow, that's how it seemed. That he put that time in, all of it, himself.

"Don't it take you back, Gordon?" he heard McKee say, a man who never once had a place to go back to, who had done nothing but try to go forward all of his life.

"I tell you how—" he began, and poked his elbow in the boy, but blind as he was he could see the commotion, people jumping up like popcorn, and the boy hopped up like he'd sat down on a pin. But where the light was, out there in the bullring, he saw nothing, just the slope beyond it spotted with snow and scrub trees of some sort, blowing in the wind. He closed his eyes. He remembered where it was, and just how it had been.

WILLA CATHER

My Ántonia

LAST SUMMER, in a season of intense heat, Jim Burden and I happened to be crossing Iowa on the same train. He and I are old friends, we grew up together in the same Nebraska town, and we had a great deal to say to each other. While the train flashed through never-ending miles of ripe wheat, by country towns and bright-flowered pastures and oak groves wilting in the sun, we sat in the observation car, where the woodwork was hot to touch and red dust lay deep over everything. The dust and heat, the burning wind, reminded us of many things. We were talking about what it is like to spend one's childhood in little towns like these, buried in wheat and corn, under stimulating extremes of climate: burning summers when the world lies green and billowy beneath a brilliant sky, when one is fairly stifled in vegetation, in the colour and smell of strong weeds and heavy harvests; blustery winters with little snow, when the whole country is stripped bare and grey as sheet-iron. We agreed that no one who had not grown up in a little prairie town could know anything about it. It was a kind of freemasonry, we said. . . .

He told us we had a long night drive ahead of us, and had better be on the hike. He led us to a hitching-bar where two farm-wagons were tied, and I saw the foreign family crowding into one of them. The other was for us. Jake got on the front seat with Otto Fuchs, and I rode on the straw in the bottom of the wagon-box, covered up with a buffalo hide. The immigrants rumbled off into the empty darkness, and we followed them.

I tried to go to sleep, but the jolting made me bite my tongue and I soon began to ache all over. When the straw settled down, I had a hard bed. Cautiously I slipped from under the buffalo hide, got up on my knees and peered over the side of the wagon. There seemed to be nothing to see; no fences, no creeks or trees, no hills or fields. If there was a road, I could not make it out in the faint starlight. There was nothing but land: not a country at all, but the material

out of which countries are made. No, there was nothing but land—
slightly undulating, I knew, because often our wheels ground
against the brake as we went down into a hollow and lurched up
again on the other side. I had the feeling that the world was left
behind, that we had got over the edge of it, and were outside man's
jurisdiction. I had never before looked up at the sky when there was
not a familiar mountain ridge against it. But this was the complete
dome of heaven, all there was of it. I did not believe that my dead
father and mother were watching me from up there; they would still
be looking for me at the sheepfold down by the creek, or along the
white road that led to the mountain pastures. I had left even their
spirits behind me. The wagon jolted on, carrying me I knew not
whither. I don't think I was homesick. If we never arrived anywhere, it did not matter. Between that earth and that sky I felt
erased, blotted out. I did not say my prayers that night: here, I felt,
what would be would be. . . .

On the afternoon of that same Sunday I took my first long ride on
my pony, under Otto's direction. After that Dude and I went twice
a week to the post-office, six miles east of us, and I saved the men a
good deal of time by riding on errands to our neighbours. When we
had to borrow anything, or to send about word that there would be
preaching at the sod schoolhouse, I was always the messenger. Formerly Fuchs attended to such things after working hours.

All the years that have passed have not dimmed my memory of
that first glorious autumn. The new country lay open before me:
there were no fences in those days, and I could choose my own way
over the grass uplands, trusting the pony to get me home again.
Sometimes I followed the sunflower-bordered roads. Fuchs told me
that the sunflowers were introduced into that country by the Mormons; that at the time of the persecution, when they left Missouri
and struck out into the wilderness to find a place where they could
worship God in their own way, the members of the first exploring
party, crossing the plains to Utah, scattered sunflower seed as they
went. The next summer, when the long trains of wagons came
through with all the women and children, they had the sunflower
trail to follow. I believe that botanists do not confirm Fuchs's story,
but insist that the sunflower was native to those plains. Nevertheless, that legend has stuck in my mind, and sunflower-bordered
roads always seem to me the roads to freedom.

SHERWOOD ANDERSON

Departure from Winesburg

YOUNG GEORGE WILLARD got out of bed at four in the morning. It was April and the young tree leaves were just coming out of their buds. The trees along the residence streets in Winesburg are maple and the seeds are winged. When the wind blows they whirl crazily about, filling the air and making a carpet underfoot.

George came down stairs into the hotel office carrying a brown leather bag. His trunk was packed for departure. Since two o'clock he had been awake thinking of the journey he was about to take and wondering what he would find at the end of his journey. The boy who slept in the hotel office lay on a cot by the door. His mouth was open and he snored lustily. George crept past the cot and went out into the silent deserted main street. The east was pink with the dawn and long streaks of light climbed into the sky where a few stars still shone.

Beyond the last house on Trunion Pike in Winesburg there is a great stretch of open fields. The fields are owned by farmers who live in town and drive homeward at evening along Trunion Pike in light creaking wagons. In the fields are planted berries and small fruits. In the late afternoon in the hot summers when the road and the fields are covered with dust, a smoky haze lies over the great flat basin of land. To look across it is like looking out across the sea. In the spring when the land is green the effect is somewhat different. The land becomes a wide green billiard table on which tiny human insects toil up and down.

All through his boyhood and young manhood George Willard had been in the habit of walking on Trunion Pike. He had been in the midst of the great open place on winter nights when it was covered with snow and only the moon looked down at him; he had been there in the fall when bleak winds blew and on summer evenings when the air vibrated with the song of insects. On the April morning he wanted to go there again, to walk again in the silence. He did walk to where the road dipped down by a little stream two miles from town and then turned and walked silently back again. When he got to Main Street clerks were sweeping the sidewalks before the stores. "Hey, you George. How does it feel to be going away?" they asked.

The west bound train leaves Winesburg at seven forty-five in the morning. Tom Little is conductor. His train runs from Cleveland to where it connects with a great trunk line railroad with terminals in Chicago and New York. Tom has what in railroad circles is called an "easy run." Every evening he returned to his family. In the fall and spring he spends his Sundays fishing in Lake Erie. He has a round red face and small blue eyes. He knows the people in the towns along his railroad better than a city man knows the people who live in his apartment building.

George came down the little incline from the New Willard House at seven o'clock. Tom Willard carried his bag. The son had become taller than the father.

On the station platform everyone shook the young man's hand. More than a dozen people waited about. Then they talked of their own affairs. Even Will Henderson, who was lazy and often slept until nine, had got out of bed. George was embarrassed. Gertrude Wilmot, a tall thin woman of fifty who worked in the Winesburg post office, came along the station platform. She had never before paid any attention to George. Now she stopped and put out her hand. In two words she voiced what everyone felt. "Good luck," she said sharply and then turning went on her way.

When the train came into the station George felt relieved. He scampered hurriedly aboard. Helen White came running along Main Street hoping to have a parting word with him, but he had found a seat and did not see her. When the train started Tom Little punched his ticket, grinned and, although he knew George well and knew on what adventure he was just setting out, made no comment. Tom had seen a thousand George Willards go out of their towns to the city. It was a commonplace enough incident with him. In the smoking car there was a man who had just invited Tom to go on a fishing trip to Sandusky Bay. He wanted to accept the invitation and talk over details.

George glanced up and down the car to be sure no one was looking then took out his pocketbook and counted his money. His mind was occupied with a desire not to appear green. Almost the last words his father had said to him concerned the matter of his behavior when he got to the city. "Be a sharp one," Tom Willard had said. "Keep your eyes on your money. Be awake. That's the ticket. Don't let any one think you're a greenhorn."

After George counted his money he looked out of the window and was surprised to see that the train was still in Winesburg.

The young man, going out of his town to meet the adventure of life, began to think but he did not think of anything very big or dramatic. Things like his mother's death, his departure from Winesburg, the uncertainty of his future life in the city, the serious and larger aspects of his life did not come into his mind.

He thought of little things—Turk Smallet wheeling boards through the main street of his town in the morning, a tall woman, beautifully gowned, who had once stayed over night at his father's hotel, Butch Wheeler the lamp lighter of Winesburg hurrying through the streets on a summer evening and holding a torch in his hand, Helen White standing by a window in the Winesburg post office and putting a stamp on an envelope.

The young man's mind was carried away by his growing passion for dreams. One looking at him would not have thought him particularly sharp. With the recollection of little things occupying his mind he closed his eyes and leaned back in the car seat. He stayed that way for a long time and when he aroused himself and again looked out of the car window the town of Winesburg had disappeared and his life there had become but a background on which to paint the dreams of his manhood.

4

The Mountains

INSTEAD OF EXTENDING steadily westward, the American frontier made great jumps—from the Mississippi to the Rocky Mountains with the fur trade, and over the Rockies to Oregon and California with the wagon trains. For at least forty years the plains were the Great American Desert, a wasteland to be traversed but not settled, a challenge but not a reward.

The rewards were to be found in the mountains, where game was plentiful and life was free. Encouraged by high prices for beaver pelts, the mountain men roamed through the Rockies, sometimes trading, living, or fighting with the Indians, always studying out the country, learning the courses of the rivers, the ridges of the mountains, and the ways of the animals.

The mountain men now seem to have been frontiersmen bigger than life size, just as the grizzly and the bull buffalo seem monstrous when compared to brown bears and deer. Names like Jim Bridger, Jedediah Smith, and Kit Carson have long appealed to the American imagination, and they have been celebrated as "men to match our mountains."

Perhaps no other author has been so dedicated to the description of early Rocky Mountain life and the evocation of its history as Vardis Fisher, whose descriptions of the grizzly and the buffalo are reprinted here. The most dramatic presentation of the character of the mountain man is that by Frederick Manfred in *Lord Grizzly*, a fictional recreation of a nearly fabulous exploit. And Manfred's work is complemented by the quiet and eloquent treatment of mountain men in A. B. Guthrie's *The Big Sky* and by Guthrie's almost elegiac reprise of the mountain men's era in a brief passage from *The Way West*.

The explorations of the mountain men were succeeded by the invasion of the cattlemen and the sheepmen who settled at the foot of the mountains, irrigated the deserts, began cutting the pines and firs, and converted high meadows to summer range. Their first view of the country is beautifully presented by Harvey Fergusson in the brief excerpt from his novel *Grant of Kingdom*.

At about the same time, in the mountains of Colorado, Dakota, Idaho, and Montana, prospectors opened the way to an entirely different frontier. Mining communities sprang up, evolving a special way of life, unique laws and customs, and even a legendry and literature of their own. That development was strangely reflected and distorted in the Deadwood Dick dime novels. Though written by a "sensational novelist" who never traveled west of Pennsylvania, they helped to form a popular tradition that still colors our attitudes toward the history of the West.

VARDIS FISHER

The Grizzly and the Buffalo

SUDDENLY DAVID MOVED. *There was that smell again* and there was no other smell in the world like it. In the next moment he had let his duffel slip off his shoulders and over his head. It was strange how a man could feel this sort of thing: he had heard nothing, had seen nothing, but he knew it was there and he knew what it was. The silvertip was meanest when leanest but he was mean any time he saw a poacher in his berry thicket. David softly took his gun, reached around to see if the dagger was at his waist, jerked his blanket around so that he could use it, and very slowly rose to his feet.

Chills went all over him, for there it was, looking at him. God Almighty, he had seen grizzlies but never such a monster as this. The monster, as though to show off all his dreadful size, rose to his hind legs, his small eyes fixed on David, his fury and outrage rising in heat under his deep fur. That was the trouble with a silvertip: the awful beast would attack anything any time, especially poachers in his domains or among his meat caches. David had killed a number of them. He knew them well. He knew that this giant would stand only a few moments and then soundlessly would sink to four feet, and rush forward and rise again. It was fatal to turn your back on this creature. It was fatal to retreat. The silvertip's small dim mind was confused by anything that had the gall to stand and face it; and so, instead of rushing furiously to the kill, it advanced in charges, showing, not fear, but a slight paralysis of its will. It might rise twice or three times. You had to watch it and figure out how it was feeling about things. You knew that when it was six or eight or ten feet from you all you had to do to make it stand again was to toss your hat or jacket or blanket over its face. The stupid monster would then rear up and give you a moment to shoot it right

These two brief selections are from Fisher's novel *Pemmican,* in which David McDonald is "the post manager, chief trader, botanist, concocter of pemmican, and bully boy" for the Hudson's Bay Company. [Ed. note]

128

through its brain. Men whose aim was bad or whose nerve faltered left their bones where they stood.

He had rushed twice and he was coming again and there he was, only a few feet from David, this mightiest of all killers; and a moment later he had the blanket over his eyes and with his tiny mind bewildered and his will frozen he got to his hind legs; and in the next moment he had a bullet through his brain and he came down as soundlessly as the flight of an owl and looked like nothing but a huge pelt in a berry thicket. He hardly shuddered but David shuddered and felt a little weak. It took just about all a man had to stand his ground when that monster came charging. Alexander Henry had told of shooting a bear that ran away and hid and of trailing it by its blood and shooting it again; and of how he discovered that his first bullet had gone through the heart. David supposed the man had lied. A deer might run fifty or even a hundred yards after being shot through the heart but it was fantastic to say that a bear had gone a quarter of a mile and was found licking its wound. David rammed powder and ball home, for there might be another; and he stared at the beast and wondered again what a man would do if his gun missed fire. A grizzly could gut a horse or a buffalo from shoulder blade to thigh bone with one stroke of his dreadful talons. One sweep down a man's frame would take half the ribs and all the organs out of him. . . .

Well, there he was, as dead as the bear grease on a squaw's braids. . . .

The breeze was from the southwest. "I can smell them," David said.

Pierre lifted his nose like a dog. In that low voice, so deadly in its quietness, he said, "Heap big stink."

That, David reflected, was true, for the buffalo was a filthy beast. It had reason to be. In springtime it shook and shuddered and itched and rubbed itself against stones and trees, trying to shed the mattings of dead hair, alive with vermin and caked with old sweat and mud and scabs; and when patches fell off, leaving naked and bleeding areas, clouds of its enemies moved in, chief of which was the one men here called the bulldog, a large vicious and bloodthirsty fly that, like a tick, was never done with feeding until it was all gut and stupor. And there were ticks by the millions: they dug in so deep that in dislodging one you pulled its body off its head, leaving the head buried; and the itching was horrible. There were fleas and wood lice and monstrous black horseflies and deer flies and mosquitoes—in fact the pests in certain seasons were so dreadful that men dared not sleep at all but sat choking all night in a smudge. Horses sometimes were so desperate with pain that they would hurl themselves into water or roll in mud. The buffalo, poor old bastard, had dim eyes at best, and when matted forelocks hung over them or hordes of insects fed and drank at their rims, it might better have had none at all. David had often looked with astonishment at the ravages the buffalo had made in woods with its rubbings and the great piles of hair at the foot of trees and the bark brightly polished as high as it reached. And if it wasn't a skyful of pests eating him alive it was the early-summer sun blistering hell out of his naked skin where the winter mats had fallen, or flocks of magpies or crows riding his raw back and eating until, goaded with pain, the grotesque monster went bellowing into the wind or tumbled like a hog into the first mudhole and burrowed and snorted until he was sheathed over with prairie clay. Or it was the prairie fires, set by lightning or by Indians; David had seen the wretched creatures with the hair burnt off them and their eyes burnt out, staggering round and round, knocking themselves senseless against trees, falling into rivers, and drowning by the hundreds or thousands or toppling over to die. Men here told of having seen so many drowned buffalo that a flowing river was continuously full of them for more than two days and two nights, and the stench along the shores was something a man had to smell to believe; and he had to see the squaws opening the bellies to take the fat out of the stinking things to believe that.

David had used to watch the bulls fight, but no more. When he first came from Scotland, his emotions green and tender and credulity like altar candles in his eyes, he thought the monsters would kill one another. In the rutting season when struggling for the cows their bellows shook the heavens and their feet tore the earth into clouds, blowing snot and rage from their nostrils, their flanks heaving, their dim eyes inflamed and bulging with erotic ardor, and their thick skulls crashing bone on bone with such power that the impact could be heard a mile away. God, how they fought and bellowed! David had expected to see crushed skulls and gutted bellies everywhere, but never once had he seen a bull hurt by another bull. Like the pedlars, they packed an awful lot of brag.

And what ridiculous things they were to look at! Most of a buffalo, almost four fifths of its bulk and weight, was from the penis sheath forward, rising into the enormous and largely useless hump of the shoulders and the massive depth of the neck and the skull, all covered over with enough hair to fill a half dozen mattresses; while from the middle on back the monster looked naked, as if it had been shorn, because the hair was so short compared to the shaggy manes and masses and beards of the front half. Even more ridiculous was the smallness of the rear quarters, compared to the front:

the grotesquely tiny thighs, with the great pouch of testicles hanging between them and flinging wildly back and forth and all around when the beast fought or ran; and the short useless tail; and the absurdly small feet, so small under the huge bulk that they cut narrow trenches across the prairie, a foot or a foot and half in depth, and no wider than that. And to top everything there were the silly little horns, looking like two tusks growing out of the skull.

On seeing the skulls opened David had been surprised to learn that the beasts actually had brains. They had brains but most of the time they never used them. Back from the precipice the Indians would set a V-shaped ambush of pickets, and then by waving robes and uttering a cry that the dull-witted creature thought friendly they would stampede a whole heard into the V and over a precipice; though if the cow who led refused to jump but turned back, as now and then she did, the Indians behind the herd had no chance to escape being trampled to death. And what a sight it was to see the squaws rush in with hatchets and knives like avengers ejected out of hell, to strike and stab and thrust until the whole ground under the precipice was wet with blood and guts and the squaws were red and wet too, while stuffing their mouths with raw liver; and the whole earth steamed and stank of the gut and kidney and heart and womb and testicle smells of living creatures, living a few moments ago, roaring and bellowing, but now hacked and laid open and still, eyes glazed, black tongues hanging down over lower-jaw teeth and only the muscles in thigh or neck still twitching. But that was not where he had seen them at their most stupid: after all, even a man could be ambushed.

He had seen Indians with fire or with plain whoop and holler stampede them into a river, where they drowned by hundreds as the moving masses behind shoved forward in snorting and terrified violence and beasts made a bridge for beasts or pontoons, and you saw a big bull standing precariously and amazingly upon the bulls and cows under him, as if walking across and resting a moment from his labors, and in another moment down he went under, never to come up until dead, but you could see the air from his lungs coming up, and the Indians there behind the dark and heaving and rolling mass, driving them on, beast upon beast, a bridge drowning, and beasts falling through the bridge, until the whole damn river was black and choked with them and the air from dying lungs was making a multitude of tiny fountains in the rolling tides and the Indians were giving no mercy, no quarter until the last hapless, unlucky, dimwitted and filled-with-terror thing lost his footing and went down. . . . And then you saw the acreage of them, dead, drifting with the current, beaching; and Indians out among them, push-

ing, shoving and yelling like mad; and then the beach heavy with
them, the heavens steaming with heat from their insides, and red
people choking down raw livers, eating like dogs. . . .

David preferred the flesh of the red deer or of young moose or of
mountain sheep; though in the early fall, when the rear short-haired
part was smooth with fat and the great pelage of the front half had
shed all its mattings and scabs and accumulated filth from mudholes
and wallows, the flesh was pretty good, particularly from the older
calves and the young barren cows. Indians were fond of the
dépouille, or back fat, which they melted to make pemmican but
would eat raw, though of all fats they ate raw their favorite was that
around the kidneys. They thought it was good for sore mouths.
And, hell, maybe it was, David had told himself; you could call it
superstition if you wanted to, but the Indians had a lot of fine remedies besides spruce beer for scurvy and cankerroot for canker and
balsam sap for flesh wounds.

FREDERICK F. MANFRED

Survival

IT TOOK HIM two full days to make up his mind to set the leg himself.

Cost him what it might in inhuman pain, it had to be done. It was that or give up forever being a mountain man in the free country.

Once his mind was made up, he went about it doggedly. He crawled over to a sturdy little chokecherry tree with a crotch a foot off the ground. Grimacing, cursing, he lifted the bad leg into it, hooked the heel and toe well down in the crotch, with his hands caught hold of another nearby stubby trunk—then heaved.

Pain filled him from tip to toe. He passed out a few seconds.

When he came to, he rested a while, panting desperately.

The mourning dove souled in the gully: ooah—koooo—koooo.

When he thought he could stand it again, he set himself and once more gave his leg a mighty wrenching pull. There was a crack; something gave; and he passed out again.

He came to gently, easily, up out of black into blue into yellow light.

He rested a little.

A magpie scolded a squirrel in some bullberry bushes across the brook. The squirrel skirled back.

Breath caught, he felt of his leg carefully, finger tips probing through the swollen rawhide flesh. Ho-ah. The bone had popped back into place. Ae. And now to splint it.

Working patiently, doggedly, saving his breath, he broke off a half-dozen straight chokecherry saplings about an inch thick. With his crude stone chisel he jammed off a long strip from the grizzly hide and built a tight splint around his leg. The strap of raw bearhide was still moist. In time it would shrink and make the splint fit snug.

This passage is taken from *Lord Grizzly,* a novel that describes the ordeals of a mountain man who has been terribly mauled by a grizzly bear and then deserted by his companions. [Ed. note]

The sun was almost directly overhead when he finished. Heat boiled out of the gully in waves. A dead calm radiated over the land. The vultures lay back waiting, wondering at all the movement of him. They turned slow wheels. It puzzled them that a stinking, filty, hairy skeleton of a creature could show so much life.

Hugh crawled back to the stream and in the shadow of the bullberry bushes let the water run along his back. He splashed water over his face and chest and belly and legs. The water was wondrous cool, wondrous soothing.

He napped.

He dreamt. And in the dream he heard Jim and Fitz talking about him.

But while the dream was very clear and very real, the talk in it was muttery, unclear. He couldn't make out what they were saying. He could see their mouths going, and could make out it was about him, but he couldn't make out the sense of what they said.

He dreamt. And in the dream he dreamt he had died alone in a gully, his leathers and meat torn to shreds, his bones picked over by green snakenecked buzzards. He cried out in his sleep; awoke in a buzzing stupor.

Afternoon came on. Water washed him. Minnies lipped him. Afternoon waned. Water soaked him. Minnies tickled him.

Toward evening, the air cooling, he revived again. He dug up a few of the rattler steaks he'd stashed in the sand and roasted them. For greens he ate grass tips. For fruit he had some buffalo berries and chokecherries. Ripe plums hung near; they looked very inviting, but he couldn't get himself to touch them. He washed his supper down with cool spring water. The meat and the greens and the fruit and the water strengthened him.

Later, when the sun had set and the stars and the mosquitoes came out and the wolves and coyotes began padding around him on the sand, he recalled his nightmare dreams of the afternoon. Though again he couldn't make out what it was Jim and Fitz had said in the dream.

"Wonder where the lads went to? Can't understand it. There must be some reason for the lads not bein' around. 'Tis a deep puzzle to this old coon."

He rolled it over in his mind. He couldn't wait any longer for the lads to show up. He had to begin thinking about himself.

He nodded. Yes, think of himself. He had to get out of that gully and that part of the wild country soon or he was a gone goose.

He rolled it over in his mind some more. The first thing was to get back to the settlements some way. As the crow flies it was at least some two hundred miles north to Henry's Post on the Yellowstone and Missouri. And Ft. Kiowa was some two hundred miles back the other way. Either way the country was buzzing with Rees as mad as hornets. There were also the rapidly increasing number of Sioux war parties. Even some Mandans.

He thought on it. One thing was certain—he couldn't follow the Grand River back to the Missouri and then follow that back to the fort. Too many mad Rees that way. They were thicker in that direction than in any other. So if he went back to the fort he'd have to cut across the open country to the south.

He puzzled over his broken leg. He wouldn't be able to crawl on that for at least a month, let alone walk on it. He either had to lay around until it knitted or somehow drag it after him. The first alternative meant he might starve to death, if he didn't freeze first; the second meant excruciating pain.

He puzzled over his splinted leg. If he could somehow carry it off the ground he might be able to crawl along on his elbows and one knee.

He puzzled on it. And finally decided to make himself a slape—travois, as the pork-eaters called it—a pair of shafts such as the squaws hooked up to dogs and ponies to dray their possessions. He remembered seeing Bending Reed make one down in Pawnee land along the Platte.

"I feel queersome," he said, and presently fell asleep.

Mosquitoes hummed over him. A light breeze came up and tousled his gray hair.

A cold nose woke him.

He made a grab for the cold nose and the whitegray wolf that went with it.

But he missed. He wasn't quite quick enough and the wolf had been a trace too stealthy. So it was no fresh meat for breakfast that morning.

He dug up what was left of the rattler and set about roasting it. He topped off the meat with grass tips and buffalo berries again, washing it all down with fine morning-cool water.

It was when he'd had his fill of water that he decided on Bending Reed and Ft. Kiowa two hundred miles away. He had to have the benefit of her cooking, her care, her potent herbs. She'd heal him. She'd put him back on his feet. Good old Reed. What a fine mate she'd made him all these years in that far country.

Calmly he set to work. He built a slape out of two long willow poles. He bound one to each side of his bad leg, starting at the hip socket and extending well out beyond his toes so that the entire leg rode well above the ground and had the benefit of the springy tips to absorb shock.

He knew there'd be a lot of prickly-pear cactus most of the way back. He had to find some protection for his elbows and arms, for his one good knee and leg. Looking around he hit on it. Cut out patches from the old she-rip. With his crude chisel he jammed off a set of patches, with tie-strings, and bound them on tight. He sloughed off what dried fat and meat was still stuck to the rest of the bear hide and cut armholes in it and drew it on over his back.

He also collected the grizzly's four claws. Bending Reed had often lamented that while he might have counted coup on many a brave in battle and had scalps to show for it, he still hadn't counted coup on a grizzly. She wanted to see her brave decked out with a necklace of grizzly claws. Well, he'd at last got his grizzly, and in a hand-to-hand fight at that.

He laughed when he thought of what she'd do with the claws. She'd hold a victory dance around them; then string them on a deer sinew; then drape them around his hoary old neck.

He planned his trip carefully. It would be safest to crawl at night; sleep during the day. Best, too, to take a creek up one gully to the top of a divide: cross on the hogback ridge; take a gully down on the other side, and so on until he crossed the Moreau River and got to the Cheyenne. At the Cheyenne he'd be far enough south and out of range of the Rees to once again head toward the Missouri.

He began the terrible odyssey on the evening of the ninth of September, the ninth day of the Moon of Maize Ripening.

A. B. GUTHRIE, Jr.

The Way West

FROM THE SLOPE to the southeast the frost shone white in afternoon sun except where the long shadows of the trees fell across. Spotted on the bottom were the tepees that the Sioux had pitched, looking white, too, or tan, depending on their age. There was movement below, men and women coming and going, children dodging among the lodges, the thin Indian dogs limping, nosing low for scraps, and, farther out, the horses beginning to graze as the afternoon cooled.

Summers sat his horse and watched, thinking how things had changed. This country was young, like himself, when he saw it first, young and wild like himself, without the thought of age. There wasn't a post on it then, nor any tame squaw begging calico, but only buffalo and beaver and the long grass waving in the Laramie bottoms. The wind had blown lonesome, the sound of emptiness in it, the breath of far-off places where no white foot had stepped. A man snuggling in his robe had felt alone and strong and good, telling himself he would see where the wind came from.

Now there wasn't a buffalo within fifty miles or beaver either—the few that were left of them—and the wind brought words and the hammer of hammers and the bray of mules and the smells of living under roof. The far post near the neck of the Laramie and the Platte would be Fort Platte, built after Summers had left the mountains; the near one Fort Laramie, or William, as some had called it, but even it had changed. Change coming on change, he thought. He remembered it from 'thirty-six—or was it 'thirty-seven?—when it was a cottonwood post like any other. Now it was 'dobe and white and spiked at the top like a castle might be, and the trade was in buffalo skins that a true mountain man wouldn't mess with.

Beyond, the Black Hills climbed away, dark with their scrub cedar and pine, with Laramie Peak rising oversized among them. Farther on, out of sight, there were the Red Buttes and the Sweet-

This passage describes the thoughts and feelings of an old mountain man and two members of the wagon train he is guiding to Oregon. [Ed. note]

water and the Southern Pass and the Green, where he had spent his young years like a trapper spent his beaver, thinking there was always more where that came from. On the near side of the pass, to the north, the Popo Agie. The Popo Agie. He formed the words with his lips, remembering how a Crow girl had got the sound of running water in them. Ashia, the Crow word for stream. Popo Ashia. The liquid sound, the girl warm at his side and both of them fulfilled for the time and easy, and she laughing while he practiced the tongue. Even her name was lost to him now, and she was dead or old, one, and the laughter gone from her, and did she remember at all the Long Knife who had bedded with her? He couldn't bring her face back. What he remembered was the warmness and swell of her and the young-skinned thighs. They went along with the Popo Agie, with water running white and blue and the green trees rising and the Wind Mountains higher still and the rich lift from the dam that never had seen a trap before.

He ought to be getting back to the train, but he stayed a minute longer while memory wakened to things seen. Laramie. It was the gate to the mountains once and before that a part of the mountains themselves, and a man traveling had to keep his eye out and his hand ready, watching the way of his horse for Indian sign, watching the way of buffalo while he hung to his Hawken rifle. There was danger still, from Pawnees and Sioux and maybe Blackfeet farther on, but it struck him as different, as somehow piddling. A cornfield, even like the sorry patch by the fort, didn't belong with war whoops and scalping knives. It belonged with cabins and women and children playing safe in the sun. It belonged with the dull pleasures, with the fat belly and the dim eye of safety.

He hadn't let himself think, back there in Missouri, how much of the old mountains there was still in him. He had butchered hogs and tended crops and dickered for oxen or mules and laid down at night by Mattie, shutting out the thought of beaver streams and canyons opening sweet to the eye and squaws who had comforted him and gone on, joining with the lost and wanted things. Popo Ashia, like running water.

He was a mountain man underneath, and always would be, even if he went to plowing and hoeing and slopping hogs again—and there was no place in the world these days for a mountain man, and less and less of it all the time. A few years more and a man fool enough to trap like as not would stumble on to a picnic. The buffalo were thinning, for all that greenhorns said that three calves were dropped for every cow killed. In not so long a time now people in the mountains would be living on hog meat, unknowing the flavor and strength of fleece fat and hump ribs. Unknowing, either, how keen an enemy the Rees and the Blackfeet were. He almost wished for the old Rees, for the old Blackfeet that the white man's pox had undone. They had given spirit to life; every day lived was a day won.

Well, he had set out, hunting old things remembered as new, and he would go on hunting, finding a kind of pleasure in awakening memory, feeling the heart turn at the proof in mountain or park or river that, sure enough, once he had played here, once he had set traps and counted beaver and spreed at rendezvous and seen the wild moon rise. At the nub of it did he just want his youth back? Beaver, streams, squaws, danger—were they just names for his young time?

Summers shook himself. Christ, a man could moon his life away! Better to make the most of what was left. There wasn't anything in feeling sorry for yourself.

He reined around and rode back to the train.

Rebecca Evans said, "I can't hardly wait to get to the fort." She had stepped ahead, so as to walk beside Lije, letting the single yoke of oxen hitched to her wagon follow by itself.

"That much farther along," Lije said as if he knew what she meant. "Be there pretty soon."

"How long will we be stayin'?"

"No longer'n need be. Day and a half. Maybe two days. We got to get on."

"Ain't Laramie halfway, Lije?"

"Now, Becky, hopin' it's so won't make it so."

"How far?"

"Dick says somep'n over six hundred mile."

"And from there on?"

"Maybe thirteen hundred."

"An' it's the worst?"

He didn't answer to that but walked along pulling on a dead pipe, his face cheery, watching the wagons ahead and now and then looking back, making sure all was all right. They had slanted out a piece from the river, to upland where the grass ran crisp under the wagon tires. With the thought of Laramie in their heads the teamsters were popping their whips or punching the oxen with sticks. The oxen didn't pay much notice. A sore-footed or worn-out ox never did.

"We might have to stay longer, the way the critters limp," Rebecca said, but Lije just got a bite on his pipe and shook his head.

She sighed inside, thinking it would be good to stay at the fort the rest of her life and so be done with dirt and hard travel and eyes teary with camp smoke and the back sore from stooping over a fire and the legs cramped from sitting on the ground. There she wouldn't have the grainy feel of sand forever in her shoes.

"We're comin' along fine."

"Yes," she said. "Fine." Men were queer, she thought. Even Lije was queer, taking such a real and simple pleasure in the work of his muscles and the roll of wheels. The more miles they made the better-spirited he was, as if there wasn't any aim in life but to leave tracks, no time in it but for go. He didn't mind eating mush with blown sand in it.

She knew they had to get to Oregon all right. She knew they had to travel, but she couldn't be so all-fired pleased, come night, that they were far gone from the morning. At night she felt tired and a little sad with tiredness and didn't like to think about tomorrow; and she got to wondering then if Oregon was what it was cracked up to be.

Lije liked the sun and even the wind and walked through the dust as if he had put it out of his mind, since he couldn't still it. She found the sun cruel sometimes, lonely-cruel for all its brightness, and the wind sad-rough, and she hated the grind of sand between shoe and foot.

"There's Dick."

Ahead she saw Summers in his buckskins, waving the train on. She had to squint to see him, for the sun shone straight in her face unless she kept it tucked down under the shade of her poke bonnet. Her face, she knew, was a sight, reddened by the sun and coarsened by the wind until it was more man's face than woman's. For all that God had made her big and stout and not dainty, she wanted to feel womanlike, to be clean and smooth-skinned and sometimes nice-dressed, not for Lije alone but for herself, for herself as a woman, so's to feel she was a rightful being and had a rightful place. She thought ahead to the fort, to clear, hot water and time to wash up and maybe to ease the long ache of her bones; and she thought backwards, too, to Missouri and the old springhouse and the fresh coolness of it and the milk creaming there in its pans. She thought of oak shade and trees fruiting and cupboards for dishes and victuals and chests for clothes and cookies baking and the smell of them following her around as the smell of camp smoke followed her now. She had had a home in Missouri, a place that stayed fixed, and, looking out door or window, she had known what she would see. She had been cozy there, seeing the hills and trees close and the sky bent down. And when she was tired, she had had a place to rest.

It was the time of the month, she knew, for she had been doing better lately in body and mind both, but now she felt she couldn't go on. Lije or no Lije, Brownie or no Brownie, she couldn't go beyond Laramie. She wanted to slack down right here on the prairie and let the train roll on while the wind blew and the sun burned and the dog-tiredness eased away and the disquiet died and dust went back to dust.

She stood still, not wanting Lije to catch sight of her face, and watched him push ahead while her own team came up. She fell into step alongside, saying to herself Lije was so gone on to Oregon he wouldn't think there was anything in her mind but to see to her wagon.

She bent her head from the sun, watching one foot step out and then the other and wondering that they did so, the way it was with her. Rock trotted up from somewhere and brushed her side and slowed and gazed into her face as if he could scent the trouble inside her. While she patted Rock, she heard Summers' voice. Summers had ridden up and turned about and was riding half around in the saddle while he talked to Lije. "Laramie Fork ain't so high. Best camp is west of the fort."

Lije nodded.

"You'd best be callin' on the bourgeois, too, Lije."

"Sure. Who is he?"

"Somewhere I heerd that Jim Bordeau was now. How you, Mrs. Evans? Rock ain't dead yet, I see."

"He just this minute come up. I'm tolerable."

"That's slick. I'll be gettin' along, Lije."

The lead wagons were sinking from sight down a slope that Rebecca figured led to the Laramie. It was as if the wheels were sinking into the earth pair by pair, and then the beds and then the swaying tops.

Lije whoaed his oxen when he came to the top of the hill. Rebecca walked up to him and saw the train winding down and, below it, Fort Laramie, white as fresh wash, with trees waving and shade dark on the grass and the river fringed with woods. She said, "I never thought to be so glad just to see a building."

"It's Fort Laramie. Sure."

"Not because it's a fort. Just because it's a building."

"It's Fort Laramie all the same."

"You reckon they've got chairs there, Lije? Real chairs."

There was a light in his eyes. He said, "Sure," and cut a little caper with his feet and sang out:

> "To the far-off Pacific sea,
>   Will you go, will you go, old girl, with me?"

She said, "I just want to set in a chair."

HARVEY FERGUSSON

Virgin Earth

THE WATERSHED of the Dark River lies on the eastern slope of the southern Rockies, where the mountains reach down from their bald rocky summits in long wooded ridges to the edge of the great plains. Rio Oscuro, the Mexicans named it, and so it was known when Ballard first saw it, but the Americans changed the name to Dark River. It could be called a river only in the Southwest, where any stream that carries water all the year around is a river. In fact, it is only a large trout stream which runs about twenty-five miles from its source to the foot of the mountains and then sinks back into the earth. It rises in a little lake at the foot of a peak above timber line, beginning as a bright thread of water creeping among the roots of the grass, then plunging suddenly into a long, dark, narrow canyon, alternately foaming through rocky gorges and disappearing into forests of spruce so dense that sunlight barely touches the water. This long dark cleft in the country is what gave the river its name. But below the box canyon, as the mountain men called such a gorge, the river emerges into a valley that widens as it falls toward the plain, the ridges dwindling and parting on either hand, the spruce giving way to tall forests of yellow pine, the stream running under a covert of wind-rippled willow, through open meadows, with here and there a tall perfect fir offering shade and shelter.

In this month of September, after the heavy rains of late summer, the country was at its best. On the upland meadows the short grass was so thick it felt like a heavy-piled carpet under the feet, and it was richly colored with the late blooming flowers of the high country. Down in the valley the wild oats would brush the belly of a deer and the river ran full and clear, with feeding trout marking perfect circles on the smooth green pools. The wild turkeys with their well-grown broods had come down into the canyons to hunt

This brief selection from the novel *Grant of Kingdom* is reprinted here because of its description of the unspoiled mountain country of New Mexico. [Ed. note]

grasshoppers in the tall grass. Up on the ridges the black-tail bucks were thrashing the velvet off their new-grown antlers, getting ready for the season of lust and battle. Higher up in thick timber the bull clk were beginning to bugle. Black bears were feeding like pigs in the berry patches, turning over logs and rocks in search of ants and grubs, laying on fat against the winter sleep. The whole country was astir with the autumn business of feeding and breeding, in the last warm days of the year and under the full September moon.

This was a country that would look good to any man who loved country for its own sake, who wanted only to spread his blankets under a tree and take his meat where he found it. And it would also look good to any man who knew the value of things and wanted to own them and use them, for here was timber enough to build a city and a thousand acres of rich bottom land that could be plowed and irrigated, and range on the lower ridges and down on the flats for thousands of cattle and sheep and horses. Whether a man was looking for peace or for power, whether he loved the earth as it was or wanted to seize it and make it over in the image of his restless desire, this was a country that would stir his blood.

Jean Ballard rode over the divide from the other side of the mountains, crossing the summit twelve thousand feet above sea level, where wild sheep with great curling horns snorted and ran for the peaks, and a golden eagle, on rigid wings, wheeled around the sun. He rode alone, for this was a venture he would not ask anyone to share. He was mounted on his big chestnut and led a pack horse with a light load. His rifle was across the saddle before him and his long knife hung at his belt. For the first time in a year he was back on the trail, feeling alert and alive and glad of solitude and hazard. He rode across the alpine meadows, his horses sinking to their fetlocks in the lush, damp sod, and out upon a rocky spur from which he could overlook the whole of the watershed, spread at his feet like a great map in massive relief. There he pulled up and dismounted and sat down on a rock to look. A rare excitement pounded in his blood. He felt big and tense with hope and desire. For the momentous, the incredible thing was that all he saw, clear down to the wide valley and the vague spread of the plain, was his dominion if he could take it and use it.

EDWARD L. WHEELER

Calamity Jane

WE HAVE DESCRIBED the eccentric dare-devil of the Black Hills in other works of this series, but as some may not have read them, it will require but little time to describe her again.

A female of no given age, although she might have ranged safely anywhere between seventeen and twenty-three, she was the possessor of a form both graceful and womanly, and a face that was peculiarly handsome and attractive, though upon it were lines drawn by the unmistakable hand of dissipation and hard usage, lines never to be erased from a face that in innocent childhood had been a pretty one. The lips and eyes still retained in themselves their girlish beauty; the lips their full, rosy plumpness, and the eyes their dark, magnetic sparkle, and the face proper had the power to become stern, grave or jolly in expression, wreathed partially as it was in a semi-framework of long, raven hair that reached below a faultless waist.

Her dress was buckskin trowsers, met at the knee by fancifully beaded leggings, with slippers of dainty pattern upon the feet; a velvet vest, and one of those luxuries of the mines, a boiled shirt, open at the throat, partially revealing a breast of alabaster purity; a short, velvet jacket, and Spanish broad-brimmed hat, slouched upon one side of a regally beautiful head. There were diamond rings upon her hands, a diamond pin in her shirt-bosom, a massive gold chain strung across her vest front.

For she had riches, this girl, and none knew better than she how to find them in the auriferous earth or at the gaming-table of Deadwood, the third Baden Baden of two continents.

A belt around her waist contained a solitary revolver of large caliber; and this, along with a rifle strapped to her back, comprised her outfit, except we mentioned the fiery little Mexican black she rode, and the accompanying trappings, which were richly decorated and bespangled, after lavish Mexican taste.

"I guess the coast is clear, Trick; so go ahead," and a jerk at the cruel Spanish bit and an application of spurs sent the spiteful cayuse clattering wildly down the canyon, while Calamity Jane rocked not ungracefully from side to side with the reckless freedom peculiar to the California buchario. Indeed, I think that any person who has witnessed the dare-devil riding of this eccentric girl, in her mad career through the Black Hills country, will agree with me that she has of her sex no peer in the saddle or on horseback.

The first time it was ever my fortune to see her, was when Deadwood was but an infant city of a few shanties, but many tents.

She dashed madly down through the gulch one day, standing erect upon the back of her unsaddled cayuse, and the animal running at the top of its speed, leaping sluices and other obstructions— still the dare-devil retained her position as if glued to the animal's back, her hair flowing wildly back from beneath her slouch hat, her eyes dancing occasionally with excitement, as she recognized some wondering pilgrim, every now and then her lips giving vent to a ringing whoop, which was creditable in imitation if not in volume and force to that of a full-blown Comanche warrior.

Now, she dashed away through the narrow gulch, catching with delight long breaths of the perfume of flowers which met her nostrils at every onward leap of her horse, piercing the gloom of the night with her dark lovely eyes, searchingly, lest she should be surprised; lighting a cigar at full motion—dashing on, on, this strange girl of the Hills went, on her flying steed.

The glowing end of her cigar attracted the notice of four men who were crouching in the dense shadows, further down the gulch, even as the hoofstrokes broke upon their hearing.

"That's her!" growled one, knocking the ashes out of his pipe, with an oath. "Reckoned she wouldn't be all night, ef we only hed patience. Grab yer weepons, an' git ready, boys. She mustn't escape us this time."

Calamity Jane came on; she was not aware of her danger, until she saw four dark shadows cross her path, and her cayuse reared upon its haunches.

"Whoa! Trick; don't git skeered; hold up, you devils. I reckon you're barkin' up ther wrong tree!" she cried.

Then there were three flashes of light in the darkness followed by as many pistol-shots—howls of pain and rage, and curses too vile to repeat here—a yell, wild and clear, a snort from the horse—then the dare-devil rode down the man at the bits, and dashed away down the canyon, with a yell of laughter that echoed and re-echoed up and down the canyon walls.

"I wonder who composed thet worthy quartette?" Calamity mused, as she gazed back over her shoulder. "Reckon at least a couple of 'em bit ther dust, ef not more. Could it have been—but no! I do not believe so. Deadwood Dick's men ain't on the rampage any more, and it couldn't hev been them. Whoever it was wanted my life, that's plain, and I shall have to look out fer breakers ahead, or next time I shall not get off with a simple scratch."

5

The Old Southwest

TWENTIETH-CENTURY popular literature about the Old South, from
The Clansman (1905) to *Gone with the Wind* (1936), has established
the picture of a gracious, settled aristocratic society in the antebel-
lum plantation days. That image has struck in the minds of the
American people, in the North as well as in the South, and they easily forget that the early Southwest frontier, stretching west from
Georgia to Arkansas, reaching north to Tennessee and Kentucky,
was once the fiercest, bloodiest, and most terrifying of all.

The men who conquered this area in the early nineteenth century
were among the most lawless, violent, and vainglorious barbarians
America has ever known. They robbed and slaughtered Indians,
fought and murdered one another, and laughed and lied as they
killed. The unashamed violence of the Old Southwest repels many
modern readers, but they must also be fascinated by the brutal gusto
and barbaric humor of the time and place.

Here are the first renderings of classic frontier toughs and ruf-
fians, the ring-tailed roarers who boast that they are half alligator,
half panther, who claim that they can lick their weight in wildcats
with one hand tied behind them. Here is a primitive code duello
that boasts of a thumb in the eye, a knee in the groin, and a knife
in the ribs. And here is the exaggeration of primitive epic—the
king-size mosquitoes, the bears as big as houses, and men who ride
the lightning and move the sun.

We can wince at the chauvinism, crudity, and cruelty of *Nick of
the Woods* or *Georgia Scenes, Characters, and Incidents.* And we
may find the outrageous hyperbole of "The Big Bear of Arkansas"
less amusing than it was for our grandfathers. But in all of this early
work we cannot fail to feel the vitality and irresistible thrust of the
frontier, qualities that have persisted in much of American literature ever since.

With the work of Mark Twain we move away from mere melodrama, journalism, or folklore. But we abandon none of them. They

are incorporated and transformed into art and social criticism, and they survive in the days of Twain's resplendent steamboats.

In the nostalgic, almost atypically gentle selection reprinted here, Twain describes learning, not fighting. His world is more complex than that of the older Southwest, the judgments more difficult, the actions less simply heroic.

Yet we can always feel the pulse of the older culture. The violence is latent, suggested rather than explicit. The humor is more subtle, sometimes tempered by melancholy. But the essential vitality remains.

ROBERT MONTGOMERY BIRD

The Jibbenainosay

"WHAT'S THE MATTER, Tom Bruce?" said the father, eyeing him with surprise.

"Matter enough," responded the young giant, with a grin of mingled awe and delight; "the Jibbenainosay is up again!"

"Whar?" cried the senior, eagerly,—"not in our limits?"

"No, by Jehoshaphat!" replied Tom; "but nigh enough to be neighborly,—on the north bank of Kentuck, whar he has left his mark right in the middle of the road, as fresh as though it war but the work of the morning!"

"And a clear mark, Tom?—no mistake in it?"

"Right to an iota!" said the young man;—"a reggelar cross on the breast, and good tomahawk dig right through the skull; and a long-legg'd fellow, too, that looked as though he might have fou't old Sattan himself!"

"It's the Jibbenainosay, sure enough; and so good luck to him!" cried the commander: "thar's a harricane coming!"

"Who is the Jibbenainosay?" demanded Forrester.

"Who?" cried Tom Bruce: "Why Nick,—Nick of the Woods."

"And who, if you please, is Nick of the Woods?"

"Thar," replied the junior, with another grin, "thar, strannger, you're too hard for me. Some think one thing, and some another; but thar's many reckon he's the devil."

"And his mark, that you were talking of in such mysterious terms, —what is that?"

"Why, a dead Injun, to be sure, with Nick's mark on him,—a knife-cut, or a brace of 'em, over the ribs in the shape of a cross. That's the way the Jibbenainosay marks all the meat of his killing. It has been a whole year now since we h'ard of him."

"Captain," said the elder Bruce, "you don't seem to understand the affa'r altogether; but if you were to ask Tom about the Jibbenainosay till doomsday, he could tell you no more than he has told already. You must know, thar's a creatur' of some sort or other that

ranges the woods round about our station h'yar, keeping a sort of
guard over us like, and killing all the brute Injuns that ar' onlucky
enough to come in his way, besides scalping them and marking
them with his mark. The Injuns call him *Jibbenainosay*, or a word
of that natur', which them that know more about the Injun gabble
than I do, say means the Spirit-that-walks; and if we can believe any
such lying devils as Injuns, (which I am loath to do, for the truth
ar'nt in 'em,) he is neither man nor beast, but a great ghost or devil
that knife cannot harm nor bullet touch; and they have always had
an idea that our fort h'yar in partickelar, and the country round
about, war under his friendly protection—many thanks to him,
whether he be a devil or not; for that war the reason the savages so
soon left off a worrying of us."

"Is it possible," said Roland, "that any one can believe such an
absurd story?"

"Why not?" said Bruce, stoutly. "Thar's the Injuns themselves,
Shawnees, Hurons, Delawares, and all,—but partickelarly the Shawnees, for he beats all creation a-killing of Shawnees,—that believe in
him, and hold him in such etarnal dread, that thar's scarce a brute
of 'em has come within ten miles of the station h'yar this three y'ar:
because as how, he haunts about our woods h'yar in partickelar, and
kills 'em wheresomever he catches 'em,—especially the Shawnees, as I
said afore, against which the creatur' has a most butchering spite;
and there's them among the other tribes that call him *Shawneewan-
naween*, or the Howl of the Shawnees, because of his keeping them
ever a howling. And thar's his marks, captain,—what do you make of
that? When you find an Injun lying scalped and tomahawked, it
stands to reason thar war something to kill him."

"Ay, truly," said Forrester; "but I think you have human beings
enough to give the credit to, without referring it to a supernatural
one."

"Strannger," said Big Tom Bruce the younger, with a sagacious
nod, "when you kill an Injun yourself, I reckon,—meaning no offence—you will be willing to take all the honor that can come of it,
without leaving it to be scrambled after by others. Thar's no man
'arns a scalp in Kentucky, without taking great pains to show it to
his neighbors."

"And besides, captain," said the father, very gravely, "thar are
men among us who have *seen* the creatur'!"

"*That,*" said Roland, who perceived his new friends were not well
pleased with his incredulity, "is an argument I can resist no longer."

"Thar war Ben Jones, and Samuel Sharp, and Peter Smalleye and
a dozen more, who all had a glimpse of him stalking through the
woods, at different times; and, they agree, he looks more like a devil

nor a mortal man,—a great tall fellow with horns and a hairy head like a buffalo-bull, and a little devil that looks like a black b'ar, that walks before him to point out the way. He war always found in the deepest forests, and that's the reason we call him Nick of the Woods; wharby we mean *Old Nick* of the Woods; for we hold him to be the devil, though a friendly one to all but Injuns. Now, captain, I war never superstitious in my life,—but I go my death on the Jibbenainosay! I never seed the creatur' himself, but I have seen, in my time, two different savages of his killing. It's a sure sign, if you see him in the woods, that thar's Injuns at hand: and it's a good sign, when you find his mark, without seeing himself; for then you may be sure the brutes are off,—for they can't stand old Nick of the Woods no how! At first, he war never h'ard of afar from our station; but he has begun to widen his range. Last year he left his marks down Salt River in Jefferson; and now, you see, he is striking game north of the Kentucky; and I've h'ard of them that say he kills Shawnees even in their own country; though consarning *that* I'll not be so partickelar. No, no, captain, thar's no mistake in Nick of the Woods; and if you are so minded, we will go and h'ar the whole news of him. But, I say, Tom," continued the Kentuckian, as the three left the porch together, "who brought the news?"

"Captain Ralph,—Roaring Ralph Stackpole," replied Tom Bruce, with a knowing and humorous look.

"What!" cried the father, in sudden alarm: "Look to the horses, Tom!"

"I will," said the youth, laughing: "it war no sooner known that Captain Ralph war among us than it was resolved to have six Regulators in the range all night! Thar's some of these new colts, (not to speak of our own creatur's,) and especially that blooded brown beast of the captain's called Brown Briery, or some such name, would set a better man than Roaring Ralph Stackpole's mouth watering."

"And who," said Roland, "is Roaring Ralph Stackpole? and what has he to do with Brown Briareus?"

"A proper fellow as ever you saw!" replied Tom, approvingly;— "killed two Injuns once, single-handed, on Bear-Grass, and has stolen more horses from them than ar another man in Kentucky. A prime creatur'! but he has his fault, poor fellow, and sometimes mistakes a Christian's horse for an Injun's, thar's the truth of it!"

"And such scoundrels you make officers of?" demanded the soldier, indignantly.

"Oh," said the elder Bruce, "thar's no reggelar commission in the case. But whar thar's a knot of our poor folks out of horses, and inclined to steal a lot from the Shawnees, (which is all fa'r plundering, you see, for thar's not a horse among them, the brutes, that they did not steal from Kentucky,) they send for Roaring Ralph and make him their captain; and a capital one he is, too, being all fight from top to bottom; and as for the stealing part, thar's no one can equal him. But, as Tom says, he sometimes *does* make mistakes, having stolen horses so often from the Injuns, he can scarce keep his hands off a Christian's and that makes us wrathy."

By this time the speakers had reached the gate of the fort, and passed among the cabins outside, where they found a throng of the villagers, surrounding the captain of horse-thieves, and listening with great edification to, and deriving no little amusement from, his account of the last achievement of the Jibbenainosay. Of this, as it related no more than the young Bruce had already repeated,—namely, that, while riding that morning from the north side, he had stumbled upon the corse of an Indian, which bore all the marks of having been a late victim to the wandering demon of the woods,—we shall say nothing:—but the appearance and conduct of the narrator, one of the first, and perhaps the parent, of the race of men who have made Salt River so renowned in story, were such as to demand a less summary notice. He was a stout, bandy-legged, broad-shouldered, and bull-headed tatterdemalion, ugly, mean, and villainous of look; yet with an impudent, swaggering, joyous self-esteem traced in every feature and expressed in every action of body, that rather disposed the beholder to laugh than to be displeased at his appearance. An old blanket-coat, or wrap-rascal, once white, but now of the same muddy brown hue that stained his visage—and once also of sufficient length to defend his legs, though the skirts had long since been transferred to the cuffs and elbows, where they appeared in huge patches—covered the upper part of his body; while the lower boasted a pair of buckskin breeches and leather wrappers, somewhat its junior in age, but its rival in mud and maculation. An old round fur hat, intended originally for a boy, and only made to fit his head by being slit in sundry places at the bottom, thus leaving a dozen yawning gaps, through which, as through the chinks of a lattice, stole out as many stiff bunches of black hair, gave to the capital excrescence an air as ridiculous as it was truly uncouth; which was not a little increased by the absence on one side of the brim, and by a loose fragment of it hanging down on the other. To give something martial to an appearance in other respects so outlandish and ludicrous, he had his rifle, and other usual equipments of a woodsman, including the knife and tomahawk, the first of which he carried in his hand, swinging it about at every moment, with a vigor and apparent carelessness well fit to discompose a nervous person, had any such happened among his auditors. As if there was not enough in his figure, visage, and attire to move the mirth of beholders, he added to his other attractions a variety of gestures and antics of the most extravagant kinds, dancing, leaping and dodging about, clapping his hands and cracking his heels together, with the activity, restlessness, and, we may add, the grace, of a jumping-jack. Such was the worthy, or unworthy, son of Salt River, a man wholly unknown to history, though not to local and traditionary fame, and much less to the then inhabitants of Bruce's Station, to whom he related his news of the Jibbenainosay with that emphasis and importance of tone and manner which are most significantly expressed in the phrase of "laying down the law."

As soon as he saw the commander of the Station approaching, he cleared the throng around him by a skip and a hop, seized the colonel by the hand, and doing the same with the soldier, before Roland could repel him, as he would have done, exclaimed, "Glad to see you, cunnel;—same to you, strannger——What's the news from Virginnie? Strannger, my name's Ralph Stackpole, and I'm a ring-tailed squealer!"

"Then, Mr. Ralph Stackpole, the ring-tailed squealer," said Roland, disengaging his hand, "be so good as to pursue your business, without regarding or taking any notice of me."

" 'Tarnal death to me!" cried the captain of horse-thieves, indignant at the rebuff, "I'm a gentleman, and my name's *Fight!* Foot and hand, tooth and nail, claw and mud-scraper, knife, gun, and tomahawk, or any other way you choose to take me, I'm your man! Cock-a-doodle-doo!" And with that the gentleman jumped into the air, and flapped his wings, as much to the amusement of the provoker of his wrath as of any other person present.

"Come, Ralph," said the commander of the Station, "whar'd' you steal that brown mar' thar?"—a question whose abruptness somewhat quelled the ferment of the man's fury, while it drew a roar of laughter from the lookers-on.

"Thar it is!" said he, striking an attitude and clapping a hand on his breast, like a man who felt his honor unjustly assailed. "Steal! *I* steal any horse but an Injun's! Whar's the man dar's insinivate that? Blood and massacree-ation! whar's the man?"

"H'yar," said Bruce, very composedly. "I know that old mar' belongs to Peter Harper, on the north side."

"You're right, by Hooky!" cried Roaring Ralph: at which seeming admission of his knavery the merriment of the spectators was greatly increased; nor was it much lessened when the fellow proceeded to aver that he had borrowed it, and that with the express stipulation that it should be left at Bruce's Station, subject to the orders of its owner. "Thar, cunnel," said he, "thar's the beast; take it; and just tell me whar's the one you mean to lend me,—for I must be off afore sunset."

"And whar are you going?" demanded Bruce.

"To St. Asaphs,"—which was a Station some twenty or thirty miles off,—replied Captain Stackpole.

"Too far for the Regulators to follow, Ralph," said Colonel Bruce; at which the young men present laughed louder than ever, and eyed the visitor in a way that seemed both to disconcert and offend him.

"Cunnel," said he, "you're a man in authority, and my superior officer; wharfo' thar' can be no scalping between us. But my name's Tom Dowdle, the rag-man!" he screamed, suddenly skipping into the thickest of the throng, and sounding a note of defiance; "my name's Tom Dowdle, the rag-man, and I'm for any man that insults me! log-leg or leather-breeches, green-shirt or blanket-coat, land-trotter or river-roller,—I'm the man for a massacree!" Then giving himself a twirl upon his foot that would have done credit to a dancing-master, he proceeded to other antic demonstrations of hostility, which when performed in after years on the banks of the Lower Mississippi, by himself and his worthy imitators, were, we suspect, the cause of their receiving the name of the mighty alligator. It is said, by naturalists, of this monstrous reptile, that he delights, when the returning warmth of spring has brought his fellows from their holes, and placed them basking along the banks of a swampy lagoon, to dart into the centre of the expanse, and challenge the whole field to combat. He roars, he blows the water from his nostrils, he lashes it with his tail, he whirls round and round, churning the water into foam; until, having worked himself into a proper fury, he darts back again to the shore, to seek an antagonist. Had the gallant captain of horse-thieves boasted the blood, as he afterwards did the name, of an "alligator half breed," he could have scarce conducted himself in a way more worthy of his parentage. He leaped into the centre of the throng, where, having found elbow-room for his purpose, he performed the gyration mentioned before, following it up by other feats expressive of his hostile humor. He flapped his wings and crowed, until every chanticleer in the settlement replied to the note of battle; he snorted and neighed like a horse; he bellowed like a bull; he barked like a dog; he yelled like an Indian; he whined like a panther; he howled like a wolf; until one would have thought he was a living menagerie, comprising within his single body the spirit of every animal noted for its love of conflict. Then, not content with such a display of readiness to fight the field, he darted from the centre of the area allowed him for his exercise, and invited the lookers-on individually to battle. "Whar's your buffalo-bull," he cried, "to cross horns with the roarer of Salt River? Whar's your full-blood colt that can shake a saddle off? h'yar's an old nag can kick off the top of a buck-eye! Whar's your cat of the Knobs? your wolf of the Rolling Prairies? h'yar's the old brown b'ar can claw the bark off a gum-tree! H'yar's a man for you, Tom Bruce! Same to you, Sim Roberts! to you, Jimmy Big-nose! to you, and to you, and to you! Ar'n't I a ring-tailed squealer? Can go down Salt on my back, and swim up the Ohio! Whar's the man to fight Roaring Ralph Stackpole?"

Now, whether it happened that there were none present inclined to a contest with such a champion, or whether it was that the young men looked upon the exhibition as a mere bravado meant rather to amuse them than to irritate, it so occurred that not one of them accepted the challenge; though each, when personally called on, did his best to add to the roarer's fury, if fury it really were, by letting off sundry jests in relation to borrowed horses and Regulators.* That the fellow's rage was in great part assumed, Roland, who was, at first, somewhat amused at his extravagance, became soon convinced; and growing at last weary of it, he was about to signify to his host his inclination to return into the fort, when the appearance of another individual on the ground suddenly gave promise of new entertainment.

* It is scarce necessary to inform the reader, that by this term must be understood those public-spirited citizens, amateur jack-ketches, who administer Lynch-law in districts where regular law is but inefficiently, or not at all established. [Author's note]

AUGUSTUS BALDWIN LONGSTREET

The Fight

IN THE YOUNGER DAYS of the Republic there lived in the county of—
two men, who were admitted on all hands to be the very *best men*
in the county; which, in the Georgia vocabulary, means they could
flog any other two men in the county. Each, through many a hard-
fought battle, had acquired the mastery of his own battalion; but
they lived on opposite sides of the Courthouse, and in different battalions: consequently, they were but seldom thrown together. When
they met, however, they were always very friendly; indeed, at their
first interview, they seemed to conceive a wonderful attachment to
each other, which rather increased than diminished as they became
better acquainted; so that, but for the circumstance which I am
about to mention, the question, which had been a thousand times
asked, "Which is the best man, Billy Stallions (Stallings) or Bob
Durham?" would probably never have been answered.

Billy ruled the upper battalion, and Bob the lower. The former
measured six feet and an inch in his stockings, and, without a single
pound of cumbrous flesh about him, weighed a hundred and eighty.
The latter was an inch shorter than his rival, and ten pounds
lighter; but he was much the most active of the two. In running and
jumping he had but few equals in the county; and in wrestling, not
one. In other respects they were nearly equal. Both were admirable
specimens of human nature in its finest form. Billy's victories had
generally been achieved by the tremendous power of his blows, one
of which had often proved decisive of his battles; Bob's, by his ad-
roitness in bringing his adversary to the ground. This advantage he
had never failed to gain at the onset, and, when gained he never
failed to improve it to the defeat of his adversary. These points of
difference have involved the reader in a doubt as to the probable
issue of a contest between them. It was not so, however, with the
two battalions. Neither had the least difficulty in determining the
point by the most natural and irresistible deductions *à priori;* and
though, by the same course of reasoning, they arrived at directly op-

posite conclusions, neither felt its confidence in the least shaken by this circumstance. The upper battalion swore "that Billy only wanted one lick at him to knock his heart, liver, and lights out of him, and if he got two at him, he'd knock him into a cocked hat." The lower battalion retorted, "that he wouldn't have time to double his fist before Bob would put his head where his feet ought to be; and that, by the time he hit the ground, the meat would fly off his face so quick, that people would think it was shook off by the fall." These disputes often led to the *argumentum ad hominem,* but with such equality of success on both sides as to leave the main question just where they found it. They usually ended, however, in the common way, with a bet; and many a quart of old Jamaica (whiskey had not then supplanted rum) were staked upon the issue. Still, greatly to the annoyance of the curious, Billy and Bob continued to be good friends.

Now there happened to reside in the county just alluded to a lit-- tle fellow by the name of Ransy Sniffle: a sprout of Richmond, who, in his earlier days, had fed copiously upon red clay and blackberries. This diet had given to Ransy a complexion that a corpse would have disdained to own, and an abdominal rotundity that was quite unprepossessing. Long spells of the fever and ague, too, in Ransy's youth, had conspired with clay and blackberries to throw him quite out of the order of nature. His shoulders were fleshless and elevated; his head large and flat; his neck slim and translucent; and his arms, hands, fingers, and feet were lengthened out of all proportion to the rest of his frame. His joints were large and his limbs small; and as for flesh, he could not, with propriety, be said to have any. Those parts which nature usually supplies with the most of this article—the calves of the legs, for example—presented in him the appearance of so many well-drawn blisters. His height was just five feet nothing; and his average weight in blackberry season, ninety-five. I have been thus particular in describing him, for the purpose of showing what a great matter a little fire sometimes kindleth. There was nothing on this earth which delighted Ransy so much as a fight. He never seemed fairly alive except when he was witnessing, fomenting, or talking about a fight. Then, indeed, his deep-sunken gray eye assumed something of a living fire, and his tongue acquired a volubility that bordered upon eloquence. Ransy had been kept for more than a year in the most torturing suspense as to the comparative manhood of Billy Stallings and Bob Durham. He had resorted to all his usual expedients to bring them in collision, and had entirely failed. He had faithfully reported to Bob all that had been said by the people in the upper battalion "agin him," and "he was sure Billy Stallings started it. He heard Billy say himself to Jim Brown,

that he could whip him, *or any other man in his battalion;*" and
this he told to Bob; adding, "Dod darn his soul, if he was a little
bigger, if he'd let any man *put upon* his battalion in such a way."
Bob replied, "If he (Stallings) thought so, he'd better come and try
it." This Ransy carried to Billy, and delivered it with a spirit becoming his own dignity and the character of his battalion, and with
a colouring well calculated to give it effect. These, and many other
schemes which Ransy laid for the gratification of his curiosity, entirely failed of their object. Billy and Bob continued friends, and
Ransy had began to lapse into the most tantalizing and hopeless despair, when a circumstance occurred which led to a settlement of the
long-disputed question.

It is said that a hundred gamecocks will live in perfect harmony
together if you do not put a hen with them; and so it would have
been with Billy and Bob had there been no women in the world.
But there were women in the world, and from them each of our
heroes had taken to himself a wife. The good ladies were no strangers to the prowess of their husbands, and, strange as it may seem,
they presumed a little upon it.

The two battalions had met at the Courthouse upon a regimental
parade. The two champions were there, and their wives had accompanied them. Neither knew the other's lady, nor were the ladies
known to each other. The exercises of the day were just over, when
Mrs. Stallings and Mrs. Durham stepped simultaneously into the
store of Zephaniah Atwater, from "down east."

"Have you any Turkey-red?" said Mrs. S.

"Have you any curtain calico?" said Mrs. D. at the same moment.

"Yes, ladies," said Mr. Atwater, "I have both."

"Then help me first," said Mrs. D., "for I'm in a hurry."

"I'm in as great a hurry as she is," said Mrs. S., "and I'll thank
you to help me first."

"And, pray, who are you, madam?" continued the other.

"Your betters, madam," was the reply.

At this moment Billy Stallings stepped in. "Come," said he,
"Nancy, let's be going; it's getting late."

"I'd a been gone half an hour ago," she replied, "if it hadn't a'
been for that impudent huzzy."

"Who do you call an impudent huzzy, you nasty, good-for-noth-
ing, snaggle-tooth gaub of fat, you?" returned Mrs. D.

"Look here, woman," said Billy, "have you got a husband here? If
you have, I'll *lick* him till he learns to teach you better manners,
you *sassy* heifer you." At this moment something was seen to rush
out of the store as if ten thousand hornets were stinging it; crying,
"Take care—let me go—don't hold me—where's Bob Durham?" It

was Ransy Sniffle, who had been listening in breathless delight to all
that had passed.

"Yonder's Bob, setting on the Courthouse steps," cried one.
"What's the matter?"

"Don't talk to me!" said Ransy, "Bob Durham, you'd better go
long yonder, and take care of your wife. They're playing h—l with
her there, in Zeph Atwater's store. Dod etarnally darn my soul, if
any man was to talk to my wife as Bill Stallions is talking to yours,
if I wouldn't drive blue blazes through him in less than no time."

Bob sprang to the store in a minute, followed by a hundred
friends; for the bully of a county never wants friends.

"Bill Stallions," said Bob, as he entered, "what have you been saying to my wife?"

"Is that your wife?" inquired Billy, obviously much surprised and
a little disconcerted.

"Yes, she is, and no man shall abuse her, I don't care who he is."

"Well," rejoined Billy, "it an't worth while to go over it; I've said
enough for a fight: and, if you'll step out, we'll settle it!"

"Billy," said Bob, "are you for a fair fight?"

"I am," said Billy. "I've heard much of your manhood, and I believe I'm a better man than you are. If you will go into a ring with
me, we can soon settle the dispute."

"Choose your friends," said Bob; "make your ring, and I'll be in
with mine as soon as you will."

They both stepped out, and began to strip very deliberately, each
battalion gathering round its champion, except Ransy, who kept
himself busy in a most honest endeavour to hear and see all that
transpired in both groups at the same time. He ran from one to the
other in quick succession; peeped here and listened there; talked to
this one, then to that one, and then to himself; squatted under one's
legs and another's arms and, in the short interval between stripping
and stepping into the ring, managed to get himself trod on by half
of both battalions. But Ransy was not the only one interested upon
this occasion; the most intense interest prevailed everywhere. Many
were the conjectures, doubts, oaths, and imprecations uttered while
the parties were preparing for the combat. All the knowing ones
were consulted as to the issue, and they all agreed, to a man, in one
of two opinions: either that Bob would flog Billy, or Billy would
flog Bob. We must be permitted, however, to dwell for a moment
upon the opinion of Squire Thomas Loggins; a man who, it was
said, had never failed to predict the issue of a fight in all his life.
Indeed, so unerring had he always proved in this regard, that it
would have been counted the most obstinate infidelity to doubt for
a moment after he had delivered himself. Squire Loggins was a man

who said but little, but that little was always delivered with the most imposing solemnity of look and cadence. He always wore the aspect of profound thought, and you could not look at him without coming to the conclusion that he was elaborating truth from its most intricate combinations.

"Uncle Tommy," said Sam Reynolds, "you can tell us all about it if you will; how will the fight go?"

The question immediately drew an anxious group around the squire. He raised his teeth slowly from the head of his walking cane, on which they had been resting; pressed his lips closely and thoughtfully together; threw down his eyebrows, dropped his chin, raised his eyes to an angle of twenty-three degrees, paused about half a minute, and replied, "Sammy, watch Robert Durham close in the beginning of the fight; take care of William Stallions in the middle of it; and see who has the wind at the end." As he uttered the last member of the sentence, he looked slyly at Bob's friends, and winked very significantly; where upon they rushed, with one accord, to tell Bob what Uncle Tommy had said. As they retired, the squire turned to Billy's friends, and said, with a smile, "Them boys think I mean that Bob will whip."

Here the other party kindled into joy, and hastened to inform Billy how Bob's friends had deceived themselves as to Uncle Tommy's opinion. In the mean time the principals and seconds were busily employed in preparing themselves for the combat. The plan of attack and defence, the manner of improving the various turns of the conflict, "the best mode of saving wind," &c., &c., were all discussed and settled. At length Billy announced himself ready, and his crowd were seen moving to the centre of the Courthouse Square; he and his five seconds in the rear. At the same time, Bob's party moved to the same point, and in the same order. The ring was now formed, and for a moment the silence of death reigned through both battalions. It was soon interrupted, however, by the cry of "Clear the way!" from Billy's seconds; when the ring opened in the centre of the upper battalion (for the order of march had arranged the centre of the two battalions on opposite sides of the circle), and Billy stepped into the ring from the east, followed by his friends. He was stripped to the trousers, and exhibited an arm, breast, and shoulders of the most tremendous portent. His step was firm, daring, and martial; and as he bore his fine form a little in advance of his friends, an involuntary burst of triumph broke from his side of the ring; and, at the same moment, an uncontrollable thrill of awe ran along the whole curve of the lower battalion.

"Look at him!" was heard from his friends; "just look at him."

"Ben, how much you ask to stand before that man two seconds?"

"Pshaw, don't talk about it! Just thinkin' about it's broke three o' my ribs a'ready!"

"What's Bob Durham going to do when Billy let's that arm loose upon him?"

"God bless your soul, he'll think thunder and lightning a mint julep to it."

"Oh, look here, men, go take Bill Stallions out o' that ring, and bring in Phil Johnson's stud horse, so that Durham may have some chance! I don't want to see the man killed right away."

These and many other like expressions, interspersed thickly with oaths of the most modern coinage, were coming from all points of the upper battalion, while Bob was adjusting the girth of his pantaloons, which walking had discovered not to be exactly right. It was just fixed to his mind, his foes becoming a little noisy, and his friends a little uneasy at his delay, when Billy called out, with a smile of some meaning, "Where's the bully of the lower battalion? I'm getting tired of waiting."

"Here he is," said Bob, lighting, as it seemed, from the clouds into the ring, for he had actually bounded clear of the head of Ransy Sniffle into the circle. His descent was quite as imposing as Billy's entry, and excited the same feelings, but in opposite bosoms.

Voices of exultation now rose on his side.

"Where did he come from?"

"Why," said one of his seconds (all having just entered), "we were girting him up, about a hundred yards out yonder, when he heard Billy ask for the bully; and he fetched a leap over the Courthouse, and went out of sight; but I told them to come on, they'd find him here."

Here the lower battalion burst into a peal of laughter, mingled with a look of admiration, which seemed to denote their entire belief of what they had heard.

"Boys, widen the ring, so as to give him room to jump."

"Oh, my little flying wild-cat, hold him if you can! and, when you get him fast, hold lightning next."

"Ned, what do you think he's made of?"

"Steel springs and chicken-hawk, God bless you!"

"Gentlemen," said one of Bob's seconds, "I understand it is to be a fair fight; catch as catch can, rough and tumble: no man touch till one or the other halloos."

"That's the rule," was the reply from the other side.

"Are you ready?"

"We are ready."

"Then blaze away, my game cocks!"

At the word, Bob dashed at his antagonist at full speed; and Bill squared himself to receive him with one of his most fatal blows. Making his calculation from Bob's velocity, of the time when he would come within striking distance, he let drive with tremendous force. But Bob's onset was obviously planned to avoid this blow; for, contrary to all expectations, he stopped short just out of arm's reach, and, before Billy could recover his balance, Bob had him "all under-hold." The next second, sure enough, "found Billy's head where his feet ought to be." How it was done no one could tell; but, as if by supernatural power, both Billy's feet were thrown full half his own height in the air, and he came down with a force that seemed to shake the earth. As he struck the ground, commingled shouts, screams, and yells burst from the lower battalion, loud enough to be heard for miles. "Hurra, my little hornet!" "Save him!" "Feed him!" "Give him the Durham physic till his stomach turns!" Billy was no sooner down than Bob was on him, and lending him awful blows about the face and breast. Billy made two efforts to rise by main strength, but failed. "Lord bless you, man, don't try to get up! *Lay* still and take it! you *bleege* to have it!"

Billy now turned his face suddenly to the ground, and rose upon his hands and knees. Bob jerked up both his hands and threw him on his face. He again recovered his late position, of which Bob endeavoured to deprive him as before; but, missing one arm, he failed, and Billy rose. But he had scarcely resumed his feet before they flew up as before, and he came again to the ground. "No fight, gentlemen!" cried Bob's friends; "the man can't stand up! Bouncing feet are bad things to fight in." His fall, however, was this time comparatively light; for, having thrown his right arm round Bob's neck, he carried his head down with him. This grasp, which was obstinately maintained, prevented Bob from getting on him, and they lay head to head, seeming, for a time, to do nothing. Presently they rose, as if by mutual consent; and, as they rose, a shout burst from both battalions. "Oh, my lark!" cried the east, "has he foxed you? Do you begin to feel him! He's only beginning to fight; he ain't got warm yet."

"Look yonder!" cried the west; "didn't I tell you so! He hit the ground so hard it jarred his nose off. Now ain't he a pretty man as he stands? He shall have my sister Sal just for his pretty looks. I want to get in the breed of them sort o' men, to drive ugly out of my kinfolks."

I looked, and saw that Bob had entirely lost his left ear, and a large piece from his left cheek. His right eye was a little discoloured, and the blood flowed profusely from his wounds.

Bill presented a hideous spectacle. About a third of his nose, at the lower extremity, was bit off, and his face so swelled and bruised that it was difficult to discover in it anything of the human visage, much more the fine features which he carried into the ring.

They were up only long enough for me to make the foregoing discoveries, when down they went again, precisely as before. They no sooner touched the ground than Bill relinquished his hold upon Bob's neck. In this he seemed to all to have forfeited the only advantage which put him upon an equality with his adversary. But the movement was soon explained. Bill wanted this arm for other purposes than defence; and he had made arrangements whereby he knew that he could make it answer these purposes; for, when they rose again, he had the middle finger of Bob's left hand in his mouth. He was now secure from Bob's annoying trips; and he began to lend his adversary tremendous blows, every one of which was hailed by a shout from his friends. "Bullets!" "*Hoss*-kicking!" "Thunder!" "That'll do for his face; now feel his short ribs, Billy!"

I now considered the contest settled. I deemed it impossible for any human being to withstand for five seconds the loss of blood which issued from Bob's ear, cheek, nose, and finger, accompanied with such blows as he was receiving. Still he maintained the conflict, and gave blow for blow with considerable effect. But the blows of each became slower and weaker after the first three or four; and it became obvious that Bill wanted the room which Bob's finger occupied for breathing. He would therefore, probably, in a short time, have let it go, had not Bob anticipated his politeness by jerking away his hand, and making him a present of the finger. He now seized Bill again, and brought him to his knees, but he recovered. He again brought him to his knees, and he again recovered. A third effort, however, brought him down, and Bob on top of him. These efforts seemed to exhaust the little remaining strength of both; and they lay, Bill undermost and Bob across his breast, motionless, and panting for breath. After a short pause, Bob gathered his hand full of dirt and sand, and was in the act of grinding it in his adversary's eyes, when Bill cried "ENOUGH!" Language cannot describe the scene that followed; the shouts, oaths, frantic gestures, taunts, replies, and little fights, and therefore I shall not attempt it. The champions were borne off by their seconds and washed; when many a bleeding wound and ugly bruise was discovered on each which no eye had seen before.

Many had gathered round Bob, and were in various ways congratulating and applauding him, when a voice from the centre of the circle cried out, "Boys, hush and listen to me!" It proceeded from Squire Loggins, who had made his way to Bob's side, and had gathered his face up into one of its most flattering and intelligible expressions. All were obedient to the squire's command. "Gentlemen," continued he, with a most knowing smile, "is—Sammy—Reynold—in —this—company—of—gentlemen?"

"Yes," said Sam, "here I am."

"Sammy," said the squire, winking to the company and drawing the head of his cane to his mouth with an arch smile as he closed, "I—wish—you—to tell—cousin—Bobby—and—these—gentlemen here present—what—your—Uncle—Tommy—said—before—the—fight—began?"

"Oh! get away, Uncle Tom," said Sam, smiling (the squire winked), "you don't know nothing about *fighting*." (The squire winked again.) "All you know about it is how it'll begin, how it'll go on, how it'll end; that's all. Cousin Bob, when you going to fight again, just go to the old man, and let him tell you all about it. If he can't, don't ask nobody else nothing about it, I tell you."

The squire's foresight was complimented in many ways by the bystanders; and he retired, advising "the boys to be at peace, as fighting was a bad business."

Durham and Stallings kept their beds for several weeks, and did not meet again for two months. When they met, Billy stepped up to Bob and offered his hand, saying, "Bobby, you've *licked* me a fair fight; but you wouldn't have done it if I hadn't been in the wrong. I oughtn't to have treated your wife as I did; and I felt so through the whole fight; and it sort o' cowed me."

"Well, Billy," said Bob, "let's be friends. Once in the fight, when you had my finger in your mouth, and was pealing me in the face and breast, I was going to halloo; but I thought of Petsy, and knew the house would be too hot for me if I got whipped when fighting for her, after always whipping when I fought for myself."

"Now that's what I always love to see," said a bystander. "It's true I brought about the fight, but I wouldn't have done it if it hadn't o' been on account of *Miss* (Mrs.) Durham. But dod etarnally darn my soul, if I ever could stand by and see any woman put upon, much less *Miss* Durham. If Bobby hadn't been there, I'd o' took it up myself, be darned if I wouldn't, even if I'd o' got whipped for it. But we're all friends now." The reader need hardly be told that this was Ransy Sniffle.

Thanks to the Christian religion, to schools, colleges, and benevolent associations, such scenes of barbarism and cruelty as that which I have been just describing are now of rare occurrence, though they may still be occasionally met with in some of the new counties. Wherever they prevail, they are a disgrace to that community. The peace-officers who countenance them deserve a place in the Penitentiary.

THOMAS BANGS THORPE

The Big Bear of Arkansas

A STEAMBOAT on the Mississippi frequently, in making her regular trips, carries between places varying from one to two thousand miles apart; and as these boats advertise to land passengers and freight at "all intermediate landings," the heterogeneous character of the passengers of one of these up-country boats can scarcely be imagined by one who has never seen it with his own eyes. Starting from New Orleans in one of these boats, you will find yourself associated with men from every state in the Union, and from every portion of the globe; and a man of observation need not lack for amusement or instruction in such a crowd, if he will take the trouble to read the great book of character so favourably opened before him. Here may be seen jostling together the wealthy Southern planter, and the pedlar of tin-ware from New England—the Northern merchant, and the Southern jockey—a venerable bishop, and a desperate gambler—the land speculator, and the honest farmer—professional men of all creeds and characters—Wolvereens, Suckers, Hoosiers, Buckeyes, and Corn-crackers, beside a "plentiful sprinkling" of the half-horse and half-alligator species of men, who are peculiar to "old Mississippi," and who appear to gain a livelihood simply by going up and down the river. In the pursuit of pleasure or business, I have frequently found myself in such a crowd.

On one occasion, when in New Orleans, I had occasion to take a trip of a few miles up the Mississippi, and I hurried on board the well-known "high-pressure-and-beat-every-thing" steamboat *Invincible,* just as the last note of the last bell was sounding; and when the confusion and bustle that is natural to a boat's getting under way had subsided, I discovered that I was associated in as heterogeneous a crowd as was ever got together. As my trip was to be of a few hours' duration only, I made no endeavours to become acquainted with my fellow passengers, most of whom would be together many days. Instead of this, I took out of my pocket the "latest paper," and more critically than usual examined its contents; my fellow passengers at the same time disposed themselves in little groups. While I was thus busily employed in reading, and my companions were more busily employed in discussing such subjects as suited their humours best, we were startled most unexpectedly by a loud Indian whoop, uttered in the "social hall," that part of the cabin fitted off for a bar; then was to be heard a loud crowing, which would not have continued to have interested us—such sounds being quite common in that place of spirits—had not the hero of these windy accomplishments stuck his head into the cabin and hallooed out, "Hurra for the Big Bar of Arkansaw!" and then might be heard a confused hum of voices, unintelligible, save in such broken sentences as "horse," "screamer," "lightning is slow," &c. As might have been expected, this continued interruption attracted the attention of every one in the cabin; all conversation dropped, and in the midst of this surprise the "Big Bar" walked into the cabin, took a chair, put his feet on the stove, and looking back over his shoulder, passed the general and familiar salute of "Strangers, how are you?" He then expressed himself as much at home as if he had been at "the Forks of Cypress," and "perhaps a little more so." Some of the company at this familiarity looked a little angry, and some astonished; but in a moment every face was wreathed in a smile. There was something about the intruder that won the heart on sight. He appeared to be a man enjoying perfect health and contentment: his eyes were as sparkling as diamonds, and good-natured to simplicity. Then his perfect confidence in himself was irresistibly droll. "Perhaps," said he, "gentlemen," running on without a person speaking, "perhaps you have been to New Orleans often; I never made *the first visit before,* and I don't intend to make another in a crow's life. I am thrown away in that ar place, and useless, that ar a fact. Some of the gentlemen thar called me *green*—well, perhaps I am, said I, *but I arn't so at home;* and if I ain't off my trail much, the heads of them perlite chaps themselves wern't much the hardest; for according to my notion, they were real *know-nothings,* green as a pumpkin-vine—couldn't, in farming, I'll bet, raise a crop of turnips: and as for shooting, they'd miss a barn if the door was swinging, and that, too, with the best rifle in the country. And then they talked to me 'bout hunting, and laughed at my calling the principal game in Arkansaw poker, and high-low-jack. 'Perhaps,' said I, 'you prefer chickens and rolette'; at this they laughed harder than ever, and asked me if I lived in the woods, and didn't know what *game* was? At this I rather think I laughed. 'Yes,' I roared, and says, 'Strangers, if you'd asked me *how we got our meat* in Arkansaw, I'd a told you at once, and given you a list of varmints that would make a caravan, beginning with the bar, and ending off with the cat; that's *meat* though, not game.' Game, indeed, that's what city folks call it; and with them it means chippen-birds and shite-pokes; maybe such trash live in my diggens, but I arn't noticed them yet: a bird any way is too trifling. I never did shoot at but one, and I'd never forgiven myself for that, had it weighed less than forty pounds. I wouldn't draw a rifle on any thing less than that; and when I meet with another wild turkey of the same weight I will drap him."

"A wild turkey weighing forty pounds!" exclaimed twenty voices in the cabin at once.

"Yes, strangers, and wasn't it a whopper? You see, the thing was so fat that it couldn't fly far; and when he fell out of the tree, after I shot him, on striking the ground he bust open behind, and the way the pound gobs of tallow rolled out of the opening was perfectly beautiful."

"Where did all that happen?" asked a cynical-looking Hoosier.

"Happen! happened in Arkansaw: where else could it have happened, but in the creation state, the finishing-up country—a state where the *sile* runs down to the centre of the 'arth, and government gives you a title to every inch of it? Then its airs—just breathe them, and they will make you snort like a horse. It's a state without a fault, it is."

"Excepting mosquitoes," cried the Hoosier.

"Well, stranger, except them; for it ar a fact that they are rather *enormous*, and do push themselves in somewhat troublesome. But, stranger, they never stick twice in the same place; and give them a fair chance for a few months, and you will get as much above noticing them as an alligator. They can't hurt my feelings, for they lay under the skin; and I never knew but one case of injury resulting from them, and that was to a Yankee: and they take worse to foreigners, any how, than they do to natives. But the way they used that fellow up! first they punched him until he swelled up and busted; then he su-per-a-ted, as the doctor called it, until he was as raw as beef; then he took the ager, owing to the warm weather, and finally he took a steamboat and left the country. He was the only man that ever took mosquitoes to heart that I know of. But mosquitoes is natur, and I never find fault with her. If they ar large, Arkansaw is large, her varmints ar large, her trees ar large, her rivers ar large, and a small mosquito would be of no more use in Arkansaw than preaching in a cane-brake."

This knock-down argument in favour of big mosquitoes used the Hoosier up, and the logician started on a new track, to explain how numerous bear were in his "diggins," where he represented them to be "about as plenty as blackberries, and a little plentifuler."

Upon the utterance of this assertion, a timid little man near me inquired if the bear in Arkansaw ever attacked the settlers in numbers.

"No," said our hero, warming with the subject, "no, stranger, for you see it ain't the natur of bar to go in droves; but the way they squander about in pairs and single ones is edifying. And then the way I hunt them the old black rascals know the crack of my gun as well as they know a pig's squealing. They grow thin in our parts, it frightens them so, and they do take the noise dreadfully, poor things. That gun of mine is perfect *epidemic among bar;* if not watched closely, it will go off as quick on a warm scent as my dog Bowie-knife will: and then that dog—whew! why the fellow thinks that the world is full of bar, he finds them so easy. It's lucky he don't talk as well as think; for with his natural modesty, if he should suddenly learn how much he is acknowledged to be ahead of all other dogs in the universe, he would be astonished to death in two minutes. Strangers, the dog knows a bar's way as well as a horse-jockey knows a woman's: he always barks at the right time, bites at the exact place, and whips without getting a scratch. I never could tell whether he was made expressly to hunt bar, or whether bar was made expressly for him to hunt: any way, I believe they were ordained to go together as naturally as Squire Jones says a man and woman is, when he moralizes in marrying a couple. In fact, Jones once said, said he, 'Marriage according to law is a civil contract of divine origin; it's common to all countries as well as Arkansaw, and people take to it as naturally as Jim Doggett's Bowie-knife takes to bar.' "

"What season of the year do your hunts take place?" inquired a gentlemanly foreigner, who, from some peculiarities of his baggage, I suspected to be an Englishman, on some hunting expedition, probably at the foot of the Rocky Mountains.

"The season for bar hunting, stranger," said the man of Arkansaw, "is generally all the year round, and the hunts take place about as regular. I read in history that varmints have their fat season, and their lean season. That is not the case in Arkansaw, feeding as they do upon the *spontenacious* productions of the sile, they have one continued fat season the year round: though in winter things in this way is rather more greasy than in summer, I must admit. For that reason bar with us run in warm weather, but in winter, they only waddle. Fat, fat! it's an enemy to speed; it tames everything that has plenty of it. I have seen wild turkeys, from its influence, as gentle as chickens. Run a bar in this fat condition, and the way it improves the critter for eating is amazing; it sort of mixes the ile up with the meat, until you can't tell t'other from which. I've done this often. I recollect one perty morning in particular, of putting an old fellow on the stretch, and considering the weight he carried, he run well. But the dogs soon tired him down, and when I came up with him wasn't he in a beautiful sweat—I might say fever; and then to see his tongue sticking out of his mouth a foot, and his sides sinking and opening like a bellows, and his cheeks so fat he couldn't look cross. In this fix I blazed at him, and pitch me naked into a briar patch if the steam didn't come out of the bullet-hole ten foot in a straight line. The fellow, I reckon, was made on the high-pressure system, and the lead sort of bust his biler."

"That column of steam was rather curious, or else the bear must have been *warm*," observed the foreigner, with a laugh.

"Stranger, as you observe, that bar was WARM, and the blowing off of the steam show'd it, and also how hard the varmint had been run. I have no doubt if he had kept on two miles farther his insides would have been stewed; and I expect to meet with a varmint yet of extra bottom, who will run himself into a skinfull of bar's grease: it is possible, much onlikelier things have happened."

"Whereabouts are these bears so abundant?" inquired the foreigner, with increasing interest.

"Why, stranger, they inhabit the neighbourhood of my settlement, one of the prettiest places on old Mississippi—a perfect location, and no mistake; a place that had some defects until the river made the 'cut-off' at 'Shirt-tail bend,' and that remedied the evil, as it brought my cabin on the edge of the river—a great advantage in wet weather, I assure you, as you can now roll a barrel of whiskey into my yard in high water from a boat, as easy as falling off a log. It's a great improvement, as toting it by land in a jug, as I used to do, *evaporated* it too fast, and it became expensive. Just stop with me, stranger, a month or two, or a year if you like, and you will appreciate my place. I can give you plenty to eat; for beside hog and hominy, you can have bar-ham, and bar-sausages, and a mattrass of bar-skins to sleep on, and a wildcat-skin, pulled off hull, stuffed with corn-shucks, for a pillow. That bed would put you to sleep if you had the rheumatics in every joint in your body. I call that ar bed a *quietus*. Then look at my land—the government ain' got another such a piece to dispose of. Such timber, and such bottom land, why you can't preserve any thing natural you plant in it unless you pick it young, things thar will grow out of shape so quick. I once planted in those diggins a few potatoes and beets: they took a fine start, and after that an ox team couldn't have kept them from growing. About that time I went off to old Kentuck on bisiness, and did not hear from them things in three months, when I accidentally stumbled on a fellow who had stopped at my place, with an idea of buying me out. 'How did you like things?' said I. 'Pretty well,' said he; 'the cabin is convenient, and the timber land is good; but that bottom land ain't worth the first red cent.' 'Why?' said I. ' 'Cause,' said he.

' 'Cause what?' said I. ' 'Cause it's full of cedar stumps and Indian mounds,' said he, *and it can't be cleared.* 'Lord,' said I, 'them ar "cedar stumps" is beets, and them ar "Indian mounds" ar tater hills.' As I expected, the crop was overgown and useless: the sile is too rich, *and planting in Arkansaw is dangerous.* I had a good-sized sow killed in that same bottom land. The old thief stole an ear of corn, and took it down where she slept at night to eat. Well, she left a grain or two on the ground, and lay down on them: before morning the corn shot up, and the percussion killed her dead. I don't plant any more: natur intended Arkansaw for a hunting ground, and I go according to natur."

The questioner who thus elicited the description of our hero's settlement, seemed to be perfectly satisfied, and said no more; but the "Big Bar of Arkansaw" rambled on from one thing to another with a volubility perfectly astonishing, occasionally disputing with those around him, particularly with a "live Sucker" from Illinois, who had the daring to say that our Arkansaw friend's stories "smelt rather tall."

In this manner the evening was spent; but conscious that my own association with so singular a personage would probably end before morning, I asked him if he would not give me a description of some particular bear hunt; adding that I took great interest in such things, though I was no sportsman. The desire seemed to please him, and he squared himself round towards me, saying, that he could give me an idea of a bar hunt that was never beat in this world, or in any other. His manner was so singular, that half of his story consisted in his excellent way of telling it, the great peculiarity of which was, the happy manner he had of emphasizing the prominent parts of his conversation. As near as I can recollect, I have italicized them, and given the story in his own words.

"Stranger," said he, "in bar hunts *I am numerous,* and which particular one, as you say, I shall tell, puzzles me. There was the old she devil I shot at the Hurricane last fall—then there was the old hog thief I popped over at the Bloody Crossing, and then—Yes, I have it! I will give you an idea of a hunt, in which the greatest bar was killed that ever lived, *none excepted;* about an old fellow that I hunted, more or less, for two or three years; and if that ain't a particular bar hunt, I ain't got one to tell. But in the first place, stranger, let me say, I am pleased with you, because you ain't ashamed to gain information by asking, and listening, and that's what I say to Countess's pups every day when I'm home; and I have got great hopes of them ar pups, because they are continually *nosing* about; and though they stick it sometimes in the wrong place, they gain experience any how, and may learn something useful to boot.

Well, as I was saying about this big bar, you see when I and some more first settled in our region, we were drivin to hunting naturally; we soon liked it, and after that we found it an easy matter to make the thing our business. One old chap who had pioneered 'afore us, gave us to understand that we had settled in the right place. He dwelt upon its merits until it was affecting, and showed us, to prove his assertions, more marks on the sassafras trees than I ever saw on a tavern door 'lection time. 'Who keeps that ar reckoning?' said I. 'The bar,' said he. 'What for?' said I. 'Can't tell,' said he; 'but so it is: the bar bite the bark and wood too, at the highest point from the ground they can reach, and you can tell, by the marks,' said he, 'the length of the bar to an inch.' 'Enough,' said I; 'I've learned something here a'ready, and I'll put it in practice.'

"Well, stranger, just one month from that time I killed a bar, and told its exact length before I measured it, by those very marks; and when I did that, I swelled up considerable—I've been a prouder man ever since. So I went on, larning something every day, until I was reckoned a buster, and allowed to be decidedly the best bar hunter in my district; and that is a reputation as much harder to earn than to be reckoned first man in Congress, as an iron ramrod is harder than a toadstool. Did the varmints grow over-cunning by being fooled with by green-horn hunters, and by this means get troublesome, they send for me as a matter of course; and thus I do my own hunting, and most of my neighbours'. I walk into the varmints though, and it has become about as much the same to me as drinking. It is told in two sentences—a bar is started, and he is killed. The thing is somewhat monotonous now—I know just how much they will run, where they will tire, how much they will growl, and what a thundering time I will have in getting them home. I could give you this history of the chase with all particulars at the commencement, I know the signs so well—*Stranger, I'm certain.* Once I met with a match though, and I will tell you about it; for a common hunt would not be worth relating.

"On a fine fall day, long time ago, I was trailing about for bar, and what should I see but fresh marks on the sassafras trees, about eight inches above any in the forests that I knew of. Says I, 'them marks is a hoax, or it indicates the d——t bar that was ever grown.' In fact, stranger, I couldn't believe it was real, and I went on. Again I saw the same marks, at the same height, and *I knew the thing lived.* That conviction came home to my soul like an earthquake. Says I, 'here is something a-purpose for me: that bar is mine, or I give up the hunting business.' The very next morning what should I see but a number of buzzards hovering over my cornfield. 'The rascal has been there,' said I, 'for that sign is certain:' and, sure

enough, on examining, I found the bones of what had been as beautiful a hog the day before, as was ever raised by a Buckeye. Then I
tracked the critter out of the field to the woods, and all the marks
he left behind, showed me that he was *the bar*.

"Well, stranger, the first fair chase I ever had with that big critter,
I saw him no less than three distinct times at a distance: the dogs
run him over eighteen miles and broke down, my horse gave out,
and I was as nearly used up as a man can be, made on *my* principle,
which is patent. Before this adventure, such things were unknown
to me as possible; but, strange as it was, that bar got me used to it
before I was done with him; for he got so at last, that he would
leave me on a long chase *quite easy*. How he did it, I never could
understand. That a bar runs at all, is puzzling; but how this one
could tire down and bust up a pack of hounds and a horse, that
were used to overhauling everything they started after in no time,
was past my understanding. Well, stranger, that bar finally got so
sassy, that he used to help himself to a hog off my premises whenever he wanted one; the buzzards followed after what he left, and so
between *bar and buzzard,* I rather think I was *out of pork*.

"Well, missing that bar so often took hold of my vitals, and I
wasted away. The thing had been carried too far, and it reduced me
in flesh faster than an ager. I would see that bar in every thing I
did: *he hunted me,* and that, too, like a devil, which I began to
think he was. While in this fix, I made preparations to give him a
last brush, and be done with it. Having completed every thing to
my satisfaction, I started at sunrise, and to my great joy, I discovered from the way the dogs run, that they were near him; finding
his trail was nothing, for that had become as plain to the pack as a
turnpike road. On we went, and coming to an open country, what
should I see but the bar very leisurely ascending a hill, and the dogs
close at his heels, either a match for him in speed, or else he did not
care to get out of their way—I don't know which. But wasn't he a
beauty, though? I loved him like a brother.

"On he went, until he came to a tree, the limbs of which formed a
crotch about six feet from the ground. Into this crotch he got and
seated himself, the dogs yelling all around it; and there he sat
eyeing them as quiet as a pond in low water. A green-horn friend of
mine, in company, reached shooting distance before me, and blazed
away, hitting the critter in the centre of his forehead. The bar
shook his head as the ball struck it, and then walked down from
that tree as gently as a lady would from a carriage. 'Twas a beautiful sight to see him do that—he was in such a rage that he seemed to
be as little afraid of the dogs as if they had been sucking pigs; and
the dogs warn't slow in making a ring around him at a respectful

distance, I tell you; even Bowie-knife, himself, stood off. Then the way his eyes flashed—why the fire of them would have singed a cat's hair; in fact that bar was in a *wrath all over*. Only one pup came near him, and he was brushed out so totally with the bar's left paw, that he entirely disappeared; and that made the old dogs more cautious still. In the mean time, I came up, and taking deliberate aim as a man should do, at his side, just back of his foreleg, *if my gun did not snap,* call me a coward, and I won't take it personal. Yes, stranger, *it snapped,* and I could not find a cap about my person. While in this predicament, I turned round to my fool friend—says I, 'Bill,' says I, 'you're an ass—you're a fool—you might as well have tried to kill that bar by barking the tree under his belly, as to have done it by hitting him in the head. Your shot has made a tiger of him, and blast me, if a dog gets killed or wounded when they come to blows, I will stick my knife into your liver, I will—' my wrath was up. I had lost my caps, my gun had snapped, the fellow with me had fired at the bar's head, and I expected every moment to see him close in with the dogs, and kill a dozen of them at least. In this thing I was mistaken, for the bar leaped over the ring formed by the dogs, and giving a fierce growl, was off—the pack, of course, in full cry after him. The run this time was short, for coming to the edge of a lake the varmint jumped in, and swam to a little island in the lake, which it reached just a moment before the dogs. 'I'll have him now,' said I, for I had found my caps in the *lining of my coat*—so, rolling a log into the lake, I paddled myself across to the island, just as the dogs had cornered the bar in a thicket. I rushed up and fired —at the same time the critter leaped over the dogs and came within three feet of me, running like mad; he jumped into the lake, and tried to mount the log I had just deserted, but every time he got half his body on it, it would roll over and send him under; the dogs, too, got around him, and pulled him about, and finally Bowie-knife clenched with him, and they sunk into the lake together. Stranger, about this time, I was excited, and I stripped off my coat, drew my knife, and intended to have taken a part with Bowie-knife myself, when the bar rose to the surface. But the varmint staid under—Bowie-knife came up alone, more dead than alive, and with the pack came ashore. 'Thank God', said I, 'the old villain has got his deserts at last.' Determined to have the body, I cut a grape-vine for a rope, and dove down where I could see the bar in the water, fastened my queer rope to his leg, and fished him, with great difficulty, ashore. Stranger, may I be chawed to death by young alligators, if the thing I looked at wasn't a *she bar, and not the old critter after all*. The way matters got mixed on that island was onaccountably curious, and thinking of it made me more than ever convinced that I was hunting the devil himself. I went home that night and took to my bed—the thing was killing me. The entire team of Arkansaw in bar-hunting, acknowledged himself used up, and the fact sunk into my feelings like a snagged boat will in the Mississippi. I grew as cross as a bar with two cubs and a sore tail. The thing got out 'mong my neighbours, and I was asked how come on that individu-al that never lost a bar when once started? and if that same individ-u-al didn't wear telescopes when he turned a she bar, of ordinary size, into an old he one, a little larger than a horse? 'Perhaps,' said I, 'friends'—getting wrathy—'perhaps you want to call somebody a liar,' 'Oh, no,' said they, 'we only heard such things as being *rather common* of late, but we don't believe one word of it; oh, no,'—and then they would ride off and laugh like so many hyenas over a dead nig-ger. It was too much, and I determined to catch that bar, go to Texas, or die,—and I made my preparations accordin'. I had the pack shut up and rested. I took my rifle to pieces and iled it. I put caps in every pocket about my person, *for fear of the lining.* I then told my neighbours, that on Monday morning—naming the day—I would start THAT BAR, and bring him home with me, or they might divide my settlement among them, the owner having disap-peared. Well, stranger, on the morning previous to the great day of my hunting expedition, I went into the woods near my house, tak-ing my gun and Bowie-knife along, just *from habit,* and there sit-ting down also from habit, what should I see, getting over my fence, but *the bar!* Yes, the old varmint was within a hundred yards of me, and the way he walked *over that fence*—stranger, he loomed up like a *black mist,* he seemed so large, and he walked right towards me. I raised myself, took deliberate aim, and fired. Instantly the varmint wheeled, gave a yell, and *walked through the fence* like a falling tree would through a cobweb. I started after, but was tripped up by my inexpressibles, which either from habit, or the excitement of the moment, were about my heels, and before I had really gathered my-self up, I heard the old varmint groaning in a thicket near by, like a thousand sinners, and by the time I reached him he was a corpse. Stranger, it took five niggers and myself to put that carcase on a mule's back, and old long-ears waddled under the load, as if he was foundered in every leg of his body, and with a common whopper of a bar, he would have trotted off, and enjoyed himself. 'Twould as-tonish you to know how big he was: I made a *bed-spread of his skin,* and the way it used to cover my bar mattress, and leave several feet on each side to tuck up, would have delighted you. It was in fact a creation bar, and if it had lived in Samson's time, and had met him, in a fair fight, it would have licked him in the twinkling of a dice-box. But, strangers, I never like the way I hunted, and *missed him.*

There is something curious about it, I could never understand,—and I never was satisfied at his giving in so easy at last. Prehaps, he had heard of my preparations to hunt him the next day, so he jist come in, like Capt. Scott's coon, to save his wind to grunt with in dying; but that ain't likely. My private opinion is, that that bar was an *unhuntable bar, and died when his time come*."

When the story was ended, our hero sat some minutes with his auditors in a grave silence; I saw there was a mystery to him connected with the bear whose death he had just related, that had evidently made a strong impression on his mind. It was also evident that there was some superstitious awe connected with the affair,—a feeling common with all "children of the wood," when they meet with any thing out of their everyday experience. He was the first one, however, to break the silence, and jumping up, he asked all present to "liquor" before going to bed,—a thing which he did, with a number of companions, evidently to his heart's content.

Long before day, I was put ashore at my place of destination, and I can only follow with the reader, in imagination, our Arkansas friend, in his adventures at the "Forks of Cypress" on the Mississippi.

MARK TWAIN

Life on the Mississippi

WHEN I WAS a boy, there was but one permanent ambition among my comrades in our village on the west bank of the Mississippi River. That was, to be a steamboatman. We had transient ambitions of other sorts, but they were only transient. When a circus came and went, it left us all burning to become clowns; the first negro minstrel show that ever came to our section left us all suffering to try that kind of life; now and then we had a hope that, if we lived and were good, God would permit us to be pirates. These ambitions faded out, each in its turn; but the ambition to be a steamboatman always remained.

Once a day a cheap, gaudy packet arrived upward from St. Louis, and another downward from Keokuk. Before these events, the day was glorious with expectancy; after them, the day was a dead and empty thing. Not only the boys, but the whole village, felt this. After all these years I can picture that old time to myself now, just as it was then: the white town drowsing in the sunshine of a summer's morning; the streets empty, or pretty nearly so; one or two clerks sitting in front of the Water Street stores, with their splint-bottomed chairs tilted back against the walls, chins on breasts, hats slouched over their faces, asleep—with shingle-shavings enough around to show what broke them down; a sow and a litter of pigs loafing along the sidewalk, doing a good business in watermelon rinds and seeds; two or three lonely little freight piles scattered about the "levee"; a pile of "skids" on the slope of the stone-paved wharf, and the fragrant town drunkard asleep in the shadow of them; two or three wood flats at the head of the wharf, but nobody to listen to the peaceful lapping of the wavelets against them; the great Mississippi, the majestic, the magnificent Mississippi, rolling its mile-wide tide along, shining in the sun; the dense forest away on the other side; the "point" above the town, and the "point" below, bounding the river-glimpse and turning it into a sort of sea, and withal a very still and brilliant and lonely one. Presently a film

of dark smoke appears above one of those remote "points"; instantly
a negro drayman, famous for his quick eye and prodigious voice,
lifts up the cry, "S-t-e-a-m-b-o-a-t a-comin'!" and the scene changes!
The town drunkard stirs, the clerks wake up, a furious clatter of
drays follows, every house and store pours out a human contribu-
tion, and all in a twinkling the dead town is alive and moving.
Drays, carts, men, boys, all go hurrying from many quarters to a common center, the wharf. Assembled there, the people fasten their eyes
upon the coming boat as upon a wonder they are seeing for the first
time. And the boat *is* rather a handsome sight, too. She is long and
sharp and trim and pretty; she has two tall, fancy-topped chimneys,
with a gilded device of some kind swung between them; a fanciful
pilot-house, all glass and "gingerbread," perched on top of the
"texas" deck behind them; the paddle-boxes are gorgeous with a picture or with gilded rays above the boat's name; the boiler-deck, the
hurricane-deck, and the texas deck are fenced and ornamented with
clean white railings; there is a flag gallantly flying from the jack-
staff; the furnace doors are open and the fires glaring bravely; the
upper decks are black with passengers; the captain stands by the big
bell, calm, imposing, the envy of all; great volumes of the blackest
smoke are rolling and tumbling out of the chimneys—a husbanded
grandeur created with a bit of pitch-pine just before arriving at a
town; the crew are grouped on the forecastle; the broad stage is run
far out over the port bow, and an envied deck-hand stands pictur-
esquely on the end of it with a coil of rope in his hand; the pent
steam is screaming through the gauge-cocks; the captain lifts his
hand, a bell rings, the wheels stop; then they turn back, churning
the water to foam, and the steamer is at rest. Then such a scramble
as there is to get aboard, and to get ashore, and to take in freight
and to discharge freight, all at one and the same time; and such a
yelling and cursing as the mates facilitate it all with! Ten minutes
later the steamer is under way again, with no flag on the jack-staff
and no black smoke issuing from the chimneys. After ten more minutes the town is dead again, and the town drunkard asleep by the
skids once more.

My father was a justice of the peace, and I supposed he possessed
the power of life and death over all men, and could hang anybody
that offended him. This was distinction enough for me as a general
thing; but the desire to be a steamboatman kept intruding, nevertheless. I first wanted to be a cabin-boy, so that I could come out
with a white apron on and shake a table-cloth over the side, where
all my old comrades could see me; later I thought I would rather be
the deck-hand who stood on the end of the stage-plank with the coil
of rope in his hand, because he was particularly conspicuous. But

these were only day-dreams—they were too heavenly to be contemplated as real possibilities. By and by one of our boys went away. He was not heard of for a long time. At last he turned up as apprentice engineer or "striker" on a steamboat. This thing shook the bottom out of all my Sunday-school teachings. That boy had been notoriously worldly, and I just the reverse; yet he was exalted to this eminence, and I left in obscurity and misery. There was nothing generous about this fellow in his greatness. He would always manage to have a rusty bolt to scrub while his boat tarried at our town, and he would sit on the inside guard and scrub it, where we all could see him and envy him and loathe him. And whenever his boat was laid up he would come home and swell around the town in his blackest and greasiest clothes, so that nobody could help remembering that he was a steamboatman; and he used all sorts of steamboat technicalities in his talk, as if he were so used to them that he forgot common people could not understand them. He would speak of the "labboard" side of a horse in an easy, natural way that would make one wish he was dead. And he was always talking about "St. Looy" like an old citizen; he would refer casually to occasions when he was "coming down Fourth Street," or when he was "passing by the Planter's House," or when there was a fire and he took a turn on the brakes of "the old Big Missouri"; and then he would go on and lie about how many towns the size of ours were burned down there that day. Two or three of the boys had long been persons of consideration among us because they had been to St. Louis once and had a vague general knowledge of its wonders, but the day of their glory was over now. They lapsed into a humble silence, and learned to disappear when the ruthless "cub"-engineer approached. This fellow had money, too, and hair-oil. Also an ignorant silver watch and a showy brass watch-chain. He wore a leather belt and used no suspenders. If ever a youth was cordially admired and hated by his comrades, this one was. No girl could withstand his charms. He "cut out" every boy in the village. When his boat blew up at last, it diffused a tranquil contentment among us such as we had not known for months. But when he came home the next week, alive, renowned, and appeared in church all battered up and bandaged, a shining hero, stared at and wondered over by everybody, it seemed to us that the partiality of Providence for an undeserving reptile had reached a point where it was open to criticism.

This creature's career could produce but one result, and it speedily followed. Boy after boy managed to get on the river. The minister's son became an engineer. The doctor's and the postmaster's sons became "mud clerks"; the wholesale liquor dealer's son became a barkeeper on a boat; four sons of the chief merchant, and two sons of the county judge, became pilots. Pilot was the grandest position of all. The pilot, even in those days of trivial wages, had a princely salary—from a hundred and fifty to two hundred and fifty dollars a month, and no board to pay. Two months of his wages would pay a preacher's salary for a year. Now some of us were left disconsolate. We could not get on the river—at least our parents would not let us.

So, by and by, I ran away. I said I would never come home again till I was a pilot and could come in glory. But somehow I could not manage it. I went meekly aboard a few of the boats that lay packed together like sardines at the long St. Louis wharf, and humbly inquired for the pilots, but got only a cold shoulder and short words from mates and clerks. I had to make the best of this sort of treatment for the time being, but I had comforting day-dreams of a future when I should be a great and honored pilot, with plenty of money, and could kill some of these mates and clerks and pay for them. . . .

Months afterward the hope within me struggled to a reluctant death, and I found myself without an ambition. But I was ashamed to go home. I was in Cincinnati, and I set to work to map out a new career. I had been reading about the recent exploration of the river Amazon by an expedition sent out by our government. It was said that the expedition, owing to difficulties, had not thoroughly explored a part of the country lying about the headwaters, some four thousand miles from the mouth of the river. It was only about fifteen hundred miles from Cincinnati to New Orleans, where I could doubtless get a ship. I had thirty dollars left; I would go and complete the exploration of the Amazon. This was all the thought I gave to the subject. I never was great in matters of detail. I packed my valise, and took passage on an ancient tub called the *Paul Jones,* for New Orleans. For the sum of sixteen dollars I had the scarred and tarnished splendors of "her" main saloon principally to myself, for she was not a creature to attract the eye of wiser travelers.

When we presently got under way and went poking down the broad Ohio, I became a new being, and the subject of my own admiration. I was a traveler! A word never had tasted so good in my mouth before. I had an exultant sense of being bound for mysterious lands and distant climes which I never have felt in so uplifting a degree since. I was in such a glorified condition that all ignoble feelings departed out of me, and I was able to look down and pity the untraveled with a compassion that had hardly a trace of contempt in it. Still, when we stopped at villages and wood-yards, I could not help lolling carelessly upon the railings of the boiler-deck to enjoy the envy of the country boys on the bank. If they did not seem to discover me, I presently sneezed to attract their attention, or moved to a position where they could not help seeing me. And as soon as I knew they saw me I gaped and stretched, and gave other signs of being mightily bored with traveling.

I kept my hat off all the time, and stayed where the wind and the sun could strike me, because I wanted to get the bronzed and weather-beaten look of an old traveler. Before the second day was half gone I experienced a joy which filled me with the purest gratitude; for I saw that the skin had begun to blister and peel off my face and neck. I wished that the boys and girls at home could see me now.

We reached Louisville in time—at least the neighborhood of it. We stuck hard and fast on the rocks in the middle of the river, and lay there four days. I was now beginning to feel a strong sense of being a part of the boat's family, a sort of infant son to the captain and younger brother to the officers. There is no estimating the pride I took in this grandeur, or the affection that began to swell and grow in me for those people. I could not know how the lordly steamboatman scorns that sort of presumption in a mere landsman. I particularly longed to acquire the least trifle of notice from the big stormy mate, and I was on the alert for an opportunity to do him a service to that end. It came at last. The riotous pow-wow of setting a spar was going on down on the forecastle, and I went down there and stood around in the way—or mostly skipping out of it—till the mate suddenly roared a general order for somebody to bring him a capstan bar. I sprang to his side and said: "Tell me where it is—I'll fetch it!"

If a rag-picker had offered to do a diplomatic service for the Emperor of Russia, the monarch could not have been more astounded than the mate was. He even stopped swearing. He stood and stared down at me. It took him ten seconds to scrape his disjointed remains together again. Then he said impressively: "Well, if this don't beat h——l!" and turned to his work with the air of a man who had been confronted with a problem too abstruse for solution.

I crept away, and courted solitude for the rest of the day. I did not go to dinner; I stayed away from supper until everybody else had finished. I did not feel so much like a member of the boat's family now as before. However, my spirits returned, in instalments, as we pursued our way down the river. I was sorry I hated the mate so, because it was not in (young) human nature not to admire him. He was huge and muscular, his face was bearded and whiskered all over; he had a red woman and a blue woman tattooed on his right arm—one on each side of a blue anchor with a red rope to it; and in the matter of profanity he was sublime. When he was getting out cargo at a landing, I was always where I could see and hear. He felt all the majesty of his great position, and made the world feel it, too. When he gave even the simplest order, he discharged it like a blast of lightning, and sent a long, reverberating peal of profanity thundering after it. I could not help contrasting the way in which the average landsman would give an order with the mate's way of doing it. If the landsman should wish the gangplank moved a foot farther forward, he would probably say: "James, or William, one of you push that plank forward, please"; but put the mate in his place, and he would roar out: "Here, now, start that gang-plank for'ard! Livley, now! *What*'re you about! Snatch it! *snatch* it! There! there! Aft again! aft again! Don't you hear me? Dash it to dash! are you going to *sleep* over it! *'Vast* heaving. *'Vast* heaving, I tell you! Going to heave it clear astern? WHERE 're you going with that barrel! *for'ard* with it 'fore I make you swallow it, you dash-dash-dash-*dashed* split between a tired mud-turtle and a crippled hearse-horse!"

I wished I could talk like that.

When the soreness of my adventure with the mate had somewhat worn off, I began timidly to make up to the humblest official connected with the boat—the night watchman. He snubbed my advances at first, but I presently ventured to offer him a new chalk pipe, and that softened him. So he allowed me to sit with him by the big bell on the hurricane-deck, and in time he melted into conversation. He could not well have helped it, I hung with such homage on his words and so plainly showed that I felt honored by his notice. He told me the names of dim capes and shadowy islands as we glided by them in the solemnity of the night, under the winking stars, and by and by got to talking about himself. He seemed oversentimental for a man whose salary was six dollars a week—or rather he might have seemed so to an older person than I. But I drank in his words hungrily, and with a faith that might have moved mountains if it had been applied judiciously. What was it to me that he was soiled and seedy and fragrant with gin? What was it to me that his grammar was bad, his construction worse, and his profanity so void of art that it was an element of weakness rather than strength in his conversation? He was a wronged man, a man who had seen trouble, and that was enough for me. As he mellowed into his plaintive history his tears dripped upon the lantern in his lap, and I cried, too, from sympathy. He said he was the son of an English nobleman—either an earl or an alderman, he could not remember which, but believed was both; his father, the nobleman, loved him, but his mother hated him from the cradle; and so while he was still a little boy he was sent to "one of them old, ancient colleges"—he couldn't remember which; and by and by his father died and his mother seized the property and "shook" him as he phrased it. After his mother shook him, members of the nobility with whom he was acquainted used their influence to get him the position of "loblolly-boy in a ship"; and from that point my watchman threw off all trammels of date and locality and branched out into a narrative that bristled all along with incredible adventures; a narrative that was so reeking with bloodshed, and so crammed with hair-breadth escapes and the most engaging and unconscious personal villainies, that I sat speechless, enjoying, shuddering, wondering, worshiping.

It was a sore blight to find out afterward that he was a low, vulgar, ignorant, sentimental, half-witted humbug, an untraveled native of the wilds of Illinois, who had absorbed wildcat literature and appropriated its marvels, until in time he had woven odds and ends of the mess into this yarn, and then gone on telling it to fledglings like me, until he had come to believe it himself.

What with lying on the rocks four days at Louisville, and some other delays, the poor old *Paul Jones* fooled away about two weeks in making the voyage from Cincinnati to New Orleans. This gave me a chance to get acquainted with one of the pilots, and he taught me how to steer the boat, and thus made the fascination of river life more potent than ever for me.

It also gave me a chance to get acquainted with a youth who had taken deck passage—more's the pity; for he easily borrowed six dollars of me on a promise to return to the boat and pay it back to me the day after we should arrive. But he probably died or forgot, for he never came. It was doubtless the former, since he had said his parents were wealthy, and he only traveled deck passage because it was cooler.

I soon discovered two things. One was that a vessel would not be likely to sail for the mouth of the Amazon under ten or twelve years; and the other was that the nine or ten dollars still left in my pocket would not suffice for so impossible an exploration as I had planned, even if I could afford to wait for a ship. Therefore it followed that I must contrive a new career. The *Paul Jones* was now bound for St. Louis. I planned a siege against my pilot, and at the end of three hard days he surrendered. He agreed to teach me the Mississippi River from New Orleans to St. Louis for five hundred dollars, payable out of the first wages I should receive after graduating. I entered upon the small enterprise of "learning" twelve or thirteen hundred miles of the great Mississippi River with the easy confidence of my time of life. If I had really known what I was about to require of my faculties, I should not have had the courage to begin. I supposed that all a pilot had to do was to keep his boat in the river, and I did not consider that that could be much of a trick, since it was so wide.

The boat backed out from New Orleans at four in the afternoon, and it was "our watch" until eight. Mr. Bixby, my chief, "straightened her up," plowed her along past the sterns of the other boats that lay at the Levee, and then said, "Here, take her; shave those steamships as close as you'd peel an apple." I took the wheel, and my heartbeat fluttered up into the hundreds; for it seemed to me that we were about to scrape the side off every ship in the line, we were so close. I held my breath and began to claw the boat away from the danger; and I had my own opinion of the pilot who had known no better than to get us into such peril, but I was too wise to express it. In half a minute I had a wide margin of safety intervening between the *Paul Jones* and the ships; and within ten seconds more I was set aside in disgrace, and Mr. Bixby was going into danger again and flaying me alive with abuse of my cowardice. I was stung, but I was obliged to admire the easy confidence with which my chief loafed from side to side of his wheel, and trimmed the ships so closely that disaster seemed ceaselessly imminent. When he had cooled a little he told me that the easy water was close ashore and the current outside, and therefore we must hug the bank, upstream, to get the benefit of the former, and stay well out, downstream, to take advantage of the latter. In my own mind I resolved to be a down-stream pilot and leave the up-streaming to people dead to prudence.

Now and then Mr. Bixby called my attention to certain things. Said he, "This is Six-Mile Point." I assented. It was pleasant enough information, but I could not see the bearing of it. I was not conscious that it was a matter of any interest to me. Another time he said, "This is Nine-Mile Point." Later he said, "This is Twelve-Mile Point." They were all about level with the water's edge; they all looked about alike to me; they were monotonously unpicturesque. I hoped Mr. Bixby would change the subject. But no; he would crowd up around a point, hugging the shore with affection, and then say: "The slack water ends here, abreast this bunch of China trees; now we cross over." So he crossed over. He gave me the wheel once or twice, but I had no luck. I either came near chipping off the edge of a sugar-plantation, or I yawed too far from shore, and so dropped back into disgrace again and got abused.

The watch was ended at last, and we took supper and went to bed. At midnight the glare of a lantern shone in my eyes, and the night watchman said:

"Come, turn out!"

And then he left. I could not understand this extraordinary procedure; so I presently gave up trying to, and dozed off to sleep. Pretty soon the watchman was back again, and this time he was gruff. I was annoyed. I said:

"What do you want to come bothering around here in the middle of the night for? Now, as like as not, I'll not get to sleep again to-night."

The watchman said:

"Well, if this ain't good, I'm blessed."

The "off-watch" was just turning in, and I heard some brutal laughter from them, and such remarks as "Hello, watchman! ain't the new cub turned out yet? He's delicate, likely. Give him some sugar in a rag, and send for the chambermaid to sing 'Rock-a-by Baby,' to him."

About this time Mr. Bixby appeared on the scene. Something like a minute later I was climbing the pilot-house steps with some of my clothes on and the rest in my arms. Mr. Bixby was close behind, commenting. Here was something fresh—this thing of getting up in the middle of the night to go to work. It was a detail in piloting that had never occurred to me at all. I knew that boats ran all night, but somehow I had never happened to reflect that somebody had to get up out of a warm bed to run them. I began to fear that piloting was not quite so romantic as I had imagined it was; there was something very real and worklike about this new phase of it.

It was a rather dingy night, although a fair number of stars were out. The big mate was at the wheel, and he had the old tub pointed at a star and was holding her straight up the middle of the river. The shores on either hand were not much more than half a mile apart, but they seemed wonderfully far away and ever so vague and indistinct. The mate said:

"We've got to land at Jones's plantation, sir."

The vengeful spirit in me exulted. I said to myself, "I wish you joy of your job, Mr. Bixby; you'll have a good time finding Mr. Jones's plantation such a night as this; and I hope you never *will* find it as long as you live."

Mr. Bixby said to the mate:

"Upper end of the plantation, or the lower?"

"Upper."

"I can't do it. The stumps there are out of water at this stage. It's no great distance to the lower, and you'll have to get along with that."

"All right, sir. If Jones don't like it, he'll have to lump it, I reckon."

And then the mate left. My exultation began to cool and my wonder to come up. Here was a man who not only proposed to find this plantation on such a night, but to find either end of it you preferred. I dreadfully wanted to ask a question, but I was carrying about as many short answers as my cargo-room would admit of, so I held my peace. All I desired to ask Mr. Bixby was the simple question whether he was ass enough to really imagine he was going to find that plantation on a night when all plantations were exactly alike and all of the same color. But I held in. I used to have fine inspirations of prudence in those days.

Mr. Bixby made for the shore and soon was scraping it, just the same as if it had been daylight. And not only that, but singing:

"Father in heaven, the day is declining," etc.

It seemed to me that I had put my life in the keeping of a peculiarly reckless outcast. Presently he turned on me and said:

"What's the name of the first point above New Orleans?"

I was gratified to be able to answer promptly, and I did. I said I didn't know.

"Don't *know?*"

This manner jolted me. I was down at the foot again, in a moment. But I had to say just what I had said before.

"Well, you're a smart one!" said Mr. Bixby. "What's the name of the *next* point?"

Once more I didn't know.

"Well, this beats anything. Tell me the name of *any* point or place I told you."

I studied awhile and decided that I couldn't.

"Look here! What do you start out from, above Twelve-Mile Point, to cross over?"

"I–I—don't know."

"You—you—don't know?" mimicking my drawling manner of speech. "What *do* you know?"

"I–I—nothing, for certain."

"By the great Cæsar's ghost, I believe you! You're the stupidest dunderhead I ever saw or ever heard of, so help me Moses! The idea of *you* being a pilot—*you!* Why, you don't know enough to pilot a cow down a lane."

Oh, but his wrath was up! He was a nervous man, and he shuffled from one side of his wheel to the other as if the floor was hot. He would boil awhile to himself, and then overflow and scald me again.

"Look here! What do you suppose I told you the names of those points for?"

I tremblingly considered a moment, and then the devil of temptation provoked me to say:

"Well to–to—be entertaining, I thought."

This was a red rag to the bull. He raged and stormed so (he was crossing the river at the time) that I judged it made him blind, because he ran over the steering-oar of a trading-scow. Of course the traders sent up a volley of red-hot profanity. Never was a man so grateful as Mr. Bixby was; because he was brimful, and here were subjects who could *talk back*. He threw open a window, thrust his head out, and such an irruption followed as I never had heard before. The fainter and farther away the scowmen's curses drifted, the higher Mr. Bixby lifted his voice and the weightier his adjectives grew. When he closed the window he was empty. You could have drawn a seine through his system and not caught curses enough to disturb your mother with. Presently he said to me in the gentlest way:

"My boy, you must get a little memorandum-book; and every time I tell you a thing, put it down right away. There's only one way to be a pilot, and that is to get this entire river by heart. You have to know it just like A B C."

That was a dismal revelation to me; for my memory was never loaded with anything but blank cartridges. However, I did not feel discouraged long. I judged that it was best to make some allowances, for doubtless Mr. Bixby was "stretching." Presently he pulled a rope and struck a few strokes on the big bell. The stars were all gone now, and the night was as black as ink. I could hear the wheels churn along the bank, but I was not entirely certain that I could see the shore. The voice of the invisible watchman called up from the hurricane-deck:

"What's this, sir?"

"Jones's plantation."

I said to myself, "I wish I might venture to offer a small bet that it isn't." But I did not chirp. I only waited to see. Mr. Bixby handled the engine-bells, and in due time the boat's nose came to the land, a torch glowed from the forecastle, a man skipped ashore, a darky's voice on the bank said: "Gimme de k'yarpet-bag, Mass' Jones," and the next moment we were standing up the river again, all serene. I reflected deeply awhile, and then said—but not aloud— "Well, the finding of that plantation was the luckiest accident that ever happened; but it couldn't happen again in a hundred years." And I fully believed it *was* an accident, too.

By the time we had gone seven or eight hundred miles up the river, I had learned to be a tolerably plucky up-stream steersman, in daylight; and before we reached St. Louis I had made a trifle of progress in night work, but only a trifle. I had a note-book that fairly bristled with the names of towns, "points," bars, islands, bends, reaches, etc.; but the information was to be found only in the note-book—none of it was in my head. It made my heart ache to think I had only got half of the river set down; for as our watch was four hours off and four hours on, day and night, there was a long four-hour gap in my book for every time I had slept since the voyage began.

My chief was presently hired to go on a big New Orleans boat, and I packed my satchel and went with him. She was a grand affair. When I stood in her pilot-house I was so far above the water that I seemed perched on a mountain; and her decks stretched so far away, fore and aft, below me, that I wondered how I could ever have considered the little *Paul Jones* a large craft. There were other differences, too. The *Paul Jones's* pilot-house was a cheap, dingy, battered rattletrap, cramped for room; but here was a sumptuous glass temple; room enough to have a dance in; showy red and gold window-curtains; an imposing sofa; leather cushions and a back to the high bench where visiting pilots sit, to spin yarns and "look at the river"; bright, fanciful "cuspidores," instead of a broad wooden box filled with sawdust; nice new oilcloth on the floor; a hospitable big stove for winter; a wheel as high as my head, costly with inlaid work; a wire tiller-rope; bright brass knobs for the bells; and a tidy, white-aproned, black "texas-tender," to bring up tarts and ices and coffee during mid-watch, day and night. Now this was "something like"; and so I began to take heart once more to believe that piloting was a romantic sort of occupation after all. The moment we were under way I began to prowl about the great steamer and fill myself with joy. She was as clean and as dainty as a drawing-room; when I looked down her long, gilded saloon, it was like gazing through a splendid tunnel; she had an oil-picture, by some gifted sign-painter, on every stateroom door; she glittered with no end of prism-fringed chandeliers; the clerk's office was elegant, the bar was marvelous, and the barkeeper had been barbered and upholstered at incredible cost. The boiler-deck (*i.e.*, the second story of the boat, so to speak) was as spacious as a church, it seemed to me; so with the forecastle; and there was no pitiful handful of deck-hands, firemen, and roust-abouts down there, but a whole battalion of men. The fires were fiercely glaring from a long row of furnaces, and over them were eight huge boilers! This was unutterable pomp. The mighty engines —but enough of this. I had never felt so fine before. And when I found that the regiment of natty servants respectfully "sir'd" me, my satisfaction was complete.

When I returned to the pilot-house St. Louis was gone, and I was lost. Here was a piece of river which was all down in my book, but I could make neither head nor tail of it: you understand, it was turned around. I had seen it when coming up-stream, but I had never faced about to see how it looked when it was behind me. My heart broke again, for it was plain that I had got to learn this troublesome river *both ways*.

The pilot-house was full of pilots, going down to "look at the river." What is called the "upper river" (the two hundred miles between St. Louis and Cairo, where the Ohio comes in) was low; and the Mississippi changes its channel so constantly that the pilots used to always find it necessary to run down to Cairo to take a fresh look, when their boats were to lie in port a week; that is, when the water was at a low stage. A deal of this "looking at the river" was done by poor fellows who seldom had a berth, and whose only hope of getting one lay in their being always freshly posted and therefore ready to drop into the shoes of some reputable pilot, for a single trip, on account of such pilot's sudden illness, or some other necessity. And a good many of them constantly ran up and down inspecting the river, not because they ever really hoped to get a berth, but because (they being guests of the boat) it was cheaper to "look at the river" than stay ashore and pay board. In time these fellows grew dainty in their tastes, and only infested boats that had an established reputation for setting good tables. All visiting pilots were useful, for they were always ready and willing, winter or summer, night or day, to go out in the yawl and help buoy the channel or assist the boat's pilots in any way they could. They were likewise welcomed because all pilots are tireless talkers, when gathered together, and as they talk only about the river they are always understood and are always interesting. Your true pilot cares nothing about anything on earth but the river, and his pride in his occupation surpasses the pride of kings.

We had a fine company of these river inspectors along this trip. There were eight or ten, and there was abundance of room for them in our great pilot-house. Two or three of them wore polished silk hats, elaborate shirt-fronts, diamond breastpins, kid gloves, and patent-leather boots. They were choice in their English, and bore themselves with a dignity proper to men of solid means and prodigious reputation as pilots. The others were more or less loosely clad, and wore upon their heads tall felt cones that were suggestive of the days of the Commonwealth.

I was a cipher in this august company, and felt subdued, not to say torpid. I was not even of sufficient consequence to assist at the wheel when it was necessary to put the tiller hard down in a hurry; the guest that stood nearest did that when occasion required—and this was pretty much all the time, because of the crookedness of the channel and the scant water. I stood in a corner; and the talk I listened to took the hope all out of me. One visitor said to another:

"Jim, how did you run Plum Point, coming up?"

"It was in the night, there, and I ran it the way one of the boys on the *Diana* told me; started out about fifty yards above the wood-pile on the false point, and held on the cabin under Plum Point till I raised the reef—quarter less twain—then straightened up for the middle bar till I got well abreast the old one-limbed cottonwood in the bend, then got my stern on the cottonwood, and head on the low place above the point, and came through a-booming—nine and a half."

"Pretty square crossing, an't it?"

"Yes, but the upper bar's working down fast."

Another pilot spoke up and said:

"I had better water than that, and ran it lower down; started out from the false point—mark twain—raised the second reef abreast the big snag in the bend, and had quarter less twain."

One of the gorgeous ones remarked:

"I don't want to find fault with your leadsmen, but that's a good deal of water for Plum Point, it seems to me."

There was an approving nod all around as this quiet snub dropped on the boaster and "settled" him. And so they went on talk-talk-talking. Meantime, the thing that was running in my mind was, "Now, if my ears hear aright, I have not only to get the names of all the towns and islands and bends, and so on, by heart, but I must even get up a warm personal acquaintanceship with every old snag and one-limbed cottonwood and obscure wood-pile that orna-ments the banks of this river for twelve hundred miles; and more than that, I must actually know where these things are in the dark, unless these guests are gifted with eyes that can pierce through two miles of solid blackness. I wish the piloting business was in Jericho and I had never thought of it."

6

The Far West

THE FRONTIER of the Far West developed its own customs, laws, and literature. It attracted a heterogeneous population from many states and foreign countries, and it evolved laws to deal with conflicting claims for land, water, timber, or pay dirt. From Portland to San Diego, from Sacramento to Tombstone, each environment and its special population created a life style of its own.

The life was shaped by the immensity and solitude of the country. Prospectors ventured all through the foothills of the Sierra Nevada and broad wastes of the Southwest, naming the places they passed— Mosquito Flat, Hell for Sure Pass, Dead Mule Meadow, Rattlesnake Gulch. Many of them died in remote places, victims of accidents, Indians, bandits, disease, exposure, or thirst. Others finally stumbled out of the wilderness to settle down as laborers for other men's ranches or mines. And a few struck it rich, staking claims that became the sites of camps and towns.

Their lonely lives have always captured the imagination of writers and readers. For Jack London, the trials of men alone in the wilderness—whether that be the mountains of the Mother Lode country or the snowfields of Alaska—were the raw material of literature. He admired their individualism, their courage, and their violent struggles. Always an admirer of Nietzsche, London found supermen on the mining frontier.

The best of the works of Walter Van Tilburg Clark, a distinguished contemporary writer, also deals with lonely men. But his stories and novels are infused with a sense of larger community, even when that community is one only of animal life disturbed by a human intruder. And it is this sense of relationship within a hostile environment that distinguishes much of the literature of the Far West.

The excerpt from *Honey in the Horn,* by H. L. Davis, illustrates the loneliness and the complementary need for human relationships that permeate the literature of the Far West. Old Simmons typifies the fifty-odd settlers on the slopes of the Cascade Mountains who chose lonely lives: "one thing that had kept these mountain people from developing any sort of community life, probably, was the fear that they would all talk one another to death the first time they got together." He also typifies the frontier eccentric, the man who lives on his own acres, pursuing his own interests and taking his own peculiar revenge on society, yet feeling the need for other human beings, if only as an audience.

Old Simmons can be compared with his most famous counterpart, the narrator of "The Celebrated Jumping Frog of Calaveras County." Simon Wheeler is another frontiersman as storyteller, one of Mark Twain's favorite personae. But Wheeler (Twain) is more than a lonely monologist; he is an artist who takes his materials from the life of Angel's Camp. His story is not merely a tall tale; it is a recreation of the life, the interests, and the personalities of the inhabitants of the Mother Lode. And it has, of course, the unique combination of understatement and overstatement that characterizes the best of Twain's work.

The restraint and emotional economy of Twain's "monotonous narrative" are quite unlike the didactic sentimentality of Bret Harte's "Outcasts of Poker Flat." For Harte made the mining West the subject of popular fiction. He combined the clichés of melodrama—the prostitute with a heart of gold, the drunken reprobate, the gentleman rascal—with the exotic local color of the California Sierra —the soaring cliffs, the serried pines, and the treacherous weather. His combination was immediately successful, and it inspired innumerable imitations in fiction, in poetry like that of Robert W. Service, and in dramas like *The Girl of the Golden West*.

Frank Norris shared the taste of his contemporaries for violence, for melodrama, and even for sentimentality. But he added a journalist's concern for verisimilitude of detail, and he wrote with the zeal of a social reformer. He described a West that was beginning to face the problems of maturity, a country dominated by banks and railroads and torn by the conflict of warring classes. His West was a country in which the natural frontier had disappeared; it would be replaced by the sharp elbows and raw antagonisms of a settled community.

Small wonder that many Americans, facing west from California, began even in the nineteenth century to realize that expansion had to end. The circle was almost closed, but Utopia was still unachieved, even undefined. Stopped by the Pacific Ocean, beyond which lay the oldest cultures and most populated lands of the world, the pioneers found Walt Whitman's question inescapable: "Where is what I started for so long ago? And why is it yet unfound?"

JACK LONDON

All Gold Canyon

IT WAS THE GREEN HEART of the canyon, where the walls swerved back from the rigid plan and relieved their harshness of line by making a little sheltered nook and filling it to the brim with sweetness and roundness and softness. Here all things rested. Even the narrow stream ceased its turbulent downrush long enough to form a quiet pool. Knee-deep in the water, with drooping head and half-shut eyes, drowsed a red-coated, many-antlered buck.

On one side, beginning at the very lip of the pool, was a tiny meadow, a cool, resilient surface of green that extended to the base of the frowning wall. Beyond the pool a gentle slope of earth ran up and up to meet the opposing wall. Fine grass covered the slope— grass that was spangled with flowers, with here and there patches of color, orange and purple and golden. Below, the canyon was shut in. There was no view. The walls leaned together abruptly and the canyon ended in a chaos of rocks, moss-covered and hidden by a green screen of vines and creepers and boughs of trees. Up the canyon rose far hills and peaks, the big foot-hills, pine-covered and remote. And far beyond, like clouds upon the border of the sky, towered minarets of white, where the Sierra's eternal snows flashed austerely the blazes of the sun.

There was no dust in the canyon. The leaves and flowers were clean and virginal. The grass was young velvet. Over the pool three cotton-woods sent their snowy fluffs fluttering down the quiet air. On the slope the blossoms of the wine-wooded manzanita filled the air with springtime odors, while the leaves, wise with experience, were already beginning their vertical twist against the coming aridity of summer. In the open spaces on the slope beyond the farthest shadow-reach of the manzanita, poised the mariposa lilies, like so many flights of jewelled moths suddenly arrested and on the verge of trembling into flight again. Here and there that woods harlequin, the madrone, permitting itself to be caught in the act of changing its pea-green trunk to madder-red, breathed its fragrance into the air from great clusters of waxen bells. Creamy-white were these bells, shaped like lilies-of-the-valley, with the sweetness of perfume that is of the springtime.

There was not a sigh of wind. The air was drowsy with its weight of perfume. It was a sweetness that would have been cloying had the air been heavy and humid. But the air was sharp and thin. It was as starlight transmuted into atmosphere, shot through and warmed by sunshine, and flower-drenched with sweetness.

An occasional butterfly drifted in and out through the patches of light and shade. And from all about rose the low and sleepy hum of mountain bees—feasting Sybarites that jostled one another good-naturedly at the board, nor found time for rough discourtesy. So quietly did the little stream drip and ripple its way through the canyon that it spoke only in faint and occasional gurgles. The voice of the stream was as a drowsy whisper, ever interrupted by dozings and silences, ever lifted again in the awakenings.

The motion of all things was a drifting in the heart of the canyon. Sunshine and butterflies drifted in and out among the trees. The hum of the bees and the whisper of the stream were a drifting of sound. And the drifting sound and drifting color seemed to weave together in the making of a delicate and intangible fabric which was the spirit of the place. It was a spirit of peace that was not of death, but of smooth-pulsing life, of quietude that was not silence, of movement that was not action, of repose that was quick with existence without being violent with struggle and travail. The spirit of the place was the spirit of the peace of the living, somnolent with the easement and content of prosperity, and undisturbed by rumors of far wars.

The red-coated, many-antlered buck acknowledged the lordship of the spirit of the place and dozed knee-deep in the cool, shaded pool. There seemed no flies to vex him and he was languid with rest. Sometimes his ears moved when the stream awoke and whispered; but they moved lazily, with foreknowledge that it was merely the stream grown garrulous at discovery that it had slept.

But there came a time when the buck's ears lifted and tensed with swift eagerness for sound. His head was turned down the canyon. His sensitive, quivering nostrils scented the air. His eyes could not pierce the green screen through which the stream rippled away, but to his ears came the voice of a man. It was a steady, monotonous, singsong voice. Once the buck heard the harsh clash of metal upon rock. At the sound he snorted with a sudden start that jerked him through the air from water to meadow, and his feet sank into the young velvet, while he pricked his ears and again scented the air. Then he stole across the tiny meadow, pausing once and again to listen, and faded away out of the canyon like a wraith, soft-footed and without sound.

The clash of steel-shod soles against the rocks began to be heard, and the man's voice grew louder. It was raised in a sort of chant and became distinct with nearness, so that the words could be heard:

> "Tu'n around an' tu'n yo' face
> Untoe them sweet hills of grace
> (D' pow'rs of sin yo' am scornin'!),
> Look about an' look aroun',
> Fling yo' sin-pack on d' groun'
> (Yo' will meet wid d' Lord in d' mornin'!)."

A sound of scrambling accompanied the song, and the spirit of the place fled away on the heels of the red-coated buck. The green screen was burst asunder, and a man peered out at the meadow and the pool and the sloping side-hill. He was a deliberate sort of man. He took in the scene with one embracing glance, then ran his eyes over the details to verify the general impression. Then, and not until then, did he open his mouth in vivid and solemn approval:

"Smoke of life an' snakes of purgatory! Will you just look at that! Wood an' water an' grass an' a side-hill! A pocket-hunter's delight an' a cayuse's paradise! Cool green for tired eyes! Pink pills for pale people ain't in it. A secret pasture for prospectors and a resting-place for tired burros, by damn!"

He was a sandy-complexioned man in whose face geniality and humor seemed the salient characteristics. It was a mobile face, quick-changing to inward mood and thought. Thinking was in him a visible process. Ideas chased across his face like wind-flaws across the surface of a lake. His hair, sparse, and unkempt of growth, was as indeterminate and colorless as his complexion. It would seem that all the color of his frame had gone into his eyes, for they were startlingly blue. Also, they were laughing and merry eyes, within them much of the naïveté and wonder of the child; and yet, in an unassertive way, they contained much of calm self-reliance and strength of purpose founded upon self-experience and experience of the world.

From out the screen of vines and creepers he flung ahead of him a miner's pick and shovel and gold-pan. Then he crawled out himself into the open. He was clad in faded overalls and black cotton shirt, with hobnailed brogans on his feet, and on his head a hat whose shapelessness and stains advertised the rough usage of wind and rain and sun and camp-smoke. He stood erect, seeing wide-eyed the secrecy of the scene and sensuously inhaling the warm, sweet breath of the canyon-garden through nostrils that dilated and quivered with delight. His eyes narrowed to laughing slits of blue, his face wreathed itself in joy, and his mouth curled in a smile as he cried aloud:

"Jumping dandelions and happy hollyhocks, but that smells good to me! Talk about your attar o' roses an' cologne factories! They ain't in it!"

He had the habit of soliloquy. His quick-changing facial expressions might tell every thought and mood, but the tongue, perforce, ran hard after, repeating, like a second Boswell.

The man lay down on the lip of the pool and drank long and deep of its water. "Tastes good to me," he murmured, lifting his head and gazing across the pool at the side-hill, while he wiped his mouth with the back of his hand. The side-hill attracted his attention. Still lying on his stomach, he studied the hill formation long and carefully. It was a practised eye that travelled up the slope to the crumbling canyon-wall and back and down again to the edge of the pool. He scrambled to his feet and favored the side-hill with a second survey.

"Looks good to me," he concluded, picking up his pick and shovel and gold-pan.

He crossed the stream below the pool, stepping agilely from stone to stone. Where the side-hill touched the water he dug up a shovelful of dirt and put it into the gold-pan. He squatted down, holding the pan in his two hands, and partly immersing it in the stream. Then he imparted to the pan a deft circular motion that sent the water sluicing in and out through the dirt and gravel. The larger and the lighter particles worked to the surface, and these, by a skilful dipping movement of the pan, he spilled out and over the edge. Occasionally, to expedite matters, he rested the pan and with his fingers raked out the large pebbles and pieces of rock.

The contents of the pan diminished rapidly until only fine dirt and the smallest bits of gravel remained. At this stage he began to work very deliberately and carefully. It was fine washing, and he washed fine and finer, with a keen scrutiny and delicate and fastidious touch. At last the pan seemed empty of everything but water; but with a quick semicircular flirt that sent the water flying over the shallow rim into the stream, he disclosed a layer of black sand on the bottom of the pan. So thin was this layer that it was like a streak of paint. He examined it closely. In the midst of it was a tiny golden speck. He dribbled a little water in over the depressed edge of the pan. With a quick flirt he sent the water sluicing across the bottom, turning the grains of black sand over and over. A second tiny golden speck rewarded his effort.

The washing had now become very fine—fine beyond all need of ordinary placer-mining. He worked the black sand, a small portion at a time, up the shallow rim of the pan. Each small portion he examined sharply, so that his eyes saw every grain of it before he allowed it to slide over the edge and away. Jealously, bit by bit, he let the black sand slip away. A golden speck, no larger than a pin-point, appeared on the rim, and by his manipulation of the water it returned to the bottom of the pan. And in such fashion another speck was disclosed, and another. Great was his care of them. Like a shepherd he herded his flock of golden specks so that not one should be lost. At last, of the pan of dirt nothing remained but his golden herd. He counted it, and then, after all his labor, sent it flying out of the pan with one final swirl of water.

But his blue eyes were shining with desire as he rose to his feet. "Seven," he muttered aloud, asserting the sum of the specks for which he had toiled so hard and which he had so wantonly thrown away. "Seven," he repeated, with the emphasis of one trying to impress a number on his memory.

He stood still a long while, surveying the hillside. In his eyes was a curiosity, new-aroused and burning. There was an exultance about his bearing and a keenness like that of a hunting animal catching the fresh scent of game.

He moved down the stream a few steps and took a second panful of dirt.

Again came the careful washing, the jealous herding of the golden specks, and the wantonness with which he sent them flying into the stream when he had counted their number.

"Five," he muttered, and repeated, "five."

He could not forbear another survey of the hill before filling the pan farther down the stream. His golden herds diminished. "Four, three, two, two, one," were his memory tabulations as he moved down the stream. When but one speck of gold rewarded his washing, he stopped and built a fire of dry twigs. Into this he thrust the gold-pan and burned it till it was blue-black. He held up the pan and examined it critically. Then he nodded approbation. Against such a color-background he could defy the tiniest yellow speck to elude him.

Still moving down the stream, he panned again. A single speck was his reward. A third pan contained no gold at all. Not satisfied with this, he panned three times again, taking his shovels of dirt within a foot of one another. Each pan proved empty of gold, and the fact, instead of discouraging him, seemed to give him satisfaction. His elation increased with each barren washing, until he arose, exclaiming jubilantly:

"If it ain't the real thing, may God knock off my head with sour apples!"

Returning to where he had started operations, he began to pan up the stream. At first his golden herds increased—increased prodigiously. "Fourteen, eighteen, twenty-one, twenty-six," ran his memory tabulations. Just above the pool he struck his richest pan—thirty-five colors.

"Almost enough to save," he remarked regretfully as he allowed the water to sweep them away.

The sun climbed to the top of the sky. The man worked on. Pan by pan, he went up the stream, the tally of results steadily decreasing.

"It's just booful, the way it peters out," he exulted when a shovelful of dirt contained no more than a single speck of gold.

And when no specks at all were found in several pans, he straightened up and favored the hillside with a confident glance.

"Ah, ha! Mr. Pocket!" he cried out, as though to an auditor hidden somewhere above him beneath the surface of the slope. "Ah, ha! Mr. Pocket! I'm a-comin', I'm a-comin,' an' I'm shorely gwine to get yer! You heah me, Mr. Pocket? I'm gwine to get yer as shore as punkins ain't cauliflowers!"

He turned and flung a measuring glance at the sun poised above him in the azure of the cloudless sky. Then he went down the canyon, following the line of shovel-holes he had made in filling the pans. He crossed the stream below the pool and disappeared through the green screen. There was little opportunity for the spirit of the place to return with its quietude and repose, for the man's voice, raised in ragtime song, still dominated the canyon with possession.

After a time, with a greater clashing of steel-shod feet on rock, he returned. The green screen was tremendously agitated. It surged back and forth in the throes of a struggle. There was a loud grating and clanging of metal. The man's voice leaped to a higher pitch and was sharp with imperativeness. A large body plunged and panted. There was a snapping and ripping and rending, and amid a shower of falling leaves a horse burst through the screen. On its back was a pack, and from this trailed broken vines and torn creepers. The animal gazed with astonished eyes at the scene into which it had been precipitated, then dropped its head to the grass and began contentedly to graze. A second horse scrambled into view, slipping once on the mossy rocks and regaining equilibrium when its hoofs sank into the yielding surface of the meadow. It was riderless, though on its back was a high-horned Mexican saddle, scarred and discolored by long usage.

The man brought up the rear. He threw off pack and saddle, with an eye to camp location, and gave the animals their freedom to graze. He unpacked his food and got out frying-pan and coffeepot. He gathered an armful of dry wood, and with a few stones made a place for his fire.

"My!" he said, "but I've got an appetite. I could scoff iron filings an' horseshoe nails an' thank you kindly, ma'am, for a second helpin'."

He straightened up, and, while he reached for matches in the pocket of his overalls, his eyes travelled across the pool to the side-hill. His fingers had clutched the match-box, but they relaxed their hold and the hand came out empty. The man wavered perceptibly. He looked at his preparations for cooking and he looked at the hill.

"Guess I'll take another whack at her," he concluded, starting to cross the stream.

"They ain't no sense in it, I know," he mumbled apologetically. "But keepin' grub back an hour ain't goin' to hurt none, I reckon."

A few feet back from his first line of test-pans he started a second line. The sun dropped down the western sky, the shadows lengthened, but the man worked on. He began a third line of test-pans. He was cross-cutting the hill-side, line by line, as he ascended. The centre of each line produced the richest pans, while the ends came where no colors showed in the pan. And as he ascended the hillside the lines grew perceptibly shorter. The regularity with which their length diminished served to indicate that somewhere up the slope the last line would be so short as to have scarcely length at all, and that beyond could come only a point. The design was growing into an inverted "V." The converging sides of this "V" marked the boundaries of the gold-bearing dirt.

The apex of the "V" was evidently the man's goal. Often he ran his eye along the converging sides and on up the hill, trying to divine the apex, the point where the gold-bearing dirt must cease. Here resided "Mr. Pocket"—for so the man familiarly addressed the imaginary point above him on the slope, crying out:

"Come down out o' that, Mr. Pocket! Be right smart an' agreeable, an' come down!"

"All right," he would add later, in a voice resigned to determination. "All right, Mr. Pocket. It's plain to me I got to come right up an' snatch you out bald-headed. An' I'll do it! I'll do it!" he would threaten still later.

Each pan he carried down to the water to wash, and as he went higher up the hill the pans grew richer, until he began to save the gold in an empty baking-powder can which he carried carelessly in his hip-pocket. So engrossed was he in his toil that he did not notice the long twilight of oncoming night. It was not until he tried vainly to see the gold colors in the bottom of the pan that he realized the passage of time. He straightened up abruptly. An expression of whimsical wonderment and awe overspread his face as he drawled:

"Gosh darn my buttons! if I didn't plumb forget dinner!"

He stumbled across the stream in the darkness and lighted his long-delayed fire. Flapjacks and bacon and warmed-over beans constituted his supper. Then he smoked a pipe by the smouldering coals, listening to the night noises and watching the moonlight stream through the canyon. After that he unrolled his bed, took off his heavy shoes, and pulled the blankets up to his chin. His face showed white in the moonlight, like the face of a corpse. But it was a corpse that knew its resurrection, for the man rose suddenly on one elbow and gazed across at his hillside.

"Good night, Mr. Pocket," he called sleepily. "Good night."

He slept through the early gray of morning until the direct rays of the sun smote his closed eyelids, when he awoke with a start and looked about him until he had established the continuity of his existence and identified his present self with the days previously lived.

To dress, he had merely to buckle on his shoes. He glanced at his fireplace and at his hillside, wavered, but fought down the temptation and started the fire.

"Keep yer shirt on, Bill; keep yer shirt on," he admonished himself. "What's the good of rushin'? No use in gettin' all het up an' sweaty. Mr. Pocket'll wait for you. He ain't a-runnin' away before you can get yer breakfast. Now, what you want, Bill, is something fresh in yer bill o' fare. So it's up to you to go an' get it."

He cut a short pole at the water's edge and drew from one of his pockets a bit of line and a draggled fly that had once been a royal coachman.

"Mebbe they'll bite in the early morning," he muttered, as he made his first cast into the pool. And a moment later he was gleefully crying: "What 'd I tell you, eh? What 'd I tell you?"

He had no reel, nor any inclination to waste time, and by main strength, and swiftly, he drew out of the water a flashing ten-inch trout. Three more, caught in rapid succession, furnished his breakfast. When he came to the stepping-stones on his way to his hillside, he was struck by a sudden thought, and paused.

"I'd just better take a hike down-stream a ways," he said. "There's no tellin' what cuss may be snoopin' around."

But he crossed over on the stones, and with a "I really oughter take that hike," the need of the precaution passed out of his mind and he fell to work.

At nightfall he straightened up. The small of his back was stiff from stooping toil, and as he put his hand behind him to soothe the protesting muscles, he said:

"Now what d'ye think of that, by damn? I clean forgot my dinner again! If I don't watch out, I'll sure be degeneratin' into a two-meal-a-day crank."

"Pockets is the damnedest things I ever see for makin' a man absent-minded," he communed that night, as he crawled into his blankets. Nor did he forget to call up the hillside, "Good night, Mr. Pocket! Good night!"

Rising with the sun, and snatching a hasty breakfast, he was early at work. A fever seemed to be growing in him, nor did the increasing richness of the test-pans allay this fever. There was a flush in his cheek other than that made by the heat of the sun, and he was oblivious to fatigue and the passage of time. When he filled a pan with dirt, he ran down the hill to wash it; nor could he forbear running up the hill again, panting and stumbling profanely, to refill the pan.

He was now a hundred yards from the water, and the inverted "V" was assuming definite proportions. The width of the pay-dirt steadily decreased, and the man extended in his mind's eye the sides of the "V" to their meeting-place far up the hill. This was his goal. the apex of the "V," and he panned many times to locate it.

"Just about two yards above that manzanita bush an' a yard to the right," he finally concluded.

Then the temptation seized him. "As plain as the nose on your face," he said, as he abandoned his laborious cross-cutting and climbed to the indicated apex. He filled a pan and carried it down the hill to wash. It contained no trace of gold. He dug deep, and he dug shallow, filling and washing a dozen pans, and was unrewarded even by the tiniest golden speck. He was enraged at having yielded to the temptation, and cursed himself blasphemously and pridelessly. Then he went down the hill and took up the cross-cutting.

"Slow an' certain, Bill; slow an' certain," he crooned. "Short-cuts to fortune ain't in your line, an' it's about time you know it. Get wise, Bill; get wise. Slow an' certain's the only hand you can play; so go to it, an' keep to it, too."

As the cross-cuts decreased, showing that the sides of the "V" were converging, the depth of the "V" increased. The gold-trace was dipping into the hill. It was only at thirty inches beneath the surface that he could get colors in his pan. The dirt he found at twenty-five inches from the surface, and at thirty-five inches, yielded barren pans. At the base of the "V," by the water's edge, he had found the gold colors at the grass roots. The higher he went up the hill, the deeper the gold dipped. To dig a hole three feet deep in order to get one test-pan was a task of no mean magnitude; while between the man and the apex intervened an untold number of such holes to be dug. "An' there's no tellin' how much deeper it'll pitch," he sighed, in a moment's pause, while his fingers soothed his aching back.

Feverish with desire, with aching back and stiffening muscles, with pick and shovel gouging and mauling the soft brown earth, the man toiled up the hill. Before him was the smooth slope, spangled with flowers and made sweet with their breath. Behind him was devastation. It looked like some terrible eruption breaking out on the smooth skin of the hill. His slow progress was like that of a slug, befouling beauty with a monstrous trail.

Though the dipping gold-trace increased the man's work, he found consolation in the increasing richness of the pans. Twenty cents, thirty cents, fifty cents, sixty cents, were the values of the gold found in the pans, and at nightfall he washed his banner pan, which gave him a dollar's worth of gold-dust from a shovelful of dirt.

"I'll just bet it's my luck to have some inquisitive cuss come buttin' in here on my pasture," he mumbled sleepily that night as he pulled the blankets up to his chin.

Suddenly he sat upright. "Bill!" he called sharply. "Now, listen to me, Bill; d'ye hear! It's up to you, to-morrow mornin', to mosey round an' see what you can see. Understand? To-morrow morning, an' don't you forget it!"

He yawned and glanced across at his side-hill. "Good night, Mr. Pocket," he called.

In the morning he stole a march on the sun, for he had finished breakfast when its first rays caught him, and he was climbing the wall of the canyon where it crumbled away and gave footing. From the outlook at the top he found himself in the midst of loneliness. As far as he could see, chain after chain of mountains heaved themselves into his vision. To the east his eyes, leaping the miles between range and range and between many ranges, brought up at last against the white-peaked Sierras—the main crest, where the backbone of the Western world reared itself against the sky. To the north and south he could see more distinctly the cross-systems that broke through the main trend of the sea of mountains. To the west the ranges fell away, one behind the other, diminishing and fading into the gentle foothills that, in turn, descended into the great valley which he could not see.

And in all that mighty sweep of earth he saw no sign of man nor of the handiwork of man—save only the torn bosom of the hillside at his feet. The man looked long and carefully. Once, far down his own canyon, he thought he saw in the air a faint hint of smoke. He looked again and decided that it was the purple haze of the hills made dark by a convolution of the canyon wall at its back.

"Hey, you, Mr. Pocket!" he called down into the canyon. "Stand out from under! I'm a-comin', Mr. Pocket! I'm a-comin'!"

The heavy brogans on the man's feet made him appear clumsy-footed, but he swung down from the giddy height as lightly and airily as a mountain goat. A rock, turning under his foot on the edge of the precipice, did not disconcert him. He seemed to know the precise time required for the turn to culminate in disaster, and in the meantime he utilized the false footing itself for the momentary earth-contact necessary to carry him on into safety. Where the earth sloped so steeply that it was impossible to stand for a second upright, the man did not hesitate. His foot pressed the impossible surface for but a fraction of the fatal second and gave him the bound that carried him onward. Again, where even the fraction of a second's footing was out of the question, he would swing his body past by a moment's hand-grip on a jutting knob of rock, a crevice, or a precariously rooted shrub. At last, with a wild leap and yell, he exchanged the face of the wall for an earth-slide and finished the descent in the midst of several tons of sliding earth and gravel.

His first pan of the morning washed out over two dollars in coarse gold. It was from the centre of the "V." To either side the diminution in the values of the pans was swift. His lines of cross-cutting holes were growing very short. The converging sides of the inverted "V" were only a few yards apart. Their meeting-point was only a few yards above him. But the pay-streak was dipping deeper and deeper into the earth. By early afternoon he was sinking the test-holes five feet before the pans could show the gold-trace.

For that matter, the gold-trace had become something more than a trace; it was a placer mine in itself, and the man resolved to come back after he had found the pocket and work over the ground. But the increasing richness of the pans began to worry him. By late afternoon the worth of the pans had grown to three and four dollars. The man scratched his head perplexedly and looked a few feet up the hill at the manzanita bush that marked approximately the apex of the "V." He nodded his head and said oracularly:

"It's one o' two things, Bill; one o' two things. Either Mr. Pocket's spilled himself all out an' down the hill, or else Mr. Pocket's that damned rich you maybe won't be able to carry him all away with you. And that 'd be hell, wouldn't it, now?" He chuckled at contemplation of so pleasant a dilemma.

Nightfall found him by the edge of the stream, his eyes wrestling with the gathering darkness over the washing of a five-dollar pan.

"Wisht I had an electric light to go on working," he said.

He found sleep difficult that night. Many times he composed himself and closed his eyes for slumber to overtake him; but his blood pounded with too strong desire, and as many times his eyes opened and he murmured wearily, "Wisht it was sun-up."

Sleep came to him in the end, but his eyes were open with the first paling of the stars, and the gray of dawn caught him with breakfast finished and climbing the hillside in the direction of the secret abiding-place of Mr. Pocket.

The first cross-cut the man made, there was space for only three holes, so narrow had become the paystreak and so close was he to the fountainhead of the golden stream he had been following for four days.

"Be ca'm, Bill; be ca'm," he admonished himself, as he broke ground for the final hole where the sides of the "V" had at last come together in a point.

"I've got the almighty cinch on you, Mr. Pocket, an' you can't lose me," he said many times as he sank the hole deeper and deeper.

Four feet, five feet, six feet, he dug his way down into the earth. The digging grew harder. His pick grated on broken rock. He examined the rock. "Rotten quartz," was his conclusion as, with the shovel, he cleared the bottom of the hole of loose dirt. He attacked the crumbling quartz with the pick, bursting the disintegrating rock asunder with every stroke.

He thrust his shovel into the loose mass. His eye caught a gleam of yellow. He dropped the shovel and squatted suddenly on his heels. As a farmer rubs the clinging earth from fresh-dug potatoes, so the man, a piece of rotten quartz held in both hands, rubbed the dirt away.

"Sufferin' Sardanopolis!" he cried. "Lumps an' chunks of it! Lumps an' chunks of it!"

It was only half rock he held in his hand. The other half was virgin gold. He dropped it into his pan and examined another piece. Little yellow was to be seen, but with his strong fingers he crumbled the rotten quartz away till both hands were filled with glowing yellow. He rubbed the dirt away from fragment after fragment, tossing them into the gold-pan. It was a treasure-hole. So much had the quartz rotted away that there was less of it than there was of gold. Now and again he found a piece to which no rock clung—a piece that was all gold. A chunk, where the pick had laid open the heart of the gold, glittered like a handful of yellow jewels, and he cocked his head at it and slowly turned it around and over to observe the rich play of the light upon it.

"Talk about yer Too Much Gold diggin's!" the man snorted contemptuously. "Why, this diggin' 'd make it look like thirty cents. This diggin' is All Gold. An' right here an' now I name this yere canyon 'All Gold Canyon,' b'gosh!"

Still squatting on his heels, he continued examining the fragments and tossing them into the pan. Suddenly there came to him a premonition of danger. It seemed a shadow had fallen upon him. But there was no shadow. His heart had given a great jump up into his throat and was choking him. Then his blood slowly chilled and he felt the sweat of his shirt cold against his flesh.

He did not spring up nor look around. He did not move. He was considering the nature of the premonition he had received, trying to locate the source of the mysterious force that had warned him, striving to sense the imperative presence of the unseen thing that threatened him. There is an aura of things hostile, made manifest by messengers too refined for the senses to know; and this aura he felt, but knew not how he felt it. His was the feeling as when a cloud passes over the sun. It seemed that smothering and menacing; a gloom, as it were, that between him and life had passed something dark and swallowed up life and made for death—his death.

Every force of his being impelled him to spring up and confront the unseen danger, but his soul dominated the panic, and he remained squatting on his heels, in his hands a chunk of gold. He did not dare to look around, but he knew by now that there was something behind him and above him. He made believe to be interested in the gold in his hand. He examined it critically, turned it over and over, and rubbed the dirt from it. And all the time he knew that something behind him was looking at the gold over his shoulder.

Still feigning interest in the chunk of gold in his hand, he listened intently and he heard the breathing of the thing behind him. His eyes searched the ground in front of him for a weapon, but they saw only the uprooted gold, worthless to him now in his extremity. There was his pick, a handy weapon on occasion; but this was not such an occasion. The man realized his predicament. He was in a narrow hole that was seven feet deep. His head did not come to the surface of the ground. He was in a trap.

He remained squatting on his heels. He was quite cool and collected; but his mind, considering every factor, showed him only his helplessness. He continued rubbing the dirt from the quartz fragments and throwing the gold into the pan. There was nothing else for him to do. Yet he knew that he would have to rise up, sooner or later, and face the danger that breathed at his back. The minutes passed, and with the passage of each minute he knew that by so much he was nearer the time when he must stand up, or else—and his wet shirt went cold against his flesh again at the thought—or else he might receive death as he stooped there over his treasure.

Still he squatted on his heels, rubbing dirt from gold and debating in just what manner he should rise up. He might rise up with a rush and claw his way out of the hole to meet whatever threatened on the even footing above ground. Or he might rise up slowly and carelessly, and feign casually to discover the thing that breathed at his back. His instinct and every fighting fibre of his body favored the mad, clawing rush to the surface. His intellect, and the craft thereof, favored the slow and cautious meeting with the thing that menaced and which he could not see. And while he debated, a loud, crashing noise burst on his ear. At the same instant he received a stunning blow on the left side of the back, and from the point of impact felt a rush of flame through his flesh. He sprang up into the air, but halfway to his feet collapsed. His body crumpled in like a leaf withered in sudden heat, and he came down, his chest across his pan of gold, his face in the dirt and rock, his legs tangled and twisted because of the restricted space at the bottom of the hole. His legs twitched convulsively several times. His body was shaken as with a mighty ague. There was a slow expansion of the lungs, accompanied by a deep sigh. Then the air was slowly, very slowly, exhaled, and his body as slowly flattened itself down into inertness.

Above, revolver in hand, a man was peering down over the edge of the hole. He peered for a long time at the prone and motionless body beneath him. After a while the stranger sat down on the edge of the hole so that he could see into it, and rested the revolver on his knee. Reaching his hand into a pocket, he drew out a wisp of brown paper. Into this he dropped a few crumbs of tobacco. The combination became a cigarette, brown and squat, with the ends turned in. Not once did he take his eyes from the body at the bottom of the hole. He lighted the cigarette and drew its smoke into his lungs with a caressing intake of the breath. He smoked slowly. Once the cigarette went out and he relighted it. And all the while he studied the body beneath him.

In the end he tossed the cigarette stub away and rose to his feet. He moved to the edge of the hole. Spanning it, a hand resting on each edge, and with the revolver still in the right hand, he muscled his body down into the hole. While his feet were yet a yard from the bottom he released his hands and dropped down.

At the instant his feet struck bottom he saw the pocket-miner's arm leap out, and his own legs knew a swift, jerking grip that overthrew him. In the nature of the jump his revolver-hand was above his head. Swiftly as the grip had flashed about his legs, just as swiftly he brought the revolver down. He was still in the air, his fall in process of completion, when he pulled the trigger. The explosion was deafening in the confined space. The smoke filled the hole so that he could see nothing. He struck the bottom on his back, and like a cat's the pocket-miner's body was on top of him. Even as the miner's body passed on top, the stranger crooked in his right arm to fire; and even in that instant the miner, with a quick thrust of elbow, struck his wrist. The muzzle was thrown up and the bullet thudded into the dirt of the side of the hole.

The next instant the stranger felt the miner's hand grip his wrist. The struggle was now for the revolver. Each man strove to turn it against the other's body. The smoke in the hole was clearing. The stranger, lying on his back, was beginning to see dimly. But suddenly he was blinded by a handful of dirt deliberately flung into his eyes by his antagonist. In that moment of shock his grip on the revolver was broken. In the next moment he felt a smashing darkness descend upon his brain, and in the midst of the darkness even the darkness ceased.

But the pocket-miner fired again and again, until the revolver was empty. Then he tossed it from him and, breathing heavily, sat down on the dead man's legs.

The miner was sobbing and struggling for breath. "Measly skunk!" he panted; "a-campin' on my trail an' lettin' me do the work, an' then shootin' me in the back!"

He was half crying from anger and exhaustion. He peered at the face of the dead man. It was sprinkled with loose dirt and gravel, and it was difficult to distinguish the features.

"Never laid eyes on him before," the miner concluded his scrutiny. "Just a common an' ordinary thief, damn him! An' he shot me in the back! He shot me in the back!"

He opened his shirt and felt himself, front and back, on his left side.

"Went clean through, and no harm done!" he cried jubilantly. "I'll bet he aimed all right all right; but he drew the gun over when he pulled the trigger—the cuss! But I fixed 'm! Oh, I fixed 'm!"

His fingers were investigating the bullet-hole in his side; and a shade of regret passed over his face. "It's goin' to be stiffer'n hell," he said. "An' it's up to me to get mended and get out o' here."

He crawled out of the hole and went down the hill to his camp. Half an hour later he returned, leading his pack-horse. His open shirt disclosed the rude bandages with which he had dressed his wound. He was slow and awkward with his left-hand movements, but that did not prevent his using the arm.

The bight of the pack-rope under the dead man's shoulders enabled him to heave the body out of the hole. Then he set to work gathering up his gold. He worked steadily for several hours, pausing often to rest his stiffening shoulder and to exclaim:

"He shot me in the back, the measly skunk! He shot me in the back!"

When his treasure was quite cleaned up and wrapped securely into a number of blanket-covered parcels, he made an estimate of its value.

"Four hundred pounds, or I'm a Hottentot," he concluded. "Say two hundred in quartz an' dirt—that leaves two hundred pounds of gold. Bill! Wake up! Two hundred pounds of gold! Forty thousand dollars! An' it's yourn—all yourn!"

He scratched his head delightedly and his fingers blundered into an unfamiliar groove. They quested along it for several inches. It was a crease through his scalp where the second bullet had ploughed.

He walked angrily over to the dead man.

"You would, would you?" he bullied. "You would, eh? Well, I fixed you good an' plenty, an' I'll give you decent burial, too. That's more'n you'd have done for me."

He dragged the body to the edge of the hole and toppled it in. It struck the bottom with a dull crash, on its side, the face twisted up to the light. The miner peered down at it.

"An' you shot me in the back!" he said accusingly. With pick and shovel he filled the hole. Then he loaded the gold on his horse. It was too great a load for the animal, and when he had gained his camp he transferred part of it to his saddle-horse. Even so, he was compelled to abandon a portion of his outfit—pick and shovel and gold pan, extra food and cooking utensils, and divers odds and ends.

The sun was at the zenith when the man forced the horses at the screen of vines and creepers. To climb the huge boulders the animals were compelled to uprear and struggle blindly through the tangled mass of vegetation. Once the saddle-horse fell heavily and the man removed the pack to get the animal on its feet. After it started on its way again the man thrust his head out from among the leaves and peered up at the hillside.

"The measly skunk!" he said, and disappeared.

There was a ripping and tearing of vines and boughs. The trees surged back and forth, marking the passage of the animals through the midst of them. There was a clashing of steel-shod hoofs on stone, and now and again an oath or a sharp cry of command. Then the voice of the man was raised in song:—

> "Tu'n around and tu'n yo' face
> Untoe them sweet hills of grace

(D' pow'rs of sin yo' am scornin'!).
Look about an' look aroun',
Fling yo' sin-pack on d' groun'
(Yo' will meet wid d' Lord in d' mornin'!))."

The song grew faint and fainter, and through the silence crept back the spirit of the place. The stream once more drowsed and whispered; the hum of the mountain bees rose sleepily. Down through the perfume-weighted air fluttered the snowy fluffs of the cottonwoods. The butterflies drifted in and out among the trees, and overall blazed the quiet sunshine. Only remained the hoof-marks in the meadow and the torn hillside to mark the boisterous trail of the life that had broken the peace of the place and passed on.

WALTER VAN TILBURG CLARK

The Indian Well

In this dead land, like a vast relief model, the only allegiance was to sun. Even night was not strong enough to resist; earth stretched gratefully under it, but had no hope that day would not return. Such living things as hoarded a little juice at their cores were secret about it, and only the most ephemeral existences, the air at dawn and sunset, the amethyst shadows in the mountains, had any freedom. The Indian Well alone, of lesser creations, was in constant revolt. Sooner or later all minor, breathing rebels came to its stone basin under the spring in the cliff, and from its overflow grew a meadow delta and two columns of willows and aspens holding a tiny front against the valley. The pictograph of a starving, ancient journey, cut in rock above the basin, a sun-warped shack on the south wing of the canyon, and an abandoned mine above it, were the last minute and practically contemporary tokens of man's participation in the cycles of the well's resistance, each of which was an epitome of centuries, and perhaps of the wars of the universe.

The day before Jim Suttler came up in the early spring to take his part in one cycle was a busy day. The sun was merely lucid after four days of broken showers and one rain of an hour with a little cold wind behind it, and under the separate cloud shadows sliding down the mountain and into the valley, the canyon was alive. A rattler emerged partially from a hole in the mound on which the cabin stood, and having gorged in the darkness, rested with his head on a stone. A road-runner, stepping long and always about to sprint, came down the morning side of the mound, and his eye, quick to perceive the difference between the live and the inanimate of the same color, discovered the coffin-shaped head on the stone. At once he broke into a reaching sprint, his neck and tail stretched level, his beak agape with expectation. But his shadow arrived a step before him. The rattler recoiled, his head scarred by the sharp beak but his eye intact. The road-runner said nothing, but peered warily into the hole without stretching his neck, then walked off stiffy, leaning forward again as if about to run. When he had gone twenty feet he turned, balanced for an instant, and charged back, checking abruptly just short of the hole. The snake remained withdrawn. The road-runner paraded briefly before the hole, talking to himself, and then ran angrily up to the spring, where he drank at the overflow, sipping and stretching his neck, lifting his feet one at a time, ready to go into immediate action. The road-runner lived a dangerous and exciting life.

In the upper canyon the cliff swallows, making short harp notes, dipped and shot between the new mud under the aspens and their high community on the forehead of the cliff. Electrical bluebirds appeared to dart the length of the canyon at each low flight, but turned up tilting half way down. Lizards made similar unexpected flights and stops on the rocks, and when they stopped did rapid push-ups, like men exercising on a floor. They were variably pugnacious and timid.

Two of them arrived simultaneously upon a rock below the road-runner. One of them immediately skittered to a rock two feet off, and they faced each other, exercising. A small hawk coming down over the mountain, but shadowless under a cloud, saw the lizards. Having overfled the difficult target, he dropped to the canyon mouth swiftly and banked back into the wind. His trajectory was cleared of swallows but one of them, fluttering hastily up, dropped a pellet of mud between the lizards. The one who had retreated disappeared. The other flattened for an instant, then sprang and charged. The road-runner was on him as he struck the pellet, and galloped down the canyon in great, tense strides on his toes, the lizard lashing the air from his beak. The hawk swooped at the road-runner, thought better of it, and rose against the wind to the head of the canyon, where he turned back and coasted out over the desert, his shadow a little behind him and farther and farther below.

The swallows became the voice of the canyon again, but in moments when they were all silent the lovely smaller sounds emerged, their own feathering, the liquid overflow, the snapping and clicking of insects, a touch of wind in the new aspens. Under these lay still more delicate tones, erasing, in the most silent seconds, the difference between eye and ear, a white cloud shadow passing under the water of the well, a dark cloud shadow on the cliff, the aspen patterns on the stones. Deepest was the permanent background of the rocks, the lost on the canyon floor, and those yet strong, the thinking cliffs. When the swallows began again it was impossible to understand the cliffs, who could afford to wait.

At noon a red and white range cow with one new calf, shining and curled, came slowly up from the desert, stopping often to let the calf rest. At each stop the calf would try vigorously to feed, but the cow would go on. When they reached the well the cow drank slowly for a long time; then she continued to wrinkle the water with her muzzle, drinking a little and blowing, as if she found it hard to leave. The calf worked under her with spasmodic nudgings. When she was done playing with the water, she nosed and licked him out from under her and up to the well. He shied from the surprising coolness and she put him back. When he stayed, she drank again. He put his nose into the water also, and bucked up as if bitten. She continued to pretend, and he returned, got water up his nostrils and took three jumps away. The cow was content and moved off toward the canyon wall, tonguing grass tufts from among the rocks. Against the cliff she rubbed gently and continuously with a mild voluptuous look, occasionally lapping her nose with a serpent tongue. The loose winter shag came off in tufts on the rock. The calf lost her, became panicked and made desperate noises which stopped prematurely, and when he discovered her, complicated her toilet. Finally she led him down to the meadow where, moving slowly, they both fed until he was full and went to sleep in a ball in the sun. At sunset they returned to the well, where the cow drank again and gave him a second lesson. After this they went back into the brush and northward into the dusk. The cow's size and relative immunity to sudden death left an aftermath of peace, rendered gently humorous by the calf.

Also at sunset, there was a resurgence of life among the swallows. The thin golden air at the cliff tops, in which there were now no clouds so that the eastern mountains and the valley were flooded with unbroken light, was full of their cries and quick maneuvers among a dancing myriad of insects. The direct sun gave them, when they perched in rows upon the cliff, a dramatic significance like that of men upon an immensely higher promontory. As dusk rose out of the canyon, while the eastern peaks were still lighted, the swallows gradually became silent creatures with slightly altered flight, until, at twilight, the air was full of velvet, swooping bats.

In the night jack-rabbits multiplied spontaneously out of the brush of the valley, drank in the rivulet, their noses and great ears continuously searching the dark, electrical air, and played in fits and starts on the meadow, the many young hopping like rubber, or made thumping love among the aspens and the willows.

A coyote came down canyon on his belly and lay in the brush with his nose between his paws. He took a young rabbit in a quiet spring and snap, and went into the brush again to eat it. At the slight rending of his meal the meadow cleared of leaping shadows and lay empty in the starlight. The rabbits, however, encouraged by newcomers, returned soon, and the coyote killed again and went off heavily, the jack's great hind legs dragging.

In the dry-wash below the meadow an old coyote, without family, profited by the second panic, which came over him. He ate what his loose teeth could tear, leaving the open remnant in the sand, drank at the basin and, carefully circling the meadow, disappeared into the dry wilderness.

Shortly before dawn, when the stars had lost luster and there was no sound in the canyon but the rivulet and the faint, separate clickings of mice in the gravel, nine antelope in loose file, with three silently flagging fawns, came on trigger toe up the meadow and drank at the well, heads often up, muzzles dripping, broad ears turning. In the meadow they grazed and the fawns nursed. When there was as much gray as darkness in the air, and new wind in the canyon, they departed, the file weaving into the brush, merging into the desert, to nothing, and the swallows resumed the talkative day shift.

Jim Suttler and his burro came up into the meadow a little after noon, very slowly, though there was only a spring-fever warmth. Suttler walked pigeon-toed, like an old climber, but carefully and stiffly, not with the loose walk natural to such a long-legged man. He stopped in the middle of the meadow, took off his old black sombrero, and stared up at the veil of water shining over the edge of the basin.

"We're none too early, Jenny," he said to the burro.

The burro had felt water for miles, but could show no excitement. She stood with her head down and her four legs spread unnaturally, as if to postpone a collapse. Her pack reared higher than Suttler's head, and was hung with casks, pails, canteens, a pick, two shovels, a crowbar and a rifle in a sheath. Suttler had the cautious uncertainty of his trade. His other burro had died two days before in the mountains east of Beatty, and Jenny and he bore its load.

Suttler shifted his old six shooter from his rump to his thigh, and studied the well, the meadow, the cabin and the mouth of the mine as if he might choose not to stay. He was not a cinema prospector. If he looked like one of the probably mistaken conceptions of Christ, with his red beard and red hair to his shoulders, it was because he had been long away from barbers and without spare water for shaving. He was unlike Christ in some other ways also.

"It's kinda run down," he told Jenny, "but we'll take it."

He put his sombrero back on, let his pack fall slowly to the ground, showing the sweat patch in his bleached brown shirt, and began to unload Jenny carefully, like a collector handling rare vases, and put everything into one neat pile.

"Now," he said, "we'll have a drink." His tongue and lips were so swollen that the words were unclear, but he spoke casually, like a club-man sealing a minor deal. One learns to do business slowly with deserts and mountains. He picked up a bucket and started for the well. At the upper edge of the meadow he looked back. Jenny was still standing with her head down and her legs apart. He did not particularly notice her extreme thinness for he had seen it coming on gradually. He was thinner himself, and tall, and so round-shouldered that when he stood his straightest he seemed to be peering ahead with his chin out.

"Come on, you old fool," he said. "It's off you now."

Jenny came, stumbling in the rocks above the meadow, and stopping often as if to decide why this annoyance recurred. When she became interested, Suttler would not let her get to the basin, but for ten minutes gave her water from his cupped hands, a few licks at a time. Then he drove her off and she stood in the shade of the canyon wall watching him. He began on his thirst in the same way, a gulp at a time, resting between gulps. After ten gulps he sat on a rock by the spring and looked at the little meadow and the big desert, and might have been considering the courses of the water through his body, but noticed also the antelope tracks in the mud.

After a time he drank another half dozen gulps, gave Jenny half a pailful, and drove her down to the meadow, where he spread a dirty blanket in the striped sun and shadow under the willows. He sat on the edge of the blanket, rolled a cigarette and smoked it while he watched Jenny. When she began to graze with her rump to the canyon, he flicked his cigarette onto the grass, rolled over with his back to the sun and slept until it became chilly after sunset. Then he woke, ate a can of beans, threw the can into the willows and led Jenny up to the well, where they drank together from the basin for a long time. While she resumed her grazing, he took another blanket and his rifle from the pile, removed his heel-worn boots, stood his rifle against a fork, and, rolling up in both blankets, slept again.

In the night many rabbits played in the meadow in spite of the strong sweat and tobacco smell of Jim Suttler lying under the willows, but the antelope, when they came in the dead dark before dawn, were nervous, drank less, and did not graze but minced quickly back across the meadow and began to run at the head of the dry wash. Jenny slept with her head hanging, and did not hear them come or go.

Suttler woke lazy and still red-eyed, and spent the morning drinking at the well, eating and dozing on his blanket. In the afternoon, slowly, a few things at a time, he carried his pile to the cabin. He had a bachelor's obsession with order, though he did not mind dirt, and puttered until sundown making a brush bed and arranging his gear. Much of this time, however, was spent studying the records, on the cabin walls, of the recent human life of the well. He had to be careful, because among the still legible names and dates, after Frank

Davis, 1893, Willard Harbinger, 1893, London, England, John Mason, June 13, 1887, Bucksport, Maine, Matthew Kenling from Glasgow, 1891, Penelope and Martin Reave, God Guide Us, 1885, was written Frank Hayward, 1492, feeling my age. There were other wits too. John Barr had written, Giv it back to the injuns, and Kenneth Thatcher, two years later, had written under that, Pity the noble redskin, while another man, whose second name was Evans, had written what was already a familiar libel, since it was not strictly true: Fifty miles from water, a hundred miles from wood, a million miles from God, three feet from hell. Someone unnamed had felt differently, saying, God is kind. We may make it now. Shot an antelope here July 10, 188—and the last number blurred. Arthur Smith, 1881, had recorded, Here berried my beloved wife Semantha, age 22, and my soul. God let me keep the child. J.M. said cryptically, Good luck, John, and Bill said, Ralph, if you come this way, am trying to get to Los Angeles. B. Westover said he had recovered from his wound there in 1884, and Galt said, enigmatically and without date, Bart and Miller burned to death in the Yellow Jacket. I don't care now. There were poets too, of both parties. What could still be read of Byron Cotter's verses, written in 1902, said,

> . . . here alone
> Each shining dawn I greet,
> The Lord's wind on my forehead
> And where he set his feet
> One mark of heel remaining
> Each day filled up anew,
> To keep my soul from burning,
> With clear, celestial dew.
> Here in His Grace abiding
> The mortal years and few
> I shall . . .

but you can't tell what he intended, while J.A. had printed,

> My brother came out in '49
> I came in '51
> At first we thought we liked it fine
> But now, by God, we're done.

Suttler studied these records without smiling, like someone reading a funny paper, and finally, with a heavy blue pencil, registered, Jim and Jenny Suttler, damn dried out, March—and paused, but had no way of discovering the day—1940.

In the evening he sat on the steps watching the swallows in the golden upper canyon turn bats in the dusk, and thought about the antelope. He had seen the new tracks also, and it alarmed him a little that the antelope could have passed twice in the dark without waking him.

Before false dawn he was lying in the willows with his carbine at ready. Rabbits ran from the meadow when he came down, and after that there was no movement. He wanted to smoke. When he did see them at the lower edge of the meadow, he was startled, yet made no quick movement, but slowly pivoted to cover them. They made poor targets in that light and backed by the pale desert, appearing and disappearing before his eyes. He couldn't keep any one of them steadily visible, and decided to wait until they made contrast against the meadow. But his presence was strong. One of the antelope advanced onto the green, but then threw its head up, spun, and ran back past the flank of the herd, which swung after him. Suttler rose quickly and raised the rifle, but let it down without firing. He could hear the light rattle of their flight in the wash, but had only a belief that he could see them. He had few cartridges, and the report and ponderous echo under the cliffs would scare them off for weeks.

His energies, however, were awakened by the frustrated hunt. While there was still more light than heat in the canyon, he climbed to the abandoned mine tunnel at the top of the alluvial wing of the cliff. He looked at the broken rock in the dump, kicked up its pack with a boot toe, and went into the tunnel, peering closely at its sides, in places black with old smoke smudges. At the back he struck two matches and looked at the jagged dead end and the fragments on the floor, then returned to the shallow beginning of a side tunnel. At the second match here he knelt quickly, scrutinized a portion of the rock, and when the match went out at once lit another. He lit six matches, and pulled at the rock with his hand. It was firm.

"The poor chump," he said aloud.

He got a loose rock from the tunnel and hammered at the projection with it. It came finally, and he carried it into the sun on the dump.

"Yessir," he said aloud, after a minute.

He knocked his sample into three pieces and examined each minutely.

"Yessir, yessir," he said with malicious glee, and, grinning at the tunnel, "The poor chump."

Then he looked again at the dump, like the mound before a gigantic gopher hole. "Still, that's a lot of digging," he said.

He put sample chips into his shirt pocket, keeping a small, black, heavy one that had fallen neatly from a hole like a borer's, to play with in his hand. After trouble he found the claim pile on the side hill south of the tunnel, its top rocks tumbled into the shale. Under the remaining rocks he found what he wanted, a ragged piece of yellowed paper between two boards. The writing was in pencil, and not diplomatic. "I hereby clame this whole damn side hill as far as I can shoot north and south and as far as I can dig in. I am a good shot. Keep off. John Barr, April 11, 1897."

Jim Suttler grinned. "Tough guy, eh?" he said.

He made a small ceremony of burning the paper upon a stone from the cairn. The black tinsel of ash blew off and broke into flakes.

"O.K., John Barr?" he asked.

"O.K., Suttler," he answered himself.

In blue pencil, on soiled paper from his pocket, he slowly printed, "Becus of the lamented desease of the late clament, John Barr, I now clame these diggins for myself and partner Jenny. I can shoot too." And wrote rather than printed, "James T. Suttler, March—" and paused.

"Make it an even month," he said, and wrote, "11, 1940." Underneath he wrote, "Jenny Suttler, her mark," and drew a skull with long ears.

"There," he said, and folded the paper, put it between the two boards, and rebuilt the cairn into a neat pyramid above it.

In high spirit he was driven to cleanliness. With scissors, soap and razor he climbed to the spring. Jenny was there, drinking.

"When you're done," he said, and when she lifted her head, pulled her ears and scratched her.

"Maybe we've got something here Jenny," he said.

Jenny observed him soberly and returned to the meadow.

"She doesn't believe me," he said, and began to perfect himself. He sheared off his red tresses in long hanks, then cut closer, and went over yet a third time, until there remained a brush, of varying density, of stiff red bristles, through which his scalp shone whitely. He sheared the beard likewise, then knelt to the well for mirror and shaved painfully. He also shaved his neck and about his ears. He arose younger and less impressive, with jaws as pale as his scalp, so that his sunburn was a red domino. He burned tresses and beard ceremoniously upon a sage bush, and announced, "It is spring."

He began to empty the pockets of his shirt and breeches onto a flat stone, yelling, "In the spring a young man's fancy," to a kind of tune, and paused, struck by the facts.

"Oh yeah?" he said. "Fat chance."

"Fat," he repeated with obscene consideration. "Oh, well," he said, and finished piling upon the rock notebooks, pencils stubs, cartridges, tobacco, knife, stump pipe, matches, chalk, samples, and three wrinkled photographs. One of the photographs he observed at length before weighting it down with a .45 cartridge. It showed a round, blonde girl with a big smile on a stupid face, in a patterned calico house dress, in front of a blossoming rhododendron bush.

He added to this deposit his belt and holster with the big .45.

Then he stripped himself, washed and rinsed his garments in the spring, and spread them upon stones and brush, and carefully arranged four flat stones into a platform beside the trough. Standing there he scooped water over himself, gasping, made it a lather, and at last, face and copper bristles also foaming, gropingly entered the basin, and submerged, flooding the water over in a thin and soapy sheet. His head emerged at once. "My God," he whispered. He remained under, however, till he was soapless, and goose pimpled as a file, when he climbed out cautiously onto the rock platform and performed a dance of small, revolving patterns with a great deal of up and down.

At one point in his dance he observed the pictograph journey upon the cliff, and danced nearer to examine it.

"Ignorant," he pronounced. "Like a little kid," he said.

He was intrigued, however, by more recent records, names smoked and cut upon the lower rock. One of these, in script, like a gigantic handwriting deeply cut, said ALVAREZ BLANCO DE TOLEDO, Anno Di 1624. A very neat, upright cross was chiseled beneath it.

Suttler grinned. "Oh, yeah?" he asked, with his head upon one side. "Nuts," he said, looking at it squarely.

But it inspired him, and with his jack-knife he began scraping beneath the possibly Spanish inscription. His knife, however, made scratches, not incisions. He completed a bad Jim and Jenny and quit, saying, "I should kill myself over a phony wop."

Thereafter, for weeks, while the canyon became increasingly like a furnace in the daytime and the rocks stayed warm at night, he drove his tunnel farther into the mountain and piled the dump farther into the gully, making, at one side of the entrance, a heap of ore to be worked, and occasionally adding a peculiarly heavy pebble to the others in his small leather bag with a draw string. He and Jenny thrived upon this fixed and well-watered life. The hollows disappeared from his face and he became less stringy, while Jenny grew round, her battleship-gray pelt even lustrous and its black markings distinct and ornamental. The burro found time from her grazing to come to the cabin door in the evenings and attend solemnly to Suttler playing with his samples and explaining their future.

"Then, old lady," Suttler said, "you will carry only small chil-

dren, one at a time, for never more than half an hour. You will
have a bedroom with French windows and a mattress, and I will
paint your feet gold.

"The children," he said, "will probably be redheaded, but maybe
blonde. Anyway, they will be beautiful.

"After we've had a holiday, of course," he added. "For one hundred and thirty-three nights," he said dreamily. "Also," he said, "just
one hundred and thirty-three quarts. I'm no drunken bum.

"For you, though," he said, "for one hundred and thirty-three
nights a quiet hotel with other old ladies. I should drag my own
mother in the gutter." He pulled her head down by the ears and
kissed her loudly upon the nose. They were very happy together.

Nor did they greatly alter most of the life of the canyon. The antelope did not return, it is true, the rabbits were fewer and less playful because he sometimes snared them for meat, the little, clean
mice and desert rats avoided the cabin they had used, and the road-
runner did not come in daylight after Suttler, for fun, narrowly
missed him with a piece of ore from the tunnel mouth. Suttler's violence was disproportionate perhaps, when he used his .45 to blow
apart a creamy rat who did invade the cabin, but the loss was insig-
nificant to the pattern of the well, and more than compensated
when he one day caught the rattler extended at the foot of the
dump in a drunken stupor from rare young rabbit, and before it
could recoil held it aloft by the tail and snapped its head off, leaving the heavy body to turn slowly for a long time among the rocks.
The dominant voices went undisturbed, save when he sang badly at
his work or said beautiful things to Jenny in a loud voice.

There were, however, two more noticeable changes, one of which,
at least, was important to Suttler himself. The first was the execu-
tion of the range cow's calf in the late fall, when he began to suggest
a bull. Suttler felt a little guilty about this because the calf might
have belonged to somebody, because the cow remained near the
meadow bawling for two nights, and because the calf had come to
meet the gun with more curiosity than challenge. But when he had
the flayed carcass hung in the mine tunnel in a wet canvas, the sensation of providence overcame any qualms.

The other change was more serious. It occurred at the beginning
of such winter as the well had, when there was sometimes a light
rime on the rocks at dawn, and the aspens held only a few yellow
leaves. Suttler thought often of leaving. The nights were cold, the
fresh meat was eaten, his hopes had diminished as he still found
only occasional nuggets, and his dreams of women, if less violent,
were more nostalgic. The canyon held him with a feeling he would

have called lonesome but at home, yet he probably would have gone except for this second change.

In the higher mountains to the west, where there was already snow, and at dawn a green winter sky, hunger stirred a buried memory in a cougar. He had twice killed antelope at the well, and felt there had been time enough again. He came down from the dwarfed trees and crossed the narrow valley under the stars, sometimes stopping abruptly to stare intently about, like a house-cat in a strange room. After each stop he would at once resume a quick, noiseless trot. From the top of the mountain above the spring he came down very slowly on his belly, but there was nothing at the well. He relaxed, and leaning on the rim of the basin, drank, listening between laps. His nose was clean with fasting, and he knew of the man in the cabin and Jenny in the meadow, but they were strange, not what he remembered about the place. But neither had his past made him fearful. It was only habitual hunting caution which made him go down into the willows carefully, and lie there head up, watching Jenny, but still waiting for antelope, which he had killed before near dawn. The strange smells were confusing and therefore irritating. After an hour he rose and went silently to the cabin, from which the strangest smell came strongly, a carnivorous smell which did not arouse appetite, but made him bristle nervously. The tobacco in it was like pins in his nostrils. He circled the cabin, stopping frequently. At the open door the scent was violent. He stood with his front paws up on the step, moving his head in serpent motions, the end of his heavy tail furling and unfurling constantly. In a dream Suttler turned over without waking, and muttered. The cougar crouched, his eyes intent, his ruff lifting. Then he swung away from the door, growling a little, and after one pause, crept back down to the meadow again and lay in the willows, but where he could watch the cabin also.

When the sky was alarmingly pale and the antelope had not come, he crawled a few feet at a time, behind the willows, to a point nearer Jenny. There he crouched, working his hind legs slowly under him until he was set, and sprang, raced the three or four jumps to the drowsy burro, and struck. The beginning of her mortal scream was severed, but having made an imperfect leap, and from no height, the cat did not at once break her neck, but drove her to earth, where her small hooves churned futilely in the sod, and chewed and worried until she lay still.

Jim Suttler was nearly awakened by the fragment of scream, but heard nothing after it, and sank again.

The cat wrestled Jenny's body into the willows, fed with uncertain relish, drank long at the well, and went slowly over the crest, stopping often to look back. In spite of the light and the beginning talk of the swallows, the old coyote also fed and was gone before Suttler woke.

When Suttler found Jenny, many double columns of regimented ants were already at work, streaming in and out of the interior and mounting like bridge workers upon the ribs. Suttler stood and looked down. He desired to hold the small muzzle in the hollow of his hand, feeling that this familiar gesture would get through to Jenny, but couldn't bring himself to it because of what had happened to that side of her head. He squatted and lifted one hoof on its stiff leg and held that. Ants emerged hurriedly from the fetlock, their lines of communication broken. Two of them made disorganized excursions on the back of his hand. He rose, shook them off, and stood staring again. He didn't say anything because he spoke easily only when cheerful or excited, but a determination was beginning in him. He followed the drag to the spot torn by the small hoofs. Among the willows again, he found the tracks of both the cougar and the coyote, and the cat's tracks again at the well and by the cabin doorstep. He left Jenny in the willows with a canvas over her during the day, and did not eat.

At sunset he sat on the doorstep, cleaning his rifle and oiling it until he could spring the lever almost without sound. He filled the clip, pressed it home, and sat with the gun across his knees until dark, when he put on his sheepskin, stuffed a scarf into the pocket, and went down to Jenny. He removed the canvas from her, rolled it up and held it under his arm.

"I'm sorry, old woman," he said. "Just tonight."

There was a little cold wind in the willows. It rattled the upper branches lightly.

Suttler selected a spot thirty yards down wind, from which he could see Jenny, spread the canvas and lay down upon it, facing toward her. After an hour he was afraid of falling asleep and sat up against a willow clump. He sat there all night. A little after midnight the old coyote came into the dry-wash below him. At the top of the wash he sat down, and when the mingled scents gave him a clear picture of the strategy, let his tongue loll out, looked at the stars for a moment with his mouth silently open, rose and trotted back into the desert.

At the beginning of daylight the younger coyote trotted in from the north, and turned up toward the spring, but saw Jenny. He sat down and looked at her for a long time. Then he moved to the west and sat down again. In the wind was only winter, and the water, and faintly the acrid bat dung in the cliffs. He completed the circle, but not widely enough, walking slowly through the willows, down the edge of the meadow and in again not ten yards in front of the following muzzle of the carbine. Like Jenny, he felt his danger too late. The heavy slug caught him at the base of the skull in the middle of the first jump, so that it was amazingly accelerated for a fraction of a second. The coyote began it alive, and ended it quite dead, but with a tense muscular movement conceived which resulted in a grotesque final leap and twist of the hindquarters alone, leaving them propped high against a willow clump while the head was half buried in the sand, red welling up along the lips of the distended jaws. The cottony underpelt of the tail and rump stirred gleefully in the wind.

When Suttler kicked the body and it did not move, he suddenly dropped his gun, grasped it by the upright hind legs, and hurled it out into the sage-brush. His face appeared slightly insane with fury for that instant. Then he picked up his gun and went back to the cabin, where he ate, and drank half of one of his last three bottles of whiskey.

In the middle of the morning he came down with his pick and shovel, dragged Jenny's much lightened body down into the dry-wash, and dug in the rock and sand for two hours. When she was covered, he erected a small cairn of stone, like the claim post, above her.

"If it takes a year," he said, and licked the salt sweat on his lips.

That day he finished the half bottle and drank all of a second one, and became very drunk, so that he fell asleep during his vigil in the willows, sprawled wide on the dry turf and snoring. He was not disturbed. There was a difference in his smell after that day which prevented even the rabbits from coming into the meadow. He waited five nights in the willows. Then he transferred his watch to a niche in the cliff, across from and just below the spring.

All winter, while the day wind blew long veils of dust across the desert, regularly repeated, like waves or the smoke of line artillery fire, and the rocks shrank under the cold glitter of night, he did not miss a watch. He learned to go to sleep at sundown, wake within a few minutes of midnight, go up to his post and become at once clear headed and watchful. He talked to himself in the mine and the cabin, but never in the niche. His supplies ran low, and he ate less, but would not risk a startling shot. He rationed his tobacco, and when it was gone worked up to a vomiting sickness every three days for nine days, but did not miss a night in the niche. All winter he did not remove his clothes, bathe, shave, cut his hair or sing. He worked the dead mine only to be busy, and became thin again, with sunken eyes which yet were not the eyes he had come with the spring before. It was April, his food almost gone, when he got his chance.

There was a half moon that night, which made the canyon walls black, and occasionally gleamed on wrinkles of the overflow. The cat came down so quietly that Suttler did not see him until he was beside the basin. The animal was suspicious. He took the wind, and twice started to drink, and didn't, but crouched. On Suttler's face there was a set grin which exposed his teeth.

"Not even a drink, you bastard," he thought.

The cat drank a little though, and dropped again, softly, trying to get the scent from the meadow. Suttler drew slowly upon his soul in the trigger. When it gave, the report was magnified impressively in the canyon. The cougar sprang straight into the air and screamed outrageously. The back of Suttler's neck was cold and his hands trembled, but he shucked the lever and fired again. This shot ricocheted from the basin and whined away thinly. The first, however, had struck near enough. The cat began to scramble rapidly on the loose stone, at first without voice, then screaming repeatedly. It doubled upon itself snarling and chewing in a small furious circle, fell and began to throw itself in short, leaping spasms upon the stones, struck across the rim of the tank and lay half in the water, its head and shoulders raised in one corner and resting against the cliff. Suttler could hear it breathing hoarsely and snarling very faintly. The soprano chorus of swallows gradually became silent.

Suttler had risen to fire again, but lowered the carbine and advanced, stopping at every step to peer intently and listen for the hoarse breathing, which continued. Even when he was within five feet of the tank the cougar did not move, except to gasp so that the water again splashed from the basin. Suttler was calmed by the certainty of accomplishment. He drew the heavy revolver from his holster, aimed carefully at the rattling head, and fired again. The canyon boomed, and the east responded faintly and a little behind, but Suttler did not hear them, for the cat thrashed heavily in the tank, splashing him as with a bucket, and then lay still on its side over the edge, its muzzle and forepaws hanging. The water was settling quietly in the tank, but Suttler stirred it again, shooting five more times with great deliberation into the heavy body, which did not move except at the impact of the slugs.

The rest of the night, even after the moon was gone, he worked fiercely, slitting and tearing with his knife. In the morning, under the swallows, he dragged the marbled carcass, still bleeding a little in places, onto the rocks on the side away from the spring, and dropped it. Dragging the ragged hide by the neck, he went unsteadily down the canyon to the cabin, where he slept like a drunkard, although his whiskey had been gone for two months.

In the afternoon, with dreaming eyes, he bore the pelt to Jenny's grave, took down the stones with his hands, shoveled the earth from her, covered her with the skin, and again with earth and the cairn.

He looked at this monument. "There," he said.

That night, for the first time since her death, he slept through.

In the morning, at the well, he repeated his cleansing ritual of a year before, save that they were rags he stretched to dry, even to the dance upon the rock platform while drying. Squatting naked and clean, shaven and clipped, he looked for a long time at the grinning countenance, now very dirty, of the plump girl in front of the blossoming rhododendrons, and in the resumption of his dance he made singing noises accompanied by the words, "Spring, spring, beautiful spring." He was a starved but revived and volatile spirit.

An hour later he went south, his boot soles held on by canvas strips, and did not once look back.

The disturbed life of the spring resumed. In the second night the rabbits loved in the willows, and at the end of a week the rats played in the cabin again. The old coyote and a vulture cleaned the cougar, and his bones fell apart in the shale. The road-runner came up one day, tentatively, and in front of the tunnel snatched up a horned toad and ran with it around the corner, but no farther. After a month the antelope returned. The well brimmed, and in the gentle sunlight the new aspen leaves made a tiny music of shadows.

H. L. DAVIS

Honey in the Horn

FLEM SIMMONS' land-holding was a half mile-square homestead claim astraddle of a creek bottom full of devil's-club stalks and skunk cabbage and wild-currant bushes and alder saplings. There was a round hundred and sixty acres of land in the claim, as provided by the Act of Congress of 1864 to encourage settlement on and development of the public domain; but old Simmons had never got round to using anywhere near all of it, and there were parts of it that he had never even had occasion to set foot on. A six-acre strip of beaver-dam meadow below his cabin produced sufficient hay to winter his horses, and he had fenced that in with an enclosure of dried brush, less because it would hold livestock than because the government required a certain portion of a homestead to be fenced as a symbol of permanence. His cabin was also laid according to land-office regulations, for it contained two rooms, two glass windows, and one stove, all of which the homestead inspectors required a settler's cabin to have, whether the settler needed them or not. There were several stools made by sawing rounds of a log and driving pegs into them for legs, a table topped with split cedar shakes that weren't nailed down and were therefore liable to rise up and slap a man in the face if he leaned too close to the edge, and a bed made by joining four small logs in a rectangle and filling the enclosure with the tips of fir boughs. Above the bed were two enlarged family portraits in black and white. One was of Grandma Simmons, who had been made by the artist to look like an iron-chinned old wampus with her hair done up so tight that she appeared to be keeping her mouth shut against the pull by bearing down with all her strength. The other was of Peg Leg Simmons, a large old gentleman with a hat pulled square across his eyebrows and a godly scowl set on his countenance as if it had been nailed there by a professional horseshoer. The bed was covered with an elaborately-pieced quilt which was a family inheritance, and there was a big grandfather's clock in a corner that must at one time have been considerable of a machine. The dial was rigged to register not only the hour of the day, but also the seconds, and there was an outside scale that kept track of even the days of the month and the phases of the moon. There was also a charge of mysterious liquid in a glass tube attached to the case, and it was supposed to cloud up ahead of any important change in the weather, and there was a set of directions lettered alongside so a man could read off exactly what kind of change it presaged. The liquid had turned sulky from overwork or lack of appreciation or something, though, and it was stalled on "Violent Storms." Old Simmons said it had stayed there without budging for fifteen years, and that it was a blamed sensible thing to do, because, instead of working itself limp trying to keep up with the weather, it simply got a long way ahead and waited for the weather to catch up.

The timekeeping department of the thing was badly used up. The second hand was gone, the minute hand was bent so it pointed out accusingly into the room instead of at figures as it should, and one of the weights was missing. Simmons had taken it to kill a skunk, and it had got lost before the smell wore off so it could be brought back. So the clock didn't run. But it was handy to hang things from and lean things against, and old Simmons couldn't have kept house without it. His father had freighted it all the way across the plains in the early days, and any clock that had been that much trouble to import was too good to throw away. It did give a comfortable feeling to the homestead cabin, the light from the stove shining against it in the half-dark that represented warmth because the dawn in the snow outside was so eye-hurtingly dazzling and white.

Simmons had planted fruit-trees and berry-bushes in the yard outside his door. They weren't of any particular use to him, but he kept them because he had always been accustomed to seeing such things around places where people lived. Some of his nursery experiments actually were doing well. A couple of rows of currant-bushes had borne so heavily that the birds hadn't managed to strip them in a whole summer of hard work. But old Simmons never picked any of the currants, because they required cooking and canning to be any good, and he had no time to fool away on such squaw's business. He had also set out a patch of strawberries, and, now that the frost had killed the weeds in it, you could see the red leaves shining under the snow as clear and pretty as flowers; and he had several runty peach- and apple-trees which he had installed before discovering that the season at that altitude was too short for them to mature their fruit. Closest to the door, within easy reach in case of unexpected illness, was a chittim-tree, the bark of which, boiled in a tea, was a reliable and violent purgative if the patient was man enough to get it down.

There were certain rules for barking a chittim-tree for physic, and a good deal of hard luck was apt to hit the constipated sufferer who guzzled a dose that hadn't been peeled carefully from up to down. If stripped on the bias, or round and round, the bark would take one's innards in that direction too, and grind the patient back and forth and sideways like gravel in a stamp-mill without ever turning anything loose. If peeled up, it was liable to fetch his entire system up, like turning a sock wrong side out, and there was a story to the effect that somebody in the country had once actually hauled his own toe nails plumb up into his ankles trying to heave up a slug of chittim that had been peeled the wrong way of the limb. Chittim-trees grew wild on that slope of the mountains, and Simmons made a considerable chunk of extra money every year by peeling the wild bark to ship to patent-medicine manufacturers in the East. Sometimes they didn't pay him much for it, and then he evened up, not by sulking and refusing to deal with them any more, but by selling them a shipment of bark that had been peeled round and sideways and hind side to. The thought of the patent-medicine factory being jumped by indignant customers who had heaved up the insoles of their boots getting rid of the medicine, and by others who hadn't been able to get rid of it at all, gave Simmons more genuine entertainment than he could have bought himself by getting a decent price for his chittim bark.

The entertainment, of course, was purely a matter of guess-work and imagination. Simmons had no way of knowing whether his mispeeled laxative had worked on patent-medicine users as awfully as it was legendarily supposed to. His snickering himself through a whole winter with so little actual information to go on showed how easy he was to entertain. Even his own conversation was enough to hold him spellbound, and he could take the measliest little episode that had happened to him and string it out and wool it around and supple it and driddle it along for hours as joyful and preoccupied as an old squaw tanning a stolen buckskin. He couldn't simply state what had happened to him, exhibit the scars to prove it, and then start talking about something else. He had to start with the way the weather had looked when he woke up and what he had thought about it, what fuel he had started the fire with, which sock he had put on first, what he had had for breakfast and how it tasted, whether he had left his team in the barn or turned them out to pasture, and the most infernal rigmarole of particulars that had no purpose whatever except to keep Clay and the Indian boy from squabbling about whether they were going over the mountains together, separately, or at all. The most they could do, while old Simmons cooked breakfast and talked, was to make faces at one another across the table.

They did so, and old Simmons set instalments of victuals in front of them and told a story that began with his getting his boots wet so he had to grease them with tallow before he could put them on, and how on that identical day he had trapped a red-fox pelt worth every nickel of eighty-five dollars. It wasn't very easy on the ears, but breakfast made up for it. There were fried bacon and onions and potatoes, sliced venison-liver and big saddle-blanket pancakes with sugar syrup, country sausage and brown flour-gravy and eggs fried with their eyes open, and a plate of fried headcheese because old Simmons had recently killed his hog. There was also coffee. He didn't fry that, but boiled it in a tin bucket with a rag in it. When the rag rose and floated, the coffee was strong enough to drink, and Simmons, cantering along with his story, set it on the table.

According to the story, he had set his trap out on the sidehill in the middle of a line of tracks which he thought belonged to a coyote. He had been delayed visiting it by the arrival of a horse-trader's outfit heading across the mountains with a big string of medium-grade saddle stock and a couple of women. While the women got down to use old Simmons' backhouse, Simmons undertook to persuade the man not to risk taking them on over the mountains in such weather. Simmons said that God and he had argued high and low with him, but the horse-trader was a stubborn kind of character, soured on the country and suspicious of any advice he got in it, so Christ, he stuck to his notion of going on, and God and old Simmons couldn't budge his determination a single peg. The women came out and backed him up, so Christ and they all got in and went on, and God and old Simmons remembered that he had intended to chase up and look at that damned trap. Well, and then——

"It was yesterday they come past here?" Clay inquired. "They didn't mention whether there was any news from down in the valley, did they?"

Simmons said that God and he had asked them what was going on down below, but to save his gizzard he couldn't recollect whether they had told him anything special or not. His own thoughts and concerns had grown on him with isolation until he couldn't take enough interest in outside events to remember whether there had been any. The one thing he felt sure of was that they hadn't told him anything out of the ordinary run. "Well, God and I moseyed along up to the trap, not expectin' to see anything except a blamed chicken-stealin' coyote, and Christ and this fox was nabbed right down into it. And me without anything to shoot him with, and I didn't dast leave for fear he'd chaw his foot off and slope on me. Well, God and I picked up a club and peeled him one over the head, and Christ, he squalled bloody murder and halfway made to pull loose, and God and I edged around to git him by the tail. . . ."

He laid the frying-pan down in the middle of the floor and stalked it dramatically to show how he had edged around the fox. Then he got down on his hands and knees and showed how the fox had glowered up at him. To complete the performance, he picked up the frying-pan and whacked himself across the head with it and keeled over with his eyes walled up and a big black patch of soot on his bald spot where the frying-pan had landed. It was spiritedly rendered. The Indian boy remarked that a fox dying usually kicked his legs, so Simmons lay down again and kicked his. Then he got up, put more wood in the stove, and set a tin cup full of melted bacon grease on the table to serve as butter. "Set up to her, boys," he invited. "Well, when I see that fox was dead, I got out my knife and opened the little blade and set down to pelt him out. So God and I ——"

"Them horse-traders didn't mention anything about Wade Shiveley, did they?" Clay asked. He did his best to sound offhanded, but he might as well have saved himself the trouble. Simmons never noticed overtones in anybody's conversation except his own, and not any hell of a lot in that. He said he hadn't heard a word about Wade Shiveley since Adam was a cowboy, and what was the newest cussedness he had been up to?

"They put him in jail," Clay said, cautiously. "But he busted out on 'em, so now he's loose again." The statement sounded flat and scrawny, cut so close to the bone. He felt slightly disappointed to realize that what had cost him so much strain and so many tall emotions to live through could be put into words so simply and with so low an emotional content. There wasn't enough in it to get old Simmons interested, and he didn't care enough about it to feel disappointed. So he said uhuh and tied into his breakfast, combining it with a long story about how he had figured on having honey for his pancakes from a swarm of wild bees he had caught, only a damned thieving bear had sneaked in and raided the stand the night before he was ready to rob it. It was even longer-winded than his stories usually were, because the only real action came off right at the start, and the rest was a painstaking catalogue of the things he had done about it, the upshot of the whole business being that he hadn't managed to do anything. He shot at the bear in the dark, and when daylight came he found blood on the ground, so he feathered up and trailed it across the mountains onto the headwaters of Wokus Creek.

There the trail petered out, and from then on the story went sort of wallowing along without being about much of anything.

One thing kept it mildly entertaining. It was nothing to listen to, but it was rather worth watching because old Simmons could eat and talk at the same time. Most of the settlers who had slung down to live in the Cascade Mountain passes into eastern Oregon could do that, and most of them did as often as they could get hold of anybody to listen to them. One thing that had kept those mountain people from developing any sort of community life, probably, was the fear that they would all talk one another to death the first time they got together. Loneliness is supposed to make people reserved and taciturn, but it didn't work that way with them, except when they happened to be of Scandinavian stock and therefore unable to think up anything to say. What solitude had lost them was the habit, not of talking, but of listening. They did so little listening themselves that they actually didn't realize what kind of a job it was, and so it never struck them that their seven-year-itch style of bush-beating narrative was any less fun to hear than it was to perform.

It was no use undertaking to explain to them about it, either. Either they refused to believe it or else they got mad about it; and in either case they went right on talking. Old Joel Farlow, who trapped cougar at the Dog River Meadows, had actually brought permanent scandal on his family name by refusing to let his daughter's marriage ceremony proceed until he had told all his life experiences to a bashful young preacher whom he had imported from the lower valley on a rush call to take charge of the splicing. He forgot all about the emergency under the witchery of being able to tell about himself, and he took up close to two days doing it, with the bride fidgeting herself into a sick spell, the groom being detained under guard in the smoke-house till they were ready for him, and the young preacher twisting and trying to get started on the wedding and being yanked back into his chair by the necktie as often as he got up to find his Bible and call the witnesses. Before it was over, the guards had got tired and left, the groom had escaped through a hole in the smoke-house roof, and the bride had taken to her bed and given birth to a prosperous infant that, according to the squaw who attended as midwife, didn't look like the vanished groom at all, so there was no chance of ever shotgunning him into acknowledging it. And besides old Farlow, there was also Mrs. Yarbro, who raised bees in the fireweed slashings on Upper Thief Creek. She was so enslaved to the practice of unbosoming herself before strangers that she deliberately worked into a lawsuit regularly every year so she could explain to the jury, from the witness-stand, what a hard life she led, and how worthless her last four husbands had been, and how much trouble her children had given her to raise, and how her roof leaked and her cow had run off with a stray bull and her bees swarmed when they weren't supposed to and stung her when she went after them, and how her female disorders (which she described in minute detail) gave her hell all the time and no doctor in the country had been able to do them a lick of good.

Sometimes Mrs. Yarbro's lawsuit would come off before a strange judge who would undertake to make her confine her testimony to the lawsuit instead of rambling along about which intimate organs were almost killing her. But no judge ever tried that more than once. It merely made her get mad and yell, and when that was over she would be unable to recollect where she had left off, so she would have to back up and start her story all over again from the beginning. The only way Mrs. Yarbro could tell anything was to start from raw and tell everything, like a school-kid who has learned the multiplication table but can only tell what nine times eight is by starting at nine times one and singsonging his way up to it.

It would have been unreasonable, of course, to blame the mountain air or water or scenery for the talkativeness of Mrs. Yarbro and old Farlow and Flem Simmons. But there did seem to be something about the section that drew long-winded people to it, because, out of the fifty-odd lone trappers and hand-loggers and wild-cattle-skinners scattered along that slope of the divide there was not one who couldn't talk the hind leg off a mule with ease, fluency, and relish. In one sense it was a good thing, because it made them better able to stand the only kind of life they were fit for. But there was something out of gear about a life that people could stand up to only by becoming a set of windies. It wasn't the right way to be, even if they did like it and even if it did keep old Simmons from taking any interest in news from the lower country and from being suspicious about Clay and the Indian boy and the circumstances under which he had found them.

MARK TWAIN

The Celebrated Jumping Frog
of Calaveras County

IN COMPLIANCE with the request of a friend of mine, who wrote me
from the East, I called on good-natured, garrulous old Simon
Wheeler, and inquired after my friend's friend, Leonidas W. Smiley,
as requested to do, and I hereunto append the result. I have a lurking suspicion that *Leonidas W.* Smiley is a myth; that my friend
never knew such a personage; and that he only conjectured that if I
asked old Wheeler about him, it would remind him of his infamous
Jim Smiley, and he would go to work and bore me to death with
some exasperating reminiscence of him as long and as tedious as it
should be useless to me. If that was the design, it succeeded.

I found Simon Wheeler dozing comfortably by the barroom stove
of the dilapidated tavern in the decayed mining camp of Angel's,
and I noticed that he was fat and bald-headed, and had an expression of winning gentleness and simplicity upon his tranquil countenance. He roused up, and gave me good-day. I told him a friend of
mine had commissioned me to make some inquiries about a cher-
ished companion of his boyhood named *Leonidas W.* Smiley—*Rev.
Leonidas W.* Smiley, a young minister of the Gospel, who he had
heard was at one time a resident of Angel's Camp. I added that if
Mr. Wheeler could tell me anything about this Rev. Leonidas W.
Smiley, I would feel under many obligations to him.

Simon Wheeler backed me into a corner and blockaded me there
with his chair, and then sat down and reeled off the monotonous
narrative which follows this paragraph. He never smiled, he never
frowned, he never changed his voice from the gentle-flowing key to
which he tuned his initial sentence, he never betrayed the slightest
suspicion of enthusiasm; but all through the interminable narrative
there ran a vein of impressive earnestness and sincerity, which
showed me plainly that, so far from his imagining that there was
anything ridiculous or funny about his story, he regarded it as a
really important matter, and admired its two heroes as men of tran-

scendent genius in *finesse*. I let him go on in his own way, and never interrupted him once.

"Rev. Leonidas W. H'm, Reverend Le—well, there was a feller here once by the name of *Jim* Smiley, in the winter of '49—or may be it was the spring of '50—I don't recollect exactly, somehow, though what makes me think it was one or the other is because I remember the big flume warn't finished when he first come to the camp; but any way, he was the curiosest man about always betting on anything that turned up you ever see, if he could get anybody to bet on the other side; and if he couldn't he'd change sides. Any way that suited the other man would suit *him*—any way just so's he got a bet, *he* was satisfied. But still he was lucky, uncommon lucky; he most always come out winner. He was always ready and laying for a chance; there couldn't be no solit'ry thing mentioned but that feller'd offer to bet on it, and take ary side you please, as I was just telling you. If there was a horse-race, you'd find him flush or you'd find him busted at the end of it; if there was a dog-fight, he'd bet on it; if there was a cat-fight, he'd bet on it; if there was a chicken-fight, he'd bet on it; why, if there was two birds setting on a fence, he would bet you which one would fly first; or if there was a camp-meeting, he would be there reg'lar to bet on Parson Walker, which he judged to be the best exhorter about here, and so he was too, and a good man. If he even see a straddle-bug start to go anywheres, he would bet you how long it would take him to get to—to wherever he was going to, and if you took him up, he would foller that straddle-bug to Mexico but what he would find out where he was bound for and how long he was on the road. Lots of the boys here has seen that Smiley, and can tell you about him. Why, it never made no difference to *him*—he'd bet on *any* thing—the dangdest feller. Parson Walker's wife laid very sick once, for a good while, and it seemed as if they warn't going to save her; but one morning he come in, and Smiley up and asked him how she was, and he said she was considable better—thank the Lord for his inf'nite mercy—and coming on so smart that with the blessing of Prov'dence she'd get well yet; and Smiley, before he thought, says, "Well, I'll resk two-and-a-half she don't anyway."

Thish-yer Smiley had a mare—the boys called her the fifteen-minute nag, but that was only in fun, you know, because of course she was faster than that—and he used to win money on that horse, for all she was so slow and always had the asthma, or the distemper, or the consumption, or something of that kind. They used to give her two or three hundred yards start, and then pass her under way; but always at the fag end of the race she'd get excited and desperate like, and come cavorting and straddling up, and scattering her legs around limber, sometimes in the air, and sometimes out to one side among the fences, and kicking up m-o-r-e dust and raising m-o-r-e racket with her coughing and sneezing and blowing her nose—and *always* fetch up at the stand just about a neck ahead, as near as you could cipher it down.

And he had a little small bull-pup, that to look at him you'd think he warn't worth a cent but to set around and look ornery and lay for a chance to steal something. But as soon as money was up on him he was a different dog; his under-jaw'd begin to stick out like the fo'castle of a steamboat, and his teeth would uncover and shine like the furnaces. And a dog might tackle him and bully-rag him, and bite him, and throw him over his shoulder two or three times, and Andrew Jackson—which was the name of the pup—Andrew Jackson would never let on but what *he* was satisfied, and hadn't expected nothing else—and the bets being doubled and doubled on the other side all the time, till the money was all up; and then all of a sudden he would grab that other dog jest by the j'int of his hind leg and freeze to it—not chaw, you understand, but only just grip and hang on till they throwed up the sponge, if it was a year. Smiley always come out winner on that pup, till he harnessed a dog once that didn't have no hind legs, because they'd been sawed off in a circular saw, and when the thing had gone along far enough, and the money was all up, and he come to make a snatch for his pet holt, he see in a minute how he'd been imposed on, and how the other dog had him in the door, so to speak, and he 'peared surprised, and then he looked sorter discouraged-like, and didn't try no more to win the fight, and so he got shucked out bad. He give Smiley a look, as much as to say his heart was broke, and it was *his* fault, for putting up a dog that hadn't no hind legs for him to take holt of, which was his main dependence in a fight, and then he limped off a piece and laid down and died. It was a good pup, was that Andrew Jackson, and would have made a name for hisself if he'd lived, for the stuff was in him and he had genius—I know it, because he hadn't no opportunities to speak of, and it don't stand to reason that a dog could make such a fight as he could under them circumstances if he hadn't no talent. It always makes me feel sorry when I think of that last fight of his'n, and the way it turned out.

Well, thish-yer Smiley had rat-tarriers, and chicken cocks, and tomcats and all them kind of things, till you couldn't rest, and you couldn't fetch nothing for him to bet on but he'd match you. He ketched a frog one day, and took him home, and said he cal'lated to educate him; and so he never done nothing for three months but set in his back yard and learn that frog to jump. And you bet you he *did* learn him, too. He'd give him a little punch behind, and the next minute you'd see that frog whirling in the air like a doughnut —see him turn one summerset, or may be a couple, if he got a good start, and come down flat-footed and all right, like a cat. He got him up so in the matter of ketching flies, and kep' him in practice so constant, that he'd nail a fly every time as fur as he could see him. Smiley said all a frog wanted was education, and he could do 'most anything—and I believe him. Why, I've seen him set Dan'l Webster down here on this floor—Dan'l Webster was the name of the frog— and sing out, "Flies, Dan'l, flies!" and quicker'n you could wink he'd spring straight up and snake a fly off'n the counter there, and flop down on the floor ag'in as solid as a gob of mud, and fall to scratching the side of his head with his hind foot as indifferent as if he hadn't no idea he'd been doin' any more'n any frog might do. You never see a frog so modest and straightfor'ard as he was, for all he was so gifted. And when it come to fair and square jumping on a dead level, he could get over more ground at one straddle than any animal of his breed you ever see. Jumping on a dead level was his strong suit, you understand; and when it come to that, Smiley would ante up money on him as long as he had a red. Smiley was monstrous proud of his frog, and well he might be, for fellers that had traveled and been everywheres all said he laid over any frog that ever *they* see.

Well, Smiley kep' the beast in a little lattice box, and he used to fetch him down town sometimes and lay for a bet. One day a feller —a stranger in the camp, he was—come acrost him with his box, and says:

"What might it be that you've got in the box?"

And Smiley says, sorter indifferent-like, "It might be a parrot, or it might be a canary, maybe, but it ain't—its only just a frog."

And the feller took it, and looked at it careful, and turned it round this way and that, and says, "H'm—so 'tis. Well, what's *he* good for?"

"Well," Smiley says, easy and careless, "he's good enough for *one* thing, I should judge—he can outjump any frog in Calaveras county."

The feller took the box again, and took another long, particular look, and give it back to Smiley, and says, very deliberate, "Well," he says, "I don't see no p'ints about that frog that's any better'n any other frog."

"Maybe you don't," Smiley says. "Maybe you understand frogs and maybe you don't understand 'em; maybe you've had experience, and maybe you ain't only a amature, as it were. Anyways, I've got *my* opinion, and I'll resk forty dollars that he can outjump any frog in Calaveras county."

And the feller studied a minute, and then says, kinder sad like, "Well, I'm only a stranger here, and I ain't got no frog; but if I had a frog, I'd bet you."

And then Smiley says, "That's all right—that's all right—if you'll hold my box a minute, I'll go and get you a frog." And so the feller took the box, and put up his forty dollars along with Smiley's, and set down to wait.

So he set there a good while thinking and thinking to hisself, and then he got the frog out and prized his mouth open and took a tea-spoon and filled him full of quail shot—filled him pretty near up to his chin—and set him on the floor. Smiley he went to the swamp and slopped around in the mud for a long time, and finally he ketched a frog, and fetched him in, and give him to this feller, and says:

"Now, if you're ready, set him alongside of Dan'l, with his fore-paws just even with Dan'l's, and I'll give the word." Then he says, "One—two—three—*git!*" and him and the feller touched up the frogs from behind, and the new frog hopped off lively, but Dan'l give a heave, and hysted up his shoulders—so—like a Frenchman, but it warn't no use—he couldn't budge; he was planted as solid as a church, and he couldn't no more stir than if he was anchored out. Smiley was a good deal surprised, and he was disgusted too, but he didn't have no idea what the matter was, of course.

The feller took the money and started away; and when he was going out at the door, he sorter jerked his thumb over his shoulder —so—at Dan'l, and says again, very deliberate, "Well," he says, "*I* don't see no p'ints about that frog that's any better'n any other frog."

Smiley he stood scratching his head and looking down at Dan'l a long time, and at last he says, "I do wonder what in the nation that frog throw'd off for—I wonder if there ain't something the matter with him—he 'pears to look mighty baggy, somehow." And he ketched Dan'l by the nap of the neck, and hefted him, and says, "Why blame my cats if he don't weigh five pound!" and turned him upside down and he belched out a double handful of shot. And then he see how it was, and he was the maddest man—he set the frog down and took out after that feller, but he never ketched him. And ——"

[Here Simon Wheeler heard his name called from the front yard, and got up to see what was wanted.] And turning to me as he moved away, he said: "Just set where you are, stranger, and rest easy —I ain't going to be gone a second."

But, by your leave, I did not think that a continuation of the history of the enterprising vagabond *Jim* Smiley would be likely to afford me much information concerning the Rev. *Leonidas W.* Smiley, and so I started away.

At the door I met the sociable Wheeler returning, and he button-
holed me and re-commenced:

"Well, thish-yer Smiley had a yaller one-eyed cow that didn't have
no tail, only just a short stump like a bannanner, and——"

However, lacking both time and inclination, I did not wait to
hear about the afflicted cow, but took my leave.

BRET HARTE

The Outcasts of Poker Flat

As MR. JOHN OAKHURST, gambler, stepped into the main street of Poker Flat on the morning of the 23d of November, 1850, he was conscious of a change in its moral atmosphere since the preceding night. Two or three men, conversing earnestly together, ceased as he approached, and exchanged significant glances. There was a Sabbath lull in the air, which, in a settlement unused to Sabbath influences, looked ominous.

Mr. Oakhurst's calm, handsome face betrayed small concern in these indications. Whether he was conscious of any predisposing cause was another question. "I reckon they're after somebody," he reflected; "likely it's me." He returned to his pocket the handkerchief with which he had been whipping away the red dust of Poker Flat from his neat boots, and quietly discharged his mind of any further conjecture.

In point of fact, Poker Flat was "after somebody." It had lately suffered the loss of several thousand dollars, two valuable horses, and a prominent citizen. It was experiencing a spasm of virtuous reaction, quite as lawless and ungovernable as any of the acts that had provoked it. A secret committee had determined to rid the town of all improper persons. This was done permanently in regard of two men who were then hanging from the boughs of a sycamore in the gulch, and temporarily in the banishment of certain other objectionable characters. I regret to say that some of these were ladies. It is but due to the sex, however, to state that their impropriety was professional, and it was only in such easily established standards of evil that Poker Flat ventured to sit in judgment.

Mr. Oakhurst was right in supposing that he was included in this category. A few of the committee had urged hanging him as a possible example and a sure method of reimbursing themselves from his pockets of the sums he had won from them. "It's agin justice," said Jim Wheeler, "to let this yer young man from Roaring Camp—an entire stranger—carry away our money." But a crude sentiment of equity residing in the breasts of those who had been fortunate enough to win from Mr. Oakhurst overruled this narrower local prejudice.

Mr. Oakhurst received his sentence with philosophic calmness, none the less coolly that he was aware of the hesitation of his judges. He was too much of a gambler not to accept fate. With him life was at best an uncertain game, and he recognized the usual percentage in favor of the dealer.

A body of armed men accompanied the deported wickedness of Poker Flat to the outskirts of the settlement. Besides Mr. Oakhurst, who was known to be a coolly desperate man, and for whose intimidation the armed escort was intended, the expatriated party consisted of a young woman familiarly known as "The Duchess;" another who had won the title of "Mother Shipton;" and "Uncle Billy," a suspected sluice-robber and confirmed drunkard. The cavalcade provoked no comments from the spectators, nor was any word uttered by the escort. Only when the gulch which marked the uttermost limit of Poker Flat was reached, the leader spoke briefly and to the point. The exiles were forbidden to return at the peril of their lives.

As the escort disappeared, their pent-up feelings found vent in a few hysterical tears from the Duchess, some bad language from Mother Shipton, and a Parthian volley of expletives from Uncle Billy. The philosophic Oakhurst alone remained silent. He listened calmly to Mother Shipton's desire to cut somebody's heart out, to the repeated statements of the Duchess that she would die in the road, and to the alarming oaths that seemed to be bumped out of Uncle Billy as he rode forward. With the easy good humor characteristic of his class, he insisted upon exchanging his own riding-horse, "Five-Spot," for the sorry mule which the Duchess rode. But even this act did not draw the party into any closer sympathy. The young woman readjusted her somewhat draggled plumes with a feeble, faded coquetry; Mother Shipton eyed the possessor of "Five-Spot" with malevolence, and Uncle Billy included the whole party in one sweeping anathema.

The road to Sandy Bar—a camp that, not having as yet experienced the regenerating influences of Poker Flat, consequently seemed to offer some invitation to the emigrants—lay over a steep mountain range. It was distant a day's severe travel. In that advanced season the party soon passed out of the moist, temperate regions of the foothills into the dry, cold, bracing air of the Sierras. The trail was narrow and difficult. At noon the Duchess, rolling out of her saddle upon the ground, declared her intention of going no farther, and the party halted.

The spot was singularly wild and impressive. A wooded amphitheatre, surrounded on three sides by precipitous cliffs of naked granite, sloped gently toward the crest of another precipice that overlooked the valley. It was, undoubtedly, the most suitable spot for a camp, had camping been advisable. But Mr. Oakhurst knew that scarcely half the journey to Sandy Bar was accomplished, and the party were not equipped or provisioned for delay. This fact he pointed out to his companions curtly, with a philosophic commentary on the folly of "throwing up their hand before the game was played out." But they were furnished with liquor, which in this emergency stood them in place of food, fuel, rest, and prescience. In spite of his remonstrances, it was not long before they were more or less under its influence. Uncle Billy passed rapidly from a bellicose state into one of stupor, the Duchess became maudlin, and Mother Shipton snored. Mr. Oakhurst alone remained erect, leaning against a rock, calmly surveying them.

Mr. Oakhurst did not drink. It interfered with a profession which required coolness, impassiveness, and presence of mind, and, in his own language, he "couldn't afford it." As he gazed at his recumbent fellow exiles, the loneliness begotten of his pariah trade, his habits of life, his very vices, for the first time seriously oppressed him. He bestirred himself in dusting his black clothes, washing his hands and face, and other acts characteristic of his studiously neat habits, and for a moment forgot his annoyance. The thought of deserting his weaker and more pitiable companions never perhaps occurred to him. Yet he could not help feeling the want of that excitement which, singularly enough, was most conducive to that calm equanimity for which he was notorious. He looked at the gloomy walls that rose a thousand feet sheer above the circling pines around him, at the sky ominously clouded, at the valley below, already deepening into shadow; and, doing so, suddenly he heard his own name called.

A horseman slowly ascended the trail. In the fresh, open face of the newcomer Mr. Oakhurst recognized Tom Simson, otherwise known as "The Innocent," of Sandy Bar. He had met him some months before over a "little game," and had, with perfect equanimity, won the entire fortune—amounting to some forty dollars—of that guileless youth. After the game was finished, Mr. Oakhurst drew the youthful speculator behind the door and thus addressed him: "Tommy, you're a good little man, but you can't gamble worth a cent. Don't try it over again." He then handed him his money back, pushed him gently from the room, and so made a devoted slave of Tom Simson.

There was a remembrance of this in his boyish and enthusiastic greeting of Mr. Oakhurst. He had started, he said, to go to Poker

Flat to seek his fortune. "Alone?" No, not exactly alone; in fact (a giggle), he had run away with Piney Woods. Didn't Mr. Oakhurst remember Piney? She that used to wait on the table at the Temperance House? They had been engaged a long time, but old Jake Woods had objected, and so they had run away, and were going to Poker Flat to be married, and here they were. And they were tired out, and how lucky it was they had found a place to camp, and company. All this the Innocent delivered rapidly, while Piney, a stout, comely damsel of fifteen, emerged from behind the pine-tree, where she had been blushing unseen, and rode to the side of her lover.

Mr. Oakhurst seldom troubled himself with sentiment, still less with propriety; but he had a vague idea that the situation was not fortunate. He retained, however, his presence of mind sufficiently to kick Uncle Billy, who was about to say something, and Uncle Billy was sober enough to recognize in Mr. Oakhurst's kick a superior power that would not bear trifling. He then endeavored to dissuade Tom Simson from delaying further, but in vain. He even pointed out the fact that there was no provision, nor means of making a camp. But, unluckily, the Innocent met this objection by assuring the party that he was provided with an extra mule loaded with provisions, and by the discovery of a rude attempt at a log house near the trail. "Piney can stay with Mrs. Oakhurst," said the Innocent, pointing to the Duchess, "and I can shift for myself."

Nothing but Mr. Oakhurst's admonishing foot saved Uncle Billy from bursting into a roar of laughter. As it was, he felt compelled to retire up the cañon until he could recover his gravity. There he confided the joke to the tall pine-trees, with many slaps of his leg, contortions of his face, and the usual profanity. But when he returned to the party, he found them seated by a fire—for the air had grown strangely chill and the sky overcast—in apparently amicable conversation. Piney was actually talking in an impulsive girlish fashion to the Duchess, who was listening with an interest and animation she had not shown for many days. The Innocent was holding forth, apparently with equal effect, to Mr. Oakhurst and Mother Shipton, who was actually relaxing into amiability. "Is this yer a d—d picnic?" said Uncle Billy, with inward scorn, as he surveyed the sylvan group, the glancing firelight, and the tethered animals in the foreground. Suddenly an idea mingled with the alcoholic fumes that disturbed his brain. It was apparently of a jocular nature, for he felt impelled to slap his leg again and cram his fist into his mouth.

As the shadows crept slowly up the mountain, a slight breeze rocked the tops of the pine-trees and moaned through their long and gloomy aisles. The ruined cabin, patched and covered with pine boughs, was set apart for the ladies. As the lovers parted, they unaffectedly exchanged a kiss, so honest and sincere that it might have been heard above the swaying pines. The frail Duchess and the malevolent Mother Shipton were probably too stunned to remark upon this last evidence of simplicity, and so turned without a word to the hut. The fire was replenished, the men lay down before the door, and in a few minutes were asleep.

Mr. Oakhurst was a light sleeper. Toward morning he awoke benumbed and cold. As he stirred the dying fire, the wind, which was now blowing strongly, brought to his cheek that which caused the blood to leave it,—snow!

He started to his feet with the intention of awakening the sleepers, for there was no time to lose. But turning to where Uncle Billy had been lying, he found him gone. A suspicion leaped to his brain, and a curse to his lips. He ran to the spot where the mules had been tethered—they were no longer there. The tracks were already rapidly disappearing in the snow.

The momentary excitement brought Mr. Oakhurst back to the fire with his usual calm. He did not waken the sleepers. The Innocent slumbered peacefully, with a smile on his good-humored, freckled face; the virgin Piney slept beside her frailer sisters as sweetly as though attended by celestial guardians; and Mr. Oakhurst, drawing his blanket over his shoulders, stroked his mustaches and waited for the dawn. It came slowly in a whirling mist of snowflakes that dazzled and confused the eye. What could be seen of the landscape appeared magically changed. He looked over the valley, and summed up the present and future in two words, "Snowed in!"

A careful inventory of the provisions, which, fortunately for the party, had been stored within the hut, and so escaped the felonious fingers of Uncle Billy, disclosed the fact that with care and prudence they might last ten days longer. "That is," said Mr. Oakhurst *sotto voce* to the Innocent, "if you're willing to board us. If you ain't— and perhaps you'd better not—you can wait till Uncle Billy gets back with provisions." For some occult reason, Mr. Oakhurst could not bring himself to disclose Uncle Billy's rascality, and so offered the hypothesis that he had wandered from the camp and had accidentally stampeded the animals. He dropped a warning to the Duchess and Mother Shipton, who of course knew the facts of their associate's defection. "They'll find out the truth about us *all* when they find out anything," he added significantly, "and there's no good frightening them now."

Tom Simson not only put all his worldly store at the disposal of Mr. Oakhurst, but seemed to enjoy the prospect of their enforced seclusion. "We'll have a good camp for a week, and then the snow'll melt, and we'll all go back together." The cheerful gayety of the young man and Mr. Oakhurst's calm infected the others. The Innocent, with the aid of pine boughs, extemporized a thatch for the

roofless cabin, and the Duchess directed Piney in the rearrangement
of the interior with a taste and tact that opened the blue eyes of
that provincial maiden to their fullest extent. "I reckon now you're
used to fine things at Poker Flat," said Piney. The Duchess turned
away sharply to conceal something that reddened her cheeks
through their professional tint, and Mother Shipton requested
Piney not to "chatter." But when Mr. Oakhurst returned from a
weary search for the trail, he heard the sound of happy laughter
echoed from the rocks. He stopped in some alarm, and his thoughts
first naturally reverted to the whiskey, which he had prudently
cachéd. "And yet it don't somehow sound like whiskey," said the
gambler. It was not until he caught sight of the blazing fire through
the still blinding storm, and the group around it, that he settled to
the conviction that it was "square fun."

Whether Mr. Oakhurst had cachéd his cards with the whiskey as
something debarred the free access of the community, I cannot say.
It was certain that, in Mother Shipton's words, he "didn't say 'cards'
once" during that evening. Haply the time was beguiled by an accordion, produced somewhat ostentatiously by Tom Simson from
his pack. Notwithstanding some difficulties attending the manipulation of this instrument, Piney Woods managed to pluck several reluctant melodies from its keys, to an accompaniment by the Innocent on a pair of bone castanets. But the crowning festivity of the
evening was reached in a rude camp-meeting hymn, which the lovers, joining hands, sang with great earnestness and vociferation. I
fear that a certain defiant tone and Covenanter's swing to its chorus,
rather than any devotional quality, caused it speedily to infect the
others, who at last joined in the refrain:—

> "I'm proud to live in the service of the Lord,
> And I'm bound to die in His army."

The pines rocked, the storm eddied and whirled above the miserable group, and the flames of their altar leaped heavenward, as if in
token of the vow.

At midnight the storm abated, the rolling clouds parted, and the
stars glittered keenly above the sleeping camp. Mr. Oakhurst, whose
professional habits had enabled him to live on the smallest possible
amount of sleep, in dividing the watch with Tom Simson somehow
managed to take upon himself the greater part of that duty. He excused himself to the Innocent by saying that he had "often been a
week without sleep." "Doing what?" asked Tom. "Poker!" replied
Oakhurst sententiously. "When a man gets a streak of luck, he don't
get tired. The luck gives in first. Luck," continued the gambler re-
flectively, "is a mighty queer thing. All you know about it for cer-

tain is that it's bound to change. And it's finding out when it's going to change that makes you. We've had a streak of bad luck since we left Poker Flat,—you come along, and slap you get into it, too. If you can hold your cards right along you're all right. For," added the gambler, with cheerful irrelevance—

> " 'I'm proud to live in the service of the Lord,
> And I'm bound to die in His army.' "

The third day came, and the sun, looking through the white-curtained valley, saw the outcasts divide their slowly decreasing store of provisions for the morning meal. It was one of the peculiarities of that mountain climate that its rays diffused a kindly warmth over the wintry landscape, as if in regretful commiseration of the past. But it revealed drift on drift of snow piled high around the hut,—a hopeless, uncharted, trackless sea of white lying below the rocky shores to which the castaways still clung. Through the marvelously clear air the smoke of the pastoral village of Poker Flat rose miles away. Mother Shipton saw it, and from a remote pinnacle of her rocky fastness hurled in that direction a final malediction. It was her last vituperative attempt, and perhaps for that reason was invested with a certain degree of sublimity. It did her good, she privately informed the Duchess. "Just you go out there and cuss, and see." She then set herself to the task of amusing "the child," as she and the Duchess were pleased to call Piney. Piney was no chicken, but it was a soothing and original theory of the pair thus to account for the fact that she didn't swear and wasn't improper.

When night crept up again through the gorges, the reedy notes of the accordion rose and fell in fitful spasms and long-drawn gasps by the flickering campfire. But music failed to fill entirely the aching void left by insufficient food, and a new diversion was proposed by Piney,—storytelling. Neither Mr. Oakhurst nor his female companions caring to relate their personal experiences, this plan would have failed too, but for the Innocent. Some months before he had chanced upon a stray copy of Mr. Pope's ingenious translation of the Iliad. He now proposed to narrate the principal incidents of that poem—having thoroughly mastered the argument and fairly forgotten the words—in the current vernacular of Sandy Bar. And so for the rest of that night the Homeric demigods again walked the earth. Trojan bully and wily Greek wrestled in the winds, and the great pines in the cañon seemed to bow to the wrath of the son of Peleus. Mr. Oakhurst listened with quiet satisfaction. Most especially was he interested in the fate of "Ash-heels," as the Innocent persisted in denominating the "swift-footed Achilles."

So, with small food and much of Homer and the accordion, a

week passed over the heads of the outcasts. The sun again forsook
them, and again from leaden skies the snowflakes were sifted over
the land. Day by day closer around them drew the snowy circle,
until at last they looked from their prison over drifted walls of dazzling white, that towered twenty feet above their heads. It became
more and more difficult to replenish their fires, even from the fallen
trees beside them, now half hidden in the drifts. And yet no one
complained. The lovers turned from the dreary prospect and looked
into each other's eyes, and were happy. Mr. Oakhurst settled himself coolly to the losing game before him. The Duchess, more cheerful than she had been, assumed the care of Piney. Only Mother
Shipton—once the strongest of the party—seemed to sicken and fade.
At midnight on the tenth day she called Oakhurst to her side. "I'm
going," she said, in a voice of querulous weakness, "but don't say
anything about it. Don't waken the kids. Take the bundle from
under my head, and open it." Mr. Oakhurst did so. It contained
Mother Shipton's rations for the last week, untouched. "Give 'em to
the child," she said, pointing to the sleeping Piney. "You've starved
yourself," said the gambler. "That's what they call it," said the
woman querulously, as she lay down again, and, turning her face to
the wall, passed quietly away.

The accordion and the bones were put aside that day, and Homer
was forgotten. When the body of Mother Shipton had been committed to the snow, Mr. Oakhurst took the Innocent aside, and showed
him a pair of snowshoes, which he had fashioned from the old
pack-saddle. "There's one chance in a hundred to save her yet," he
said, pointing to Piney; "but it's there," he added, pointing toward
Poker Flat. "If you can reach there in two days she's safe." "And
you?" asked Tom Simson. "I'll stay here," was the curt reply.

The lovers parted with a long embrace. "You are not going, too?"
said the Duchess, as she saw Mr. Oakhurst apparently waiting to ac-
company him. "As far as the cañon," he replied. He turned suddenly
and kissed the Duchess, leaving her pallid face aflame, and her trembling limbs rigid with amazement.

Night came, but not Mr. Oakhurst. It brought the storm again
and the whirling snow. Then the Duchess, feeding the fire, found
that some one had quietly piled beside the hut enough fuel to last a
few days longer. The tears rose to her eyes, but she hid them from
Piney.

The women slept but little. In the morning, looking into each
other's faces, they read their fate. Neither spoke, but Piney, accepting the position of the stronger, drew near and placed her arm
around the Duchess's waist. They kept this attitude for the rest of
the day. That night the storm reached its greatest fury, and, rending
asunder the protecting vines, invaded the very hut.

Toward morning they found themselves unable to feed the fire, which gradually died away. As the embers slowly blackened, the Duchess crept closer to Piney, and broke the silence of many hours: "Piney, can you pray?" "No, dear," said Piney simply. The Duchess, without knowing exactly why, felt relieved, and, putting her head upon Piney's shoulder, spoke no more. And so reclining, the younger and purer pillowing the head of her soiled sister upon her virgin breast, they fell asleep.

The wind lulled as if it feared to waken them. Feathery drifts of snow, shaken from the long pine boughs, flew like white winged birds, and settled about them as they slept. The moon through the rifted clouds looked down upon what had been the camp. But all human stain, all trace of earthly travail, was hidden beneath the spotless mantle mercifully flung from above.

They slept all that day and the next, nor did they waken when voices and footsteps broke the silence of the camp. And when pitying fingers brushed the snow from their wan faces, you could scarcely have told from the equal peace that dwelt upon them which was she that had sinned. Even the law of Poker Flat recognized this, and turned away, leaving them still locked in each other's arms.

But at the head of the gulch, on one of the largest pine-trees, they found the deuce of clubs pinned to the bark with a bowie-knife. It bore the following, written in pencil in a firm hand:—

†

BENEATH THIS TREE
LIES THE BODY

OF

JOHN OAKHURST,

WHO STRUCK A STREAK OF BAD LUCK
ON THE 23D OF NOVEMBER 1850,

AND

HANDED IN HIS CHECKS
ON THE 7TH DECEMBER, 1850.

✝

And pulseless and cold, with a Derringer by his side and a bullet in his heart, though still calm as in life, beneath the snow lay he who was at once the strongest and yet the weakest of the outcasts of Poker Flat.

FRANK NORRIS

Wheat

UPON DESCENDING from his train at Port Costa, S. Behrman asked to be directed at once to where the barque *Swanhilda* was taking on grain. Though he had bought and greatly enlarged his new elevator at this port, he had never seen it. The work had been carried on through agents, S. Behrman having far too many and more pressing occupations to demand his presence and attention. Now, however, he was to see the concrete evidence of his success for the first time.

He picked his way across the railroad tracks to the line of warehouses that bordered the docks, numbered with enormous Roman numerals and full of grain in bags.

The sight of these bags of grain put him in mind of the fact that among all the other shippers he was practically alone in his way of handling his wheat. They handled the grain in bags; he, however, preferred it in the bulk. Bags were sometimes four cents apiece, and he had decided to build his elevator and bulk his grain therein, rather than to incur this expense. Only a small part of his wheat— that on Number Three division—had been sacked. All the rest, practically two thirds of the entire harvest of Los Muertos, now found itself warehoused in his enormous elevator at Port Costa.

To a certain degree it had been the desire of observing the working of his system of handling the wheat in bulk that had drawn S. Behrman to Port Costa. But the more powerful motive had been curiosity, not to say downright sentiment. So long had he planned for this day of triumph, so eagerly had he looked forward to it, that now, when it had come, he wished to enjoy it to its fullest extent, wished to miss no feature of the disposal of the crop. He had watched it harvested, he had watched it hauled to the railway, and now would watch it as it poured into the hold of the ship, would even watch the ship as she cleared and got under way.

He passed through the warehouses and came out upon the dock

This selection is from *The Octopus*, the first of two novels Norris completed in a projected trilogy about the growing, marketing, and uses of wheat. [Ed. note]

that ran parallel with the shore of the bay. A great quantity of shipping was in view, barques for the most part, Cape Horners, great,
deep-sea tramps, whose iron-shod forefeet had parted every ocean
the world round from Rangoon to Rio Janeiro, and from Melbourne to Christiania. Some were still in the stream, loaded with
wheat to the Plimsoll mark, ready to depart with the next tide. But
many others laid their great flanks alongside the docks and at that
moment were being filled by derrick and crane with thousands upon
thousands of bags of wheat. The scene was brisk; the cranes creaked
and swung incessantly with a rattle of chains; stevedores and wharf-
ingers toiled and perspired; boatswains and dock-masters shouted
orders, drays rumbled, the water lapped at the piles; a group of sailors, painting the flanks of one of the great ships, raised an occasional chanty; the trade wind sang æolian in the cordages, filling the
air with the nimble taint of salt. All around were the noises of ships
and the feel and flavour of the sea.

S. Behrman soon discovered his elevator. It was the largest structure discernible, and upon its red roof, in enormous white letters,
was his own name. Thither, between piles of grain bags, halted
drays, crates, and boxes of merchandise, with an occasional pyramid
of salmon cases, S. Behrman took his way. Cabled to the dock, close
under his elevator, lay a great ship with lofty masts and great spars.
Her stern was toward him as he approached and, upon it, in raised
golden letters, he could read the words "*Swanhilda*—Liverpool."

He went aboard by a very steep gangway and found the mate on
the quarter deck. S. Behrman introduced himself.

"Well," he added, "how are you getting on?"

"Very fairly, sir," returned the mate, who was an Englishman.
"We'll have her all snugged down tight by this time day after to-
morrow. It's a great saving of time shunting the stuff in her like
that, and three men can do the work of seven."

"I'll have a look 'round, I believe," returned S. Behrman.

"Right—oh," answered the mate with a nod.

S. Behrman went forward to the hatch that opened down into the
vast hold of the ship. A great iron chute connected this hatch with
the elevator, and through it was rushing a veritable cataract of
wheat.

It came from some gigantic bin within the elevator itself, rushing
down the confines of the chute to plunge into the roomy, gloomy
interior of the hold with an incessant, metallic roar, persistent,
steady, inevitable. No men were in sight. The place was deserted.
No human agency seemed to be back of the movement of the wheat.
Rather, the grain seemed impelled with a force of its own, a resistless, huge force, eager, vivid, impatient for the sea.

S. Behrman stood watching, his ears deafened with the roar of the hard grains against the metallic lining of the chute. He put his hand once into the rushing tide, and the contact rasped the flesh of his fingers and like an undertow drew his hand after it in its impetuous dash.

Cautiously he peered down into the hold. A musty odour rose to his nostrils, the vigorous, pungent aroma of the raw cereal. It was dark. He could see nothing; but all about and over the opening of the hatch the air was full of a fine, impalpable dust that blinded the eyes and choked the throat and nostrils.

As his eyes became used to the shadows of the cavern below him, he began to distinguish the grey mass of the wheat, a great expanse, almost liquid in its texture, which, as the cataract from above plunged into it, moved and shifted in long, slow eddies. As he stood there, this cataract on a sudden increased in volume. He turned about, casting his eyes upward toward the elevator to discover the cause. His foot caught in a coil of rope, and he fell headforemost into the hold.

The fall was a long one and he struck the surface of the wheat with the sodden impact of a bundle of damp clothes. For the moment he was stunned. All the breath was driven from his body. He could neither move nor cry out. But, by degrees, his wits steadied themselves and his breath returned to him. He looked about and above him. The daylight in the hold was dimmed and clouded by the thick chaff-dust thrown off by the pour of grain, and even this dimness dwindled to twilight at a short distance from the opening of the hatch, while the remotest quarters were lost in impenetrable blackness. He got upon his feet only to find that he sank ankle deep in the loose-packed mass underfoot.

"Hell," he muttered, "here's a fix."

Directly underneath the chute, the wheat, as it poured in, raised itself in a conical mound, but from the sides of this mound it shunted away incessantly in thick layers, flowing in all directions with the nimbleness of water. Even as S. Behrman spoke, a wave of grain poured around his legs and rose rapidly to the level of his knees. He stepped quickly back. To stay near the chute would soon bury him to the waist.

No doubt, there was some other exit from the hold, some companion ladder that led up to the deck. He scuffled and waded across the wheat, groping in the dark with outstretched hands. With every inhalation he choked, filling his mouth and nostrils more with dust than with air. At times he could not breathe at all, but gagged and gasped, his lips distended. But search as he would, he could find no outlet to the hold, no stairway, no companion ladder. Again and again, staggering along in the black darkness, he bruised his knuckles and forehead against the iron sides of the ship. He gave up the attempt to find any interior means of escape and returned laboriously to the space under the open hatchway. Already he could see that the level of the wheat was raised.

"God," he said, "this isn't going to do at all." He uttered a great shout. "Hello, on deck there, somebody! For God's sake."

The steady, metallic roar of the pouring wheat drowned out his voice. He could scarcely hear it himself above the rush of the cataract. Besides this, he found it impossible to stay under the hatch. The flying grains of wheat, spattering as they fell, stung his face like wind-driven particles of ice. It was a veritable torture; his hands smarted with it. Once he was all but blinded. Furthermore, the succeeding waves of wheat, rolling from the mound under the chute, beat him back, swirling and dashing against his legs and knees, mounting swiftly higher, carrying him off his feet.

Once more he retreated, drawing back from beneath the hatch. He stood still for a moment and shouted again. It was in vain. His voice returned upon him, unable to penetrate the thunder of the chute, and horrified, he discovered that so soon as he stood motionless upon the wheat, he sank into it. Before he knew it, he was knee-deep again, and a long swirl of grain sweeping outward from the ever-breaking, ever-reforming pyramid below the chute, poured around his thighs, immobilizing him.

A frenzy of terror suddenly leaped to life within him. The horror of death, the Fear of The Trap, shook him like a dry reed. Shouting, he tore himself free of the wheat and once more scrambled and struggled toward the hatchway. He stumbled as he reached it and fell directly beneath the pour. Like a storm of small shot, mercilessly, pitilessly, the unnumbered multitude of hurtling grains flagellated and beat and tore his flesh. Blood streamed from his forehead and, thickening with the powder-like chaff-dust, blinded his eyes. He struggled to his feet once more. An avalanche from the cone of wheat buried him to his thighs. He was forced back and back and back, beating the air, falling, rising, howling for aid. He could no longer see; his eyes, crammed with dust, smarted as if transfixed with needles whenever he opened them. His mouth was full of the dust, his lips were dry with it; thirst tortured him, while his outcries choked and gagged in his rasped throat.

And all the while without stop, incessantly, inexorably, the wheat, as if moving with a force all its own, shot downward in a prolonged roar, persistent, steady, inevitable.

He retreated to a far corner of the hold and sat down with his back against the iron hull of the ship and tried to collect his thoughts, to calm himself. Surely there must be some way of escape; surely he was not to die like this, die in this dreadful substance that was neither solid nor fluid. What was he to do? How make himself heard?

But even as he thought about this, the cone under the chute broke again and sent a great layer of grain rippling and tumbling toward him. It reached him where he sat and buried his hand and one foot.

He sprang up trembling and made for another corner.

"By God," he cried, "by God, I must think of something pretty quick!"

Once more the level of the wheat rose and the grains began piling deeper about him. Once more he retreated. Once more he crawled staggering to the foot of the cataract, screaming till his ears sang and his eyeballs strained in their sockets, and once more the relentless tide drove him back.

Then began that terrible dance of death; the man dodging, doubling, squirming, hunted from one corner to another, the wheat slowly, inexorably flowing, rising, spreading to every angle, to every nook and cranny. It reached his middle. Furious and with bleeding hands and broken nails, he dug his way out to fall backward, all but exhausted, gasping for breath in the dust-thickened air. Roused again by the slow advance of the tide, he leaped up and stumbled away, blinded with the agony in his eyes, only to crash against the metal hull of the vessel. He turned about, the blood streaming from his face, and paused to collect his senses, and with a rush, another wave swirled about his ankles and knees. Exhaustion grew upon him. To stand still meant to sink; to lie or sit meant to be buried the quicker; and all this in the dark, all this in an air that could scarcely be breathed, all this while he fought an enemy that could not be gripped, toiling in a sea that could not be stayed.

Guided by the sound of the falling wheat, S. Behrman crawled on hands and knees toward the hatchway. Once more he raised his voice in a shout for help. His bleeding throat and raw, parched lips refused to utter but a wheezing moan. Once more he tried to look toward the one patch of faint light above him. His eyelids, clogged with chaff, could no longer open. The Wheat poured about his waist as he raised himself upon his knees.

Reason fled. Deafened with the roar of the grain, blinded and made dumb with its chaff, he threw himself forward with clutching fingers, rolling upon his back, and lay there, moving feebly, the head rolling from side to side. The Wheat, leaping continuously from the chute, poured around him. It filled the pockets of the coat, it crept up the sleeves and trouser legs, it covered the great, protuberant stomach, it ran at last in rivulets into the distended, gasping mouth. It covered the face.

Upon the surface of the Wheat, under the chute, nothing moved but the Wheat itself. There was no sign of life. Then, for an instant, the surface stirred. A hand, fat, with short fingers and swollen veins, reached up, clutching, then fell limp and prone. In another instant it was covered. In the hold of the *Swanhilda* there was no movement but the widening ripples that spread flowing from the ever-breaking, ever-reforming cone; no sound, but the rushing of the Wheat that continued to plunge incessantly from the iron chute in a prolonged roar, persistent, steady, inevitable.

WALT WHITMAN

Facing West from California's Shores

FACING west from California's shores,
Inquiring, tireless, seeking what is yet unfound,
I, a child, very old, over waves, towards the house of maternity, the
    land of migrations, look afar,
Look off the shores of my Western sea, the circle almost circled;
For starting westward from Hindustan, from the vales of Kashmere,
From Asia, from the north, from the God, the sage, and the hero,
From the south, from the flowery peninsulas and the spice islands,
Long having wander'd since, round the earth having wander'd,
Now I face home again, very pleas'd and joyous,
(But where is what I started for so long ago?
And why is it yet unfound?)

7

The Cattleman's Frontier

LONG AFTER the wagon trains had crossed the plains, years after prospectors and miners had penetrated every mountain range except the Black Hills of Dakota, and scarcely months after the surrender at Appomattox, Texas cattlemen began the conquest of the Great American Desert. Driving enormous herds of cattle, some pushed north to Oklahoma, then known as the Indian Territory, and on to central and western Kansas. Others drove west and north into Colorado and Wyoming. Soon they spread the cattle business into Montana and the Dakotas, and the last open land was occupied.

During the thirty years after the Civil War the Indians lost their buffalo, almost all of their choicest territories, and their war with a merciless alien people. Sitting Bull, Crazy Horse, and Geronimo could win battles, but they were outnumbered, outgunned, and overpowered. The Indians who were not exterminated were herded into reservations. Then they were left with only the long, slow holding action of trying to preserve their traditions and cultures, a difficult program that they still continue.

The white–Indian conflict is central in Dorothy Johnson's "Flame on the Frontier." Her heroine, Sarah Harris, is a white girl reared among Indians but recovered by the white community. Knowing and feeling the conflicting values of both cultures, she can be wholly comfortable with neither. She lives out her life in the white community, never forgetting her Indian education.

With Stephen Crane's "The Blue Hotel" a different conflict begins to foreshadow many of the themes and concerns of both the "formula" Western and the best of modern literature. The conflict is typically "Western" in that the moral stance of many of the characters is simple and forthright, susceptible to clear statement and easy understanding. Yet the central action is thoroughly modern in its final ambiguity, its almost existential irony.

In *The Virginian,* Owen Wister introduces the archetypal hero of the cattleman's frontier. As the hero of that book climbs down from a corral gate "with the undulations of a tiger, smooth and easy," he is the glass of fashion and mold of form for Zane Grey's Lassiter, Max Brand's Destry, and even Jack Schaefer's Shane. He has the deceptively simple appearance of nature's gentleman, the noble savage in chaps, though he lives by a code that involves him in conflicts as agonizing as those in Corneille's *Cid* or Dryden's *Conquest of Granada*. He is the progenitor of a unique American genre of popular literature, the forerunner of Bill Boyd and Gary Cooper and John Wayne. The Virginian has achieved immortality himself, appearing in millions of books, a successful play, several motion pictures, and a long-running television series.

With Jack Schaefer's *Shane,* the apotheosis of hero to demigod becomes nearly complete. Now the Western is stripped of its gratuitous local color, its rustic comedy, its barnyard folklore, and its feudal or Populist social criticism—all elements that complicate the texture of *The Virginian*. The hero becomes "a knight without armor in a savage land," riding into a ravaged kingdom and saving its terrorized people. Seen through the eyes of a boy, he is a mythic figure with antecedents in the *Morte D'Arthur* and credentials from Jesse Weston's *From Ritual to Romance*. Seen in thousands of motion picture theatres, he embodies refined simplicities central to America's self-image.

Yet even this god on horseback must age, even as American simplicities are qualified and nearly baffled by increasing complexities of social organization. In *The Tin Star,* a short story made famous because it inspired the motion picture *High Noon,* John Cunningham illustrates the further development of violence and melodrama and its end of innocence—the realization that the old codes, however admirable, can become the basis of tragedy.

Clay Fisher's "The Trap" shows still another characteristic of much Western folklore and fiction, its repeated glorification of the outcast or outlaw. Like Jesse James, Butch Cassidy, or Billy the Kid, the hero of "The Trap" ends up guilty of a crime yet somehow admirable as he fights the world. He also ends up showing Clay Fisher's skill and versatility as an author, one who can take a plot device from Ambrose Bierce and make it unmistakably his own.

And finally, in a short story by Ernest Haycox, one of the greatest of Western story writers, the code of the West is dramatized by understatement. In "A Day in Town," Haycox succeeds in portraying the essential strength of character that makes the Western hero a precious part of America's cultural heritage. Haycox brings his hero back to the realities of life as a mature adult in a cruel environment —back to his burdens and responsibilities as a husband, father, and citizen of a free society.

DOROTHY JOHNSON

The Girl Called Bluejay

SARAH HARRIS, who had been called Bluejay, was hard to tame, they said in the settlement. Her mother fretted over her heathen ways. The girl could not even make bread!

"I can tan hides," Sarah claimed angrily. "I can butcher a buffalo and make pemmican. I can pitch a tepee and pack it on a horse to move."

But those skills were not valued in a white woman, and Sarah found the settlement not quite heaven. She missed the constant talk and laughter of the close-pitched tepees. She had to learn a whole new system of polite behavior. There was dickering and trading and bargaining, instead of a proud exchanging of fine gifts. A neighbor boy slouching on a bench outside the cabin, talking to her stepfather while he got up courage to ask whether Sarah was at home, was less flattering as a suitor than a young warrior, painted and feathered, showing off on a spotted horse. Sometimes Sarah felt that she had left heaven behind her.

But she never went back to it. When she was seventeen, she married the blacksmith, Herman Schwartz, and their first baby was born six months later.

Sarah's oldest child was six and her second child was three when the Indian man appeared at the door of her cabin and stood silently peering in.

"Git out of here!" she cried, seizing the broom.

He answered in the Sioux tongue, "Bluejay has forgotten."

She gave Horse Ears a shrill welcome in his own language and the three-year-old started to cry. She lifted a hand for an accustomed slap but let it fall. Indian mothers did not slap their children.

But she was **not** Indian any more, she recollected. She welcomed Horse Ears in as a white woman does an invited guest. In her Sun-

This selection is only a part of the long story "Flame on the Frontier." [Ed. note]

day-company voice she chattered politely. It was her privilege because she was a white woman. No need any more for the meek silence of the Indian woman.

She brought out bread and butter and ate with him. That was her privilege, too.

"My sister?" she asked.

He had not seen The Foreigner for a long time. He had left that village.

"Does Bluejay's man make much meat?" Horse Ears asked. "Is he a man with many honors in war?"

She laughed shrilly. "He makes much meat. He has counted coup many times. We are rich."

"I came to find out those things," he answered. "In my lodge there is only one woman."

She understood, and her heart leaped with the flattery. He had traveled far, and in some danger, to find out that all was well with her. If it was not, there was refuge in his tepee. And not only now, she realized, but any time, forever.

A shadow fell across the threshold; a hoarse voice filled the room. "What's that bloody Injun doing here?" roared Sarah's husband. "Are you all right?"

"Sure, we're all right," she answered. "I don't know who he is. He was hungry."

His eyes narrowed with anger, "Is he one of them you used to know?"

Her body tensed with fear. "I don't know him, I told you!"

Her husband spoke to the Indian in halting Sioux, but Horse Ears was wise. He did not answer.

"Git out!" the blacksmith ordered, and the Indian obeyed without a word.

As Sarah watched him go down the path, without turning, she wished fervently that she could tell him good-bye, could thank him for coming. But she could not betray him by speaking.

Herman Schwartz strode toward her in silent, awesome, blazing fury. She did not cringe; she braced her body against the table. He gave her a blow across the face that rocked her and blinded her.

She picked up the heavy iron skillet.

"Don't you ever do that again or I'll kill you," she warned.

He glared at her with fierce pride, knowing that she meant what she said.

"I don't reckon I'll have to do it again," he said complacently. "If I ever set eyes on that savage again, I'll kill him. You know that, don't you, you damn squaw?"

She shrugged. "Talk's cheap."

As she went down to the spring for a bucket of water, she was singing.

Her girlhood was gone, and her freedom was far behind her. She had two crying children and was pregnant again. But two men loved her, and both of them had just proved it.

Forty years later, her third child was elected to the state legislature, and she went, a frightened, white-haired widow, to see him there. She was proud, but never so proud as she had been on a summer day three months before he was born.

STEPHEN CRANE

The Blue Hotel

I

THE PALACE HOTEL at Fort Romper was painted a light blue, a shade that is on the legs of a kind of heron, causing the bird to declare its position against any background. The Palace Hotel, then, was always screaming and howling in a way that made the dazzling winter landscape of Nebraska seem only a grey swampish hush. It stood alone on the prairie, and when the snow was falling the town two hundred yards away was not visible. But when the traveller alighted at the railway station he was obliged to pass the Palace Hotel before he could come upon the company of low clapboard houses which composed Fort Romper, and it was not to be thought that any traveller could pass the Palace Hotel without looking at it. Pat Scully, the proprietor, had proved himself a master of strategy when he chose his paints. It is true that on clear days, when the great transcontinental expresses, long lines of swaying Pullmans, swept through Fort Romper, passengers were overcome at the sight, and the cult that knows the brown-reds and the subdivisions of the dark greens of the East expressed shame, pity, horror, in a laugh. But to the citizens of this prairie town and to the people who would naturally stop there, Pat Scully had performed a feat. With this opulence and splendour, these creeds, classes, egotisms, that streamed through Romper on the rails day after day, they had no colour in common.

As if the displayed delights of such a blue hotel were not sufficiently enticing, it was Scully's habit to go every morning and evening to meet the leisurely trains that stopped at Romper and work his seductions upon any man that he might see wavering, gripsack in hand.

One morning, when a snow-crusted engine dragged its long string of freight cars and its one passenger coach to the station, Scully performed the marvel of catching three men. One was a shaky and quick-eyed Swede, with a great shining cheap valise; one was a tall bronzed cowboy, who was on his way to a ranch near the Dakota line; one was a little silent man from the East, who didn't look it, and didn't announce it. Scully practically made them prisoners. He was so nimble and merry and kindly that each probably felt it would be the height of brutality to try to escape. They trudged off over the creaking board sidewalks in the wake of the eager little Irishman. He wore a heavy fur cap squeezed tightly down on his head. It caused his two red ears to stick out stiffly, as if they were made of tin.

At last, Scully, elaborately, with boisterous hospitality, conducted them through the portals of the blue hotel. The room which they entered was small. It seemed to be merely a proper temple for an enormous stove, which, in the centre, was humming with godlike violence. At various points on its surface the iron had become luminous and glowed yellow from the heat. Beside the stove Scully's son Johnnie was playing High-Five with an old farmer who had whiskers both grey and sandy. They were quarrelling. Frequently the old farmer turned his face toward a box of sawdust—coloured brown from tobacco juice—that was behind the stove, and spat with an air of great impatience and irritation. With a loud flourish of words Scully destroyed the game of cards, and bustled his son upstairs with part of the baggage of the new guests. He himself conducted them to three basins of the coldest water in the world. The cowboy and the Easterner burnished themselves fiery red with this water, until it seemed to be some kind of metal-polish. The Swede, however, merely dipped his fingers gingerly and with trepidation. It was notable that throughout this series of small ceremonies the three travellers were made to feel that Scully was very benevolent. He was conferring great favours upon them. He handed the towel from one to another with an air of philanthropic impulse.

Afterward they went to the first room, and, sitting about the stove, listened to Scully's officious clamour at his daughters, who were preparing the midday meal. They reflected in the silence of experienced men who tread carefully amid new people. Nevertheless, the old farmer, stationary, invincible in his chair near the warmest part of the stove, turned his face from the sawdust-box frequently and addressed a glowing commonplace to the strangers. Usually he was answered in short but adequate sentences by either the cowboy or the Easterner. The Swede said nothing. He seemed to be occupied in making furtive estimates of each man in the room. One might have thought that he had the sense of silly suspicion which comes to guilt. He resembled a badly frightened man.

Later, at dinner, he spoke a little, addressing his conversation entirely to Scully. He volunteered that he had come from New York, where for ten years he had worked as a tailor. These facts seemed to strike Scully as fascinating, and afterward he volunteered that he had lived at Romper for fourteen years. The Swede asked about the crops and the price of labour. He seemed barely to listen to Scully's extended replies. His eyes continued to rove from man to man.

Finally, with a laugh and a wink, he said that some of these Western communities were very dangerous; and after his statement he straightened his legs under the table, tilted his head, and laughed again, loudly. It was plain that the demonstration had no meaning to the others. They looked at him wondering and in silence.

II

As the men trooped heavily back into the front room, the two little windows presented views of a turmoiling sea of snow. The huge arms of the wind were making attempts—mighty, circular, futile—to embrace the flakes as they sped. A gate-post like a still man with a blanched face stood aghast amid this profligate fury. In a hearty voice Scully announced the presence of a blizzard. The guests of the blue hotel, lighting their pipes, assented with grunts of lazy masculine contentment. No island of the sea could be exempt in the degree of this little room with its humming stove. Johnnie, son of Scully, in a tone which defined his opinion of his ability as a card-player, challenged the old farmer of both grey and sandy whiskers to a game of High-Five. The farmer agreed with a contemptuous and bitter scoff. They sat close to the stove, and squared their knees under a wide board. The cowboy and the Easterner watched the game with interest. The Swede remained near the window, aloof, but with a countenance that showed signs of an inexplicable excitement.

The play of Johnnie and the grey-beard was suddenly ended by another quarrel. The old man arose while casting a look of heated scorn at his adversary. He slowly buttoned his coat, and then stalked with fabulous dignity from the room. In the discreet silence of all other men the Swede laughed. His laughter rang somehow childish. Men by this time had begun to look at him askance, as if they wished to inquire what ailed him.

A new game was formed jocosely. The cowboy volunteered to become the partner of Johnnie, and they all then turned to ask the Swede to throw in his lot with the little Easterner. He asked some questions about the game, and, learning that it wore many names, and that he had played it when it was under an alias, he accepted the invitation. He strode toward the men nervously, as if he expected to be assaulted. Finally, seated, he gazed from face to face and laughed shrilly. This laugh was so strange that the Easterner looked up quickly, the cowboy sat intent and with his mouth open, and Johnnie paused, holding the cards with still fingers.

Afterward there was a short silence. Then Johnnie said, "Well, let's get at it. Come on now!" They pulled their chairs forward until their knees were bunched under the board. They began to play, and their interest in the game caused the others to forget the manner of the Swede.

The cowboy was a board-whacker. Each time that he held superior cards he whanged them, one by one, with exceeding force, down upon the improvised table, and took the tricks with a glowing air of prowess and pride that sent thrills of indignation into the hearts of his opponents. A game with a board-whacker in it is sure to become intense. The countenances of the Easterner and the Swede were miserable whenever the cowboy thundered down his aces and kings, while Johnnie, his eyes gleaming with joy, chuckled and chuckled.

Because of the absorbing play none considered the strange ways of the Swede. They paid strict heed to the game. Finally, during a lull caused by a new deal, the Swede suddenly addressed Johnnie: "I suppose there have been a good many men killed in this room." The jaws of the others dropped and they looked at him.

"What in hell are you talking about?" said Johnnie.

The Swede laughed again his blatant laugh, full of a kind of false courage and defiance. "Oh, you know what I mean all right," he answered.

"I'm a liar if I do!" Johnnie protested. The card was halted, and the men stared at the Swede. Johnnie evidently felt that as the son of the proprietor he should make a direct inquiry. "Now, what might you be drivin' at, mister?" he asked. The Swede winked at him. It was a wink full of cunning. His fingers shook on the edge of the board. "Oh, maybe you think I have been to nowheres. Maybe you think I'm a tenderfoot?"

"I don't know nothin' about you," answered Johnnie, "and I don't give a damn where you've been. All I got to say is that I don't know what you're driving at. There hain't never been nobody killed in this room."

The cowboy, who had been steadily gazing at the Swede, then spoke: "What's wrong with you, mister?"

Apparently it seemed to the Swede that he was formidably menaced. He shivered and turned white near the corners of his mouth. He sent an appealing glance in the direction of the little Easterner. During these moments he did not forget to wear his air of advanced pot-valour. "They say they don't know what I mean," he remarked mockingly to the Easterner.

The latter answered after prolonged and cautious reflection. "I don't understand you," he said, impassively.

The Swede made a movement then which announced that he thought he had encountered treachery from the only quarter where he had expected sympathy, if not help. "Oh, I see you are all against me. I see——"

The cowboy was in a state of deep stupefaction. "Say," he cried, as he tumbled the deck violently down upon the board, "say, what are you gittin' at, hey?"

The Swede sprang up with the celerity of a man escaping from a snake on the floor. "I don't want to fight!" he shouted. "I don't want to fight!"

The cowboy stretched his long legs indolently and deliberately. His hands were in his pockets. He spat into the sawdust-box. "Well, who the hell thought you did?" he inquired.

The Swede backed rapidly toward a corner of the room. His hands were out protectingly in front of his chest, but he was making an obvious struggle to control his fright. "Gentlemen," he quavered, "I suppose I am going to be killed before I can leave this house! I suppose I am going to be killed before I can leave this house!" In his eyes was the dying-swan look. Through the windows could be seen the snow turning blue in the shadow of dusk. The wind tore at the house, and some loose thing beat regularly against the clap-boards like a spirit tapping.

A door opened, and Scully himself entered. He paused in surprise as he noted the tragic attitude of the Swede. Then he said, "What's the matter here?"

The Swede answered him swiftly and eagerly: "These men are going to kill me."

"Kill you!" ejaculated Scully. "Kill you! What are you talkin'?"

The Swede made the gesture of a martyr.

Scully wheeled sternly upon his son. "What is this, Johnnie?"

The lad had grown sullen. "Damned if I know," he answered. "I can't make no sense to it." He began to shuffle the cards, fluttering them together with an angry snap. "He says a good many men have been killed in this room, or something like that. And he says he's goin' to be killed here too. I don't know what ails him. He's crazy, I shouldn't wonder."

Scully then looked for explanation to the cowboy, but the cowboy simply shrugged his shoulders.

"Kill you?" said Scully again to the Swede. "Kill you? Man, you're off your nut."

"Oh, I know," burst out the Swede. "I know what will happen. Yes, I'm crazy—yes. Yes, of course, I'm crazy—yes. But I know one thing——" There was a sort of sweat of misery and terror upon his face. "I know I won't get out of here alive."

The cowboy drew a deep breath, as if his mind was passing into the last stages of dissolution. "Well, I'm doggoned," he whispered to himself.

Scully wheeled suddenly and faced his son. "You've been troublin' this man!"

Johnnie's voice was loud with its burden of grievance. "Why, good Gawd, I ain't done nothin' to 'im."

The Swede broke in. "Gentlemen, do not disturb yourselves. I will leave this house. I will go away, because"—he accused them dramatically with his glance—"because I do not want to be killed."

Scully was furious with his son. "Will you tell me what is the matter, you young divil? What's the matter, anyhow? Speak out!"

"Blame it!" cried Johnnie in despair, "don't I tell you I don't know? He—says we want to kill him, and that's all I know. I can't tell what ails him."

The Swede continued to repeat: "Never mind, Mr. Scully; never mind. I will leave this house. I will go away, because I do not wish to be killed. Yes, of course, I am crazy—yes. But I know one thing! I will go away. I will leave this house. Never mind, Mr. Scully; never mind. I will go away."

"You will not go 'way," said Scully. "You will not go 'way until I hear the reason of this business. If anybody has troubled you I will take care of him. This is my house. You are under my roof, and I will not allow any peaceable man to be troubled here." He cast a terrible eye upon Johnnie, the cowboy, and the Easterner.

"Never mind, Mr. Scully; never mind. I will go away. I do not wish to be killed." The Swede moved toward the door which opened upon the stairs. It was evidently his intention to go at once for his baggage.

"No, no," shouted Scully peremptorily; but the white-faced man slid by him and disappeared. "Now," said Scully severely, "what does this mane?"

Johnnie and the cowboy cried together: "Why, we didn't do nothin' to 'im!"

Scully's eyes were cold. "No," he said, "you didn't?"

Johnnie swore a deep oath. "Why, this is the wildest loon I ever see. We didn't do nothin' at all. We were jest sittin' here playin' cards, and he——"

The father suddenly spoke to the Easterner. "Mr. Blanc," he asked, "what has these boys been doin'?"

The Easterner reflected again. "I didn't see anything wrong at all," he said at last, slowly.

Scully began to howl. "But what does it mane?" He stared ferociously at his son. "I have a mind to lather you for this, me boy."

Johnnie was frantic. "Well, what have I done?" he bawled at his father.

III

"I think you are tongue-tied," said Scully finally to his son, the cowboy, and the Easterner; and at the end of this scornful sentence he left the room.

Upstairs the Swede was swiftly fastening the straps of his great valise. Once his back happened to be half turned toward the door, and, hearing a noise there, he wheeled and sprang up, uttering a loud cry. Scully's wrinkled visage showed grimly in the light of the small lamp he carried. This yellow effulgence, streaming upward, coloured only his prominent features, and left his eyes, for instance, in mysterious shadow. He resembled a murderer.

"Man! man!" he exclaimed, "have you gone daffy?"

"Oh, no! Oh, no!" rejoined the other. "There are people in this world who know pretty nearly as much as you do—understand?"

For a moment they stood gazing at each other. Upon the Swede's deathly pale cheeks were two spots brightly crimson and sharply edged, as if they had been carefully painted. Scully placed the light on the table and sat himself on the edge of the bed. He spoke ruminatively. "By cracky, I never heard of such a thing in my life. It's a complete muddle. I can't, for the soul of me, think how you ever got this idea into your head." Presently he lifted his eyes and asked: "And did you sure think they were going to kill you?"

The Swede scanned the old man as if he wished to see into his mind. "I did," he said at last. He obviously suspected that this answer might precipitate an outbreak. As he pulled on a strap his whole arm shook, the elbow wavering like a bit of paper.

Scully banged his hand impressively on the footboard of the bed. "Why, man, we're goin' to have a line of ilictric street-cars in this town next spring."

" 'Alineofelectricstreet-cars,' " repeated the Swede, stupidly.

"And," said Scully, "there's a new railroad goin' to be built down from Broken Arm to here. Not to mintion the four churches and the smashin' big brick schoolhouse. Then there's the big factory, too. Why, in two years Romper'll be a met-tro-*pol*-is."

Having finished the preparation of his baggage, the Swede straightened himself. "Mr. Scully," he said, with sudden hardihood, "how much do I owe you?"

"You don't owe me anythin'," said the old man, angrily.

"Yes, I do," retorted the Swede. He took seventy-five cents from his pocket and tendered it to Scully; but the latter snapped his fingers in disdainful refusal. However, it happened that they both stood gazing in a strange fashion at three silver pieces on the Swede's open palm.

"I'll not take your money," said Scully at last. "Not after what's been goin' on here." Then a plan seemed to strike him. "Here," he cried, picking up his lamp and moving toward the door. "Here! Come with me a minute."

"No," said the Swede, in overwhelming alarm.

"Yes," urged the old man. "Come on! I want you to come and see a picter—just across the hall—in my room."

The Swede must have concluded that his hour was come. His jaw dropped and his teeth showed like a dead man's. He ultimately followed Scully across the corridor, but he had the step of one hung in chains.

Scully flashed the light high on the wall of his own chamber. There was revealed a ridiculous photograph of a little girl. She was leaning against a balustrade of gorgeous decoration, and the formidable bang to her hair was prominent. The figure was as graceful as an upright sled-stake, and, withal, it was of the hue of lead. "There," said Scully, tenderly, "that's the picter of my little girl that died. Her name was Carrie. She had the purtiest hair you ever saw! I was that fond of her, she——"

Turning then, he saw that the Swede was not contemplating the picture at all, but, instead, was keeping keen watch on the gloom in the rear.

"Look, man!" cried Scully, heartily. "That's the picter of my little gal that died. Her name was Carrie. And then here's the picter of my oldest boy, Michael. He's a lawyer in Lincoln, an' doin' well. I gave that boy a grand eddication, and I'm glad for it now. He's a fine boy. Look at 'im now. Ain't he bold as blazes, him there in Lincoln, an honoured an' respicted gintleman! An honoured and respicted gintleman," concluded Scully with a flourish. And, so saying, he smote the Swede jovially on the back.

The Swede faintly smiled.

"Now," said the old man, "there's only one more thing." He dropped suddenly to the floor and thrust his head beneath the bed. The Swede could hear his muffled voice. "I'd keep it under me piller if it wasn't for that boy Johnnie. Then there's the old woman ——Where is it now? I never put it twice in the same place. Ah, now come out with you!"

Presently he backed clumsily from under the bed, dragging with him an old coat rolled into a bundle. "I've fetched him," he muttered. Kneeling on the floor, he unrolled the coat and extracted from its heart a large yellow-brown whisky-bottle.

His first manœuvre was to hold the bottle up to the light. Reassured, apparently, that nobody had been tampering with it, he thrust it with a generous movement toward the Swede.

The weak-kneed Swede was about to eagerly clutch this element of strength, but he suddenly jerked his hand away and cast a look of horror upon Scully.

"Drink," said the old man affectionately. He had risen to his feet, and now stood facing the Swede.

There was a silence. Then again Scully said: "Drink!"

The Swede laughed wildly. He grabbed the bottle, put it to his mouth; and as his lips curled absurdly around the opening and his throat worked, he kept his glance, burning with hatred, upon the old man's face.

IV

After the departure of Scully the three men, with the cardboard still upon their knees, preserved for a long time an astounded silence. Then Johnnie said: "That's the doddangedest Swede I ever see."

"He ain't no Swede," said the cowboy, scornfully.

"Well, what is he then?" cried Johnnie. "What is he then?"

"It's my opinion," replied the cowboy deliberately, "he's some kind of a Dutchman." It was a venerable custom of the country to entitle as Swedes all light-haired men who spoke with a heavy tongue. In consequence the idea of the cowboy was not without its daring. "Yes, sir," he repeated. "It's my opinion this feller is some kind of a Dutchman."

"Well, he says he's a Swede, anyhow," muttered Johnnie, sulkily. He turned to the Easterner: 'What do you think, Mr. Blanc?"

"Oh, I don't know," replied the Easterner.

"Well, what do you think makes him act that way?" asked the cowboy.

"Why, he's frightened." The Easterner knocked his pipe against a rim of the stove. "He's clear frightened out of his boots."

"What at?" cried Johnnie and the cowboy together.

The Easterner reflected over his answer.

"What at?" cried the others again.

"Oh, I don't know, but it seems to me this man has been reading dime novels, and he thinks he's right out in the middle of it—the shootin' and stabbin' and all."

"But," said the cowboy, deeply scandalized, "this ain't Wyoming, ner none of them places. This is Nebrasker."

"Yes," added Johnnie, "an' why don't he wait till he gits *out West?*"

The travelled Easterner laughed. "It isn't different there even— not in these days. But he thinks he's right in the middle of hell."

Johnnie and the cowboy mused long.

"It's awful funny," remarked Johnnie at last.

"Yes," said the cowboy. "This is a queer game. I hope we don't git snowed in, because then we'd have to stand this here man bein' around with us all the time. That wouldn't be no good."

"I wish pop would throw him out," said Johnnie.

Presently they heard a loud stamping on the stairs, accompanied by ringing jokes in the voice of old Scully, and laughter, evidently from the Swede. The men around the stove stared vacantly at each other. "Gosh!" said the cowboy. The door flew open, and old Scully, flushed and anecdotal, came into the room. He was jabbering at the Swede, who followed him, laughing bravely. It was the entry of two roisterers from a banquet hall.

"Come now," said Scully sharply to the three seated men, "move up and give us a chance at the stove." The cowboy and the East-erner obediently sidled their chairs to make room for the new-com-ers. Johnnie, however, simply arranged himself in a more indolent attitude, and then remained motionless.

"Come! Git over, there," said Scully.

"Plenty of room on the other side of the stove," said Johnnie.

"Do you think we want to sit in the draught?" roared the father.

But the Swede here interposed with a grandeur of confidence. "No, no. Let the boy sit where he likes," he cried in a bullying voice to the father.

"All right! All right!" said Scully, deferentially. The cowboy and the Easterner exchanged glances of wonder.

The five chairs were formed in a crescent about one side of the stove. The Swede began to talk; he talked arrogantly, profanely, an-grily. Johnnie, the cowboy, and the Easterner maintained a morose silence, while old Scully appeared to be receptive and eager, break-ing in constantly with sympathetic ejaculations.

Finally the Swede announced that he was thirsty. He moved in his chair, and said that he would go for a drink of water.

"I'll git it for you," cried Scully at once.

"No," said the Swede, contemptuously. "I'll get it for myself." He arose and stalked with the air of an owner off into the executive parts of the hotel.

As soon as the Swede was out of hearing Scully sprang to his feet and whispered intensely to the others: "Upstairs he thought I was tryin' to poison 'im."

"Say," said Johnnie, "this makes me sick. Why don't you throw 'im out in the snow?"

"Why, he's all right now," declared Scully. "It was only that he was from the East, and he thought this was a tough place. That's all. He's all right now."

The cowboy looked with admiration upon the Easterner. "You were straight," he said. "You were on to that there Dutchman."

"Well," said Johnnie to his father, "he may be all right now, but I don't see it. Other time he was scared, but now he's too fresh."

Scully's speech was always a combination of Irish brogue and idiom, Western twang and idiom, and scraps of curiously formal diction taken from the story-books and newspapers. He now hurled a strange mass of language at the head of his son. "What do I keep? What do I keep? What do I keep?" he demanded, in a voice of thunder. He slapped his knee impressively, to indicate that he himself was going to make reply, and that all should heed. "I keep a hotel," he shouted. "A hotel, do you mind? A guest under my roof has sacred privileges. He is to be intimidated by none. Not one word shall he hear that would prijudice him in favour of goin' away. I'll not have it. There's no place in this here town where they can say they iver took in a guest of mine because he was afraid to stay here." He wheeled suddenly upon the cowboy and the Easterner. "Am I right?"

"Yes, Mr. Scully," said the cowboy, "I think you're right."

"Yes, Mr. Scully," said the Easterner, "I think you're right."

V

At six-o'clock supper, the Swede fizzed like a fire-wheel. He sometimes seemed on the point of bursting into riotous song, and in all his madness he was encouraged by old Scully. The Easterner was encased in reserve; the cowboy sat in wide-mouthed amazement, forgetting to eat, while Johnnie wrathily demolished great plates of food. The daughters of the house, when they were obliged to replenish the biscuits, approached as warily as Indians, and, having succeeded in their purpose, fled with ill-concealed trepidation. The Swede domineered the whole feast, and he gave it the appearance of a cruel bacchanal. He seemed to have grown suddenly taller; he gazed, brutally disdainful, into every face. His voice rang through the room. Once when he jabbed out harpoon-fashion with his fork to pinion a biscuit, the weapon nearly impaled the hand of the Easterner, which had been stretched quietly out for the same biscuit.

After supper, as the men filed toward the other room, the Swede smote Scully ruthlessly on the shoulder. "Well, old boy, that was a good, square meal." Johnnie looked hopefully at his father; he knew that shoulder was tender from an old fall; and, indeed, it appeared for a moment as if Scully was going to flame out over the matter, but in the end he smiled a sickly smile and remained silent. The others understood from his manner that he was admitting his responsibility for the Swede's new view-point.

Johnnie, however, addressed his parent in an aside. "Why don't you license somebody to kick you downstairs?" Scully scowled darkly by way of reply.

When they were gathered about the stove, the Swede insisted on another game of High-Five. Scully gently deprecated the plan at first, but the Swede turned a wolfish glare upon him. The old man subsided, and the Swede canvassed the others. In his tone there was always a great threat. The cowboy and the Easterner both remarked indifferently that they would play. Scully said that he would presently have to go to meet the 6.58 train, and so the Swede turned menacingly upon Johnnie. For a moment their glances crossed like blades, and then Johnnie smiled and said, "Yes, I'll play."

They formed a square, with the little board on their knees. The Easterner and the Swede were again partners. As the play went on, it was noticeable that the cowboy was not board-whacking as usual. Meanwhile, Scully, near the lamp, had put on his spectacles and, with an appearance curiously like an old priest, was reading a newspaper. In time he went out to meet the 6.58 train, and, despite his precautions, a gust of polar wind whirled into the room as he opened the door. Besides scattering the cards, it chilled the players to the marrow. The Swede cursed frightfully. When Scully returned, his entrance disturbed a cosy and friendly scene. The Swede again cursed. But presently they were once more intent, their heads bent forward and their hands moving swiftly. The Swede had adopted the fashion of board-whacking.

Scully took up his paper and for a long time remained immersed in matters which were extraordinarily remote from him. The lamp burned badly, and once he stopped to adjust the wick. The newspaper, as he turned from page to page, rustled with a slow and comfortable sound. Then suddenly he heard three terrible words: "You are cheatin'!"

Such scenes often prove that there can be little of dramatic import in environment. Any room can present a tragic front; any room can be comic. This little den was now hideous as a torture-chamber. The new faces of the men themselves had changed it upon the instant. The Swede held a huge fist in front of Johnnie's face, while the latter looked steadily over it into the blazing orbs of his accuser. The Easterner had grown pallid; the cowboy's jaw had dropped in

that expression of bovine amazement which was one of his important mannerisms. After the three words, the first sound in the room
was made by Scully's paper as it floated forgotten to his feet. His
spectacles had also fallen from his nose, but by a clutch he had
saved them in air. His hand, grasping the spectacles, now remained
poised awkwardly and near his shoulder. He stared at the card-play-
ers.

Probably the silence was while a second elapsed. Then, if the floor
had been suddenly twitched out from under the men they could not
have moved quicker. The five had projected themselves headlong toward a common point. It happened that Johnnie, in rising to hurl
himself upon the Swede, had stumbled slightly because of his curiously instinctive care for the cards and the board. The loss of the
moment allowed time for the arrival of Scully, and also allowed the
cowboy time to give the Swede a great push which sent him staggering back. The men found tongue together, and hoarse shouts of
rage, appeal, or fear burst from every throat. The cowboy pushed
and jostled feverishly at the Swede, and the Easterner and Scully
clung wildly to Johnnie; but through the smoky air, above the swaying bodies of the peace-compellers, the eyes of the two warriors ever
sought each other in glances of challenge that were at once hot and
steely.

Of course the board had been overturned, and now the whole
company of cards was scattered over the floor, where the boots of
the men trampled the fat and painted kings and queens as they
gazed with their silly eyes at the war that was waging above them.

Scully's voice was dominating the yells. "Stop now! Stop, I say!
Stop, now——"

Johnnie, as he struggled to burst through the rank formed by
Scully and the Easterner, was crying, "Well, he says I cheated! He
says I cheated! I won't allow no man to say I cheated! If he says I
cheated, he's a —— ——!"

The cowboy was telling the Swede, "Quit, now! Quit, d'ye hear—
—"

The screams of the Swede never ceased: "He did cheat! I saw
him! I saw him——"

As for the Easterner, he was importuning in a voice that was not
heeded: "Wait a moment, can't you? Oh, wait a moment. What's
the good of a fight over a game of cards? Wait a moment——"

In this tumult no complete sentences were clear. "Cheat"—"Quit"
—"He says"—these fragments pierced the uproar and rang out
sharply. It was remarkable that, whereas Scully undoubtedly made
the most noise, he was the least heard of any of the riotous band.

Then suddenly there was a great cessation. It was as if each man had paused for breath; and although the room was still lighted with the anger of men, it could be seen that there was no danger of immediate conflict, and at once Johnnie, shouldering his way forward, almost succeeded in confronting the Swede. "What did you say I cheated for? What did you say I cheated for? I don't cheat, and I won't let no man say I do!"

The Swede said, "I saw you! I saw you!"

"Well," cried Johnnie, "I'll fight any man what says I cheat!"

"No, you won't," said the cowboy. "Not here."

"Ah, be still, can't you?" said Scully, coming between them.

The quiet was sufficient to allow the Easterner's voice to be heard. He was repeating, "Oh, wait a moment, can't you? What's the good of a fight over a game of cards? Wait a moment!"

Johnnie, his red face appearing above his father's shoulder, hailed the Swede again. "Did you say I cheated?"

The Swede showed his teeth. "Yes."

"Then," said Johnnie, "we must fight."

"Yes, fight," roared the Swede. He was like a demoniac. "Yes, fight! I'll show you what kind of a man I am! I'll show you who you want to fight! Maybe you think I can't fight! Maybe you think I can't! I'll show you, you skin, you card-sharp! Yes, you cheated! You cheated! You cheated!"

"Well, let's go at it, then, mister," said Johnnie, coolly.

The cowboy's brow was beaded with sweat from his efforts in intercepting all sorts of raids. He turned in despair to Scully. "What are you goin' to do now?"

A change had come over the Celtic visage of the old man. He now seemed all eagerness; his eyes glowed.

"We'll let them fight," he answered, stalwartly. "I can't put up with it any longer. I've stood this damned Swede till I'm sick. We'll let them fight."

VI

The men prepared to go out of doors. The Easterner was so nervous that he had great difficulty in getting his arms into the sleeves of his new leather coat. As the cowboy drew his fur cap down over his ears his hands trembled. In fact, Johnnie and old Scully were the only ones who displayed no agitation. These preliminaries were conducted without words.

Scully threw open the door. "Well, come on," he said. Instantly a terrific wind caused the flame of the lamp to struggle at its wick, while a puff of black smoke sprang from the chimney-top. The stove was in mid-current of the blast, and its voice swelled to equal the roar of the storm. Some of the scarred and bedabbled cards were caught up from the floor and dashed helplessly against the farther wall. The men lowered their heads and plunged into the tempest as into a sea.

No snow was falling, but great whirls and clouds of flakes, swept up from the ground by the frantic winds, were streaming southward with the speed of bullets. The covered land was blue with the sheen of an unearthly satin, and there was no other hue save where, at the low, black railway station—which seemed incredibly distant—one light gleamed like a tiny jewel. As the men floundered into a thigh-deep drift, it was known that the Swede was bawling out something. Scully went to him, put a hand on his sholder, and projected an ear. "What's that you say?" he shouted.

"I say," bawled the Swede again, "I won't stand much show against this gang. I know you'll all pitch on me."

Scully smote him reproachfully on the arm. "Tut, man!" he yelled. The wind tore the words from Scully's lips and scattered them far alee.

"You are all a gang of——" boomed the Swede, but the storm also seized the remainder of this sentence.

Immediately turning their backs upon the wind, the men had swung around a corner to the sheltered side of the hotel. It was the function of the little house to preserve here, amid this great devastation of snow, an irregular V-shape of heavily encrusted grass, which crackled beneath the feet. One could imagine the great drifts piled against the windward side. When the party reached the comparative peace of this spot it was found that the Swede was still bellowing.

"Oh, I know what kind of a thing this is! I know you'll all pitch on me. I can't lick you all!"

Scully turned upon him panther-fashion. "You'll not have to whip all of us. You'll have to whip my son Johnnie. An' the man what troubles you durin' that time will have me to dale with."

The arrangements were swiftly made. The two men faced each other, obedient to the harsh commands of Scully, whose face, in the subtly luminous gloom, could be seen set in the austere impersonal lines that are pictured on the countenances of the Roman veterans. The Easterner's teeth were chattering, and he was hopping up and down like a mechanical toy. The cowboy stood rock-like.

The contestants had not stripped off any clothing. Each was in his ordinary attire. Their fists were up, and they eyed each other in a calm that had the elements of leonine cruelty in it.

During this pause, the Easterner's mind, like a film, took lasting impressions of three men—the iron-nerved master of the ceremony; the Swede, pale, motionless, terrible; and Johnnie, serene yet ferocious, brutish yet heroic. The entire prelude had in it a tragedy greater than the tragedy of action, and this aspect was accentuated by the long, mellow cry of blizzard, as it sped the tumbling and wailing flakes into the black abyss of the south.

"Now!" said Scully.

The two combatants leaped forward and crashed together like bullocks. There was heard the cushioned sound of blows, and of a curse squeezing out from between the tight teeth of one.

As for the spectators, the Easterner's pent-up breath exploded from him with a pop of relief, absolute relief from the tension of the preliminaries. The cowboy bounded into the air with a yowl. Scully was immovable as from supreme amazement and fear at the fury of the fight which he himself had permitted and arranged.

For a time the encounter in the darkness was such a perplexity of flying arms that it presented no more detail than would a swiftly revolving wheel. Occasionally a face, as if illumined by a flash of light, would shine out, ghastly and marked with pink spots. A moment later, the men might have been known as shadows, if it were not for the involuntary utterance of oaths that came from them in whispers.

Suddenly a holocaust of warlike desire caught the cowboy, and he bolted forward with the speed of a broncho. "Go it, Johnnie! go it! Kill him! Kill him!"

Scully confronted him. "Kape back," he said; and by his glance the cowboy could tell that this man was Johnnie's father.

To the Easterner there was a monotony of unchangeable fighting that was an abomination. This confused mingling was eternal to his sense, which was concentrated in a longing for the end, the priceless end. Once the fighters lurched near him, and as he scrambled hastily backward he heard them breathe like men on the rack.

"Kill him, Johnnie! Kill him! Kill him! Kill him!" The cowboy's face was contorted like one of those agony masks in museums.

"Keep still," said Scully, icily.

Then there was a sudden loud grunt, incomplete, cut short, and Johnnie's body swung away from the Swede and fell with sickening heaviness to the grass. The cowboy was barely in time to prevent the mad Swede from flinging himself upon his prone adversary. "No, you don't," said the cowboy, interposing an arm. "Wait a second."

"Scully was at his son's side. "Johnnie! Johnnie, me boy!" His voice had a quality of melancholy tenderness. "Johnnie! Can you go on with it?" He looked anxiously down into the bloody, pulpy face of his son.

There was a moment of silence and then Johnnie answered in his ordinary voice, "Yes, I—it—yes."

Assisted by his father he struggled to his feet. "Wait a bit now till you git your wind," said the old man.

A few paces away the cowboy was lecturing the Swede. "No, you don't! Wait a second!"

The Easterner was plucking at Scully's sleeve. "Oh, this is enough," he pleaded. "This is enough! Let it go as it stands. This is enough!"

"Bill," said Scully, "git out of the road." The cowboy stepped aside."Now." The combatants were actuated by a new caution as they advanced toward collision. They glared at each other, and then the Swede aimed a lightning blow that carried with it his entire weight. Johnnie was evidently half stupid from weakness, but he miraculously dodged, and his fist sent the over-balanced Swede sprawling.

The cowboy, Scully, and the Easterner burst into a cheer that was like a chorus of triumphant soldiery, but before its conclusion the Swede had scuffed agilely to his feet and come in berserk abandon at his foe. There was another perplexity of flying arms, and Johnnie's body again swung away and fell, even as a bundle might fall from a roof. The Swede instantly staggered to a little wind-waved tree and leaned upon it, breathing like an engine, while his savage and flame-lit eyes roamed from face to face as the men bent over Johnnie. There was a splendour of isolation in his situation at this time which the Easterner felt once when, lifting his eyes from the man on the ground, he beheld that mysterious and lonely figure, waiting.

"Are you any good yet, Johnnie?" asked Scully in a broken voice.

The son gasped and opened his eyes languidly. After a moment he answered, "No—I ain't—any good—any—more." Then, from shame and bodily ill, he began to weep, the tears furrowing down through the blood-stains on his face. "He was too—too—too heavy for me."

Scully straightened and addressed the waiting figure. "Stranger," he said, evenly, "it's all up with our side." Then his voice changed into that vibrant huskiness which is commonly the tone of the most simple and deadly announcements. "Johnnie is whipped."

Without replying, the victor moved off on the route to the front door of the hotel.

The cowboy was formulating new and unspellable blasphemies. The Easterner was startled to find that they were out in a wind that seemed to come direct from the shadowed arctic floes. He heard again the wail of the snow as it was flung to its grave in the south. He knew now that all this time the cold had been sinking into him deeper and deeper, and he wondered that he had not perished. He felt indifferent to the condition of the vanquished man.

"Johnnie, can you walk?" asked Scully.

"Did I hurt—hurt him any?" asked the son.

"Can you walk, boy? Can you walk?"

Johnnie's voice was suddenly strong. There was a robust impatience in it. "I asked whether I hurt him any!"

"Yes, yes, Johnnie," answered the cowboy, consolingly; "he's hurt a good deal."

They raised him from the ground, and as soon as he was on his feet he went tottering off, rebuffing all attempts at assistance. When the party rounded the corner they were fairly blinded by the pelting of the snow. It burned their faces like fire. The cowboy carried Johnnie through the drift to the door. As they entered, some cards again rose from the floor and beat against the wall.

The Easterner rushed to the stove. He was so profoundly chilled that he almost dared to embrace the glowing iron. The Swede was not in the room. Johnnie sank into a chair and, folding his arms on his knees, buried his face in them. Scully, warming one foot and then the other at a rim of the stove, muttered to himself with Celtic mournfulness. The cowboy had removed his fur cap, and with a dazed and rueful air he was running one hand through his tousled locks. From overhead they could hear the creaking of boards, as the Swede tramped here and there in his room.

The sad quiet was broken by the sudden flinging open of a door that led toward the kitchen. It was instantly followed by an inrush of women. They precipitated themselves upon Johnnie amid a chorus of lamentation. Before they carried their prey off to the kitchen, there to be bathed and harangued with that mixture of sympathy and abuse which is a feat of their sex, the mother straightened herself and fixed old Scully with an eye of stern reproach. "Shame be upon you, Patrick Scully!" she cried. "Your own son, too. Shame be upon you!"

"There, now! Be quiet, now!" said the old man, weakly.

"Shame be upon you, Patrick Scully!" The girls, rallying to this slogan, sniffed disdainfully in the direction of those trembling accomplices, the cowboy and the Easterner. Presently they bore Johnnie away, and left the three men to dismal reflection.

VII

"I'd like to fight this here Dutchman myself," said the cowboy, breaking a silence.

Scully wagged his head sadly. "No, that wouldn't do. It wouldn't be right. It wouldn't be right."

"Well, why wouldn't it?" argued the cowboy. "I don't see no harm in it."

"No," answered Scully, with mournful heroism. "It wouldn't be right. It was Johnnie's fight, and now we mustn't whip the man just because he whipped Johnnie."

"Yes, that's true enough," said the cowboy; "but—he better not get fresh with me, because I couldn't stand no more of it."

"You'll not say a word to him," commanded Scully, and even then they heard the tread of the Swede on the stairs. His entrance was made theatric. He swept the door back with a bang and swaggered to the middle of the room. No one looked at him. "Well," he cried, insolently, at Scully, "I s'pose you'll tell me now how much I owe you?"

The old man remained stolid. "You don't owe me nothin'."

"Huh!" said the Swede, "huh! Don't owe 'im nothin'."

The cowboy addressed the Swede. "Stranger, I don't see how you come to be so gay around here."

Old Scully was instantly alert. "Stop!" he shouted, holding his hand forth, fingers upward. "Bill, you shut up!"

The cowboy spat carelessly into the sawdust-box. "I didn't say a word, did I?" he asked.

"Mr. Scully," called the Swede, "how much do I owe you?" It was seen that he was attired for departure, and that he had his valise in his hand.

"You don't owe me nothin'," repeated Scully in the same imperturbable way.

"Huh!" said the Swede. "I guess you're right. I guess if it was any way at all, you'd owe me somethin'. That's what I guess." He turned to the cowboy. " 'Kill him! Kill him! Kill him!' " he mimicked, and then guffawed victoriously. " 'Kill him!' " He was convulsed with ironical humour.

But he might have been jeering the dead. The three men were immovable and silent, staring with glassy eyes at the stove.

The Swede opened the door and passed into the storm, giving one derisive glance backward at the still group.

As soon as the door was closed, Scully and the cowboy leaped to their feet and began to curse. They trampled to and fro, waving their arms and smashing into the air with their fists. "Oh, but that was a hard minute!" wailed Scully. "That was a hard minute! Him there leerin' and scoffin'! One bang at his nose was worth forty dollars to me that minute! How did you stand it, Bill?"

"How did I stand it?" cried the cowboy in a quivering voice. "How did I stand it? Oh!"

The old man burst into sudden brogue. "I'd loike to take that Swade," he wailed, "and hould 'im down on a shtone flure and bate 'im to a jelly wid a shtick!"

. . .

The cowboy groaned in sympathy. "I'd like to git him by the neck and ha-ammer him"—he brought his hand down on a chair with a noise like a pistol-shot—"hammer that there Dutchman until he couldn't tell himself from a dead coyote!"

"I'd bate 'im until he——"

"I'd show *him* some things——"

And then together they raised a yearning, fanatic cry—"Oh-o-oh! if we only could——"

"Yes!"

"Yes!"

"And then I'd——"

"O-o-oh!"

VIII

The Swede, tightly gripping his valise, tacked across the face of the storm as if he carried sails. He was following a line of little naked, gasping trees which, he knew, must mark the way of the road. His face, fresh from the pounding of Johnnie's fists, felt more pleasure than pain in the wind and the driving snow. A number of square shapes loomed upon him finally, and he knew them as the houses of the main body of the town. He found a street and made travel along it, leaning heavily upon the wind whenever, at a corner, a terrific blast caught him.

He might have been in a deserted village. We picture the world as thick with conquering and elate humanity, but here, with the bugles of the tempest pealing, it was hard to imagine a peopled earth. One viewed the existence of man then as a marvel, and conceded a glamour of wonder to these lice which were caused to cling to a whirling, fire-smitten, ice-locked, disease-stricken, space-lost bulb. The conceit of man was explained by this storm to be the very engine of life. One was a coxcomb not to die in it. However, the Swede found a saloon.

In front of it an indomitable red light was burning, and the snow-flakes were made blood-colour as they flew through the circumscribed territory of the lamp's shining. The Swede pushed open the door of the saloon and entered. A sanded expanse was before him, and at the end of it four men sat about a table drinking. Down one side of the room extended a radiant bar, and its guardian was leaning upon his elbows listening to the talk of the men at the table. The Swede dropped his valise upon the floor and, smiling fraternally upon the barkeeper, said, "Gimme some whisky, will you?" The man placed a bottle, a whisky-glass, and a glass of ice-thick water upon the bar. The Swede poured himself an abnormal portion of whisky and drank it in three gulps. "Pretty bad night," remarked the bartender, indifferently. He was making the pretension of blindness which is usually a distinction of his class; but it could have been seen that he was furtively studying the half-erased blood-stains on the face of the Swede. "Bad night," he said again.

"Oh, it's good enough for me," replied the Swede, hardily, as he poured himself some more whisky. The barkeeper took his coin and manœuvred it through its reception by the highly nickelled cash-machine. A bell rang; a card labelled "20 cts." had appeared.

"No," continued the Swede, "this isn't too bad weather. It's good enough for me."

"So?" murmured the barkeeper, languidly.

The copious drams made the Swede's eyes swim, and he breathed a trifle heavier. "Yes, I like this weather. I like it. It suits me." It was apparently his design to impart a deep significance to these words.

"So?" murmured the bartender again. He turned to gaze dreamily at the scroll-like birds and bird-like scrolls which had been drawn with soap upon the mirrors in back of the bar.

"Well, I guess I'll take another drink," said the Swede, presently. "Have something?"

"No, thanks; I'm not drinkin'," answered the bartender. Afterward he asked, "How did you hurt your face?"

The Swede immediately began to boast loudly. "Why, in a fight. I thumped the soul out of a man down here at Scully's hotel."

The interest of the four men at the table was at last aroused.

"Who was it?" said one.

"Johnnie Scully," blustered the Swede. "Son of the man what runs it. He will be pretty near dead for some weeks, I can tell you. I made a nice thing of him, I did. He couldn't get up. They carried him in the house. Have a drink?"

Instantly the men in some subtle way encased themselves in reserve. "No, thanks," said one. The group was of curious formation. Two were prominent local business men; one was the district attorney; and one was a professional gambler of the kind known as "square." But a scrutiny of the group would not have enabled an observer to pick the gambler from the men of more reputable pursuits. He was, in fact, a man so delicate in manner, when among people of fair class, and so judicious in his choice of victims, that in the strictly masculine part of the town's life he had come to be explicitly trusted and admired. People called him a thoroughbred. The fear and contempt with which his craft was regarded was undoubtedly the reason why his quiet dignity shone conspicuous above the quiet dignity of men who might be merely hatters, billiard-markers, or grocery clerks. Beyond an occasional unwary traveller who came by rail, this gambler was supposed to prey solely upon reckless and senile farmers, who, when flush with good crops, drove into town in all the pride and confidence of an absolutely invulnerable stupidity. Hearing at times in circuitous fashion of the despoilment of such a farmer, the important men of Romper invariably laughed in contempt of the victim, and if they thought of the wolf at all, it was with a kind of pride at the knowledge that he would never dare think of attacking their wisdom and courage. Besides, it was popular that this gambler had a real wife and two real children in a neat cottage in a suburb, where he led an exemplary home life; and when any one even suggested a discrepancy in his character, the crowd immediately vociferated descriptions of this virtuous family circle. Then men who led exemplary home lives, and men who did not lead exemplary home lives, all subsided in a bunch, remarking that there was nothing more to be said.

However, when a restriction was placed upon him—as, for instance, when a strong clique of members of the new Pollywog Club refused to permit him, even as a spectator, to appear in the rooms of the organization—the candour and gentleness with which he accepted the judgment disarmed many of his foes and made his friends more desperately partisan. He invariably distinguished between himself and a respectable Romper man so quickly and frankly that his manner actually appeared to be a continual broadcast compliment.

And one must not forget to declare the fundamental fact of his entire position in Romper. It is irrefutable that in all affairs outside his business, in all matters that occur eternally and commonly between man and man, this thieving card-player was so generous, so just, so moral, that, in a contest, he could have put to flight the consciences of nine tenths of the citizens of Romper.

And so it happened that he was seated in this saloon with the two prominent local merchants and the district attorney.

The Swede continued to drink raw whisky, meanwhile babbling at the barkeeper and trying to induce him to indulge in potations. "Come on. Have a drink. Come on. What —no? Well, have a little one, then. By gawd, I've whipped a man to-night, and I want to celebrate. I whipped him good, too. Gentlemen," the Swede cried to the men at the table, "have a drink?"

"Ssh!" said the barkeeper.

The group at the table, although furtively attentive, had been pretending to be deep in talk, but now a man lifted his eyes toward the Swede and said, shortly, "Thanks. We don't want any more."

At this reply the Swede ruffled out his chest like a rooster. "Well," he exploded, "it seems I can't get anybody to drink with me in this town. Seems so, don't it? Well!"

"Ssh!" said the barkeeper.

"Say," snarled the Swede, "don't you try to shut me up. I won't have it. I'm a gentleman, and I want people to drink with me. And I want 'em to drink with me now. *Now*—do you understand?" He rapped the bar with his knuckles.

Years of experience had calloused the bartender. He merely grew sulky. "I hear you," he answered.

"Well," cried the Swede, "listen hard then. See those men over there? Well, they're going to drink with me, and don't you forget it. Now you watch."

"Hi!" yelled the barkeeper, "this won't do!"

"Why won't it?" demanded the Swede. He stalked over to the table, and by chance laid his hand upon the shoulder of the gambler. "How about this?" he asked wrathfully. "I asked you to drink with me."

The gambler simply twisted his head and spoke over his shoulder. "My friend, I don't know you."

"Oh, hell!" answered the Swede, "come and have a drink."

"Now, my boy," advised the gambler, kindly, "take your hand off my shoulder and go 'way and mind your own business." He was a little, slim man, and it seemed strange to hear him use this tone of heroic patronage to the burly Swede. The other men at the table said nothing.

"What! You won't drink with me, you little dude? I'll make you, then! I'll make you!" The Swede had grasped the gambler frenziedly at the throat, and was dragging him from his chair. The other men sprang up. The barkeeper dashed around the corner of his bar. There was a great tumult, and then was seen a long blade in the hand of the gambler. It shot forward, and a human body, this citadel of virtue, wisdom, power, was pierced as easily as if it had been a melon. The Swede fell with a cry of supreme astonishment.

The prominent merchants and the district attorney must have at once tumbled out of the place backward. The bartender found himself hanging limply to the arm of a chair and gazing into the eyes of a murderer.

"Henry," said the latter, as he wiped his knife on one of the towels that hung beneath the bar rail, "you tell 'em where to find me. I'll be home, waiting for 'em." Then he vanished. A moment afterward the barkeeper was in the street dinning through the storm for help and, moreover, companionship.

The corpse of the Swede, alone in the saloon, had its eyes fixed upon a dreadful legend that dwelt atop of the cash-machine: "This registers the amount of your purchase."

IX

Months later, the cowboy was frying pork over the stove of a little ranch near the Dakota line, when there was a quick thud of hoofs outside, and presently the Easterner entered with the letters and the papers.

"Well," said the Easterner at once, "the chap that killed the Swede has got three years. Wasn't much, was it?"

"He has? Three years?" The cowboy poised his pan of pork, while he ruminated upon the news. "Three years. That ain't much."

"No. It was a light sentence," replied the Easterner as he unbuckled his spurs. "Seems there was a good deal of sympathy for him in Romper."

"If the bartender had been any good," observed the cowboy, thoughtfully, "he would have gone in and cracked that there Dutchman on the head with a bottle in the beginnin' of it and stopped all this here murderin'."

"Yes, a thousand things might have happened," said the Easterner, tartly.

The cowboy returned his pan of pork to the fire, but his philosophy continued. "It's funny, ain't it? If he hadn't said Johnnie was cheatin' he'd be alive this minute. He was an awful fool. Game played for fun, too. Not for money. I believe he was crazy."

"I feel sorry for that gambler," said the Easterner.

"Oh, so do I," said the cowboy. "He don't deserve none of it for killin' who he did."

"The Swede might not have been killed if everything had been square."

"Might not have been killed?" exclaimed the cowboy. "Everythin' square? Why, when he said that Johnnie was cheatin' and acted like such a jackass? And then in the saloon he fairly walked up to git hurt?" With these arguments the cowboy browbeat the Easterner and reduced him to rage.

"You're a fool!" cried the Easterner, viciously. "You're a bigger jackass than the Swede by a million majority. Now let me tell you one thing. Let me tell you something. Listen! Johnnie *was* cheating!"

" 'Johnnie,' " said the cowboy, blankly. There was a minute of silence, and then he said, robustly, "Why, no. The game was only for fun."

"Fun or not," said the Easterner, "Johnnie was cheating. I saw him. I know it. I saw him. And I refused to stand up and be a man. I let the Swede fight it out alone. And you—you were simply puffing around the place and wanting to fight. And then old Scully himself! We are all in it! This poor gambler isn't even a noun. He is kind of an adverb. Every sin is the result of a collaboration. We, five of us, have collaborated in the murder of this Swede. Usually there are from a dozen to forty women really involved in every murder, but in this case it seems to be only five men—you, I, Johnnie, old Scully; and that fool of an unfortunate gambler came merely as a culmination, the apex of a human movement, and gets all the punishment."

The cowboy, injured and rebellious, cried out blindly into this fog of mysterious theory: "Well, I didn't do anythin', did I?"

OWEN WISTER

The Virginian

ENTER THE MAN

SOME NOTABLE SIGHT was drawing the passengers, both men and women, to the window; and therefore I rose and crossed the car to see what it was. I saw near the track an enclosure, and round it some laughing men, and inside it some whirling dust, and amid the dust some horses, plunging, huddling, and dodging. They were cow ponies in a corral, and one of them would not be caught, no matter who threw the rope. We had plenty of time to watch this sport, for our train had stopped that the engine might take water at the tank before it pulled us up beside the station platform of Medicine Bow. We were also six hours late, and starving for entertainment. The pony in the corral was wise, and rapid of limb. Have you seen a skilful boxer watch his antagonist with a quiet, incessant eye? Such an eye as this did the pony keep upon whatever man took the rope. The man might pretend to look at the weather, which was fine; or he might affect earnest conversation with a bystander: it was bootless. The pony saw through it. No feint hoodwinked him. This animal was thoroughly a man of the world. His undistracted eye stayed fixed upon the dissembling foe, and the gravity of his horse-expression made the matter one of high comedy. Then the rope would sail out at him, but he was already elsewhere; and if horses laugh, gayety must have abounded in that corral. Sometimes the pony took a turn alone; next he had slid in a flash among his brothers, and the whole of them like a school of playful fish whipped round the corral, kicking up the fine dust, and (I take it) roaring with laughter. Through the window-glass of our Pullman the thud of their mischievous hoofs reached us, and the strong, humorous curses of the cow-boys. Then for the first time I noticed a man who sat on the high gate of the corral, looking on. For he now climbed down with the undulations of a tiger, smooth and easy, as if his muscles flowed beneath his skin. The others had all visibly whirled the rope, some of them even shoulder high. I did not see his arm lift or move. He appeared to hold the rope down low, by his leg. But like a sudden

283

snake I saw the noose go out its length and fall true; and the thing was done. As the captured pony walked in with a sweet, church-door expression, our train moved slowly on to the station, and a passenger remarked, "That man knows his business."

But the passenger's dissertation upon roping I was obliged to lose, for Medicine Bow was my station. I bade my fellow-travellers goodby, and descended, a stranger, into the great cattle land. And here in less than ten minutes I learned news which made me feel a stranger indeed.

My baggage was lost; it had not come on my train; it was adrift somewhere back in the two thousand miles that lay behind me. And by way of comfort, the baggage-man remarked that passengers often got astray from their trunks, but the trunks mostly found them after a while. Having offered me this encouragement, he turned whistling to his affairs and left me planted in the baggage-room at Medicine Bow. I stood deserted among crates and boxes, blankly holding my check, furious and forlorn. I stared out through the door at the sky and the plains; but I did not see the antelope shining among the sagebrush, nor the great sunset light of Wyoming. Annoyance blinded my eyes to all things save my grievance: I saw only a lost trunk. And I was muttering half-aloud, "What a forsaken hole this is!" when suddenly from outside on the platform came a slow voice:—

"Off to get married *again?* Oh, don't!"

The voice was Southern and gentle and drawling; and a second voice came in immediate answer, cracked and querulous:—

"It ain't again. Who says it's again? Who told you, anyway?"

And the first voice responded caressingly:—

"Why, your Sunday clothes told me, Uncle Hughey. They are speakin' mighty loud o' nuptials."

"You don't worry me!" snapped Uncle Hughey, with shrill heat.

And the other gently continued, "Ain't them gloves the same yu' wore to your last weddin'?"

"You don't worry me! You don't worry me!" now screamed Uncle Hughey.

Already I had forgotten my trunk; care had left me; I was aware of the sunset, and had no desire but for more of this conversation. For it resembled none that I had heard in my life so far. I stepped to the door and looked out upon the station platform.

Lounging there at ease against the wall was a slim young giant, more beautiful than pictures. His broad, soft hat was pushed back; a loose-knotted, dull-scarlet handkerchief sagged from his throat; and one casual thumb was hooked in the cartridge-belt that slanted across his hips. He had plainly come many miles from somewhere across the vast horizon, as the dust upon him showed. His boots were white with it. His overalls were gray with it. The weather-beaten bloom of his face shone through it duskily, as the ripe peaches look upon their trees in a dry season. But no dinginess of travel or shabbiness of attire could tarnish the splendor that radiated from his youth and strength. The old man upon whose temper his remarks were doing such deadly work was combed and curried to a finish, a bridegroom swept and garnished; but alas for age! Had I been the bride, I should have taken the giant, dust and all.

He had by no means done with the old man.

"Why, yu've hung weddin' gyarments on every limb!" he now drawled, with admiration. "Who is the lucky lady this trip?"

The old man seemed to vibrate. "Tell you there ain't been no other! Call me a Mormon, would you?"

"Why, that—"

"Call me a Mormon? Then name some of my wives. Name two. Name one. Dare you!"

"—that Laramie wido' promised you—"

"Shucks!"

"—only her doctor suddenly ordered Southern climate and—"

"Shucks!! You're a false alarm."

"—so nothing but her lungs came between you. And next you'd most got united with Cattle Kate, only—"

"Tell you you're a false alarm!"

"—only she got hung."

"Where's the wives in all this? Show the wives! Come now!"

"That corn-fed biscuit-shooter at Rawlins yu' gave the canary—"

"Never married her. Never did marry—"

"But yu' come so near, uncle! She was the one left yu' that letter explaining how she'd got married to a young cyard-player the very day before her ceremony with you was due, and—"

"Oh, you're nothing; you're a kid; you don't amount to—"

"—and how she'd never, never forget to feed the canary."

"This country's getting full of kids," stated the old man, witheringly. "It's doomed." This crushing assertion plainly satisfied him. And he blinked his eyes with renewed anticipation. His tall tormentor continued with a face of unchanging gravity, and a voice of gentle solicitude:—

"How is the health of that unfortunate—"

"That's right! Pour your insults! Pour 'em on a sick, afflicted woman!" The eyes blinked with combative relish.

"Insults? Oh, no, Uncle Hughey!"

"That's all right! Insults goes!"

"Why, I was mighty relieved when she began to recover her mem'ry. Las' time I heard, they told me she'd got pretty near all back. Remembered her father, and her mother, and her sisters and brothers, and her friends, and her happy childhood, and all her doin's except only your face. The boys was bettin' she'd get that far too, give her time. But I reckon afteh such a turrable sickness as she had, that would be expectin' most too much."

At this Uncle Hughey jerked out a small parcel. "Shows how much you know!" he cackled. "There! See that! That's my ring she sent me back, being too unstrung for marriage. So she don't remember me, don't she? Ha-ha! Always said you were a false alarm."

The Southerner put more anxiety into his tone. "And so you're a-takin' the ring right on to the next one!" he exclaimed. "Oh, don't go to get married again, Uncle Hughey! What's the use o' being married?"

"What's the use?" echoed the bridegroom, with scorn. "Hm! When you grow up you'll think different."

"Course I expect to think different when my age is different. I'm havin' the thoughts proper to twenty-four, and you're havin' the thoughts proper to sixty."

"Fifty!" shrieked Uncle Hughey, jumping in the air.

The Southerner took a tone of self-reproach. "Now, how could I forget you was fifty," he murmured, "when you have been telling it to the boys so careful for the last ten years!"

Have you ever seen a cockatoo—the white kind with the topknot —enraged by insult? The bird erects every available feather upon its person. So did Uncle Hughey seem to swell, clothes, mustache, and woolly white beard; and without further speech he took himself on board the East-bound train, which now arrived from its siding in time to deliver him.

Yet this was not why he had not gone away before. At any time he could have escaped into the baggage-room or withdrawn to a dignified distance until his train should come up. But the old man had evidently got a sort of joy from this teasing. He had reached that inevitable age when we are tickled to be linked with affairs of gallantry, no matter how.

With him now the East-bound departed slowly into that distance whence I had come. I stared after it as it went its way to the far shores of civilization. It grew small in the unending gulf of space, until all sign of its presence was gone save a faint skein of smoke against the evening sky. And now my lost trunk came back into my thoughts, and Medicine Bow seemed a lonely spot. A sort of ship had left me marooned in a foreign ocean; the Pullman was comfortably steaming home to port, while I—how was I to find Judge Henry's ranch? Where in this unfeatured wilderness was Sunk Creek? No creek or any water at all flowed here that I could perceive. My host had written he should meet me at the station and drive me to his ranch. This was all that I knew. He was not here. The baggage-man had not seen him lately. The ranch was almost certain to be too far to walk to, to-night. My trunk—I discovered myself still star-ing dolefully after the vanished East-bound; and at the same instant I became aware that the tall man was looking gravely at me,—as gravely as he had looked at Uncle Hughey throughout their remark-able conversation.

To see his eye thus fixing me and his thumb still hooked in his cartridge-belt, certain tales of travellers from these parts forced themselves disquietingly into my recollection. Now that Uncle Hughey was gone, was I to take his place and be, for instance, in-vited to dance on the platform to the music of shots nicely aimed?

"I reckon I am looking for you, seh," the tall man now observed.

"WHEN YOU CALL ME THAT, *SMILE!*"

We cannot see ourselves as others see us, or I should know what appearance I cut at hearing this from the tall man. I said nothing, feeling uncertain.

"I reckon I am looking for you, seh," he repeated politely.

"I am looking for Judge Henry," I now replied.

He walked toward me, and I saw that in inches he was not a giant. He was not more than six feet. It was Uncle Hughey that had made him seem to tower. But in his eye, in his face, in his step, in the whole man, there dominated a something potent to be felt, I should think, by man or woman.

"The Judge sent me afteh you, seh," he now explained, in his civil Southern voice; and he handed me a letter from my host. Had I not witnessed his facetious performances with Uncle Hughey, I should have judged him wholly ungifted with such powers. There was nothing external about him but what seemed the signs of a na-ture as grave as you could meet. But I had witnessed; and therefore supposing that I knew him in spite of his appearance, that I was, so to speak, in his secret and could give him a sort of wink, I adopted at once a method of easiness. It was so pleasant to be easy with a large stranger, who instead of shooting at your heels had very civ-illy handed you a letter.

"You're from old Virginia, I take it?" I began.

He answered slowly, "Then you have taken it correct, seh."

A slight chill passed over my easiness, but I went cheerily on with a further inquiry. "Find many oddities out here like Uncle Hughey?"

"Yes seh, there is a right smart of oddities around. They come in on every train."

At this point I dropped my method of easiness.

"I wish that trunks came on the train," said I. And I told him my predicament.

It was not to be expected that he would be greatly moved at my loss; but he took it with no comment whatever. "We'll wait in town for it," said he, always perfectly civil.

Now, what I had seen of "town" was, to my newly arrived eyes, altogether horrible. If I could possibly sleep at the Judge's ranch, I preferred to do so.

"Is it too far to drive there to-night?" I inquired.

He looked at me in a puzzled manner.

"For this valise," I explained, "contains all that I immediately need; in fact, I could do without my trunk for a day or two, if it is not convenient to send. So if we could arrive there not too late by starting at once—" I paused.

"It's two hundred and sixty-three miles," said the Virginian.

To my loud ejaculation he made no answer, but surveyed me a moment longer, and then said, "Supper will be about ready now." He took my valise, and I followed his steps toward the eating-house in silence. I was dazed.

As we went, I read my host's letter—a brief, hospitable message. He was very sorry not to meet me himself. He had been getting ready to drive over, when the surveyor appeared and detained him. Therefore in his stead he was sending a trustworthy man to town, who would look after me and drive me over. They were looking forward to my visit with much pleasure. This was all.

Yes, I was dazed. How did they count distance in this country? You spoke in a neighborly fashion about driving over to town, and it meant—I did not know yet how many days. And what would be meant by the term "dropping in," I wondered. And how many miles would be considered really far? I abstained from further questioning the "trustworthy man." My questions had not fared excessively well. He did not propose making me dance, to be sure: that would scarcely be trustworthy. But neither did he propose to have me familiar with him. Why was this? What had I done to elicit that veiled and skilful sarcasm about oddities coming in on every train? Having been sent to look after me, he would do so, would even carry my valise; but I could not be jocular with him. This handsome, ungrammatical son of the soil had set between us the bar of his cold and perfect civility. No polished person could have done it better. What was the matter? I looked at him, and suddenly it came to me. If he had tried familiarity with me the first two minutes of our acquaintance, I should have resented it; by what right, then, had I tried it with him? It smacked of patronizing: on this occasion he had come off the better gentleman of the two. Here in flesh and blood was a truth which I had long believed in words, but never met before. The creature we call a *gentleman* lies deep in the hearts of thousands that are born without chance to master the outward graces of the type.

Between the station and the eating-house I did a deal of straight thinking. But my thoughts were destined presently to be drowned in amazement at the rare personage into whose society fate had thrown me.

Town, as they called it, pleased me the less, the longer I saw it. But until our language stretches itself and takes in a new word of closer fit, town will have to do for the name of such a place as was Medicine Bow. I have seen and slept in many like it since. Scattered wide, they littered the frontier from the Columbia to the Rio Grande, from the Missouri to the Sierras. They lay stark, dotted over a planet of treeless dust, like soiled packs of cards. Each was similar to the next, as one old five-spot of clubs resembles another. Houses, empty bottles, and garbage, they were forever of the same shapeless pattern. More forlorn they were than stale bones. They seemed to have been strewn there by the wind and to be waiting till the wind should come again and blow them away. Yet serene above their foulness swam a pure and quiet light, such as the East never sees; they might be bathing in the air of creation's first morning. Beneath sun and stars their days and nights were immaculate and wonderful.

Medicine Bow was my first, and I took its dimensions, twenty-nine buildings in all,—one coal shute, one water tank, the station, one store, two eating-houses, one billiard hall, two tool-houses, one feed stable, and twelve others that for one reason and another I shall not name. Yet this wretched husk of squalor spent thought upon appearances; many houses in it wore a false front to seem as if they were two stories high. There they stood, rearing their pitiful masquerade amid a fringe of old tin cans, while at their very doors began a world of crystal light, a land without end, a space across which Noah and Adam might come straight from Genesis. Into that space went wandering a road, over a hill and down out of sight, and up again smaller in the distance, and down once more, and up once more, straining the eyes, and so away.

Then I heard a fellow greet my Virginian. He came rollicking out of a door, and made a pass with his hand at the Virginian's hat. The Southerner dodged it, and I saw once more the tiger undulation of body, and knew my escort was he of the rope and the corral.

"How are yu', Steve?" he said to the rollicking man. And in his tone I heard instantly old friendship speaking. With Steve he would take and give familiarity.

Steve looked at me, and looked away—and that was all. But it was enough. In no company had I ever felt so much an outsider. Yet I liked the company, and wished that it would like me.

"Just come to town?" inquired Steve of the Virginian.

"Been here since noon. Been waiting for the train."

"Going out to-night?"

"I reckon I'll put out to-morro'."

"Beds are all took," said Steve. This was for my benefit.

"Dear me!" said I.

"But I guess one of them drummers will let yu' double up with him." Steve was enjoying himself, I think. He had his saddle and blankets, and beds were nothing to him.

"Drummers, are they?" asked the Virginian.

"Two Jews handling cigars, one American with consumption killer, and a Dutchman with jew'lry."

The Virginian set down my valise, and seemed to meditate. "I did want a bed to-night," he murmured gently.

"Well," Steve suggested, "the American looks like he washed the oftenest."

"That's of no consequence to me," observed the Southerner.

"Guess it'll be when yu' see 'em."

"Oh, I'm meaning something different. I wanted a bed myself."

"Then you'll have to build one."

"Bet yu' I have the Dutchman's."

"Take a man that won't scare. Bet yu' drinks yu' can't have the American's."

"Go yu'," said the Virginian. "I'll have his bed without any fuss. Drinks for the crowd."

"I suppose you have me beat," said Steve, grinning at him affectionately. "You're such a son-of-a——when you get down to work. Well, so-long! I got to fix my horse's hoofs."

I had expected that the man would be struck down. He had used to the Virginian a term of heaviest insult, I thought. I had marvelled to hear it come so unheralded from Steve's friendly lips. And now I marvelled still more. Evidently he had meant no harm by it, and evidently no offence had been taken. Used thus, this language was plainly complimentary. I had stepped into a world new to me indeed, and novelties were occurring with scarce any time to get breath between them. As to where I should sleep, I had forgotten that problem altogether in my curiosity. What was the Virginian going to do now? I began to know that the quiet of this man was volcanic.

"Will you wash first, sir?"

We were at the door of the eating-house, and he set my valise inside. In my tenderfoot innocence I was looking indoors for the washing arrangments.

"It's out hyeh, seh," he informed me gravely, but with strong Southern accent. Internal mirth seemed often to heighten the local flavor of his speech. There were other times when it had scarce any special accent or fault in grammar.

A trough was to my right, slippery with soapy water; and hanging from a roller above one end of it was a rag of discouraging appearance. The Virginia caught it, and it performed one whirling revolution on its roller. Not a dry or clean inch could be found on it. He took off his hat, and put his head in the door.

"Your towel, ma'am," said he, "has been too popular."

She came out, a pretty woman. Her eyes rested upon him for a moment, then upon me with disfavor; then they returned to his black hair.

"The allowance is one a day," said she, very quietly. "But when folks are particular—" She completed her sentence by removing the old towel and giving a clean one to us.

"Thank you, ma'am," said the cow-puncher.

She looked once more at his black hair, and without any word returned to her guests at supper.

A pail stood in the trough, almost empty; and this he filled for me from a well. There was some soap sliding at large in the trough, but I got my own. And then in a tin basin I removed as many of the stains of travel as I was able. It was not much of a toilet that I made in this first wash-trough of my experience, but it had to suffice, and I took my seat at supper.

Canned stuff it was,—corned beef. And one of my table companions said the truth about it. "When I slung my teeth over that," he remarked, "I thought I was chewing a hammock." We had strange coffee, and condensed milk; and I have never seen more flies. I made no attempt to talk, for no one in this country seemed favorable to me. By reason of something,—my clothes, my hat, my pronunciation, whatever it might be,—I possessed the secret of estranging people at sight. Yet I was doing better than I knew; my strict silence and attention to the corned beef made me in the eyes of the cow-boys at table compare well with the over-talkative commerical travellers.

The Virginian's entrance produced a slight silence. He had done wonders with the wash-trough, and he had somehow brushed his clothes. With all the roughness of his dress, he was now the neatest of us. He nodded to some of the other cow-boys, and began his meal in quiet.

But silence is not the native element of the drummer. An average fish can go a longer time out of water than this breed can live without talking. One of them now looked across the table at the grave, flannel-shirted Virginian; he inspected, and came to the imprudent conclusion that he understood his man.

"Good evening," he said briskly.

"Good evening," said the Virginian.

"Just come to town?" pursued the drummer.

"Just come to town," the Virginian suavely assented.

"Cattle business jumping along?" inquired the drummer.

"Oh, fair." And the Virginian took some more corned beef.

"Gets a move on your appetite, anyway," suggested the drummer.

The Virginian drank some coffee. Presently the pretty woman refilled his cup without his asking her.

"Guess I've met you before," the drummer stated next.

The Virginian glanced at him for a brief moment.

"Haven't I, now? Ain't I seen you somewheres? Look at me. You been in Chicago, ain't you? You look at me well. Remember Ikey's, don't you?"

"I don't reckon I do."

"See, now! I knowed you'd been in Chicago. Four or five years ago. Or maybe it's two years. Time's nothing to me. But I never forget a face. Yes, sir. Him and me's met at Ikey's, all right." This important point the drummer stated to all of us. We were called to witness how well he had proved old acquaintanceship. "Ain't the world small, though!" he exclaimed complacently. "Meet a man once and you're sure to run on to him again. That's straight. That's no bar-room josh." And the drummer's eye included us all in his confidence. I wondered if he had attained that high perfection when a man believes his own lies.

The Virginian did not seem interested. He placidly attended to his food, while our landlady moved between dining room and kitchen, and the drummer expanded.

"Yes, sir! Ikey's over by the stock-yards, patronized by all cattlemen that know what's what. That's where. Maybe it's three years. Time never was nothing to me. But faces! Why, I can't quiet 'em. Adults or children, male and female; onced I seen 'em I couldn't lose one off my memory, not if you were to pay me bounty, five dollars a face. White men, that is. Can't do nothing with niggers or Chinese. But you're white, all right." The drummer suddenly returned to the Virginian with this high compliment. The cowpuncher had taken out a pipe, and was slowly rubbing it. The compliment seemed to escape his attention, and the drummer went on.

"I can tell a man when he's white, put him at Ikey's or out loose here in the sage-brush." And he rolled a cigar across to the Virginian's plate.

"Selling them?" inquired the Virginian.

"Solid goods, my friend. Havana wrappers, the biggest tobacco proposition for five cents got out yet. Take it, try it, light it, watch it burn. Here." And he held out a bunch of matches.

The Virginian tossed a five-cent piece over to him.

"Oh, no, my friend! Not from you! Not after Ikey's. I don't forget you. See? I knowed your face right away. See? That's straight. I seen you at Chicago all right."

"Maybe you did," said the Virginian. "Sometimes I'm mighty careless what I look at."

"Well, py damn!" now exclaimed the Dutch drummer, hilariously. "I am ploom disappointed. I vas hoping to sell him some-dings myself."

"Not the same here," stated the American. "He's too healthy for me. I gave him up on sight."

Now it was the American drummer whose bed the Virginian had in his eye. This was a sensible man, and had talked less than his brothers in the trade. I had little doubt who would end by sleeping in his bed; but how the thing would be done interested me more deeply than ever.

The Virginian looked amiably at his intended victim, and made one or two remarks regarding patent medicines. There must be a good deal of money in them, he supposed, with a live man to manage them. The victim was flattered. No other person at the table had beeen favored with so much of the tall cow-puncher's notice. He responded, and they had a pleasant talk. I did not divine that the Virginian's genius was even then at work, and that all this was part of his satanic strategy. But Steve must have divined it. For while a few of us still sat finishing our supper, that facetious horseman returned from doctoring his horse's hoofs, put his head into the dining room, took in the way in which the Virginian was engaging his victim in conversation, remarked aloud, "I've lost!" and closed the door again.

"What's he lost?" inquired the American drummer.

"Oh, you mustn't mind him," drawled the Virginian. "He's one of those box-head jokers goes around openin' and shuttin' doors that-a-way. We call him harmless. Well," he broke off, "I reckon I'll go smoke. Not allowed in hyeh?" This last he addressed to the landlady, with especial gentleness. She shook her head, and her eyes followed him as he went out.

Left to myself I meditated for some time upon my lodging for the night, and smoked a cigar for consolation as I walked about. It was not a hotel that we had supped in. Hotel at Medicine Bow there appeared to be none. But connected with the eating-house was that place where, according to Steve, the beds were all taken, and there I went to see for myself. Steve had spoken the truth. It was a single apartment containing four or five beds, and nothing else whatever. And when I looked at these beds, my sorrow that I could sleep in none of them grew less. To be alone in one offered no temptation, and as for this courtesy of the country, this doubling up—!

"Well, they have got ahead of us." This was the Virginian standing at my elbow.

I assented.

"They have staked out their claims," he added.

In this public sleeping room they had done what one does to secure a seat in a railroad train. Upon each bed, as notice of occupancy, lay some article of travel or of dress. As we stood there, the two Jews came in and opened and arranged their valises, and folded and refolded their linen dusters. Then a railroad employee entered and began to go to bed at this hour, before dusk had wholly darkened into night. For him, going to bed meant removing his boots and placing his overalls and waistcoat beneath his pillow. He had no coat. His work began at three in the morning; and even as we still talked he began to snore.

"The man that keeps the store is a friend of mine," said the Virginian; "and you can be pretty near comfortable on his counter. Got any blankets?"

I had no blankets.

"Looking for a bed?" inquired the American drummer, now arriving.

"Yes, he's looking for a bed," answered the voice of Steve behind him.

"Seems a waste of time," observed the Virginian. He looked thoughtfully from one bed to another. "I didn't know I'd have to lay over here. Well, I have sat up before."

"This one's mine," said the drummer, sitting down on it. "Half's plenty enough room for me."

"You're cert'nly mighty kind," said the cow-puncher. "But I'd not think o' disconveniencing yu'."

"That's nothing. The other half is yours. Turn in right now if you feel like it."

"No. I don't reckon I'll turn in right now. Better keep your bed to yourself."

"See here," urged the drummer, "if I take you I'm safe from drawing some party I might not care so much about. This here sleeping proposition is a lottery."

"Well," said the Virginian (and his hesitation was truly masterly), "if you put it that way—"

"I do put it that way. Why, you're clean! You've had a shave right now. You turn in when you feel inclined, old man! I ain't retiring just yet."

The drummer had struck a slightly false note in these last remarks. He should not have said "old man." Until this I had thought him merely an amiable person who wished to do a favor. But "old man" came in wrong. It had a hateful taint of his profession; the being too soon with everybody, the celluloid good-fellowship that passes for ivory with nine in ten of the city crowd. But not so with the sons of the sagebrush. They live nearer nature, and they know better.

But the Virginian blandly accepted "old man" from his victim: he had a game to play.

"Well, I cert'nly thank yu'," he said. "After a while I'll take advantage of your kind offer."

I was surprised. Possession being nine points of the law, it seemed his very chance to intrench himself in the bed. But the cow-puncher had planned a campaign needing no intrenchments. Moreover, going to bed before nine o'clock upon the first evening in many weeks that a town's resources were open to you, would be a dull proceeding. Our entire company, drummer and all, now walked over to the store, and here my sleeping arrangements were made easily. This store was the cleanest place and the best in Medicine Bow, and would have been a good store anywhere, offering a multitude of things for sale, and kept by a very civil proprietor. He bade me make myself at home, and placed both of his counters at my disposal. Upon the grocery side there stood a cheese too large and strong to sleep near comfortably, and I therefore chose the dry-goods side. Here thick quilts were unrolled for me, to make it soft; and no condition was placed upon me, further than that I should remove my boots, because the quilts were new, and clean, and for sale. So now my rest was assured. Not an anxiety remained in my thoughts. These therefore turned themselves wholly to the other man's bed, and how he was going to lose it.

I think that Steve was more curious even than myself. Time was on the wing. His bet must be decided, and the drinks enjoyed. He stood against the grocery counter, contemplating the Virginian. But it was to me that he spoke. The Virginian, however, listened to every word.

"Your first visit to this country?"

I told him yes.

"How do you like it?"

I expected to like it very much.

"How does the climate strike you?"

I thought the climate was fine.

"Makes a man thirsty though."

This was the sub-current which the Virginian plainly looked for. But he, like Steve, addressed himself to me.

"Yes," he put in, "thirsty while a man's soft yet. You'll harden."

"I guess you'll find it a drier country than you were given to expect," said Steve.

"If your habits have been frequent that way," said the Virginian.

"There's parts of Wyoming," pursued Steve, "where you'll go hours and hours before you'll see a drop of wetness."

"And if yu' keep a-thinkin' about it," said the Virginian, "it'll seem like days and days."

Steve, at this stroke, gave up, and clapped him on the shoulder with a joyous chuckle. "You old son-of-a——!" he cried affectionately.

"Drinks are due now," said the Virginian. "My treat, Steve. But I reckon your suspense will have to linger a while yet."

Thus they dropped into direct talk from that speech of the fourth dimension where they had been using me for their telephone.

"Any cyards going to-night?" inquired the Virginian.

"Stud and draw," Steve told him. "Strangers playing."

"I think I'd like to get into a game for a while," said the Southerner. "Strangers, yu' say?"

And then, before quitting the store, he made his toilet for this little hand at poker. It was a simple preparation. He took his pistol from its holster, examined it, then shoved it between his overalls and his shirt in front, and pulled his waistcoat over it. He might have been combing his hair for all the attention any one paid to this, except myself. Then the two friends went out, and I bethought me of that epithet which Steve again had used to the Virginian as he clapped him on the shoulder. Clearly this wild country spoke a language other than mine—the word here was a term of endearment. Such was my conclusion.

The drummers had finished their dealings with the proprietor, and they were gossiping together in a knot by the door as the Virginian passed out.

"See you later, old man!" This was the American drummer accosting his prospective bed-fellow.

"Oh, yes," returned the bed-fellow, and was gone.

The American drummer winked triumphantly at his brethren. "He's all right," he observed, jerking a thumb after the Virginian. "He's easy. You got to know him to work him. That's all."

"Und vat is your point?" inquired the German drummer.

"Point is—he'll not take any goods off you or me; but he's going to talk up the killer to any consumptive he runs acrost. I ain't done with him yet. Say," (he now addressed the proprietor), "what's her name?"

"Whose name?"

"Woman runs the eating-house."

"Glen. Mrs. Glen."

"Ain't she new?"

"Been settled here about a month. Husband's a freight conductor."

"Thought I'd not seen her before. She's a good-looker."

"Hm! Yes. The kind of good looks I'd sooner see in another man's wife than mine."

"So that's the gait, is it?"

"Hm! well, it don't seem to be. She come here with that reputation. But there's been general disappointment."

"Then she ain't lacked suitors any?"

"Lacked! Are you acquainted with cow-boys?"

"And she disappointed 'em? Maybe she likes her husband?"

"Hm! well, how are you to tell about them silent kind?"

"Talking of conductors," began the drummer. And we listened to his anecdote. It was successful with his audience; but when he launched fluently upon a second I strolled out. There was not enough wit in this narrator to relieve his indecency, and I felt shame at having been surprised into laughing with him.

I left that company growing confidential over their leering stories, and I sought the saloon. It was very quiet and orderly. Beer in quart bottles at a dollar I had never met before; but saving its price, I found no complaint to make of it. Through folding doors I passed from the bar proper with its bottles and elk head back to the hall with its various tables. I saw a man sliding cards from a case, and across the table from him another man laying counters down. Near by was a second dealer pulling cards from the bottom of a pack, and opposite him a solemn old rustic piling and changing coins upon the cards which lay already exposed.

But now I heard a voice that drew my eyes to the far corner of the room.

"Why didn't you stay in Arizona?"

Harmless looking words as I write them down here. Yet at the sound of them I noticed the eyes of the others directed to that corner. What answer was given to them I did not hear, nor did I see who spoke. Then came another remark.

"Well, Arizona's no place for amatures."

This time the two card dealers that I stood near began to give a part of their attention to the group that sat in the corner. There was in me a desire to leave this room. So far my hours at Medicine Bow had seemed to glide beneath a sunshine of merriment, of easy-going jocularity. This was suddenly gone, like the wind changing to north in the middle of a warm day. But I stayed, being ashamed to go.

Five or six players sat over in the corner at a round table where counters were piled. Their eyes were close upon their cards, and one seemed to be dealing a card at a time to each, with pauses and betting between. Steve was there and the Virginian; the others were new faces.

"No place for amatures," repeated the voice; and now I saw that it was the dealer's. There was in his countenance the same ugliness that his words conveyed.

"Who's that talkin'?" said one of the men near me, in a low voice.

"Trampas."

"What's he?"

"Cow-puncher, bronco-buster, tin-horn, most anything."

"Who's he talkin' at?"

"Think it's the black-headed guy he's talking at."

"That ain't supposed to be safe, is it?"

"Guess we're all goin' to find out in a few minutes."

"Been trouble between 'em?"

"They've not met before. Trampas don't enjoy losin' to a stranger."

"Fello's from Arizona, yu' say?"

"No. Virginia. He's recently back from havin' a look at Arizona. Went down there last year for a change. Works for the Sunk Creek outfit." And then the dealer lowered his voice still further and said something in the other man's ear, causing him to grin. After which both of them looked at me.

There had been silence over in the corner; but now the man Trampas spoke again.

"*And* ten," said he, sliding out some chips from before him. Very strange it was to hear him, how he contrived to make those words a personal taunt. The Virginian was looking at his cards. He might have been deaf.

"*And* twenty," said the next player, easily.

The next threw his cards down.

It was now the Virginian's turn to bet, or leave the game, and he did not speak at once.

Therefore Trampas spoke. "Your bet, you son-of-a——."

The Virginian's pistol came out, and his hand lay on the table, holding it unaimed. And with a voice as gentle as ever, the voice that sounded almost like a caress, but drawling a very little more than usual, so that there was almost a space between each word, he issued his orders to the man Trampas:—

"When you call me that, *smile*." And he looked at Trampas across the table.

Yes, the voice was gentle. But in my ears it seemed as if somewhere the bell of death was ringing; and silence, like a stroke, fell on the large room. All men present, as if by some magnetic current, had become aware of this crisis. In my ignorance, and the total stoppage of my thoughts, I stood stock-still, and noticed various people crouching, or shifting their positions.

"Sit quiet," said the dealer, scornfully to the man near me. "Can't you see he don't want to push trouble? He has handed Trampas the choice to back down or draw his steel."

Then, with equal suddenness and ease, the room came out of its strangeness. Voices and cards, the click of chips, the puff of tobacco, glasses lifted to drink,—this level of smooth relaxation hinted no more plainly of what lay beneath than does the surface tell the depth of the sea.

For Trampas had made his choice. And that choice was not to "draw his steel." If it was knowledge that he sought, he had found it, and no mistake! We heard no further reference to what he had been pleased to style "amatures." In no company would the black-headed man who had visited Arizona be rated a novice at the cool art of self-preservation.

One doubt remained: what kind of man was Trampas? A public back-down is an unfinished thing,—for some natures at least. I looked at his face, and thought it sullen, but tricky rather than courageous.

Something had been added to my knowledge also. Once again I had heard applied to the Virginian that epithet which Steve so freely used. The same words, identical to the letter. But this time they had produced a pistol. "When you call me that, *smile!*" So I perceived a new example of the old truth, that the letter means nothing until the spirit gives it life.

JACK SCHAEFER

Shane

HE RODE into our valley in the summer of '89. I was a kid then, barely topping the backboard of father's old chuck-wagon. I was on the upper rail of our small corral, soaking in the late afternoon sun, when I saw him far down the road where it swung into the valley from the open plain beyond.

In that clear Wyoming air I could see him plainly, though he was still several miles away. There seemed nothing remarkable about him, just another stray horseman riding up the road toward the cluster of frame buildings that was our town. Then I saw a pair of cowhands, loping past him, stop and stare after him with a curious intentness.

He came steadily on, straight through the town without slackening pace, until he reached the fork a half-mile below our place. One branch turned left across the river ford and on to Luke Fletcher's big spread. The other bore ahead along the right bank where we homesteaders had pegged our claims in a row up the valley. He hesitated briefly, studying the choice, and moved again steadily on our side.

As he came near, what impressed me first was his clothes. He wore dark trousers of some serge material tucked into tall boots and held at the waist by a wide belt, both of a soft black leather tooled in intricate design. A coat of the same dark material as the trousers was neatly folded and strapped to his saddle-roll. His shirt was finespun linen, rich brown in color. The handkerchief knotted loosely around his throat was black silk. His hat was not the familiar Stetson, not the familiar gray or muddy tan. It was plain black, soft in texture, unlike any hat I had ever seen, with a creased crown and a wide curling brim swept down in front to shield the face.

All trace of newness was long since gone from these things. The dust of distance was beaten into them. They were worn and stained and several neat patches showed on the shirt. Yet a kind of magnificence remained and with it a hint of men and manners alien to my limited boy's experience.

Then I forgot the clothes in the impact of the man himself. He was not much above medium height, almost slight in build. He would have looked frail alongside father's square, solid bulk. But even I could read the endurance in the lines of that dark figure and the quiet power in its effortless, unthinking adjustment to every movement of the tired horse.

He was clean-shaven and his face was lean and hard and burned from high forehead to firm, tapering chin. His eyes seemed hooded in the shadow of the hat's brim. He came closer, and I could see that this was because the brows were drawn in a frown of fixed and habitual alertness. Beneath them the eyes were endlessly searching from side to side and forward, checking off every item in view, missing nothing. As I noticed this, a sudden chill, I could not have told why, struck through me there in the warm and open sun.

He rode easily, relaxed in the saddle, leaning his weight lazily into the stirrups. Yet even in this easiness was a suggestion of tension. It was the easiness of a coiled spring, of a trap set.

He drew rein not twenty feet from me. His glance hit me, dismissed me, flicked over our place. This was not much, if you were thinking in terms of size and scope. But what there was was good. You could trust father for that. The corral, big enough for about thirty head if you crowded them in, was railed right to true sunk posts. The pasture behind, taking in nearly half of our claim, was fenced tight. The barn was small, but it was solid, and we were raising a loft at one end for the alfalfa growing green in the north forty. We had a fair-sized field in potatoes that year and father was trying a new corn he had sent all the way to Washington for and they were showing properly in weedless rows.

Behind the house mother's kitchen garden was a brave sight. The house itself was three rooms—two really, the big kitchen where we spent most of our time indoors and the bedroom beside it. My little lean-to room was added back of the kitchen. Father was planning, when he could get around to it, to build mother the parlor she wanted.

We had wooden floors and a nice porch across the front. The house was painted too, white with green trim, rare thing in all that region, to remind her, mother said when she made father do it, of her native New England. Even rarer, the roof was shingled. I knew what that meant. I had helped father split those shingles. Few places so spruce and well worked could be found so deep in the Territory in those days.

The stranger took it all in, sitting there easily in the saddle. I saw his eyes slow on the flowers mother had planted by the porch steps, then come to rest on our shiny new pump and the trough beside it. They shifted back to me, and again, without knowing why, I felt that sudden chill. But his voice was gentle and he spoke like a man schooled to patience.

"I'd appreciate a chance at the pump for myself and the horse."

I was trying to frame a reply and choking on it, when I realized that he was not speaking to me but past me. Father had come up behind me and was leaning against the gate to the corral.

"Use all the water you want, stranger."

Father and I watched him dismount in a single flowing tilt of his body and lead the horse over to the trough. He pumped it almost full and let the horse sink its nose in the cool water before he picked up the dipper for himself.

He took off his hat and slapped the dust out of it and hung it on a corner of the trough. With his hands he brushed the dust from his clothes. With a piece of rag pulled from his saddle-roll he carefully wiped his boots. He untied the handkerchief from around his neck and rolled his sleeves and dipped his arms in the trough, rubbing thoroughly and splashing water over his face. He shook his hands dry and used the handkerchief to remove the last drops from his face. Taking a comb from his shirt pocket, he smoothed back his long dark hair. All his movements were deft and sure, and with a quick precision he flipped down his sleeves, reknotted the handkerchief, and picked up his hat.

Then, holding it in his hand, he spun about and strode directly toward the house. He bent low and snapped the stem of one of mother's petunias and tucked this into the hatband. In another moment the hat was on his head, brim swept down in swift, unconscious gesture, and he was swinging gracefully into the saddle and starting toward the road.

I was fascinated. None of the men I knew were proud like that about their appearance. In that short time the kind of magnificence I had noticed had emerged into plainer view. It was in the very air of him. Everything about him showed the effects of long use and hard use, but showed too the strength of quality and competence. There was no chill on me now. Already I was imagining myself in hat and belt and boots like those.

He stopped the horse and looked down at us. He was refreshed and I would have sworn the tiny wrinkles around his eyes were what with him would be a smile. His eyes were not restless when he looked at you like this. They were still and steady and you knew the man's whole attention was concentrated on you even in the casual glance.

"Thank you," he said in his gentle voice and was turning into the road, back to us, before father spoke in his slow, deliberate way.

"Don't be in such a hurry, stranger."

I had to hold tight to the rail or I would have fallen backwards into the corral. At the first sound of father's voice, the man and the horse, like a single being, had wheeled to face us, the man's eyes boring at father, bright and deep in the shadow of the hat's brim. (I was shivering, struck through once more. Something intangible and cold and terrifying was there in the air between us.)

I stared in wonder as father and the stranger looked at each other a long moment, measuring each other in an unspoken fraternity of adult knowledge beyond my reach. Then the warm sunlight was flooding over us, for father was smiling and he was speaking with the drawling emphasis that meant he had made up his mind.

"I said don't be in such a hurry, stranger. Food will be on the table soon and you can bed down here tonight."

The stranger nodded quiety as if he too had made up his mind. "That's mighty thoughtful of you," he said and swung down and came toward us, leading his horse. Father slipped into step beside him and we all headed for the barn.

"My name's Starrett," said father. "Joe Starrett. This here," waving at me, "is Robert MacPherson Starrett. Too much name for a boy. I make it Bob."

The stranger nodded again. "Call me Shane," he said. Then to me: "Bob it is. You were watching me for quite a spell coming up the road."

It was not a question. It was a simple statement. "Yes . . ." I stammered. "Yes. I was."

"Right," he said, "I like that. A man who watches what's going on around him will make his mark."

A man who watches . . . For all his dark appearance and lean, hard look, this Shane knew what would please a boy. The glow of it held me as he took care of his horse, and I fussed around, hanging up his saddle, forking over some hay, getting in his way and my own in my eagerness. He let me slip the bridle off and the horse, bigger and more powerful than I had thought now that I was close beside it, put its head down patiently for me and stood quietly while I helped him curry away the caked dust. Only once did he stop me. That was when I reached for his saddle-roll to put it to one side. In the instant my fingers touched it, he was taking it from me and he put it on a shelf with a finality that indicated no interference.

JOHN M. CUNNINGHAM

———•—•———

The Tin Star

SHERIFF DOANE looked at his deputy and then down at the daisies he
had picked for his weekly visit, lying wrapped in newspaper on his
desk. "I'm sorry to hear you say that, Toby. I was kind of counting
on you to take over after me."

"Don't get me wrong, Doane," Toby said, looking through the
front window. "I'm not afraid. I'll see you through this shindig. I'm
not afraid of Jordan or young Jordan or any of them. But I want to
tell you now. I'll wait till Jordan's train gets in. I'll wait to see what
he does. I'll see you through whatever happens. After that, I'm quitting."

Doane began kneading his knuckles, his face set against the pain
as he gently rubbed the misshapen, twisted bones. Using his fists all
these years hadn't helped the gout. He said nothing.

Toby looked around, his brown eyes troubled in his round, olive-
skinned face. "What's the use of holding down a job like this? Look
at you. What'd you ever get out of it? Enough to keep you eating.
And what for?"

Doane stopped kneading his arthritic hands and looked down at
the star on his shirt front. He looked from it to the smaller one on
Toby's. "That's right," he said. "They don't even hang the right
ones. You risk your life catching somebody, and the damned juries
let them go so they can come back and shoot at you. You're poor all
your life, you got to do everything twice, and in the end they pay
you off in lead. So you can wear a tin star. It's a job for a dog, son."

Toby's voice did not rise, but his eyes were a little wider in his
round, gentle face. "Then why keep on with it? What for? I been
working for you for two years—trying to keep the law so sharp-nosed
money-grabbers can get rich, while we piddle along on what the
county pays us. I've seen men I used to bust playing marbles going
up and down this street on four-hundred-dollar saddles, and what've
I got? Nothing. Not a damned thing."

There was a little smile around Doane's wide mouth. "That's

right, Toby. It's all for free. The headaches, the bullets and every-thing, all for free. I found that out long ago." The mock-grave look vanished. "But somebody's got to be around and take care of things." He looked out of the window at the people walking up and down the crazy boardwalks. "I like it free. You know what I mean? You don't get a thing for it. You've got to risk everything. And you're free inside. Like the larks. You know the larks? How they get up in the sky and sing when they want to? A pretty bird. A very pretty bird. That's the way I like to feel inside."

Toby looked at him without expression. "That's the way you look at it. I don't see it. I've only got one life. You talk about doing it all for nothing, and that gives you something. What? What've you got now, waiting for Jordan to come?"

"I don't know yet. We'll have to wait and see."

Toby turned back to the window. "All right, but I'm through. I don't see any sense in risking your neck for nothing."

"Maybe you will," Doane said, beginning to work on his hands again.

"Here comes Mettrick. I guess he don't give up so easy. He's still got that resignation in his hand."

"I guess he doesn't," Doane said. "But I'm through listening. Has young Jordan come out of the saloon yet?"

"No," Toby said, and stepped aside as the door opened. Mettrick came in. "Now listen, Doane," he burst out, "for the last time—"

"Shut up, Percy," Doane said. "Sit down over there and shut up or get out."

The flare went out of the mayor's eyes. "Doane," he moaned, "you are the biggest—"

"Shut up," Doane said. "Toby, has he come out yet?"

Toby stood a little back from the window, where the slant of golden sunlight, swarming with dust, wouldn't strike his white shirt.

"Yes. He's got a chair. He's looking this way, Doane. He's still drinking. I can see a bottle on the porch beside him."

"I expected that. Not that it makes much difference." He looked down at the bunch of flowers.

Mettrick, in the straight chair against the wall, looked up at him, his black eyes scornful in his long, hopeless face.

"Don't make much difference? Who the hell do you think you are, Doane? God? It just means he'll start the trouble without wait-ing for his stinking brother, that's all it means." His hand was shak-ing, and the white paper hanging listlessly from his fingers fluttered slightly. He looked at it angrily and stuck it out at Doane. "I gave it to you. I did the best I could. Whatever happens, don't be blaming me, Doane. I gave you a chance to resign, and if—" He left off and sat looking at the paper in his hand as though it were a dead puppy of his that somebody had run a buggy over.

Doane standing with the square almost chisel-pointed tips of his fingers just touching the flowers, turned slowly with the care of movement he would have used around a crazy horse. "I know you're my friend, Percy. Just take it easy, Percy. If I don't resign, it's not because I'm ungrateful."

"Here comes Staley with the news," Toby said from the window. "He looks like somebody just shot his grandma."

Percy Mettrick laid his paper on the desk and began smoothing it out carefully. "It's not as though it were dishonorable, Doane. You should have quit two years ago, when your hands went bad. It's not dishonorable now. You've still got time."

He glanced up at the wall clock. "It's only three. You've got an hour before it gets in, you can take your horse . . ." As he talked to himself, Doane looked slantwise at him with his little smile. He grew more cheerful. "Here." He jabbed a pen out at Doane. "Sign it and get out of town."

The smile left Doane's mouth. "This is an elective office. I don't have to take orders, even if you are mayor." His face softened. "It's simpler than you think, Percy. When they didn't hang Jordan, I knew this day would come. Five years ago, I knew it was coming, when they gave him that silly sentence. I've been waiting for it."

"But not to commit suicide," Mettrick said in a low voice, his eyes going down to Doane's gouty hands. Doane's knobby, twisted fingers closed slowly into fists, as though hiding themselves; his face flushed slightly. "I may be slow, but I can still shoot."

The mayor stood up and went slowly over to the door.

"Goodbye, Doane."

"I'm not saying goodbye, Percy. Not yet."

"Goodbye," Mettrick repeated. He went out of the door.

Toby turned from the window. His face was tight around the mouth. "You should have resigned like he said, Doane. You ain't a match for one of them, much less two of them together. And if Pierce and Frank Colby come, too, like they was all together before —"

"Shut up, shut up," Doane said. "For God's sake, shut up." He sat down suddenly at the desk and covered his face with his hands. "Maybe the pen changes a man." He was sitting stiff, hardly breathing.

"What are you going to do, Doane?"

"Nothing. I can't do anything until they start something. I can't do a thing. . . . Maybe the pen changes a man. Sometimes it does. I remember—"

"Listen, Doane," Toby said, his voice, for the first time, urgent.

"It maybe changes some men, but not Jordan. It's already planned, what they're going to do. Why else would young Jordan be over there, watching? He's come three hundred miles for this."

"I've seen men go in the pen hard as rock and come out peaceful and settle down. Maybe Jordan—"

Toby's face relapsed into dullness. He turned back to the window listlessly. Doane's hands dropped.

"You don't think that's true, Toby?"

Toby sighed. "You know it isn't so, Doane. He swore he'd get you. That's the truth."

Doane's hands came up again in front of his face, but this time he was looking at them, his big gray eyes going quickly from one to the other, almost as though he were afraid of them. He curled his fingers slowly into fists, and uncurled them slowly, pulling with all his might, yet slowly. A thin sheen on his face reflected the sunlight from the floor. He got up.

"Is he still there?" he asked.

"Sure, he's still there."

"Maybe he'll get drunk. Dead drunk."

"You can't get a Jordan that drunk."

Doane stood with feet apart, looking at the floor, staring back and forth along one of the cracks. "Why didn't they hang him?" he asked the silence in the room.

"Why didn't they hang him?" he repeated, his voice louder.

Toby kept his post by the window, not moving a muscle in his face, staring out at the man across the street. "I don't know," he said. "For murder, they should. I guess they should, but they didn't."

Doane's eyes came again to the flowers, and some of the strain went out of his face. Then suddenly his eyes closed and he gave a long sigh, and then, luxuriously, stretched his arms. "Good God!" he said, his voice easy again. "It's funny how it comes over you like that." He shook his head violently. "I don't know why it should. It's not the first time. But it always does."

"I know," Toby said.

"It just builds up and then it busts."

"I know."

"The train may be late."

Toby said nothing.

"You never can tell," Doane said, buckling on his gun belt. "Things may have changed with Jordan. Maybe he won't even come. You never can tell. I'm going up to the cemetery as soon as we hear from Staley."

"I wouldn't. You'd just tempt young Jordan to start something."

"I've been going up there every Sunday since she died."

"We'd best both just stay in here. Let them make the first move."

Feet sounded on the steps outside and Doane stopped breathing for a second. Staley came in, his face pinched, tight and dead, his eyes on the floor. Doane looked him over carefully.

"Is it on time?" he asked steadily.

Staley looked up, his faded blue eyes, distant, pointed somewhere over Doane's head. "Mr. Doane, you ain't handled this thing right. You should of drove young Jordan out of town." His hand went to his chest and he took off the deputy's badge.

"What are you doing?" Doane asked sharply.

"If you'd of handled it right, we could have beat this," Staley said, his voice louder.

"You know nobody's done nothing yet," Toby said softly, his gentle brown eyes on Staley. "There's nothing we can do until they start something."

"I'm quitting, Mr. Doane," Staley said. He looked around for someplace to put the star. He started for the desk, hesitated, and then awkwardly, with a peculiar diffidence, laid the star gently on the window sill.

Doane's jaw began to jut a little. "You still haven't answered my question. Is the train on time?"

"Yes. Four ten. Just on time." Staley stood staring at Doane, then swallowed. "I saw Frank Colby. He was in the livery putting up his horse. He'd had a long ride on that horse. I asked him what he was doing in town—friendly like." He ducked his head and swallowed again. "He didn't know I was a deputy. I had my star off." He looked up again. "They're all meeting together, Mr. Doane. Young Jordan, and Colby and Pierce. They're going to meet Jordan when he comes in. The same four."

"So you're quitting," Doane said.

"Yes, sir. It ain't been handled right."

Toby stood looking at him, his gentle eyes dull. "Get out," he said, his voice low and tight.

Staley looked at him, nodded and tried to smile, which was too weak to last. "Sure."

Toby took a step toward him. Staley's eyes were wild as he stood against the door. He tried to back out of Toby's way.

"Get out," Toby said again, and his small brown fist flashed out. Staley stepped backward and fell down the steps in a sprawling heap, scrambled to his feet and hobbled away. Toby closed the door slowly. He stood rubbing his knuckles, his face red and tight.

"That didn't do any good," Doane said softly.

Toby turned on him. "It couldn't do no harm," he said acidly, throwing the words into Doane's face.

"You want to quit, too?" Doane asked, smiling.

"Sure, I want to quit," Toby shot out. "Sure. Go on to your blasted cemetery, go on with your flowers, old man—" He sat down suddenly on the straight chair. "Put a flower up there for me, too."

Doane went to the door. "Put some water on the heater, Toby. Set out the liniment that the vet gave me. I'll try it again when I get back. It might do some good yet."

Then he let himself out and stood in the sunlight on the porch, the flowers drooping in his hand, looking against the sun across the street at the dim figure under the shaded porch.

Then he saw the two other shapes hunkered against the front of the saloon in the shade of the porch, one on each side of young Jordan, who sat tilted back in a chair. Colby and Pierce. The glare of the sun beat back from the blinding white dust and fought shimmering in the air.

Doane pulled the brim of his hat farther down in front and stepped slowly down to the board sidewalk, observing just as carefully, avoiding any pause which might be interpreted as a challenge.

Young Jordan had the bottle to his lips as Doane came out. He held it there for a moment motionless, and then, as Doane reached the walk, he passed the bottle slowly sideward to Colby and leaned forward, away from the wall, so that the chair came down softly. He sat there, leaning forward slightly, watching while Doane untied his horse. As Doane mounted, Jordan got up. Colby's hand grabbed one of his arms. He shook it off and untied his own horse from the rail.

Doane's mouth tightened and his eyes looked a little sad. He turned his horse, and holding the flowers so the jog would not rattle off the petals, headed up the street, looking straight ahead.

The hoofs of his horse made soft, almost inaudible little plops in the deep dust. Behind him he heard a sudden stamping of hoofs and then the harsh splitting and crash of wood. He looked back. Young Jordan's horse was up on the sidewalk, wild-eyed and snorting with young Jordan leaning forward half out of the saddle, pushing himself back from the horse's neck, back off the horn into the saddle, swaying insecurely. And as Jordan managed the horse off the sidewalk Doane looked quickly forward again, his eyes fixed distantly ahead and blank.

He passed men he knew, and out of the corner of his eye he saw their glances slowly follow him, calm, or gloomy, or shrewdly speculative. As he passed, he knew their glances were shifting to the man whose horse was softly coming up behind him. It was like that all the way up the street. The flowers were drooping markedly now.

The town petered out with a few Mexican shacks, the road dwindled to broad ruts, and the sage was suddenly on all sides of him, stretching away toward the heat-obscured mountains like an infinite multitude of gray-green sheep. He turned off the road and began the slight ascent up the little hill whereon the cemetery lay. Grasshoppers thrilled invisibly in the sparse, dried grass along the track, silent as he came by, and shrill again as he passed, only to become silent again as the other rider came.

He swung off at the rusty barbed wire Missouri gate and slipped the loop from the post, and the shadow of the other slid tall across his path and stopped. Doane licked his lips quickly and looked up, his grasp tightening on the now sweat-wilted newspaper. Young Jordan was sitting his horse, open-mouthed, leaning forward with his hands on the pommel to support himself, his eyes vague and dull. His lips were wet and red, and hung in a slight smile.

A lark made the air sweet over to the left, and then Doane saw it, rising into the air. It hung in the sun, over the cemetery. Moving steadily and avoiding all suddenness, Doane hung his reins over the post.

"You don't like me, do you?" young Jordan said. A long thread of saliva descended from the corner of his slackly smiling mouth.

Doane's face set into a sort of blank preparedness. He turned and started slowly through the gate, his shoulders hunched up and pulled backward.

Jordan got down from the saddle, and Doane turned toward him slowly. Jordan came forward straight enough, with his feet apart, braced against staggering. He stopped three feet from Doane, bent forward, his mouth slightly open.

"You got any objections to me being in town?"

"No," Doane said, and stood still.

Jordan thought that over, his eyes drifting idly sideways for a moment. Then they came back, to a finer focus this time, and he said, "Why not?" hunching forward again, his hands open and held away from the holsters at his hips.

Doane looked at the point of his nose. "You haven't done anything, Jordan. Except get drunk. Nothing to break the law."

"I haven't done nothing," Jordan said, his eyes squinting away at one of the small, tilting tombstones. "By God, I'll do something. Whadda I got to do?" He drew his head back, as though he were farsighted, and squinted. "Whadda I got to do to make you fight, huh?"

"Don't do anything," Doane said quietly, keeping his voice even. "Just go back and have another drink. Have a good time."

"You think I ain't sober enough to fight?" Jordan slipped his right gun out of its holster, turning away from Doane. Doane stiffened. "Wait, mister," Jordan said.

He cocked the gun. "See that bird?" He raised the gun into the air, squinting along the barrel. The bright nickel of its finish gleamed in the sun. The lark wheeled and fluttered. Jordan's arm swung unsteadily in a small circle.

He pulled the trigger and the gun blasted. The lark jumped in the air, flew away about twenty feet, and began circling again, catching insects.

"Missed 'im," Jordan mumbled, lowering his arm and wiping sweat off his forehead. "Damn it, I can't see!" He raised his arm again. Again the heavy blast cracked Doane's ears. Down in the town, near the Mexican huts, he could see tiny figures run out into the street.

The bird didn't jump this time, but darted away out of sight over the hill,

"Got him," Jordan said, scanning the sky. His eyes wandered over the graveyard for a moment, looking for the bird's body. "Now you see?" he said, turning to Doane, his eyes blurred and watering with the sun's glare. "I'm going down and shoot up the damned town. Come down and stop me, you old—"

He turned and lurched sideways a step, straightened himself out and walked more steadily toward his horse, laughing to himself. Doane turned away, his face sick, and trudged slowly up the hill, his eyes on the ground.

He stopped at one of the newer graves. The headstone was straight on this one. He looked at it, his face changing expression. "Here lies Cecelia Doane, born 1837, died 1885, the loyal wife . . ."

He stopped and pulled a weed from the side of the grave, then pulled a bunch of withered stems from a small green funnel by the headstone, and awkwardly took the fresh flowers out of the newspaper. He put the flowers into the funnel, wedging them firmly down into the bottom, and set it down again. He stood up and moved back, wiping sweat from his eyes.

A sudden shout came from the gate, and the sharp crack of a quirt. Doane turned with a befuddled look.

Jordan was back on his horse, beating Doane's. He had looped the reins over its neck so that it would run free. It was tearing away down the slope headed back for town.

Doane stood with his hat in his hand, his face suddenly beet red. He took a step after Jordan, and then stood still, shaking a little. He stared fixedly after him, watching him turn into the main road and toward the main street again. Then, sighing deeply, he turned back to the grave. Folding the newspaper, he began dusting off the heavy slab, whispering to himself. "No, Cissie, I could have gone. But, you know—it's my town."

He straightened up, his face flushed, put on his hat, and slapping the folded paper against his kneee, started down the path. He got to the Missouri gate, closed it, and started down the ruts again.

A shot came from the town, and he stopped. Then there were two more, sharp spurts of sound coming clear and definite across the sage. He made out a tiny figure in a blue shirt running along a sidewalk.

He stood stock-still, the grasshoppers singing in a contented chorus all around him in the bright yellow glare. A train whistle came faint from off the plain, and he looked far across it. He made out the tiny trailed plume of smoke.

His knees began to quiver very slightly and he began to walk, very slowly, down the road.

Then suddenly there came a splatter of shots from below. The train whistle came again, louder, a crying wail of despair in the burning, brilliant, dancing air.

He began to hurry, stumbling a little in the ruts. And then he stopped short, his face open in fear. "My God, my empty horse, those shots—Toby, no!" He began to run, shambling, awkward and stumbling, his face ashen.

From the end of the street, as he hobbled panting past the tight-shut Mexican shanties, he could see a blue patch in the dust in front of the saloon, and shambled to a halt. It wasn't Toby, whoever it was, lying there face down: face buried in the deep, pillowing dust, feet still on the board sidewalk where the man had been standing.

The street was empty. None of the faces he knew looked at him now. He drew one of his guns and cocked it and walked fast up the walk, on the saloon side.

A shot smashed ahead of him and he stopped, shrinking against a store front. Inside, through the glass door, he could see two pale faces in the murk. Blue powder smoke curled out from under the saloon porch ahead of him.

Another shot smashed, this time from his office. The spurt of smoke, almost invisible in the sunlight, was low down in the doorway. Two horses were loose in the street now, his own, standing alert up past the saloon, and young Jordan's half up on the board-walk under one of the porches.

He walked forward, past young Jordan's horse, to the corner of the saloon building. Another shot slammed out of his office door, the bullet smacking the window ahead of him. A small, slow smile grew on his mouth. He looked sideways at the body in the street.

Young Jordan lay with the back of his head open to the sun, crimson and brilliant, his bright nickel gun still in his right hand, its hammer still cocked, unfired.

The train whistle moaned again, closer.

"Doane," Toby called from the office door, invisible. "Get out of town." There was a surge of effort in the voice, a strain that made it almost a squeal. "I'm shot in the leg. Get out before they get together."

A door slammed somewhere. Doane glanced down between the saloon and the store beside it. Then he saw, fifty yards down the street, a figure come out of another side alley and hurry away down the walk toward the station. From the saloon door another shot slammed across the street. Toby held his fire.

Doane peered after the running figure, his eyes squinting thoughtfully. The train's whistle shrieked again like the ultimatum of an approaching conqueror at the edge of town, and in a moment the ground under his feet began to vibrate slightly and the hoarse roar of braking wheels came up the street.

He turned back to young Jordan's horse, petted it around the head a moment and then took it by the reins close to the bit. He guided it across the street, keeping its body between him and the front of the saloon, without drawing fire, and went on down the alley beside his office. At the rear door he hitched the horse and went inside.

Toby was on the floor, a gun in his hand, his hat beside him, peering out across the sill. Doane kept low, beneath the level of the window, and crawled up to him. Toby's left leg was twisted peculiarly and blood leaked steadily out from the boot top onto the floor. His face was sweating and very pale, and his lips were tight. "I thought he got you," Toby said keeping his eyes on the saloon across the street. "I heard those shots and then your horse came bucketing back down the street. I got Jordan. Colby got me in the leg before I got back inside."

"Never mind about that. Come on, get on your feet if you can and I'll help you on the horse in back. You can get out of town and I'll shift for myself."

"I think I'm going to pass out. I don't want to move. It won't hurt no worse getting killed than it does now. The hell with the horse! Take it yourself."

Doane looked across the street, his eyes moving over the door and the windows carefully, inch by inch.

"I'm sorry I shot him," Toby said. "It's my fault. And it's my fight now, Doane. Clear out."

Doane turned and scuttled out of the back. He mounted the horse and rode down behind four stores. He turned up another alley, dashed across the main street, down another alley, then back up behind the saloon.

He dismounted, his gun cocked in his hand. The back door of the place was open and he got through it quickly, the sound of his boot heels dimmed under the blast of a shot from the front of the saloon. From the dark rear of the room, he could see Pierce, crouched behind the bar, squinting through a bullet hole in the stained-glass bottom half of the front window.

There was a bottle of whisky standing on the bar beside Pierce; he reached out a hand and tilted the bottle up to his mouth, half turning toward Doane as he did so. Pierce kept the bottle to his lips, pretending to drink, and, with his right hand invisible behind the bar, brought his gun into line with Doane.

The tip of Pierce's gun came over the edge of the bar, the rest of him not moving a hair and Doane, gritting his teeth, squeezed slowly and painfully on his gun trigger. The gun flamed and bucked in his hand, and he dropped it, his face twisting in agony. The bottle fell out of Pierce's hand and spun slowly on the bar. Pierce sat there for a moment before his head fell forward and he crashed against the edge of the bar and slipped down out of sight.

Doane picked up his gun with his left hand and walked forward to the bar, holding his right hand like a crippled paw in front of him. The bottle had stopped revolving. Whisky inside it, moving back and forth, rocked it gently. He righted it and took a short pull at the neck, and in a moment the pain lines relaxed in his face. He went to the bat-wing doors and pushed one of them partly open.

"Toby!" he called.

There was no answer from across the street, and then he saw the barrel of a revolver sticking out of his office door, lying flat, and behind it one hand, curled loosely and uselessly around the butt.

He looked down the street. The train stood across it. A brakeman moved along the cars slowly, his head down. There was nobody else in sight.

He started to step out, and saw then two men coming up the opposite walk, running fast. Suddenly one of them stopped, grabbing the other by the arm, and pointed at him. He stared back for a moment, seeing Jordan clearly now, the square, hard face unchanged except for its pallor, bleak and bony as before.

Doane let the door swing to and continued to watch them over the top of it. They talked for a moment. Then Colby ran back down the street—well out of effective range—sprinted across it and disappeared. Down the street the engine, hidden by some building, chuffed angrily, and the cars began to move again. Jordan stood still, leaning against the front of a building, fully exposed, a hard smile on his face.

Doane turned and hurried to the back door. It opened outward. He slammed and bolted it, then hurried back to the front and waited, his gun ready. He smiled as the back door rattled, turned, fired a shot at it and listened. For a moment there was no sound. Then something solid hit it, bumped a couple of times and silence came again.

From the side of the building, just beyond the corner where Pierce's body lay, a shot crashed. The gun in the office door jumped out of the hand and spun wildly. The hand lay still.

He heard Jordan's voice from down the street, calling, the words formed slowly, slightly spaced.

"Is he dead?"

"Passed out," Colby called back.

"I'm going around back to get him. Keep Doane inside." Jordan turned and disappeared down an alley.

Doane leaned across the bar, knocked bottles off the shelves of the back bar and held his pistol on the corner of the wall, about a foot above the floor.

"Pierce," he said.

"Throw out your guns," Pierce answered.

Doane squinted at the corner, moved his gun slightly and fired. He heard a cry of pain, then curses; saw the bat-wing doors swing slightly. Then he turned and ran for the back door. He threw back the bolt and pushed on the door. It wouldn't give. He threw himself against it. It gave a little at the bottom. Colby had thrown a stake up against it to keep him locked in.

He ran back to the front.

Across the street, he could see somebody moving in his office, dimly, beyond the window. Suddenly the hand on the floor disappeared.

"Come on out, you old—" Pierce said, panting. "You only skinned me." His voice was closer than before, somewhere between the door and the corner of the building, below the level of the stained glass.

Then Doane saw Toby's white shirt beyond the window opposite. Jordan was holding him up, and moving toward the door. Jordan came out on the porch, hugging Toby around the chest, protecting himself with the limp body. With a heave he sent Toby flying down the steps, and jumped back out of sight. Toby rolled across the sidewalk and fell into the street, where he lay motionless.

Doane looked stupidly at Toby, then at young Jordan, still lying with his feet cocked up on the sidewalk.

"He ain't dead, Doane," Jordan called. "Come and get him if you want him alive." He fired through the window. Dust jumped six inches from Toby's head. "Come on out, Doane, and shoot it out. You got a chance to save him." The gun roared again, and dust jumped a second time beside Toby's head, almost in the same spot.

"Leave the kid alone," Doane called. "This fight's between you and me."

"The next shot kills him, Doane."

Doane's face sagged white and he leaned against the side of the door. He could hear Pierce breathing heavily in the silence, just outside. He pushed himself away from the door and drew a breath through clenched teeth. He cocked his pistol and strode out, swinging around. Pierce fired from the sidewalk, and Doane aimed straight into the blast and pulled as he felt himself flung violently around by Pierce's bullet.

Pierce came up from the sidewalk and took two steps toward him, opening and shutting a mouth that was suddenly full of blood, his eyes wide and wild, and then pitched down at his feet.

Doane's right arm hung useless, his gun at his feet. With his left hand he drew his other gun and stepped out from the walk, his mouth wide open, as though he were gasping for breath or were about to scream, and took two steps toward Toby as Jordan came out of the office door, firing. The slug caught Doane along the side of his neck, cutting the shoulder muscle, and his head fell over to one side. He staggered on, firing. He saw Toby trying to get up, saw Jordan fall back against the building, red running down the front of his shirt, and the smile gone.

Jordan stood braced against the building, holding his gun in both hands, firing as he slid slowly down. One bullet took Doane in the stomach, another in the knee. He went down, flopped forward and dragged himself up to where Toby lay trying to prop himself up on one elbow. Doane knelt there like a dog, puking blood into the dust, blood running out of his nose, but his gray eyes almost indifferent, as though there were one man dying and another watching.

He saw Jordan lift his gun with both hands and aim it toward Toby, and as the hammer fell, he threw himself across Toby's head and took it in the back. He rolled off onto his back and lay staring into the sky.

Upside down, he saw Toby take his gun and get up on one elbow, level it at Jordan and fire, and then saw Toby's face, over his, looking down at him as the deputy knelt in the street.

They stayed that way for a long moment, while Doane's eyes grew more and more dull and the dark of his blood in the white dust grew broader. His breath was coming hard, in small sharp gasps.

"There's nothing in it, kid," he whispered. "Only a tin star. They don't hang the right ones. You got to fight everything twice. It's a job for a dog."

"Thank you, Doane."

"It's all for free. You going to quit, Toby?"

Toby looked down at the gray face, the mouth and chin and neck crimson, the grey eyes dull. Toby shook his head. His face was hard as a rock.

Doane's face suddenly looked a little surprised, his eyes went past Toby to the sky. Toby looked up. A lark was high above them, circling and fluttering, directly overhead. "A pretty bird," Doane mumbled. "A very pretty bird."

His head turned slowly to one side, and Toby looked down at him and saw him as though fast asleep.

He took Doane's gun in his hand, and took off Doane's star, and sat there in the street while men slowly came out of stores and circled about them. He sat there unmoving, looking at Doane's half-averted face, holding the two things tightly, one in each hand, like a child with a broken toy, his face soft and blurred, his eyes unwet.

After a while the lark went away. He looked up at the men, and saw Mettrick.

"I told him he should have resigned," Mettrick said, his voice high. "He could have taken his horse—"

"Shut up," Toby said. "Shut up or get out." His eyes were sharp and his face placid and set. He turned to another of the men. "Get the doc," he said. "I've got a busted leg. And I've got a lot to do."

The man looked at him, a little startled, and then ran.

CLAY FISHER

The Trap

CANADY felt the horse beginning to go rough beneath him. He had been expecting it. On this rocky going no mount could make it for long when he was already ridden out in coming to it. "Easy, easy," he said to the laboring animal. "It's only a posse." The horse seemed to understand the tone of the words, for it slowed and went better and steadier for a ways. "We'll rest on the rise ahead," Canady said. "I can see back a few miles and you can catch some wind and we'll go on. We'll make it."

He knew they wouldn't. He knew it before they came to the rise and he got down and walked out on the overhanging spur of gray-black basalt that gave view down the canyon behind them for ten miles. It wasn't a canyon, really, but a narrowing valley. The canyon proper lay before them. Canady grinned and wiped his streaming face. It was hot, and going to get hotter. "Hoss," he said, "they're pushing. They mean to take up. They must know the country ahead. They don't ride like there's any hurry." The horse, now, did not respond with its ears and a turning of its soft eyes, as it had before. It stood, head-down, blowing out through its distended nostrils. Canady came back and squatted down and put his hand below the nose of the horse, where the moisture of its pained breathing would strike his palm. "Damn," he said softly. "Blood."

He got his field glasses from the saddle pocket and examined the pursuers through them. "Eight," he said aloud, "and six ropes. I wonder how come it is that they always fetch so many ropes? Never saw a posse yet didn't feel they'd each of them ought to have a rope."

His fingers went to his sunburned neck. They felt it tenderly, and he grinned again. "Son of a gun," he said, "it could happen."

Canady's grins were not the grimaces of a fool, or of an unfeeling man. They were the grins of a gambler. And of an outlaw. And a thief. Canady knew where he was and where he had been and, most apparently, where he was going. It did not frighten him. He would grin when they put the loop over his head. That was his kind. He wouldn't curse or revile, and he wouldn't pray. Not out loud, anyway.

"Hoss," he said, "what do you think?"

The animal, slightly recovered, moved its ears and whickered gruntingly. Canady nodded, turning his back to the approaching posse and glassing the country ahead. "Me too," he agreed. "A grunt and a whicker is all she's worth. We haven't got no place to go." He tensed, as he said it, the glasses freezing on an opening in the rearing base rock of the closing valley. It was to their right. A good horse, fresh and sound, could take a man up to that gap in the cliff. The spill of detritus and ages-old fan of boulders and stunted pine that lay below its lip would permit of perilous mounted passage. There was water up there, too, for Canady could see the small white ribbon of the stream splashing down a rainbow falls to mist up upon the lower rocks in a spume of red and yellow and turquoise green lights, splendid with beauty in the early sun. "I take it back," he said. "Maybe we do have a place to go. Pretty, too, and handy to town. You can't beat that."

Directly ahead was a level sunlit flat, dotted with tall pines and scrub juniper and house-sized boulders. The clear stream from the high hole in the right-side valley wall watered the flat, growing good mountain hay upon its sandy red loam and making a ride across it a thing to pleasure the heart of any Western man.

"Come on," said Canady to his horse. "You canter me across the flat and I'll climb the fan afoot leaving you to pack up nothing but the saddle and the grub sack. You game? Least we can do is make those birds scratch for their breakfast. And who knows? Our luck might change. We might get up there and into that hole-in-the-wall before they come up to the rise, here, and spot us. If we can do that, there's a chance they'll ride on by, up the valley, and we can double back tonight and make it free."

He was talking to Canady, now, not to the horse. It was the way of men much alone and when they needed to do some figuring. They would do it out loud, the way Canady was doing. It sounded better thay way, more convincing, and more as though it might really come off. Canady even swung into the saddle believing his own advice, telling himself what he wanted to know, then accepting it as a very good chance indeed. Again, it was his way. A man didn't live by the gun and the good fast horse without acquiring a working philosophy with lots of elastic in it.

"Move out," he repeated to the horse. "It's your part to get us across the flat in time."

The little mustang humped its back and shook itself like a wet dog. Running sweat, and caked, as well, flew from its streaked hide.

Its gathering of itself in response to the rider's words was a visible thing. The horse was like the man. It wouldn't quit short of the last second, or step, or shot. They were of a kind with the country around them. It was all the edge they had ever needed.

Canady panted. He wiped the perspiration from his eyes and started upward again. Behind him, the little horse came on, unled, the reins looped over the horn so as not to trail and be stepped on. He followed the man like a dog, panting with him, struggling where he struggled, sliding where he slid, and lunging on as he did, after each setback.

They had made nearly the top of the fan of fallen rock below and leading into the opening of the side canyon. In another four or five minutes they would be clear of the climb. They would be off the slide and safely into the notch in the high wall of the valley. They would be out of sight of the posse, and the posse still had not come into view of them on the rise back across the pine flat.

"Easy, hoss," gasped Canady. "We're going to make it."

But Canady was wrong. Thirty yards from the top, the mustang put its slender foreleg into a rock crevice and drew back quickly. The movement set the slide moving and caught the leg and crushed it like a matchstick below the knee. When the horse had freed itself and was standing hunched and trembling behind Canady, the shattered leg hung sickeningly a'swing and free of the ground, and Canady cursed with tears in his eyes. It was not the luck of it that brought his angry words, but the shame of it. It was his pity and his feeling for a gallant companion that had given its all and almost found it enough.

The hesitation, the wait there near the top of the slide, near the safety of the hole-in-the-wall, was the natural thing for a Western man. His horse was hurt. It was hopelessly hurt. He would have to leave it, but not like that. Not standing there on three legs hunched up in the middle with pain and fright. Not standing there watching him with those liquid brown eyes. No, he couldn't leave his horse like that.

But how else? He couldn't shoot the mustang, for the noise would key the posse to his location. Had he had a knife he could cut its throat. Or had he an ax he could have crushed its skull above the eye-socket and put the poor devil down painlessly. With a rock he might be able to stun the brave little brute, but he could not be sure of killing it cleanly. The same held true for the butt of his Colt or the steel-shod heel of his Winchester. He could stun the horse, likely put it to its knees, but not, still, be able to go on knowing it would not recover and try to get up again and go on, and so suffer as no horse-riding man could think to let his mount suffer. But, damn it, this was *his* life he was arguing with himself about. It wasn't the damned horse's life. If he didn't do something and do it quick, the posse would be over the rise and he and the horse could go to hell together. Well, he would use the Colt butt. He knew he could hit the exhausted animal hard enough with it to put it down for the necessary time for himself to get on into the hole-in-the-wall and for the posse to ride by and on up the valley. That was all the time he needed, or at least it was all he could ask for. He pulled the Colt and started back to the horse, sliding and stumbling in his hurry to get to the trembling beast and knock it down. But when he got up to its side, when he looked into those dark eyes, he couldn't do it. He had to be sure. "The hell with the posse," he said to the little horse, and spun the Colt in the air and caught it by the handle and put it behind the ragged ear and pulled the trigger. The smoke from the shot was still curling upward, and the little pony just going slowly down, when the first of the pursuing riders came up over the rise across the flat and yelled excitedly back to his comrades that the game was in sight, and on foot.

Canady went up the little stream. Behind him, where it fed the rainbow falls leaping outward into the main valley, the possemen were just topping the detritus fan and closing in on "the hole." Back there Canady had made a decision. It was not to stay and fight from the entrance cleft of the hole, where the little rivulet went out of the side canyon. He did not know what lay on up the side canyon, and feared there might be a way by which the possemen, familiar with this territory, could ride a circle and come in behind him. He could not risk that, he believed, and must go on up the creek as far as he could, hoping it would be far enough to find a place here he could put his back to the wall and fight without their being able to get behind him.

Now, going along, the way becoming steeper and narrower and the creek bank little more than wide enough to pass a good horse and rider, he saw ahead of him a basalt dike, or cross dam of rock, which cut across the narrowing floor of the side canyon. Here the stream took another plunge, this of about thirty feet. Above the dike, Canady could see the boles of pine trees and hence knew that the ground above the dike lay fairly level. The cross-laying of rock apparently served as a barrier against which the winter erosions of snow, ice and thaw had worked with the spring floodings of the creek to bring down and build up a tiny flat.

Canady's gray eyes lit up. His brown face relaxed and he said aloud, "By God, maybe this is it," and went on with renewed strength and some hope of keeping his life a little longer. Up there, above that rock cross-bank, a man with a good carbine and plenty of shells could hold down most eight-man posses for several afternoons. Well, two or three, anyway. Or one. For certain, until nightfall. Twelve, fifteen hours, say. It was better than nothing.

His luck held. There was a good angling trail going up that thirty-foot vertical face of rock. It was a game trail, and somewhat of a cow trail, too. He made out the droppings of elk, blacktail deer, range steers and, then, suddenly and strangely, a fairly fresh piling of horse sign. This latter find sent a chill through him. He was on his knees in the instant of the sighting, but then he straightened, grinning. It was all right. The pony was unshod. Moreover, he suspected, from the hard round prints that it left, that it never had been shod and was one of a bunch of broomtails—wild mustangs— that came into this rocky depth for the water that flowed so green and cool in the stream.

Clearing the top of the stone dam, Canady's grin widened. The flat above lay precisely as he had imagined it did. He laughed softly, as a man will who is alone. Now, then, it would be a little different from the way those hungry lawmen had planned it. This was perfect. At the apex of the triangle of the flat he saw the thick stand of sycamore and cottonwood, aspen, laurel and willow, and he knew that the water headed there. A moment later, he made out the source of the stream, a large artesian spring gushing from the native rock under great pressure. The spring was set above the grove some few feet, its stream falling rapidly to plunge into the foliage. Likely it pooled up there under the trees and at the foot of the down-plunge. That's what lured in the wild horses and the other game and the cattle, too, what few of the latter were hardy enough to come this far into the mounains for feed. All a man would need to do, now, was hole up in those boulders that girded the spring, up there above the trees, and he could command with his Winchester the whole of the small, open flat between the spring grove and the stone crossdam that Canady had just clambered up. Taking a deep breath, the fugitive started across the flat, toward the spring and its hole-up boulders. It was not until he had climbed safely into this haven at the canyon head and laid down pantingly to look back on his trail and get ready for the possemen, that he saw where he had come.

Below him in the trees the spring pooled up exactly as he had expected it would. Also the rim of the pool showed the centuries of wear of the hoofed animals coming to its banks for water. But there was something else—two other things—that he had not expected to see there, and his grin faded and his gray eyes grew taut and tired and empty.

The first thing was the wild horse. It had not gone on up out of the little side canyon as Canady had hoped, showing him the way to follow its tracks and escape over the rim where no mounted man might follow. It was still in the grove of trees that sheltered the spring-pool waterhole, and it wasn't still there because of its thirst. Beyond the trees, back where Canady had come from, and so skillfully blended and built into the natural cover of the canyon that even his range-wise eyes had missed them, were the two woven brush and pole wings of the second thing Canady had not dreamed to find there. Those were the man-made wings of a mustang corral down there. Canady had stumbled into a wild horse trap. And he was caught there, with this unfortunate lone mustang that now cowered in the trees and could not get out of the trap any more than could he, and for the same reason—the posse and the box canyon.

"Steady on," Canady called down softly to the terrified horse. "We'll think of something."

Two hours after high noon the sun was gone from the canyon. Canady could see its light splashing the far side of the main valley still, but in the side canyon all was soft shade, and hot. Canady drank enough water to keep himself from drying out, yet not enough to log him. He noted that the wild mustang did the same thing. It knew, as Canady knew, that to be ready to fight or fly called for an empty belly. "Smart," said Canady, "smart as hell." The horse heard him and looked up. "*Coo-ee, coo-ee,*" Canady called to him reassuringly. "Don't fret; I'll figure something for us." But it was a lie and he knew it was a lie.

He had gone down, right after he first lay up in the spring boulders and saw the trap and the wild broomtail in it, and closed off the narrow gate of the funnel-winged corral with his lariat. He had done that in a hurry, before the posse had worked up into the canyon and taken its position along the top of the crossdam. His one thought had been that the broomtail was a horse, wild or not, and that so long as a man had a horse he wasn't out of it in that country. And he had wanted to keep hidden from the posse the fact that he did have a horse up there in that headwaters timber. The mustang had played with him in that last part of it, lying up shy and quiet as a deer in the trees and brush, not wanting any more than Canady wanted for the men to know that it was there. "It" in this case was a scrubby little stallion, probably too small and old to hold a band of mares. The little horse had not only the fixtures but the temperament of the mongrel stud animal. Watching him lie still in the spring brush and keep his eyes following every move of the men below him, as well as of the single man above him, Canady knew that he and the trapped horse were friends. The only problem was proving it to the horse.

Sometimes these old scrub studs had been ridden long ago and would remember man's smell and voice. He tried a dozen times to talk the mustang up toward his end of the spring pool. But the animal gave no sign that the sight, scent or sound of mankind was familiar to him, or welcome. He bared his teeth silently and pinned his ears and squatted in the haunches ready to kick like a pack mule on a cold morning. He did this every time Canady said more than three or four words to him, or accompanied his talk with any movement that might mean he was coming down to see the horse, if the horse would not come up to see him.

What possible good the horse could do him, even if, by some miracle Canady might gentle him down and put his saddle and bridle on him, Canady didn't know. Then, even in thinking that far, he laughed and shrugged. His saddle and bridle were down there on that rock slide below the hole-in-the-wall. He'd had no time and no reason to take them off his dead mount. So if he went out of there astride that broomtail it would be bareback, and that was about as good a bet as that the crafty old stallion would sprout wings and fly up out of the canyon. A bridle, of sorts, he could rig from splitting and unraveling a short length of his lariat. It would be sort of a breaking hackamore arrangement and might do to give simple directions of right and left and who-up. But even if he rigged this Sioux headstall and got it on the shaggy little horse, then what? That was, even if the rascal wanted to be good, or had been ridden in the past, and remembered it of a sudden? Nothing. Not a damned thing. Canady couldn't ride out of that canyon if he had the best saddle mount in Montana waiting and eager to make the try with him. It was all crazy, thinking of that wild stud. But just finding any horse up there was bound to start a man's mind going. Especially when he had just shot his own mount and was fixing to put his back to the best rock he could find and go down with lead flying. But it was crazy all the same. All Canady could do was what the old broomtail stud could do—fight the rope to the last breath he had in him, then kill himself, if he could, before the others did it for him.

The afternoon wore on. The heat in the deep-walled little canyon was enormous. The deerflies swarmed at the spring pool and bit like mad cats. They nearly drove Canady wild, but he fought them with hand and mind and swathed neckband and, when evening came, they lifted up out of the canyon on the first stir of the night wind. In the early part of the waiting there had been some desultory talk between the posse and Canady, talk of Canady coming out peacefully and getting a fair trail, but the fugitive had not bothered to take that offer seriously. He knew the trial he would get. The posse had its own witnesses with it. They would bring up these two or three men who had "seen" the shooting and say to them, "Is that him?" and the men would say, "Yes, that's him," and the trial would be over. Witnesses! thought Canady. God, how he hated them. It wasn't that he minded being identified if he was the man. In his business no feeling was held against the witness who *had* seen something. It was those devils, like the ones with the posse, who had *not* seen the job and yet who were always ready to raise their right hands and be sworn, who were the ones Canady hated. There had not been any witnesses as to what passed between him and that teller. All the other bank people had been on the floor behind the cage, and there had been no customers in the bank, or out in front of it. The shooting had happened and Canady had made it to his horse in back of the bank, and made it away down the alley and into the sagebrush south of town before he had passed a living soul. Then, it was two farm wagons, both carrying kids and driven by women, that he had ridden by well out of Gray's Landing. How those good folks —and they were the only real witnesses, save the cashier and the other teller on the bank floor—how they could identify him as anything other than a horseman not of that area, Canady did not know. As for the three shots that had killed the teller, and they must have killed him or the posse would not have pushed so hard, those shots had been fired *after* both barrels of the .36 caliber derringer that the teller brought up out of the cash drawer had been triggered and put their slugs, one in Canady's chest, and one in the ceiling of the Second National Bank of Gray's Landing, Montana. But the only witness to that fact was dead. Canady had reacted as all men with guns in their hands react to other men with guns in their hands. He had fired by instinct, by pure conditioned reflex of long experience, when that first .36 bullet went into the pectoral muscles of his left chest.

Armed robbery? Certainly. Twenty years in the Territorial Prison? Of course. A man expected that. But to be run down like a mad dog and cornered and starved out and then strung up on a naked cottonwood like a damned Indian drunk or a common horse thief was not right or fair. Murder? Could you call it murder when the other man was a professional in his business and he could see that you were a professional in yours? When you told him he would be killed if he tried anything funny? Then, when on top of the fair warning, you gave him the first shot? Could you call it murder, then, if you shot in answer to his try at killing you? Self-defense was the actual verdict, but of course an armed robber could not plead self-defense. But he was not guilty of murder, or even of assault with a deadly weapon, or even of intent to commit murder, or of a damned thing, really, but to sack that cash drawer and clear out of Gray's Landing just as fast and peaceably as he and the old horse might manage.

Canady grinned, even as he exonerated himself.

It was no good. He knew it was no good. A man had to be honest with himself. If he was in another business he wouldn't need a gun to conduct his trade. Needing and using a gun, he was always in the peril of being forced to use it. The teller was an honest man. Frank Canady was a crook. The teller was a dead honest man and Canady was a live dishonest man. Canady was a killer.

"No!" he yelled down to the posse. "I won't do it; I shot second; I didn't mean to harm that fellow. He pulled on me and shot first. But he's dead, ain't he? Sure he is. And you say to me to come on down peaceable and you'll see I get a fair trial? With a dead teller back there on the floor of the Second National. That's rich. Really rich."

The possemen were startled. It had been two hours since the fugitive had made a sound. Previously he had refused to come down and they had thought he meant it. Now, did they detect a change? Was it that he wanted to reconsider and was only protecting his ego by the defiant outburst.

"That's right, you heard us right," the leader of the posse called up to him. "You come down here and we'll guarantee to take you back to Gray's Landing and get you to either Cheyenne or Miles City, wherever the court is sitting, by train and under armed guard. You'll get the trial we promised, and the protection beforehand." He waited a significant moment, then demanded, "What do you say? There's no use any more people getting hurt."

Canady's gray eyes grew tired again.

"That's so," he called back. "It includes me too. I don't want to see anybody else get it, either. 'Specially me. No thanks, Mr. Posseman. I'll stay up here. I don't fancy that you brung along all them ropes just to tie me up for the ride back to Gray's Landing."

There was a silence from below the cross-dam of rock in the upper throat of the canyon that lasted perhaps two, perhaps three stretching minutes. Then the posseman called back. "All right," he said, "you'll have it your way. When it's full dark we're going to come for you, and you know what that will mean. There are eight of us, all good shots, and you won't have the chance of a rat in an oatbin. We've got bulls-eye lanterns to light you out. We will set them up behind boulders where you can't snipe them, and yet where they will throw light up there around you like it was bright moonlight. We mean to stomp you out. There will be no trial and no talk of a trial. You're dead right now."

Canady sank back behind his breastwork of basalt and gray-green granite. He hawked the cottony spittle from his throat and spat grimacingly down toward the mustang stud. The animal had been crouching and listening to the exchange of voices intelligently like some big gaunt sandy-maned dog. Seeing him, and noting his apparent interest, Canady managed a trace of his quiet grin.

"What do *you* say, amigo?" he asked.

The horse looked up at him. It was the first time in all the long hours that Canady had tried gentle-talking to him that the animal had made a direct and not spooked response to the man's voice. Now he stomped a splayed and rock-split forehoof and whickered softly and gruntingly in his throat, precisely as Canady's old horse had done.

"All right," said Canady, for some reason feeling mightily warmed by the mustang's action, "so we've each got one friend in the world. That isn't too bad. As long as you have a friend you have a chance. Rest easy; let me think. We'll still make it, you and me. . . ."

It was dusk when the old steer came down the cliff trail. He was a ladino, one of those mossy-horned old rascals that had successfully hidden out from the gathers of a dozen years. He was old and crafty and cautious as any wild animal, but he had to have water and he was coming down to the spring pool to get it. He certainly saw the men of the posse, and winded their mounts, but they did not see him and he knew that they did not. His yellow buckskin hide with the dark "cruz" or cross-stripe on the shoulders, and the dark brown legs and feet, blended perfectly into the weathered face of the cliff, and he made no more sound coming down that hidden trail than a mountain doe might have made. But he had failed to see Canady or to separate his scent, or the scent of the mustang stud, from the other horse and man scents coming from below. He came on, carefully, silently, yet quickly down the wall of the canyon from the rim above and Canady, seeing him, was suddenly lifted in mind and heart. He had been right in the first place. There *was* a trail up out of that blind box of a side canyon. A track up that dizzy sheer cliff, up there, that would pass a desperate man, or a catlike wild mustang, but not a mounted man or a man going afoot leading his tamed and trained saddle mount. "Come on, come on," he heard himself whispering to the old outlaw steer. "Come on down here and let me see how you do it. Let me see how and where you get off that damned wall and down here where we are."

He grinned when he said that, when he said "we," meaning himself and the wild stud, without thinking about it. It was funny how a man took to anything for a friend when he had run out of the real McCoy and was in his last corner. He supposed that if a sidewinder crawled along at the final minute and that was all he had to talk to, a man would find some excuse to think kindly of the snake tribe. Well, anyway, he was thinking with deep kindness about the animal kingdom just then. Especially the horse and cow part of it. And extraspecially about the latter half. "Come on, keep coming on, don't slip, for God's sake," he said to the gaunt dun steer. "Easy, easy. Let me see you do it, just don't fall or spook or get a bad smell and change your mind. That's it, that's it. Easy, easy. . . ."

He talked the steer down that cliff trail as though his life depended on it, and it did. And the steer made it. He made it in a way that caused Canady to suck in his breath and shake his head in wonderment. He made it in a way that even caused Canady to think for a moment about there being something to the idea of a divine providence, for it was the sort of thing no man could have figured out by himself, the weird, crazy, wonderful kind of a last-second reprieve that no force but God Almighty could have sent to a man in Canady's place. It was a miracle.

The dun steer performed it with an easy quickness that defied belief, too. He came to that place on his side of the canyon where it seemed to Canady that the trail must end. The man could see the sheer face of the rock dropping sixty feet to the creek bed. A giant outcropping of granite hid the exact end of the rightside trail, but Canady could see, and with absolute certainty, that the trail did not continue downward past that outcrop that hid its actual terminus. But as he watched the steer disappear behind the outcrop and as he wondered what would happen next, he saw the lean yellow body launch itself in a graceful leap from behind the outer edge of the outcrop, and sail outward through the thin air of the canyon's dark throat. It appeared as though the leap would smash the ribby brute into the rearing face of the opposite, left-hand canyon wall, which lay no more than fifteen or twenty feet from the right-side wall. But again the steer disappeared, this time seemingly into the very face of the opposing cliff.

There was a tricky turn in the rock wall of the canyon's left side at just that point, however, and while Canady could see the creek's raggedly broken bottom, he could not see where the steer hit into the wall. All he was sure of for the moment was that the animal had made his landing somewhere other than in the creek bottom. Difficult as it might be to accept, that old outlaw steer had somehow made it from one side of the wall to the other. But, even so, then what? Where was he now? The questions were soon answered when the missing steer appeared to walk right out of the waterfall that came down from Canady's elevated vantage to strike into and begin following the brief section of creek bed into the pool grove. While

Canady gaped, the animal stole swiftly to the pool, drank sparingly, returned and disappeared again behind the curtain of misty water cascading down from the spring above.

So that was it. As simple and as remarkable as that. A trail ran from behind the waterfall up the left-hand wall. At a point opposite the right-side trail's end, it too, terminated. But it was obvious that there was room enough for a running jump and opposite landing, to and from either wall, with both takeoff and landing spots completely masked from the lower canyon.

Gaging the distance of the jump, Canady knew that he could make it. With his boots off and laced about his neck, or better, thrown over with his Colt and the saddlebags with the bank money, the Winchester being slung on his back, alone, he could make that distance through the air. But, then, what of that? He made the jump safely and went on up the right-side cliff trail behind the ladino steer and gained the rim; then what? He would still be afoot in a hostile land in midsummer's blazing heat without food, water, or a mount. That was the rub. Even if he made that jump and the cliff climb beyond it and got to the rim, he would have to have a horse. Otherwise, the possemen, within an hour or two of dark, having come for him and found him gone, would go back out and climb out of the main valley and cut for his sign on both rims of the side canyon, and they would still get him. They would get him easy, with them mounted and he afoot.

No, he had to take that broomy studhorse with him.

Somehow, he had to get that mustang to go with him up the cliff. If he could do that, could get the little horse to make the jump with him on its back—it would have to be that way for he could never trust the brute to follow him or to wait for him if he allowed it to jump first—if he could make that gap in the canyon on the back of that little wild horse, then stay with him, hand-leading him up the cliff trail, then oh then, by the dear good Lord, he would make it. He and the horse would make it together. Just as he had promised the raunchy little devil. Up on the rim, he would remount the tough wiry mustang and together they would race away and Canady would have his life and the broomtail stud would have his freedom and the Gray's Landing posse would have their ropes unstretched and their vengeance unadministered and left to God where it belonged.

The thought of the Almighty came very strong to Canady in that moment of desperate hope. He turned his face upward to peer out of the narrow slit of late twilight far above him where the walls of the Canyon seemed almost to touch at the top and where, far, far up there, he could now see the yellow steer climbing the last few steps

of the steep trail and humping himself over the rim and losing himself to canyon's view. Canady nodded and said to the dusk-hushed
stillness about him: "If you'll let me make it, too, Lord, me and
that little hoss down yonder, I will try to set things as right as I can.
I'll take this money, Lord, the bank don't need it and I won't want
it any more after this night, and I will give this money to the widow
of that poor teller. I will figure some way to do it, Lord, that she
don't know where it came from. And I'll turn loose this little wild
hoss, if you will let me gentle him enough to get on him and push
him to that jump, up yonder. I'm going to try it, Lord. I'm going
down there to the pool and try putting my loop on him right now.
You reckon you could help me? I surely hope so, as I think you
wouldn't send that ladino steer down here to show a man the way
out, and then not help him to make it. Nor likewise do I think you
would put that little old mustang studhorse down there in that trap
by the pool unless you wanted him used. It looks to me, Lord, as if
you truly wanted to pull me out of this here trap, and if that's the
way it is, why thank You and I'll do my best. . . ."

In the little light remaining, Canady went down from his rocks by
the spring to try for the trapped wild horse. He took his rope from
the trap gate and closed the gate, instead, with brush and poles,
hoping it would turn the stud should he break past him when he
came at him with the lariat.
The actual catching went, as such things perversely will, with a
strange easiness. Oh, the little horse fought that loop when he felt it
settle on him, but he did not do so viciously. The very fact that he
permitted Canady to come close enough to dab the loop on him to
begin with was peculiarly simple. It made the matter suspicious to
Canady and he thought the little stud was merely stalling on him,
was trying to tempt him in close where he could use his teeth and
hooves on him. He knew the small mustangs would do this. They
would fight like panthers in close, using their teeth like carnivorous
animals, and their feet with all the savagery of elk or moose fighting
off wolves. But this was not the case with the tattered broomtail in
the mustang trap. When Canady got up near enough to him, he saw
the reason why, or thought that he did. The telltale white marks of
the cinch and saddle, the places where white hair had grown in to
replace the original claybank sorrel hairs, showed clearly in the
darkening twilight. Canady's first thought that this horse had been
handled before was now assured. And it certainly explained the
change in the animal the moment the man snugged the loop high
up on his neck, under the jaw, in a way that showed the horse he
meant to hold him hard and fast, and to handle him again as he
had been handled years before. Memory is a strong force. The stud

made Canady throw him on the ground, using the loose end of the rope to make a figure-8 snake and roll it around the front legs to bring the little pony down, but once he had been thrown and permitted to stand up again, it was all over. This man had gentled many horses. He had spent his life with them. Their smell had become his smell. The very sound of his voice had a horse sound in it. The mustang had heard it the first word of the day. He had sensed his kinship with this particular man, then, and he sensed his mastery of the horsekind, now. He submitted to Canady and stood quietly, if still trembling, while the man stroked him and sweet-whispered to him and got him to ease and to stand without shaking, and without dread or apprehension.

Then Canady cut and wove the makeshift breaking halter, the Plains Indian's simple rope rein and bridle arrangement, continuing to talk all the while to the small mustang. When, in half an hour more, it was full dark and the split-ear hackamore-bridle and its short reining rope were finished and put upon the horse, the animal was to all practical purposes reduced to a useable saddle horse. It was a piece of the greatest luck, Canady knew, that he had been able to catch and work the little brute. But it was not so entirely luck that it had no sense or possibility to it, and his success only made the fugitive believe that his hunch of higher help was a true one, and this thought, in turn, strengthened him and made his spirits rise.

"Come on," he murmured to the little horse, "it's time we got shut of here. Come along, *coo-ee, coo-ee,* little hoss. That's good, that's real good. Easy, easy. . . ."

They went in behind the creek falls, as the yellow ladino steer had done. The mustang pulled back a bit at the water but once it had hit him he steadied down and followed Canady's urging pull on the lariat as well and as obediently as any horse would have done in similar straits. Beyond the sheet of the falls, the left-hand trail went sharply but safely upward and around the trunklike bulge of the canyon's wall which had hidden it from Canady's view at the spring. Around the turn was the expected straight run at the leap-over. It was better, even, than Canady hoped. There was some actual soil in its track and here and there, some clumps of tough wire grass to give footing and power for the jump.

"Steady, now," said Canady, and eased up onto the crouching mustang. The little mount flinched and deepened his crouch, but he did not break. Canady sighed gratefully and nodded upward to that power which clearly was helping him now. He took his grip on the rope rein and put the pressure of his bowed knees to the mustang's ribs. Beneath him, he felt the littls horse squat and gather himself. Then he touched him, just touched him, with his left boot-

heel. The wild stud uncoiled his tensed muscles, shot down the runway of the trail, came up to the jump-across as though he had been
trained to it since colthood. Canady felt his heart soar with the
mightly upward spring in the small brute's wiry limbs. He laughed
with the sheer joy of it. He couldn't help it. He had never in his life
felt a triumph such as this one; this sailing over that hell's pit of
blackness down there beneath him; this gliding spring, this arching,
floating burst of power that was carrying him high above those
deadly rock fangs so far below, and was carrying him, too, up and
away from those blood-hungry possemen and their winking, glaring,
prying bull's-eye lanterns, which he could just see now, from an eye-
corner, coming into view down-canyon of his deserted place at the
spring above the pool and the peaceful grove of mountain ash and
alder and willow there at the head of Rainbow Creek in Blind Canyon, sixty and more miles from the Second National Bank and that
fool of a dead teller in Gray's Landing, Montana. Oh, what a wondrous, heady thing was life! And, oh! what a beholden and humble
man was Frank Canady for this gift, this chance, this answer to his
fumbling prayer. He would never forget it. Never never, never.

They came down very hard at the far end of the jump. The con-
cussion of the horse hitting the ground rattled Canady's teeth and
cracked his jaws together as loud as a pistol shot. He saw lights behind his eyes and heard wild and strange sounds, but only for a second or two. Then all was clear again and he and the little horse
were going together up the right-side cliff trail, Canady leading the
way, the little horse following faithful as a pet dog behind him. It
seemed no more than a minute before they were where it had taken
the yellow steer half an hour to climb, and it seemed only a breath
later that they had topped out on the rim and were free.

Canady cried then. The tears came to his eyes and he could not
help himself. He didn't think that the little mustang would care,
though, and he was right. When he put his arms about the shaggy,
warm neck and hugged the skinny old stud, the mustang only
whickered deep in his throat and leaned into Frank Canady and
rested his homely jughead over the man's shoulder. They were of a
kind. They belonged to each other, and with each other, and that
was true; for that was the way that the possemen found them when
they came probing carefully up the bed of the creek in its brief run
from the deserted pool grove to the foot of the spring's waterfall.
The horse had fallen with the man beneath him, and neither had
known a flash or a spark or a hint of thought, in the instant their
lives had been crushed out among the granite snags of the creek bed
below the jumping place of the yellow ladino steer.

ERNEST HAYCOX

———————————

A Day in Town

THEY REACHED TWO DANCE around ten that morning and turned into the big lot between the courthouse and the Cattle King Hotel. Most of the homesteaders camped here when they came to town, for after a slow ride across the sage flats, underneath so hot and so yellow a sun, the shade of the huge locust trees was a comfort. Joe Blount unhitched and watered the horses and tied them to a pole. He was a long and loose and deliberate man who had worked with his hands too many years to waste motion, and if he dallied more than usual over his chores now it was because he dreaded the thing ahead of him.

His wife sat on the wagon's seat, holding the baby. She had a pin in her mouth and she was talking around it to young Tom: "Stay away from the horses on the street and don't you go near the railroad tracks. Keep hold of May's hand. She's too little to be alone, you remember. Be sure to come back by noon."

Young Tom was seven and getting pretty thin from growth. The trip to town had him excited. He kept nodding his sun-bleached head, he kept tugging at little May's hand, and then both of them ran headlong for the street and turned the corner of the Cattle King, shrilly whooping as they disappeared.

Blount looked up at his wife. She was a composed woman and not one to bother people with talk and sometimes it was hard for a man to know what was in her mind. But he knew what was there now, for all their problems were less than this one and they had gone over it pretty thoroughly the last two-three months. He moved his fingers up to the pocket of his shirt and dropped them immediately away, searching the smoky horizon with his glance. He didn't expect to see anything over there, but it was better than meeting her eyes at this moment. He said in his patiently low voice: "Think we could make it less than three hundred?"

The baby moved its arms, its warm-wet fingers aimlessly brushing Hester Blount's cheeks. She said: "I don't see how. We kept figuring —and it never gets smaller. You know best, Joe."

"No, he murmured, "it never gets any smaller. Well, three hundred. That's what I'll ask for." And yet, with the chore before him, he kept his place by the dropped wagon tongue. He put his hands in his pockets and drew a long breath and looked at the powdered earth below him with a sustained gravity, and was like this when Hester Blount spoke again. He noticed that she was pretty gentle with her words: "Why, now, Joe, you go on. It isn't like you were shiftless and hadn't tried. He knows you're a hard worker and he knows your word's good. You just go ahead."

"Guess we've both tried," he agreed. "And I guess he knows how it's been. We ain't alone." He went out toward the street, reminding himself of this. They weren't alone. All the people along Christmas Creek were burned out, so it wasn't as if he had failed because he didn't know how to farm. The thought comforted him a good deal; it restored a little of his pride. Crossing the street toward Dunmire's stable, he met Chess Roberts, with whom he had once punched cattle on the Hat outfit, and he stopped in great relief and palavered with Chess for a good ten minutes until, looking back, he saw his wife still seated on the wagon. That sight vaguely troubled him and he drawled to Chess, "Well, I'll see you later," and turned quite slowly toward the bank.

There was nothing in the bank's old-fashioned room to take a man's attention. Yet when he came into its hot, shaded silence Joe Blount removed his hat and felt ill at ease as he walked toward Lane McKercher. There was a pine desk here and on the wall a railroad map showing the counties of the Territory in colors. Over at the other side of the room stood the cage where McKercher's son waited on the trade.

McKercher was big and bony and gray and his eyes could cut. They were that penetrating, as everybody agreed. "Been a long time since you came to town. Sit down and have a talk," and his glance saw more about Joe Blount than the homesteader himself could ever tell. "How's Christmas Creek?"

Blount settled in the chiar. He said, "Why, just fine," and laid his hands over the hat in his lap. Weather had darkened him and work had thinned him and gravity remained like a stain on his cheeks. He was, McKercher recalled, about thirty years old, had once worked as a puncher on Hat and had married a girl from a small ranch over in the Yellows. Thirty wasn't so old, yet the country was having its way with Joe Blount. When he dropped his head the skin around his neck formed a loose crease and his mouth had that half-severe expression which comes from too much trouble. This was what McKercher saw. This and the blue army shirt, washed and mended until it was as thin as cotton, and the man's long hard hands lying so loose before him.

McKercher said, "A little dry over your way?"

"Oh," said Blount, "a little. Yeah, a little bit dry."

The banker sat back and waited, and the silence ran on a long while. Blount moved around in the chair and lifted his hand and reversed the hat on his lap. His eyes touched McKercher and passed quickly on to the ceiling. He stirred again, not comfortable. One hand reached up to the pocket of his shirt, dropping quickly back.

"Something on your mind, Joe?"

"Why," said Blount, "Hester and I have figured it out pretty close. It would take about three hundred dollars until next crop. Don't see how it could be less. There'd be seed and salt for stock and grub to put in and I guess some clothes for the kids. Seems like a lot but we can't seem to figure it any smaller."

"A loan?" said McKercher.

"Why, yes," said Blount, relieved that the explaining was over.

"Now let's see. You've got another year to go before you get title to your place. So that's no security. How was your wheat?

"Burnt out. No rain over there in April."

"How much stock?"

"Well, not much. Just two cows. I sold off last fall. The graze was pretty skinny." He looked at McKercher and said in the briefest way, "I got nothing to cover this loan. But I'm a pretty good worker."

McKercher turned his eyes toward the desk. There wasn't much to be seen behind the cropped gray whiskers of his face. According to the country this was why he wore them—so that a man could never tell what he figured. But his shoulders rose and dropped and he spoke regretfully: "There's no show for you on that ranch, Joe. Dry farming—it won't do. All you fellows are burned out. This country never was meant for it. It's cattle land and that about all."

He let it go like that, and waited for the homesteader to come back with a better argument. Only, there was no argument. Joe Blount's lips changed a little and his hands flattened on the peak of his hat. He said in a slow, mild voice, "Well, I can see it your way all right," and got up. His mind strayed up to the shirt pocket again, and fell away—and McKercher, looking straight into the man's eyes, saw an expression there hard to define. The banker shook his head. Direct refusal was on his tongue and it wasn't like him to postpone it, which he did. "I'll think it over. Come back about two o'clock."

"Sure," said Blount, and turned across the room, his long frame swinging loosely, his knees springing as he walked, saving energy. After he had gone out of the place McKercher remembered the way the homesteader's hand had gone toward the shirt pocket. It was a gesture that remained in the banker's mind.

Blount stopped outside the bank. Hester, at this moment, was passing down toward the dry-goods store with the baby in her arms. He waited until she had gone into the store and then walked on toward the lower end of town, not wanting her to see him just then. He knew McKercher would turn him down at two o'clock. He had heard it pretty plainly in the banker's tone, and he was thinking of all the things he had meant to explain to McKercher. He was telling McKercher that one or two bad years shouldn't count against a man. That the land on Christmas Creek would grow the best winter wheat in the world. That you had to take the dry with the wet. But he knew he'd never say any of this. The talk wasn't in him, and never had been. Young Tom and little May were across the street, standing in front of Swing's restaurant, seeing something that gripped their interest. Joe Blount looked at them from beneath the lowered brim of his hat; they were skinny with age and they needed some clothes. He went on by, coming against Chess Roberts near the saloon.

Chess said: "Well, we'll have a drink on this."

The smell of the saloon drifted out to Joe Blount, its odor of spilled whisky and tobacco smoke starting the saliva in his jaws, freshening a hunger. But Hester and the kids were on his mind and something told him it was unseemly, the way things were. He said: "Not right now, Chess. I got some chores to tend. What you doing?"

"You ain't heard? I'm riding for Hat again."

Blount said: "Kind of quiet over my way. Any jobs for a man on Hat?"

"Not now," said Chess. "We been layin' off summer help. A little bit tough this year, Joe. You havin' trouble on Christmas Creek?"

"Me? Not a bit, Chess. We get along. It's just that I like to keep workin'."

After Chess had gone, Joe Blount laid the point of his shoulder against the saloon wall and watched his two children walk hand in hand past the windows of the general store. Young Tom pointed and swung his sister around; and both of them had their faces against a window, staring in. Blount pulled his eyes away. It took the kids to do things that scraped a man's pride pretty hard, that made him feel his failure. Under the saloon's board awning lay shade, but sweat cracked through his forehead and he thought quickly of what he could do. Maybe Dunmire could use a man to break horses. Maybe he could get on hauling wood for the feed store. This was Saturday and the big ranch owners would be coming down the Two Dance grade pretty soon. Maybe there was a hole on one of those outfits. It was an hour until noon, and at noon he had to go back to Hester. He turned toward the feed store.

Hester Blount stood at the dry-goods counter of Vetten's store. Vetten came over, but she said, "I'm just trying to think." She laid the baby on the counter and watched it lift its feet straight in the air and aimlessly try to catch them with its hands; and she was thinking that the family needed a good many things. Underwear all around, and stockings and overalls. Little May had to have some material for a dress, and some ribbon. You couldn't let a girl grow up without a few pretty things, even out on Christmas Creek. It wasn't good for the girl. Copper-toed shoes for young Tom, and a pair for his father; and lighter buttoned ones for May. None of these would be less than two dollars and a half, and it was a crime the way it mounted up. And plenty of flannel for the baby.

She had not thought of herself until she saw the dark gray bolt of silk lying at the end of the counter, and when she saw it something happened to her heart. It wasn't good to be so poor that the sight of a piece of silk made you feel this way. She turned from it, ashamed of her thoughts—as though she had been guilty of extravagance. Maybe if she were young again and still pretty, and wanting to catch a man's eyes, it might not be so silly to think of clothes. But she was no longer young or pretty and she had her man. She could take out her love of nice things on little May, who was going to be a very attractive girl. As soon as Joe was sure of the three hundred dollars she's come back here and get what they all had to have—and somehow squeeze out the few pennies for dress material and the hair ribbon.

She stood here thinking of these things and so many others—a tall and rather comely woman in her early thirties, darkfaced and carrying an even, sweet-lipped gravity while her eyes sought the dry-goods shelves and her hand unconsciously patted the baby's round middle.

A woman came bustling into the store and said in a loud, accented voice: "Why, Hester Blount, of all the people I never expected to see!"

Hester said, "Now, isn't this a surprise!" and the two took each other's hands, and fell into a quick half embrace. Ten years ago they had been girls together over in the Two Dance, Hester and this Lila Evenson who had married a town man. Lila was turning into a heavy woman and, like many heavy women, she loved white and wore it now, though it made her look big as a house. Above the tight collar of the dress, her skin was a flushed red and a second chin faintly trembled when she talked. Hester Blount stood motion-

less, listening to that outpour of words, feeling the quick search of
Lila's eyes. Lila, she knew, would be taking everything in—her worn
dress, her heavy shoes, and the lines of her face.

"And another baby!" said Lila and bent over it and made a long
gurgling sound. "What a lucky woman! That's three? But ain't it a
problem, out there on Christmas Creek? Even in town here I worry
so much over my one darling."

"No," said Hester, "we don't worry. How is your husband?"

"So well," said Lila. "You know, he's bought the drugstore from
old Kerrin, who is getting old. He had done so well. We are lucky,
as we keep telling ourselves. And that reminds me. You must come
up to dinner. You really must come this minute."

They had been brought up on adjoining ranches and had ridden
to the same school and to the same dances. But that was so long ago,
and so much had changed them. And Lila was always a girl to
throw her fortunes in other people's faces. Hester said, gently, regretfully: "Now, isn't it too bad! We brought a big lunch in the
wagon, thinking it would be easier. Joe has so many chores to do
here."

"I have often wondered about you, away out there," said Lila.
"Have you been well? It's been such a hard year for everybody. So
many homesteaders going broke."

"We are well," said Hester slowly, a small, hard pride in her tone.
"Everything's been fine."

"Now, that's nice," murmured Lila, her smile remaining fixed, but
her eyes, Hester observed, were sharp and busy—and reading too
much. Lila said, "Next time you come and see us," and bobbed her
head and went out of the store, her clothes rustling in this quiet.
Hester's lips went sharp-shut and quick color burned on her cheeks.
She took up the baby and turned into the street again and saw that
Tom hadn't come yet to the wagon. The children were out of sight
and there was nothing to do but wait. Hearing the far-off halloo of a
train's whistle, she walked on under the board galleries to the depot.

Heat swirled around her and light flashed up from polished spots
on the iron rails. Around her lay the full monotony of the desert, so
familiar, so wide—and sometimes so hard to bear. Backed against
the yellow depot wall, she watched the train rush forward, a high
plume of white steam rising to the sky as it whistled to warn them.
And then it rushed by, engine and cars, in a great smash of sound
that stirred the baby in her arms. She saw men standing on the plat-
forms. Women's faces showed in the car windows, serene and idly
curious and not a part of Hester's world at all; and afterward the
train was gone, leaving behind the heated smell of steel and smoke.

When the quiet came back it was lonelier than before. She turned back to the wagon.

It was then almost twelve. The children came up, hot and weary and full of excitement. Young Tom said: "The school is right in town. They don't have to walk at all. It's right next to the houses. Why don't they have to walk three miles like us?" And May said: "I saw a china doll with real clothes and painted eyelashes. Can I have a china doll?"

Hester changed the baby on the wagon seat. She said: "Walking is good for people, Tom. Why should you expect a doll now, May? Christmas is the time. Maybe Christmas we'll remember."

"Well, I'm hungry."

"Wait till your father comes," said Hester.

When he turned in from the street, later, she knew something was wrong. He was always a deliberate man, not much given to smiling. But he walked with his shoulders down and when he came up he said only: "I suppose we ought to eat." He didn't look directly at her. He had his own strong pride and she knew this wasn't like him —to stand by the wagon's wheel, so oddly watching his children. She reached under the seat for the box of sandwiches and the cups and the jug of cold coffee. She said: "What did he say, Joe?"

"Why, nothing yet. He said come back at two. He wanted to think about it."

She murmured, "It won't hurt us to wait," and laid out the sandwiches. They sat on the shaded ground and ate, the children with a quick, starved impatience, with an excited and aimless talk. Joe Blount looked at them carefully. "What was it you saw in the restaurant, sonny?"

"It smelled nice," said young May. "The smell came out the door."

Joe Blount cleared his throat. "Don't stop like that in front of the restaurant again."

"Can we go now? Can we go down by the depot?"

"You hold May's hand," said Blount, and watched them leave. He sat cross-legged before his wife, his big hands idle, his expression unstirred. The sandwich, which was salted bacon grease spread on Hester's potato bread, lay before him. "Ain't done enough this morning to be hungry," he said.

"I know."

They were never much at talking. And now there wasn't much to say. She knew that he had been turned down. She knew that at two o'clock he would go and come back empty-handed. Until then she wouldn't speak of it, and neither would he. And she was thinking with a woman's realism of what lay before them. They had nothing except this team and wagon and two cows standing unfed in the barn lot. Going back to Christmas Creek now would be going back only to pack up and leave. For they had delayed asking for this loan until the last sack of flour in the storehouse had been emptied.

He said: "I been thinking. Not much to do on the ranch this fall. I ought to get a little outside work."

"Maybe you should."

"Fact is, I've tried a few places. Kind of quiet. But I can look around some more."

She said, "I'll wait here."

He got up, a rangy, spare man who found it hard to be idle. He looked at her carefully and his voice didn't reveal anything. "If I were you I don't believe I'd order anything at the stores until I come back."

She watched the way he looked out into the smoky horizon, the way he held his shoulders. When he turned away, not meeting her eyes, her lips made a sweet line across her dark face, a softly maternal expression showing. She said, "Joe," and waited until he turned. "Joe, we'll always get along."

He went away again, around the corner of the Cattle King. She shifted her position on the wagon's seat, her hand gently patting the baby who was a little cross from the heat. One by one she went over the list of necessary things in her mind, and one by one, erased them. It was hard to think of little May without a ribbon bow in her hair, without a good dress. Boys could wear old clothes, as long as they were warm; but a girl, a pretty girl, needed the touch of niceness. It was hard to be poor.

Coming out of the bank at noon, Lane McKercher looked into the corral space and saw the Blounts eating their lunch under the locust tree. He turned down Arapahoe Street, walking through the comforting shade of the poplars to the big square house at the end of the lane. At dinner hour his boy took care of the bank, and so he ate his meal with the housekeeper in a dining room whose shades had been tightly drawn—the heavy midday meal of a man who had developed his hunger and his physique from early days on the range. Afterward he walked to the living-room couch and lay down with a paper over his face for the customary nap.

A single fly made a racket in the deep quiet, but it was not this that kept him from sleeping. In some obscure manner the shape of

Joe Blount came before him—the long, patient and work-stiffened shape of a man whose eyes had been so blue and so calm in face of refusal. Well, there had been something behind those eyes for a moment, and then it had passed away, eluding McKercher's sharp glance.

They were mostly all patient ones and seldom speaking—these men that came off the deep desert. A hard life had made them that way, as McKercher knew, who had shared that life himself. Blount was no different than the others and many times McKercher had refused these others, without afterthoughts. It was some other thing that kept his mind on Blount. Not knowing why, he lay quietly on the couch, trying to find the reason.

The country, he told himself, was cattle country, and those who tried to dry-farm it were bound to fail. He had seen them fail, year after year. They took their wagons and their families out toward Christmas Creek, loaded high with plunder; and presently they came back with their wagons baked and their eyebrows bleached and nothing left. With their wives sitting in the wagons, old from work, with their children long and thin from lack of food. They had always failed and always would. Blount was a good man, but so were most of the rest. Why should he be thinking of Blount?

He rose at one o'clock, feeling the heat and feeling his age; and washed his hands and face with good cold water. Lighting a cigar, he strolled back down Arapahoe and walked across the square toward the Cattle King. Mrs. Blount sat on the wagon's seat, holding a baby. The older youngsters, he noticed, were in the cool runway of Dunmire's stable. He went into the saloon, though not to drink.

"Nick," he said, "Joe Blount been in for a drink yet?"

The saloonkeeper looked up from an empty poker table, "No," he said.

McKercher went out, crossing to Billy Saxton's feed store. Deep in the big shed Billy Saxton weighed hay bales on his heavy scales. He stopped and sopped the sweat off his forehead, and smiled. "Bankin'," he stated, "is easier."

"Maybe it is," said Lane McKercher. "Your know Joe Blount well?"

"Why, he's all right. Used to ride for Hat. Old man Dale liked him. He was in here a while back."

"To buy feed?"

"No, he wanted to haul wood for me."

McKercher went back up the street toward the bank. Jim Benbow was coming down the road from the Two Dance hills, kicking a long streamer of dust behind. Sun struck the windows on the north side of town, setting up a brilliant explosion of light. Joe Blount came out of the stable and turned over toward the Cattle King, waiting for Benbow.

In the bank, McKercher said to his son, "All right, you go eat," and sat down at his pine desk. Benbow put his head through the front door, calling: "I'll need five thousand this week, Mac—until the stock check comes in."

"All right."

He sat quite still at the desk, stern with himself because he could not recall why he kept thinking of Joe Blount. Men were everything to Lane McKercher, who watched them pass along this street year in and year out, who studied them with his sharp eyes and made his judgments concerning them. If there was something in a man, it had to come out. And what was it in Joe Blount he couldn't name? The echoes of the big clock on the wall rattled around the droning silence of the bank like the echo of feet striking the floor; it was then a quarter of two, and he knew he had to refuse Blount a second time. He could not understand why he had not made the first turndown final.

Blount met Jim Benbow on the corner of the Cattle King, directly after Hat's owner had left the bank. He shook Benbow's hand, warmed and pleased by the tall cattleman's smile of recognition. Benbow said: "Been a long time since I saw you. How's Christmas Creek, Joe?"

"Fine—just fine. You're lookin' good. You don't get old."

"Well, let's go have a little smile on that."

"Why, thanks, no. I was wonderin'. It's pretty quiet on my place right now. Not much to do till spring. You need a man?"

Benbow shook his head. "Not a thing doing, Joe. Sorry."

"Of course—of course," murmured Blount. "I didn't figure there would be."

He stood against the Cattle King's low porch rail after Benbow had gone down the street, his glance lifted and fixed on the smoky light of the desert beyond town. Shade lay around him but sweat began to creep below his hatbrim. He was closely and quickly thinking of places that might be open for a man, and knew there were none in town and none on the range. This was the slack season of the year. The children were over in front of the grocery store, stopped by its door, hand in hand, round, dark cheeks lifted and still. Blount swung his shoulders around, cutting them out of his sight.

Sullen Ben Drury came out of the courthouse and passed Blount, removing his cigar and speaking, and replacing the cigar again. Its smell was like acid biting at Blount's jaw corners, and suddenly he faced the bank with the odd and terrible despair of a man who has reached the end of hope, and a strange thought came to him, which was that the doors of that bank were wide open and money lay on the counter inside for the taking.

He stood very still, his head down, and after a while he thought: "An unseemly thing for a man to hold in his head." It was two o'clock then and he turned over the square, going toward the bank with his legs springing as he walked and all his muscles loose. In the quietness of the room his boots dragged up odd sound. He stood by Lane McKercher's desk, waiting without any show of expression; he knew what McKercher would say.

McKercher said, slowly and with an odd trace of irritation: "Joe, you're wasting your time on Christmas Creek. And you'd waste the loan."

Blount said, mildly and courteously: "I can understand your view. Don't blame you for not loanin' without security." He looked over McKercher's head, his glance going through the window to the far strip of horizon. "Kind of difficult to give up a thing," he mused. "I figured to get away from ridin' for other folks and ride for myself. Well, that was why we went to Christmas Creek. Maybe a place the kids could have later. Man wants his children to have somethin' better than he had."

"Not on Christmas Creek," said McKercher. He watched Joe Blount with a closer and sharper interest, bothered by a feeling he could not name. Bothered by it and turned impatient by it.

"Maybe, maybe not," said Blount. "Bad luck don't last forever." Then he said, "Well, I shouldn't be talkin'. I thank you for your time." He put on his hat, and his big hand moved up across his shirt, to the pocket there—and dropped away. He turned toward the door.

"Hold on," said Lane. "Hold on a minute." He waited till Blount came back to the desk. He opened the desk's drawer and pulled out a can of cigars, holding them up. "Smoke?"

There was a long delay, and it was strange to see the way Joe Blount looked at the cigars, with his lips closely together. He said, his voice dragging on the words, "I guess not, but thanks."

Lane McKercher looked down at the desk, his expression breaking out of its maintained strictness. The things in a man had to come out, and he knew now why Joe Blount had stayed so long in his mind. It made him look up. "I have been considering this. It won't ever be a matter of luck on Christmas Creek. It's a matter of water. When I passed the feed store today I noticed a second-hand windmill in the back. It will do. You get hold of Plummer Bodry and find out his price for driving you a well. I never stake a man unless I stake him right. We will figure the three hundred and whatever it takes to put up a tank and windmill. When you buy your supplies today, just say you've got credit here."

"Why, now—" began Joe Blount in his slow, soft voice, "I—"

But Lane McKercher said to his son, just coming back from lunch, "I want you to bring your ledger over here." He kept on talking and Joe Blount, feeling himself pushed out, turned and left the bank.

McKercher's son came over. "Made that loan after all. Why?"

McKercher said only, "He's a good man, Bob." But he knew the real reason. A man that smoked always carried his tobacco in his shirt pocket. Blount had kept reaching, out of habit, for something that wasn't there. Well, a man like Blount loved this one small comfort and never went without it unless actually destitute. But Blount wouldn't admit it, and had been too proud to take a free cigar. Men were everything—and the qualities in them came out sooner or later, as with Blount. A windmill and water was a good risk with a fellow like that.

Hester watched him cross the square and come toward her, walking slowly, with his shoulders squared. She patted the baby's back and gently rocked it, and wondered at the change. When he came up he said, casually, "I'll hitch and drive around to the store, so we can load the stuff you buy."

She watched him carefully, so curious to know how it had happened. But she only said: "We'll get along."

He was smiling then, he who seldom smiled. "I guess you need a few things for yourself. We can spare something for that."

"Only a dress and some ribbon, for May. A girl needs something nice." She paused, and afterward added, because she knew how real his need was, "Joe, you buy yourself some tobacco."

He let it out a long, long breath. "I believe I will," he said. They stood this way, both gently smiling. They needed no talk to explain anything to each other. They had been through so much these last few years. Hardship and trouble had drawn them so close together that words were unnecessary. So they were silent, remembering so much, and understanding so much, and still smiling. Presently he turned to hitch up.

8

Memory

EVERY NATION faces the temptation of sentimentalizing its past and replacing reality with a palatable myth. Thus Daniel Boone and Davy Crockett have become the heroes of the children's hour, sweetened by legend and homogenized by Walt Disney. A laundered Wyatt Earp strides bravely down the boardwalks of Dodge City, handsome, imperturbable, unstained by the weaknesses and venalities of the historical record. And innumerable types of stupid Cooper Indians immolate themselves fighting fictional supermen.

These are the cliches of motion pictures and television, but they have antecedents in our literature. Even as good a poet as Stephen Vincent Benét can surrender to the easy sentimentalities of our national self-image. In "The Ballad of William Sycamore," a skillful but facile poem, he celebrates the familiar frontiersman, invoking memories of Kentucky rifles and log cabins, the Alamo and the Little Big Horn. And he ends with a contented corpse and an elegant variation of "don't fence me in." The movement of the poem is rapid, its stereotypes have the tested effectiveness of a Norman Rockwell magazine cover, and its sentimentality is unabashed.

The grandfather of Steinbeck's "The Leader of the People" is neither dead nor contented. He, too, celebrates a conquest of the frontier, but he also mourns the end of an era. As one of the "old men along the shore hating the ocean," he believes the last battle has been won and that the kind of men who fought it have vanished. His story contains the nostalgia, the melancholy, and even the self-pity that tinge some contemporary evocations of the frontier spirit.

Many of our writers return to the basic paradox of the frontiersman's life, that he destroys the world he loves. He settles New England and produces Boston; he cuts down the forest to produce Cincinnati and Chicago; he fights the Comanches and bleeds at the Alamo to produce Dallas and Houston; and he conquers the deserts so that his children can build Phoenix, Palm Springs, and Las Vegas. He kills off the California Indians so that movie stars can relive the myths of the West on Hollywood sound stages. His children mourn even as they celebrate his achievements, and some of them join together in organizations like the Sierra Club to try to preserve a few patches of wilderness.

The basic paradox of the frontiersman's life is treated as fantasy in William Brandon's "The Buffalo Singer." One of America's authorities on Indian culture, Brandon can understand both the glories of our past and the sometimes vulgar realities of our present. His Wully and Granddaddy Thanko head for a high place and celebrate a religious mystery behind a billboard advertising beer. And so they and Brandon achieve a miracle.

Perhaps their achievement is like that of Steinbeck's leader of the people, merely a tale for little boys. But the boys will never forget. They will grow to manhood talking of "New Frontiers," of the frontiers of science or space or medicine. And even as men they will share the wish—if not the power—of William Brandon's buffalo singer: they will dream of days when the earth shook as the great herds stampeded.

STEPHEN VINCENT BENÉT

The Ballad of William Sycamore
(1790-1871)

MY FATHER, he was a mountaineer,
His fist was a knotty hammer;
He was quick on his feet as a running deer,
And he spoke with a Yankee stammer.

My mother, she was merry and brave,
And so she came to her labor,
With a tall green fir for her doctor grave
And a stream for her comforting neighbor.

And some are wrapped in the linen fine,
And some like a godling's scion;
But I was cradled on twigs of pine
In the skin of a mountain lion.

And some remember a white, starched lap
And a ewer with silver handles;
But I remember a coonskin cap
And the smell of bayberry candles.

The cabin logs, with the bark still rough,
And my mother who laughed at trifles,
And the tall, lank visitors, brown as snuff,
With their long, straight squirrel-rifles.

I can hear them dance, like a foggy song,
Through the deepest one of my slumbers,
The fiddle squeaking the boots along
And my father calling the numbers.

347

The quick feet shaking the puncheon-floor,
And the fiddle squealing and squealing,
Till the dried herbs rattled above the door
And the dust went up to the ceiling.

There are children lucky from dawn till dusk,
But never a child so lucky!
For I cut my teeth on "Money Musk"
In the Bloody Ground of Kentucky!

When I grew tall as the Indian corn,
My father had little to lend me,
But he gave me his great, old powder-horn
And his woodsman's skill to befriend me.

With a leather shirt to cover my back,
And a redskin nose to unravel
Each forest sign, I carried my pack
As far as a scout could travel.

Till I lost my boyhood and found my wife,
A girl like a Salem clipper!
A woman straight as a hunting-knife
With eyes as bright as the Dipper!

We cleared our camp where the buffalo feed,
Unheard-of streams were our flagons;
And I sowed my sons like the apple-seed
On the trail of the Western wagons.

They were right, tight boys, never sulky or slow,
A fruitful, a goodly muster.
The eldest died at the Alamo.
The youngest fell with Custer.

The letter that told it burned my hand.
Yet we smiled and said, "So be it!"
But I could not live when they fenced the land,
For it broke my heart to see it.

I saddled a red, unbroken colt
And rode him into the day there;
And he threw me down like a thunderbolt
And rolled on me as I lay there.

The hunter's whistle hummed in my ear
As the city-men tried to move me,
And I died in my boots like a pioneer
With the whole wide sky above me.

Now I lie in the heart of the fat, black soil,
Like the seed of a prairie-thistle;
It has washed my bones with honey and oil
And picked them clean as a whistle.

And my youth returns, like the rains of Spring,
And my sons, like the wild-geese flying;
And I lie and hear the meadow-lark sing
And have much content in my dying.

Go play with the towns you have built of blocks,
The towns where you would have bound me!
I sleep in my earth like a tired fox,
And my buffalo have found me.

JOHN STEINBECK

The Leader of the People

ON SATURDAY AFTERNOON Billy Buck, the ranch-hand, raked together the last of the old year's haystack and pitched small forkfuls over the wire fence to a few mildly interested cattle. High in the air small clouds like puffs of cannon smoke were driven eastward by the March wind. The wind could be heard whishing in the brush on the ridge crests, but no breath of it penetrated down into the ranch-cup.

The little boy, Jody, emerged from the house eating a thick piece of buttered bread. He saw Billy working on the last of the haystack. Jody tramped down scuffing his shoes in the way he had been told was destructive to good shoe-leather. A flock of white pigeons flew out of the black cypress tree as Jody passed, and circled the tree and landed again. A half-grown tortoise-shell cat leaped from the bunk-house porch, galloped on stiff legs across the road, whirled and galloped back again. Jody picked up a stone to help the game along, but he was too late, for the cat was under the porch before the stone could be discharged. He threw the stone into the cypress tree and started the white pigeons on another whirling flight.

Arriving at the used-up haystack, the boy leaned against the barbed wire fence. "Will that be all of it, do you think?" he asked.

The middle-aged ranch-hand stopped his careful raking and stuck his fork into the ground. He took off his black hat and smoothed down his hair. "Nothing left of it that isn't soggy from ground moisture," he said. He replaced his hat and rubbed his dry leathery hands together.

"Ought to be plenty mice," Jody suggested.

"Lousy with them," said Billy. "Just crawling with mice."

"Well, maybe, when you get all through, I could call the dogs and hunt the mice."

"Sure, I guess you could," said Billy Buck. He lifted a forkful of the damp ground-hay and threw it into the air. Instantly three mice leaped out and burrowed frantically under the hay again.

Jody sighed with satisfaction. Those plump, sleek, arrogant mice were doomed. For eight months they had lived and multiplied in the haystack. They had been immune from cats, from traps, from poison and from Jody. They had grown smug in their security, overbearing and fat. Now the time of disaster had come; they would not survive another day.

Billy looked up at the top of the hills that surrounded the ranch. "Maybe you better ask your father before you do it," he suggested.

"Well, where is he? I'll ask him now."

"He rode up to the ridge ranch after dinner. He'll be back pretty soon."

Jody slumped against the fence post. "I don't think he'd care."

As Billy went back to his work he said ominously, "You'd better ask him anyway. You know how he is."

Jody did know. His father, Carl Tiflin, insisted upon giving permission for anything that was done on the ranch, whether it was important or not. Jody sagged farther against the post until he was sitting on the ground. He looked up at the little puffs of wind-driven cloud. "Is it like to rain, Billy?"

"It might. The wind's good for it, but not strong enough."

"Well, I hope it don't rain until after I kill those damn mice." He looked over his shoulder to see whether Billy had noticed the mature profanity. Billy worked on without comment.

Jody turned back and looked at the side-hill where the road from the outside world came down. The hill was washed with lean March sunshine. Silver thistles, blue lupins and a few poppies bloomed among the sage bushes. Halfway up the hill Jody could see Doubletree Mutt, the black dog, digging in a squirrel hole. He paddled for a while and then paused to kick bursts of dirt out between his hind legs, and he dug with an earnestness which belied the knowledge he must have had that no dog had ever caught a squirrel by digging in a hole.

Suddenly, while Jody watched, the black dog stiffened, and backed out of the hole and looked up the hill toward the cleft in the ridge where the road came through. Jody looked up too. For a moment Carl Tiflin on horseback stood out against the pale sky and then he moved down the road toward the house. He carried something white in his hand.

The boy started to his feet. "He's got a letter," Jody cried. He trotted away toward the ranch house, for the letter would probably be read aloud and he wanted to be there. He reached the house before his father did, and ran in. He heard Carl dismount from his creaking saddle and slap the horse on the side to send it to the barn where Billy would unsaddle it and turn it out.

Jody ran into the kitchen. "We got a letter!" he cried.

His mother looked up from a pan of beans. "Who has?"

"Father has. I saw it in his hand."

Carl strode into the kitchen then, and Jody's mother asked, "Who's the letter from, Carl?"

He frowned quickly. "How did you know there was a letter?"

She nodded her head in the boy's direction. "Big-Britches Jody told me."

Jody was embarrassed.

His father looked down at him contemptuously. "He is getting to be a Big-Britches," Carl said. "He's minding everybody's business but his own. Got his big nose into everything."

Mrs. Tiflin relented a little. "Well, he hasn't enough to keep him busy. Who's the letter from?"

Carl still frowned on Jody. "I'll keep him busy if he isn't careful." He held out a sealed letter. "I guess it's from your father."

Mrs. Tiflin took a hairpin from her head and slit open the flap. Her lips pursed judiciously. Jody saw her eyes snap back and forth over the lines. "He says," she translated, "he says he's going to drive out Saturday to stay for a little while. Why, this is Saturday. The letter must have been delayed." She looked at the postmark. "This was mailed day before yesterday. It should have been here yesterday." She looked up questioningly at her husband, and then her face darkened angrily. "Now what have you got that look on you for? He doesn't come often."

Carl turned his eyes away from her anger. He could be stern with her most of the time, but when occasionally her temper arose, he could not combat it.

"What's the matter with you?" she demanded again.

In his explanation there was a tone of apology Jody himself might have used. "It's just that he talks," Carl said lamely. "Just talks."

"Well, what of it? You talk yourself."

"Sure I do. But your father only talks about one thing."

"Indians!" Jody broke in excitedly. "Indians and crossing the plains!"

Carl turned fiercely on him. "You get out, Mr. Big-Britches! Go on, now! Get out!"

Jody went miserably out the back door and closed the screen with elaborate quietness. Under the kitchen window his shamed, downcast eyes fell upon a curiously shaped stone, a stone of such fascination that he squatted down and picked it up and turned it over in his hands.

The voices came clearly to him through the open kitchen window. "Jody's damn well right," he heard his father say. "Just Indians and crossing the plains. I've heard that story about how the horses got driven off about a thousand times. He just goes on and on, and he never changes a word in the things he tells."

When Mrs. Tiflin answered her tone was so changed that Jody, outside the window, looked up from his study of the stone. Her voice had become soft and explanatory. Jody knew how her face would have changed to match the tone. She said quietly, "Look at it this way, Carl. That was the big thing in my father's life. He led a wagon train clear across the plains to the coast, and when it was finished, his life was done. It was a big thing to do, but it didn't last long enough. Look!" she continued, "It's as though he was born to do that, and after he finished it, there wasn't anything more for him to do but think about it and talk about it. If there'd been any farther west to go, he'd have gone. He's told me so himself. But at last there was the ocean. He lives right by the ocean where he had to stop."

She had caught Carl, caught him and entangled him in her soft tone.

"I've seen him," he agreed quietly. "He goes down and stares off west over the ocean." His voice sharpened a little. "And then he goes up to the Horseshoe Club in Pacific Grove, and he tells people how the Indians drove off the horses."

She tried to catch him again. "Well, it's everything to him. You might be patient with him and pretend to listen."

Carl turned impatiently away. "Well, if it gets too bad, I can always go down to the bunkhouse and set with Billy," he said irritably. He walked through the house and slammed the front door after him.

Jody ran to his chores. He dumped the grain to the chickens without chasing any of them. He gathered the eggs from the nests. He trotted into the house with the wood and interlaced it so carefully in the wood-box that two armloads seemed to fill it to overflowing.

His mother had finished the beans by now. She stirred up the fire and brushed off the stove-top with a turkey wing. Jody peered cautiously at her to see whether any rancor toward him remained. "Is he coming today?" Jody asked.

"That's what his letter said."

"Maybe I better walk up the road to meet him."

Mrs. Tiflin clanged the stove-lid shut. "That would be nice," she said. "He'd probably like to be met."

"I guess I'll just do it then."

Outside, Jody whistled shrilly to the dogs. "Come on up the hill," he commanded. The two dogs waved their tails and ran ahead.

Along the roadside the sage had tender new tips. Jody tore off some
pieces and rubbed them on his hands until the air was filled with
the sharp wild smell. With a rush the dogs leaped from the road
and yapped into the brush after a rabbit. That was the last Jody
saw of them, for when they failed to catch the rabbit, they went back
home.

Jody plodded on up the hill toward the ridge top. When he
reached the little cleft where the road came through, the afternoon
wind struck him and blew up his hair and ruffled his shirt. He
looked down on the little hills and ridges below and then out at the
huge green Salinas Valley. He could see the white town of Salinas
far out in the flat and the flash of its windows under the waning
sun. Directly below him, in an oak tree, a crow congress had con-
vened. The tree was black with crows all cawing at once.

Then Jody's eyes followed the wagon road down from the ridge
where he stood, and lost it behind a hill, and picked it up again on
the other side. On that distant stretch he saw a cart slowly pulled by
a bay horse. It disappeared behind the hill. Jody sat down on the
ground and watched the place where the cart would reappear again.
The wind sang on the hilltops and the puff-ball clouds hurried eastward.

Then the cart came into sight and stopped. A man dressed in
black dismounted from the seat and walked to the horse's head. Although it was so far away, Jody knew he had unhooked the check-
rein, for the horse's head dropped forward. The horse moved on,
and the man walked slowly up the hill beside it. Jody gave a glad
cry and ran down the road toward them. The squirrels bumped
along off the road, and a road-runner flirted its tail and raced over
the edge of the hill and sailed out like a glider.

Jody tried to leap into the middle of his shadow at every step. A
stone rolled under his foot and he went down. Around a little bend
he raced, and there, a short distance ahead, were his grandfather
and the cart. The boy dropped from his unseemly running and approached at a dignified walk.

The horse plodded stumble-footedly up the hill and the old man
walked beside it. In the lowering sun their giant shadows flickered
darkly behind them. The grandfather was dressed in a black broad-
cloth suit and he wore kid congress gaiters and a black tie on a short,
hard collar. He carried his black slouch hat in his hand. His white
beard was cropped close and his white eyebrows overhung his eyes
like moustaches. The blue eyes were sternly merry. About the whole
face and figure there was a granite dignity, so that every motion
seemed an impossible thing. Once at rest, it seemed the old man
would be stone, would never move again. His steps were slow and
certain. Once made, no step could ever be retraced; once headed in

a direction, the path would never bend nor the pace increase nor slow.

When Jody appeared around the bend, Grandfather waved his hat slowly in welcome, and he called, "Why, Jody! Come down to meet me, have you?"

Jody sidled near and turned and matched his step to the old man's step and stiffened his body and dragged his heels a little. "Yes, sir," he said. "We got your letter only today."

"Should have been here yesterday," said Grandfather. "It certainly should. How are all the folks?"

"They're fine, sir." He hesitated and then suggested shyly, "Would you like to come on a mouse hunt tomorrow, sir?"

"Mouse hunt, Jody?" Grandfather chuckled. "Have the people of this generation come down to hunting mice? They aren't very strong, the new people, but I hardly thought mice would be game for them."

"No, sir. It's just play. The haystack's gone. I'm going to drive out the mice to the dogs. And you can watch, or even beat the hay a little."

The stern, merry eyes turned down on him. "I see. You don't eat them, then. You haven't come to that yet."

Jody explained, "The dogs eat them, sir. It wouldn't be much like hunting Indians, I guess."

"No, not much—but then later, when the troops were hunting Indians and shooting children and burning teepees, it wasn't much different from your mouse hunt."

They topped the rise and started down into the ranch cup, and they lost the sun from their shoulders. "You've grown," Grandfather said. "Nearly an inch, I should say."

"More," Jody boasted. "Where they mark me on the door, I'm up more than an inch since Thanksgiving even."

Grandfather's rich throaty voice said, "Maybe you're getting too much water and turning to pith and stalk. Wait until you head out, and then we'll see."

Jody looked quickly into the old man's face to see whether his feelings should be hurt, but there was no will to injure, no punishing nor putting-in-your-place light in the keen blue eyes. "We might kill a pig," Jody suggested.

"Oh, no! I couldn't let you do that. You're just humoring me. It isn't the time and you know it."

"You know Riley, the big boar, sir?"

"Yes. I remember Riley well."

"Well, Riley ate a hole into that same haystack, and it fell down on him and smothered him."

"Pigs do that when they can," said Grandfather.

"Riley was a nice pig, for a boar, sir. I rode him sometimes, and he didn't mind."

A door slammed at the house below them, and they saw Jody's mother standing on the porch waving her apron in welcome. And they saw Carl Tiflin walking up from the barn to be at the house for the arrival.

The sun had disappeared from the hills by now. The blue smoke from the house chimney hung in flat layers in the purpling ranch-cup. The puff-ball clouds, dropped by the falling wind, hung listlessly in the sky.

Billy Buck came out of the bunkhouse and flung a wash basin of soapy water on the ground. He had been shaving in mid-week, for Billy held Grandfather in reverence, and Grandfather said that Billy was one of the few men of the new generation who had not gone soft. Although Billy was in middle age, Grandfather considered him a boy. Now Billy was hurrying toward the house too.

When Jody and Grandfather arrived, the three were waiting for them in front of the yard gate.

Carl said, "Hello, sir. We've been looking for you."

Mrs. Tiflin kissed Grandfather on the side of his beard, and stood still while his big hand patted her shoulder. Billy shook hands solemnly, grinning under his straw moustache. "I'll put up your horse," said Billy, and he led the rig away.

Grandfather watched him go, and then, turning back to the group, he said as he had said a hundred times before, "There's a good boy. I knew his father, old Muletail Buck. I never knew why they called him Mule-tail except he packed mules."

Mrs. Tiflin turned and led the way into the house. "How long are you going to stay, Father? Your letter didn't say."

"Well, I don't know. I thought I'd stay about two weeks. But I never stay as long as I think I'm going to."

In a short while they were sitting at the white oilcloth table eating their supper. The lamp with the tin reflector hung over the table. Outside the dining-room windows the big moths battered softly against the glass.

Grandfather cut his steak into tiny pieces and chewed slowly. "I'm hungry," he said. "Driving out here got my appetite up. It's like when we were crossing. We all got so hungry every night we could hardly wait to let the meat get done. I could eat about five pounds of buffalo meat every night."

"It's moving around does it," said Billy. "My father was a government packer. I helped him when I was a kid. Just the two of us could about clean up a deer's ham."

"I knew your father, Billy," said Grandfather. "A fine man he was. They called him Mule-tail Buck. I don't know why except he packed mules."

"That was it," Billy agreed. "He packed mules."

Grandfather put down his knife and fork and looked around the table. "I remember one time we ran out of meat—" His voice dropped to a curious low sing-song, dropped into a tonal groove the story had worn for itself. "There was no buffalo, no antelope, not even rabbits. The hunters couldn't even shoot a coyote. That was the time for the leader to be on the watch. I was the leader, and I kept my eyes open. Know why? Well, just the minute the people began to get hungry they'd start slaughtering the team oxen. Do you believe that? I've heard of parties that just ate up their draft cattle. Started from the middle and worked toward the ends. Finally they'd eat the lead pair, and then the wheelers. The leader of a party had to keep them from doing that."

In some manner a big moth got into the room and circled the hanging kerosene lamp. Billy got up and tried to clap it between his hands. Carl struck with a cupped palm and caught the moth and broke it. He walked to the window and dropped it out.

"As I was saying," Grandfather began again, but Carl interrupted him. "You'd better eat some more meat. All the rest of us are ready for our pudding."

Jody saw a flash of anger in his mother's eyes. Grandfather picked up his knife and fork. "I'm pretty hungry, all right," he said. "I'll tell you about that later."

When supper was over, when the family and Billy Buck sat in front of the fireplace in the other room, Jody anxiously watched Grandfather. He saw the signs he knew. The bearded head leaned forward; the eyes lost their sternness and looked wonderingly into the fire; the big lean fingers laced themselves on the black knees. "I wonder," he began, "I just wonder whether I ever told you how those thieving Piutes drove off thirty-five of our horses."

"I think you did," Carl interrupted. "Wasn't it just before you went up into the Tahoe country?"

Grandfather turned quickly toward his son-in-law. "That's right. I guess I must have told you that story."

"Lots of times," Carl said cruelly, and he avoided his wife's eyes. But he felt the angry eyes on him, and he said, " 'Course I'd like to hear it again."

Grandfather looked back at the fire. His fingers unlaced and laced again. Jody knew how he felt, how his insides were collapsed and empty. Hadn't Jody been called a Big-Britches that very afternoon? He arose to heroism and opened himself to the term Big-Britches again. "Tell about Indians," he said softly.

Grandfather's eyes grew stern again. "Boys always want to hear about Indians. It was a job for men, but boys want to hear about it. Well, let's see. Did I every tell you how I wanted each wagon to carry a long iron plate?"

Everyone but Jody remained silent. Jody said, "No. You didn't."

"Well, when the Indians attacked, we always put the wagons in a circle and fought from between the wheels. I thought that if every wagon carried a long plate with rifle holes, the men could stand the plates on the outside of the wheels when the wagons were in the circle and they would be protected. It would save lives and that would make up for the extra weight of the iron. But of course the party wouldn't do it. No party had done it before and they couldn't see why they should go to the expense. They lived to regret it, too."

Jody looked at his mother, and knew from her expression that she was not listening at all. Carl picked at a callus on his thumb and Billy Buck watched a spider crawling up the wall.

Grandfather's tone dropped into its narrative groove again. Jody knew in advance exactly what words would fall. The story droned on, speeded up for the attack, grew sad over the wounds, struck a dirge at the burials on the great plains. Jody sat quietly watching Grandfather. The stern blue eyes were detached. He looked as though he were not very interested in the story himself.

When it was finished, when the pause had been politely respected as the frontier of the story, Billy Buck stood up and stretched and hitched his trousers. "I guess I'll turn in," he said. Then he faced Grandfather. "I've got an old powder horn and a cap and ball pistol down to the bunkhouse. Did I ever show them to you?"

Grandfather nodded slowly. "Yes, I think you did, Billy. Reminds me of a pistol I had when I was leading the people across." Billy stood politely until the little story was done, and then he said, "Good night," and went out of the house.

Carl Tiflin tried to turn the conversation then. "How's the country between here and Monterey? I've heard it's pretty dry."

"It is dry," said Grandfather. "There's not a drop of water in the Laguna Seca. But it's a long pull from '87. The whole country was powder then, and in '61 I believe all the coyotes starved to death. We had fifteen inches of rain this year."

"Yes, but it all came too early. We could to with some now."

Carl's eye fell on Jody. "Hadn't you better be getting to bed?"

Jody stood up obediently. "Can I kill the mice in the old haystack, sir?"

"Mice? Oh! Sure, kill them all off. Billy said there isn't any good hay left."

Jody exchanged a secret and satisfying look with Grandfather. "I'll kill every one tomorrow," he promised.

Jody lay in his bed and thought of the impossible world of Indians and buffaloes, a world that had ceased to be forever. He wished he could have been living in the heroic time, but he knew he was not of heroic timber. No one living now, save possibly Billy Buck, was worthy to do the things that had been done. A race of giants had lived then, fearless men, men of a staunchness unknown in this day. Jody thought of the wide plains and of the wagons moving across like centipedes. He thought of Grandfather on a huge white horse, marshaling the people. Across his mind marched the great phantoms, and they marched off the earth and they were gone.

He came back to the ranch for a moment, then. He heard the dull rushing sound that space and silence make. He heard one of the dogs, out in the doghouse, scratching a flea and bumping his elbow against the floor with every stroke. Then the wind arose again and the black cypress groaned and Jody went to sleep.

He was up half an hour before the triangle sounded for breakfast. His mother was rattling the stove to make the flames roar when Jody went through the kitchen. "You're up early," she said. "Where are you going?"

"Out to get a good stick. We're going to kill the mice today."

"Who is 'we'?"

"Why, Grandfather and I."

"So you've got him in it. You always like to have someone in with you in case there's blame to share."

"I'll be right back," said Jody. "I just want to have a good stick ready for after breakfast."

He closed the screen door after him and went out into the cool blue morning. The birds were noisy in the dawn and the ranch cats came down from the hill like blunt snakes. They had been hunting gophers in the dark, and although the four cats were full of gopher meat, they sat in a semi-circle at the back door and mewed piteously for milk. Doubletree Mutt and Smasher moved sniffing along the edge of the brush, performing the duty with rigid ceremony, but when Jody whistled, their heads jerked up and their tails waved. They plunged down to him, wriggling their skins and yawning. Jody patted their heads seriously, and moved on to the weathered scrap pile. He selected an old broom handle and a short piece of inch-square scrap wood. From his pocket he took a shoelace and tied the ends of the sticks loosely together to make a flail. He whistled his new weapon through the air and struck the ground experimentally, while the dogs leaped aside and whined with apprehension.

Jody turned and started down past the house toward the old haystack ground to look over the field of slaughter, but Billy Buck, sitting patiently on the back steps, called to him, "You better come back. It's only a couple of minutes till breakfast."

Jody changed his course and moved toward the house. He leaned his flail against the steps. "That's to drive the mice out," he said. "I'll bet they're fat. I'll bet they don't know what's going to happen to them today."

"No, nor you either," Billy remarked philosophically, "nor me, nor anyone."

Jody was staggered by this thought. He knew it was true. His imagination twitched away from the mouse hunt. Then his mother came out on the back porch and struck the triangle, and all thoughts fell in a heap.

Grandfather hadn't appeared at the table when they sat down. Billy nodded at his empty chair. "He's all right? He isn't sick?"

"He takes a long time to dress," said Mrs. Tiflin. "He combs his whiskers and rubs up his shoes and brushes his clothes."

Carl scattered sugar on his mush. "A man that's led a wagon train across the plains has got to be pretty careful how he dresses."

Mrs. Tiflin turned on him. "Don't do that, Carl! Please don't!" There was more of threat than of request in her tone. And the threat irritated Carl.

"Well, how many times do I have to listen to the story of the iron plates, and the thirty-five horses? That time's done. Why can't he forget it, now it's done?" He grew angrier while he talked, and his voice rose. "Why does he have to tell them over and over? He came across the plains. All right! Now it's finished. Nobody wants to hear about it over and over."

The door into the kitchen closed softly. The four at the table sat frozen. Carl laid his mush spoon on the table and touched his chin with his fingers.

Then the kitchen door opened and Grandfather walked in. His mouth smiled tightly and his eyes were squinted. "Good morning," he said, and he sat down and looked at his mush dish.

Carl could not leave it there. "Did—did you hear what I said?"

Grandfather jerked a little nod.

"I don't know what got into me, sir. I didn't mean it. I was just being funny."

Jody glanced in shame at his mother, and he saw that she was looking at Carl, and that she wasn't breathing. It was an awful thing that he was doing. He was tearing himself to pieces to talk like that. It was a terrible thing to him to retract a word, but to retract it in shame was infinitely worse.

Grandfather looked sidewise. "I'm trying to get right side up," he said gently. "I'm not being mad. I don't mind what you said, but it might be true, and I would mind that."

"It isn't true," said Carl. "I'm not feeling well this morning. I'm sorry I said it."

"Don't be sorry, Carl. An old man doesn't see things sometimes. Maybe you're right. The crossing is finished. Maybe it should be forgotten, now it's done."

Carl got up from the table. "I've had enough to eat. I'm going to work. Take your time, Billy!" He walked quickly out of the dining-room. Billy gulped the rest of his food and followed soon after. But Jody could not leave his chair.

"Won't you tell any more stories?" Jody asked.

"Why, sure I'll tell them, but only when—I'm sure people want to hear them."

"I like to hear them, sir."

"Oh! Of course you do, but you're a little boy. It was a job for men, but only little boys like to hear about it."

Jody got up from his place. "I'll wait outside for you, sir. I've got a good stick for those mice."

He waited by the gate until the old man came out on the porch. "Let's go down and kill the mice now," Jody called.

"I think I'll just sit in the sun, Jody. You go kill the mice."

"You can use my stick if you like."

"No, I'll just sit here a while."

Jody turned disconsolately away, and walked down toward the old haystack. He tried to whip up his enthusiasm with thoughts of the fat juicy mice. He beat the ground with his flail. The dogs coaxed and whined about him, but he could not go. Back at the house he could see Grandfather sitting on the porch, looking small and thin and black.

Jody gave up and went to sit on the steps at the old man's feet. "Back already? Did you kill the mice?"

"No, sir. I'll kill them some other day."

The morning flies buzzed close to the ground and the ants dashed about in front of the steps. The heavy smell of sage slipped down the hill. The porch boards grew warm in the sunshine.

Jody hardly knew when Grandfather started to talk. "I shouldn't stay here, feeling the way I do." He examined his strong old hands. "I feel as though the crossing wasn't worth doing." His eyes moved up the side-hill and stopped on a motionless hawk perched on a dead limb. "I tell those old stories, but they're not what I want to tell. I only know how I want people to feel when I tell them.

"It wasn't Indians that were important, nor adventures, nor even getting out here. It was a whole bunch of people made into one big crawling beast. And I was the head. It was westering and westering. Every man wanted something for himself, but the big beast that was all of them wanted only westering. I was the leader, but if I hadn't been there, someone else would have been the head. The thing had to have a head.

"Under the little bushes the shadows were black at white noon-day. When we saw the mountains at last, we cried—all of us. But it wasn't getting here that mattered, it was movement and westering.

"We carried life out here and set it down the way those ants carry eggs. And I was the leader. The westering was as big as God, and the slow steps that made the movement piled up and piled up until the continent was crossed.

"Then we came down to the sea, and it was done." He stopped and wiped his eyes until the rims were red. "That's what I should be telling instead of stories."

When Jody spoke, Grandfather started and looked down at him. "Maybe I could lead the people some day," Jody said.

The old man smiled. "There's no place to go. There's the ocean to stop you. There's a line of old men along the shore hating the ocean because it stopped them."

"In boats I might, sir."

"No place to go, Jody. Every place is taken. But that's not the worst—no, not the worst. Westering has died out of the people. Westering isn't a hunger any more. It's all done. Your father is right. It is finished." He laced his fingers on his knee and looked at them.

Jody felt very sad. "If you'd like a glass of lemonade I could make it for you."

Grandfather was about to refuse, and then he saw Jody's face. "That would be nice," he said. "Yes, it would be nice to drink a lemonade."

Jody ran into the kitchen where his mother was wiping the last of the breakfast dishes. "Can I have a lemon to make a lemonade for Grandfather?"

His mother mimicked—"And another lemon to make a lemonade for you."

"No, ma'am. I don't want one."

"Jody! You're sick!" Then she stopped suddenly. "Take a lemon out of the cooler," she said softly. "Here, I'll reach the squeezer down to you."

WILLIAM BRANDON

·•·

The Buffalo Singer

THEY ALL PILED into the pickup and drove every which way beyond the Ridge, looking for Wully. Now and then one of the kids yelled from the back of the truck, "There he is!" but it always turned out to be something else, and Jesiah swore in Chickasaw. The rolling land to the west, usually shades of pearl and pumpkin, was stained with vermilion, and the sun sank inch by inch. The pickup's shadow was forty rods long, racing in a silent glide across rose-tinted greasewood and a sailing jackrabbit. The kids stood up full length swaying dangerously and lifted their arms to make giant gestures that all but encompassed the earth. They saw someone walking a long way off that turned into Jana Penna, walking along dancing every few steps with a transistor radio held beside her ear.

She said, "I saw Wully with Granddaddy Thanko, going some place. Are you leaving right now?"

"If we can find that daggoned Wully we are," Jesiah said.

"Granddaddy Thanko had his medicine bundle," Jana Penna said. "Can I ride as far as you go toward the Center?"

"Sure, but that might not be too far," Jesiah said. "Get in here in front."

Jana Penna climbed into the cab beside what looked like a rolled-up rag rug but was in reality Tapatopa, wearing two overcoats and topped off by a brand new blue bandanna tied around his head. She could hardly see him all shriveled mouth and burnished eyes inside the layers of coats and the starched bandanna, that looked like the bluebell crown purportedly worn by the King of the Fairies.

The two biggest boys crawled from the back of the truck onto the roof of the cab and hung their heads in at the window to ask Jana Penna to play her radio. Jana Penna turned it up loud playing rhythm and blues while Jesiah drove on.

When they reached the turn for Horny Toad Highway Jesiah began slowing up to stop but Jana Penna switched off her radio long enough to say, "I'll go along with you and see too, if you don't mind. I'm not in any big hurry to get to the Center." They both knew that if Granddaddy Thanko had his medicine bundle then he and Wully would probably have been heading for Red Sandy Hill, that being the only thing that would pass for a high place within twenty miles.

They found Wully and Granddaddy Thanko on top of the hill behind the big red white and blue beer signboard there, Wully dancing around in a circle and Granddaddy Thanko singing.

Jana Penna turned her radio down low until they could hear Granddaddy Thanko's hoarse voice over the slambanging guitar from Tulsa.

"Tag yah he ah gap yah, tag yah he cattle yah," Granddaddy Thanko sang, more or less. "Sahnn sahnn, tag yah he tag yah heee, ah gap yah ah gap yah, atta atta yah yah atta atta yah yah, yah yah yah yah, atta atta yah yah."

Wully's cowboy boots, of which he was proud, stood off to one side leaning against each other like a pair of spectators. Wully's bare feet pressed delicately against the red sand, softly and quickly step by step as if kneading the earth. He was wearing his overall pants but he had taken off his shirt and piled it on top of his head like a sort of turban. Irregular black blotches of sweat soaked the seat and beltline of his pants.

The circle Wully danced went round and round like a turning wheel in front of Granddaddy Thanko, who was sitting on the ground with his medicine bundle spread open on his knees. Occasionally Granddaddy Thanko would lift up with both hands some one of the sacred objects from the medicine bundle, and offer it to the four directions and to the sky and the earth, singing all the while.

"Should I hide?" Jana Penna whispered, there being many things considered improper for a woman, especially young and unmarried, to watch. "Naw," Jesiah said. "There ain't anything private about it or Granddaddy Thanko would of put up his sticks. Anyhow, Wully's done his vigil. Just set still and Granddaddy Thanko'll let on he don't see you. This here is his buffalo-calling song. Wully's never learned this one, and he was wanting to."

Granddaddy Thanko stopped singing and gestured to Wully with both hands with a motion as if shooting a basketball. Wully turned to dancing back and forth across the circle in a straight line and then in another straight line that ran crossways to the first, and after the two lines were tramped down enough to be visible he stopped in the center of the circle and turned up his face and sang, "Koogyah koogyah koogyah koogyah, koogyah koogyah koogyah." Then he danced to each of the four ends of the straight lines and each time he stopped and sang, "Koogyah," which was as near as he could pronounce the Kiowa word for grandfather, and sang it out seven times for the seven directions.

The sun had set. The rolling plain of vermilion had dried bone-gray. Afterglow drenched the sky with a wash of luminous green that drained slowly away, while a rising nearly-full moon became luminous at a corresponding rate so there was no darkness, only a shift of colors and shadows. Nighthawks appeared from nowhere, swooping through the tranquil air. Far away, in the direction of the willow-bordered river not visible beyond the horizon, a car's headlights twinkled and vanished like a spark.

Granddaddy Thanko leaned forward and beat with the palms of his hands on the earth, while he sang in his hoarse voice. Wully sang a response in English because he didn't know enough Kiowa words, and then Granddaddy Thanko sang the next line and Wully answered again.

The little kids in the bed of the truck watched with round eyes, in silence. The boys on the roof of the cab watched restlessly, sometimes yawning. In the cab Jana Penna's radio murmured and whispered. Jesiah leaned with crossed arms on the steering wheel and sighed.

"Grandfather buffalo in the east, white in the east, grandfather buffalo in the north, blue in the north," Wully sang, in his melodious young voice that soared up through the night like a marble column. He danced from compass point to compass point, stopping at each to sing. "Grandfather buffalo in the west, yellow in the west, grandfather buffalo in the south, red in the south."

Moonlight coated the land with silver. A tiny owl hung motionless for a moment just above the truck, and then shot noiselessly away.

Granddaddy Thanko arranged his medicine bundle on the ground and got laboriously to his feet and walked around and about, stretching his legs. He passed by the signboard and struck it several times with his fist, booming out the rhythm.

"Grandfather come down to us, grandfather," Wully sang. "Grandfather, we call, grandfather, we call to you, come to us, come to us."

Granddaddy Thanko shouted out to prompt him, and Wully sang on without missing a beat.

"As the littlest calf, with yellow hair. As the growing calf, with dark hair. As the little buffalo, with gray horns. As the young bull buffalo, as the young cow, as the old buffalo bent with age, as all, grandfather with four legs, we call to you. Run to us, run to us, come to us, come to us, down to us, down to us, grandfather come to us."

Granddaddy Thanko came to the driver's side of the truck and stood there for a while watching Wully. Then he spoke to Jesiah but he didn't notice Tapatopa and Jana Penna. Granddaddy Thanko wore his hair long, and part of it plaited into a pigtail that always fell in front of his left shoulder. A spot of red ochre, small and unobtrusive so people wouldn't make remarks, was on the lobe of his right ear. His shirt and his overall jacket were worn turned inside out but this didn't attract much attention either, one side of an old shirt and an old overall jacket being much like the other. All these things were part of the mystic vision by which Granddaddy Thanko lived. He was as fanatical as a medieval saint about living in keeping with his vision. Most people thought he was crazy.

Wully sang:

> From the world unseen to this world that we see
> we see coming into being going into life
> the cow buffalo and the bull buffalo
> we see coming into being into life
> the buffalo calf and the old buffalo
>
> From the world unseen to this world we see
> into the light of day we see
> we see them coming into being
> buffalo
> going into life
> into the light of day.

Granddaddy Thanko beat the rhythm on the truck with his fist until he hurt his hand and stopped to suck a knuckle. He was excited. He said, "Jesiah, look at that boy. Look at him."

"Yes sir I know," Jesiah said.

"He's no ordinary person," Granddaddy Thanko said. "He's different. Not only he feels more. He's different." He cupped his hands around his mouth to bellow instructions at Wully. "You listen to what I tell you, Jesiah. I tell you straight out. He's no ordinary person, that Wully. He's different."

"He is, yes sir," Jesiah said.

"I know pretty well," Granddaddy Thanko said mysteriously.

"I do too," Jesiah said. "Try to get him to carry in water some time, or the like of that."

"No no," Granddaddy Thanko said, in a voice of dictum. "He's no ordinary person."

"Not that he don't want to," Jesiah said. "He just don't remember any longer than you're standing there talking. His head is off somewhere. For chores he's as worthless as tits on a boar."

"You hear what I tell you," Granddaddy Thanko said. "He's nobody ordinary. That boy is somebody not ordinary."

Wully sang in a higher, wilder pitch, "The wind calls you, the grass the grass calls, the river the long river calls, oh wild buffalo." He sang so earnestly that his voice almost broke into a sob at the end of each line. "The earth calls," he sang, thudding his bare feet against the ground. "The earth remembers your footprints the earth remembers."

Granddaddy Thanko shouted out prompting again for the set piece about the tracks of the buffalo.

"In this way came the buffalo tracks," Wully sang, "the buffalo tracks that we see, that everywhere we see, for the tracks of those feet were made by life in this way, life that came in this way."

Granddaddy Thanko slapped his thighs to the beat and stamped a few solemn steps of the dance, shaking with excitement.

"Looka my adaykya," he said to Jesiah. "Look how he's got my adaykya to dance with him."

The dust hanging in the moonlit dance circle shifting with each movement of Wully in the dance and each quiver of the dust made it seem that the medicine bundle was also in motion, rising and falling with the steps of Wully's quick, caressing feet.

"Now take my adaykya for an example," Granddaddy Thanko said. "He don't care for it, Wully don't, because, you know, it can't be the way it ought to be. How many adaykya did there used to be, in the real old time religion? I got just the one, and it's used for everything. Whatever I sing for, I use it, and I got a something for everything in it, all the objects. Wully don't care for that. It ain't the way it ought to be to be true, is what he says. Oh, he's not ordinary."

"He don't mind abusing the truth when it comes to laying out of school," Jesiah said.

"That boy better not be in no school," Granddaddy Thanko said ominously. "You get him right out of there."

"He's out already."

"It's sacred things and thinking that's got to be true for him," Granddaddy Thanko explained. "I expect he couldn't stand it if he was made to do a thinking thing untrue. Like say a word. Like in Kiowa we call toadstools thunder-turds and of course nobody thinks so, but Wully, he wouldn't even say so without saying such as are *called* thunder-turds, he don't even stop to think about it he just says it or such as that whenever he talks Kiowa words or in English either or far as I know in Chickasaw too, but I reckon you know better than I do what I mean anyhow."

Jesiah had completely lost his way in whatever Granddaddy Thanko was trying to explain. He said, "I don't guess I do, but it's all right."

"These things are unknown," Granddaddy Thanko said.

"Ah gap yah, ah gap yah, sahnn sahnn ah gap yah," Wully sang. "Ah gap yah gah tag yah hee . . . ah gap yah gah, ah gap yah gah . . ."

"You would say he was a Ki-kya," Granddaddy Thanko said proudly. He shouted out to Wully to sing now the buffalo bull songs, and Wully sang of how the earth rumbles to the running feet of buffalo bulls and how a buffalo bull sticks his tail straight up in the air when he is angry and then curves it lashing over his back and how terrible is his humped shoulder and how he shakes his mane when he is wounded and enraged and how his curved horns are like knife blades.

"I never knew any person like him all my life," Granddaddy Thanko said. "Ary boy or man either. Why, he could do anything, you know, I mean, in the old time religion."

Wully's voice, singing, ululated like a leaping brook.

"Just listen to that there," Granddaddy Thanko said, in such admiration that he wept, and had to wipe his eyes with the back of his hand and bend over and blow his nose with a thumb to one side and then the other.

"Buffalo, buffalo, let them see," sang Wully's clarion voice. "Buffalo, buffalo, wild buffalo, come to us come to us, let us see."

"You are still fixing to go to Dallas Texas," Granddaddy Thanko said suddenly to Jesiah. Jesiah had gotten so interested in listening to Wully that he didn't understand, and so he didn't answer. "You know best what you want to do," Granddaddy Thanko said.

He sounded truculent. Jesiah said in bewilderment, "What I want to do about what?"

"About going away from here. Away from here he will be no good at all."

Jesiah said in despair, "Oh, hellsfire."

"You know best," Granddaddy Thanko said humbly.

"I don't want to argue with you or nobody, Granddaddy Thanko. Wully's big enough. He can do whatever he wants to. But he don't want to stay here by his ownself."

"He ought to stay here, though. You believe me, Jesiah. But he feels too much about the rest of you."

"Listen, I don't want to argue about it," Jesiah said, gently pounding the steering wheel for emphasis, unconsciously in the same rhythm as the beat of Wully's dance.

"Now the little calf is born, filled with life and motion," Wully sang, correctly weaving in the final verse of the song of the buffalo tracks. "Born filled with life and motion, born the newborn yellow calf standing on its feet and walks, leaving tracks, leaving footprints, buffalo, buffalo, leaving tracks."

"Away from here all his power will be gone," Granddaddy Thanko said. "In a city it will all be shut up in squares and gone."

Jesiah turned in exasperation to face him through the open cab window and said, "What the hell are you doing trying to make an argument?"

"Now on the road of the people, now on the road of the nation," Wully sang, dancing along one of the straight lines. "Let the nation see the road, buffalo buffalo let them see."

"Maybe he'll just go crazy and die," Granddaddy Thanko said, his eyes glittering. Jesiah was shocked, and Granddaddy Thanko hurriedly raised both hands as if in prayer. "You know I don't want but only good for him. And you too, Jesiah. Now don't say nothing, Jesiah. You're getting mad, so don't say nothing."

Something loomed up near the truck and then whirled and bucked and trotted away down the hillside, startling the little kids in the back of the truck so that one of them cried for a minute. Jesiah half-opened the door of the cab and looked away down the hill. He said, "Somebody's old cow. I thought at first it was a buffalo."

"Maybe so," Granddaddy Thanko said. He was standing extraordinarily tall and straight in the silver moonlight and looked bewitched, like a kingly knight in shining armor still dazzled at being suddenly materialized.

"My grandfather the buffalo," Wully sang, really singing now in a prayer. "Sing welcome my grandfather, into the visible world, my grandfather, into this visible world, grandfather the buffalo."

"Maybe you Chickasaw people just don't feel all these things so much," Granddaddy Thanko said boldly.

Jesiah, closing the cab door, leaned out and said, "You better take that back."

"I take it back, Jesiah," Granddaddy Thanko said equably.

"You're going to end up making me get mad."

"All right, Jesiah. But what did I say so terrible? Different people can need all kinds of different things, that's all I said. All right, Jesiah. I'll let up on it."

"I hope to holler you will," Jesiah said.

"Into the visible world come along," sang Wully's voice, neither breaking nor out of breath but as easily and warmly as if by no effort at all, and with a note of impetus that stepped up line by line as steadily as walking up a flight of stairs. "Come forth come forth appearing, appearing in this world we see, my grandfather the buffalo, buffalo buffalo let us see."

The biggest boy, Henry, hung over the edge of the roof and said, "Look, Dad, Wully's called one."

Jesiah stuck his head out of the window of the cab and looked back and saw a buffalo standing no more than six or eight feet behind Granddaddy Thanko. It was a giant buffalo, its hump hunching up higher than Granddaddy Thanko's head. Moonlight sprin-

kled its forelock and mane with straws of silver and made the buffalo's eyes look white and blind, so that the buffalo, standing so still,
had the appearance of a statue. It was enormous, it was half again
bigger than any horse or cow Jesiah had ever seen. Then it moved
its lower jaw, that had a beard hanging down, its lower jaw moved
from side to side in a placid chewing motion.

"Granddaddy Thanko," Jesiah said, "there's a big buffalo right
behind you."

"I been having my eyes on another one across," Granddaddy
Thanko said, without turning around.

A little way beyond the other side of the dance circle, beyond the
hanging veil of silver dust, a shadow moved, looking as big as if the
billboard was walking, and a buffalo there ambled part way around
the circle of Wully's dancing and strolled off down hill, switching its
tail and rolling its hipbones and hind legs with immense stateliness.

"Back to us now in this world on your road, you come again to us
now in this world on your road, buffalo father in the world we can
see, buffalo cow in this world on your road, buffalo calf look and
see, look and see, look and see," sang Wully, and his dancing body,
flinging silver drops of sweat, pointed and pointed this way and that
way in the cloud of shining dust. "Running with bounds and leaps,
buffalo calf, whirling from side to side, buffalo calf, bounding, turning, running straight, little tiny buffalo, look and see."

Jana Penna said in a whisper, pulling Jesiah's sleeve, "There's
some kind of things moving around all over the flats out there. It
must be more of them. Can you tell?"

Wully sang exultantly:

> Buffalo bull, great and tall,
> Come here, come here, come this way
>
> Buffalo cow, mother, mother
> Buffalo calf, little one, yellow one
> Come here, come here, come this way
> See them, hear them, hear their voices
> Come here, come here, come this way.

The rolling plain in the moonlight was stirring with motion as
far as the eye could see, and the sound of the stirring was audible in
the night, and the sound of lowing, and the distant bellow of a bull
and bleat of a calf.

"It's little bunches of buffalo all over everywhere," Jesiah said.

The great buffalo behind Granddaddy Thanko wandered away,
but now there were other buffalo near enough to the hilltop to be
in plain sight in the moonlight, not far from the truck and the cir-

cle of Wully's dance, bringing a strong dusty smell and a rustling undercurrent of sound, like a hundred thousand restless sleepers turning and muttering just beneath the grass.

Wully left the straight lines and went back to dancing around the circle, stopping at each compass point to cup his hands around his mouth and sing peal on peal at the top of his voice, "See them coming, this way that way, see them coming everywhere, see them, hear them, hear their voices, buffalo buffalo seven directions, buffalo buffalo everywhere."

There was a crack like a rifle shot and some of the buffalo jumped and ran in a rapid trot or gallop a little way, the quick bursts of their running beating the earth like practice flourishes of drums. The crack came from the signboard, swaying as a buffalo scratched himself by rubbing against it. A young bull running and bucking banged the signboard with a tinny crash and the signboard toppled and collapsed with a violent metallic clang, and a few more buffalo leapt and ran for an instant, accelerating the drum beats.

One of the little kids in the back of the truck began to laugh. From the top of the cab Henry said, "Boy, there must be a million of them." The silver of the rolling plain was by now dissolved under the black sea of moving buffalo.

"They all look like they're going the same way," Jesiah said. "I would say they're coming up from the North Fork."

"What they're doing is they're migrating," Henry said. "Ain't that so, Granddaddy Thanko?"

"Maybe," Granddaddy Thanko said.

Wully was dancing in one spot in the center of the circle. His exalted voice sang,

> See them, hear them, see them moving
> Hear the bulls they run like thunder
> See the dust like smoke above them
> See them hear them see them coming
> Buffalo buffalo everywhere.

Far, far out across the plain that vibrated with movement a slender white wand shined out and contracted and stretched. There was the faint floating echo of a distant blaring automobile horn. The white wand settled into tiny distant headlights, and the horn sounded again and again.

"That's that car we saw coming from the bridge," Jesiah said. "It's run into them."

"Koogyah koogyah koogyah koogyah, koogyah koogyah koogyah," Wully chanted. "Touch again buffalo touch again, world again buf-

falo world again, life again buffalo life again, buffalo buffalo everywhere."

The faraway automobile horn, shrilling incessantly, raised a
wind that swept in a gust over the land, as if all the restless sleepers
were springing to their feet to join Wully in the thudding rhythm
of his dance. Individual buffaloes near enough down the hillside to
be seen ran now and then like bouncing tumbleweeds until they
were stopped by running into their neighbors. The wind came
again, with a sound like the resonance inside an immense bass
drum, a sound that rumbled resonating on and on, until the earth
began to shiver gently to it, and the stanchions in the bed of the
pickup truck began to rattle. The wind was the sound of the buffalo
starting to run. They were trotting, those that could be seen down
the hillside were trotting at a quick trot, their heads unusually high
or unusually low, as if tasting the ground or tasting the air above. A
bawling calf ran headlong down the hill and was absorbed in the
black crowd of the bands, now moving so close togther they formed
one single and seemingly endless herd.

The wind exploded in the cyclone roar of the buffalo stampeding,
a roar that came like a long fast train from far out across the rolling
plains. They streamed past the foot of the hill in a desperate rush,
running at a panicked rocking gallop, tails like flagstaffs in the air.
The stanchions in the pickup rattled to the shaking earth with the
regularity of a motor. Dust blurred the moon and thickened the air
and coated faces and hair and hands, but the original dusty smell of
the buffalo was replaced by a still stronger bitter smell, the sour
urine-like smell of fear. All the expanse of land below the hill
flowed with their race to escape.

The time of their going may have been five minutes or may have
been an hour. For what seemed a long time afterward the world re-
verberated to the thundering chorus of their running. There was no
further sign of the horn or headlights of the distant car out on the
rolling plain.

A faint trembling still clung to the earth when Wully walked
over to the truck from his dance circle. He was carrying his boots
and his shirt. His body was covered with sweat that in the moonlight looked like drops of mercury rolling on his skin, his skin so
streaked with sweat-caked dust that it looked painted.

Granddaddy Thanko took out a leaf of tobacco and chewed it
and then came to Wully and gave him some of the juice of the tobacco in his nose, in each nostril, and took off his inside-out overall
jacket and put it around Wully's shoulders. Then he reached
through the window of the cab and shook Jesiah's hand. Then he
walked over to the dance circle and got his medicine bundle.

"I ought to go home and get in bed, I guess," Wully said. His teeth were chattering. He opened the door of the cab and said, "Hi, Jana Penna. I didn't know you were here."

"We can all crowd in," Jesiah said. "Granddaddy Thanko too."

"Jana and I can get in back," Wully said.

"No, ride up here. But tell those boys to get off the roof." Jesiah looked inside the coats at Tapatopa and saw the old man's eyes alight. Some time he was going to die in there, and no one would know unless they looked to see. Jesiah felt a great regard for Tapatopa, who was in fact not his father-in-law as everyone thought but had been his first wife's first husband's grandfather. He wished Tapatopa would shake hands with him as Granddaddy Thanko had done, but Tapatopa kept his hands buried in his coats.

They all piled into the cab, Wully still shivering although wrapped in Granddaddy Thanko's jacket and nearly buried under both Jana Penna and Granddaddy Thanko, and Jesiah drove down the hill and within the first hundred yards a skunk and coyote, looking dazed, ran across their headlights, the coyote's tail appearing to be blown to one side as he loped along, although since the stampede there wasn't any noticeable wind. Horny Toad Highway and even stretches of the county road were chewed up from the hooves of the buffalo and mired with their droppings. Jesiah had to motor along in creep low for miles.

Before they got home, a news bulletin on Jana Penna's radio reported an earthquake evidently centered in far western Oklahoma or northeastern New Mexico, and also reported that a hysterical refugee from a flattened oil camp was claiming it hadn't been any earthquake at all but a stampede of buffalo. The radio announcer was still making jokes about that when Tapatopa at last risked a hand outside his coats and got hold of Jana Penna's radio and turned on some rhythm and blues.

Questions For Study, Discussion, and Writing

1. ATTITUDES AND INTERPRETATIONS

WEBB: *The American Frontier Concept.* What are Webb's definitions of *frontier, boundary,* and *border?* Are his definitions determined by elements of permanence or of conflict? Considering both early adventurers and later settlers, was the westward movement a search for material advantage, such as money from the fur trade or free land, or a kind of spiritual freedom? Was the umbilical cord to the East ever severed? If you think there is a real difference between East and West, cite examples in personality or custom to support your argument. What does Webb consider the significance of Turner's thesis on the study of history? Since the American frontier was unique in many ways, why does Webb believe the American frontier concept should be applied to modern European civilization?

TURNER: *The Frontier in American History.* What effect does Turner believe the constantly moving frontier has on the basic American character? Why does Turner say the first frontier was a European one? List the natural boundary lines which Turner says were frontiers of different periods in American history. How important is the role played by agriculture in the transition from virgin land to manufacturing area?

CRÈVECOEUR: *What Is an American?* Must Crèvecoeur's statements be interpreted in light of the fact that he was a Tory and left the colony rather than take part in the war? Does this fact invalidate his observations and interpretations? Do you agree with Crèvecoeur's implication that a European emigrant had no ties to the country where he had lacked material advantage? In your opinion, does he give a factual description of the "last inhabited districts" or is it colored by his aristocratic fastidiousness?

WISTER: Preface to *The Virginian.* How important to a culture is the serious novelist who recreates a vanished time? As he is read by infinitely more people than is the historian, may he not have a greater impact in shaping the American mind? Is Wister's romanticism any less acceptable than a scholar's selecting facts to prove his thesis?

WHITMAN: *Pioneers! O Pioneers!* Whitman's poem reflects great optimism. Why? A pioneer could hardly survive on optimism alone, but could he survive without it? Consider the elements of personality required by a man who could adapt to an unknown and hostile environment. Do you think of *pioneers* as those who accepted the challenge to go to the frontier—or only as those who survived? Does the term connote success?

FROST: *The Gift Outright.* Why couldn't a colonial *belong* to the land. What is Frost's point about the reciprocal nature of the relationship? Why does Frost say "many deeds of war"? When was the change accomplished so that we "found salvation in surrender"? Has the land "vaguely realizing westward" been "realized"? Though the poet gives clues to the past, is it possible that the surrender and fulfilment are still to come? Does his "we" include all Americans, or only those with whom he can communicate through his poem?

2. THE FORESTS

BRADFORD: From *The History of the Plymouth Plantation.* Does this selection tend to support Turner's statement that the first frontier was a European one? Would you say these men are still Englishmen—or does their very activity in dealing with the frontier make them Americans? When a scouting party finds a store of "Indian corn" and beans and carries off what it wants, Bradford notes this as a special providence of God to prevent starvation. Are the action and the pious justification typical of most subsequent encounters between white men and Indians? These settlers have little fear of the Indians. Why? Although they had been scouting in the area over a month, the Pilgrims settled in a location much inferior to that of the colony eventually founded at Boston. Does this result seem typical of many frontier episodes, ruled by restlessness, often lacking in common sense? Are the two qualities mutually exclusive?

BROWN: *Escape from the Cave.* It is customary to compare Brown's writing to that of Edgar Allan Poe. Judging from this selection, what similarities can you find? Though Brown's scene and incidents are strongly American, is his work not merely the transplanting of the English melodrama to a different setting? In spite of the melodramatic events and miraculous deliveries, is the author successful in making you "feel" this experience? Is sharing the protagonist's emotion a vital factor in all frontier literature?

HAWTHORNE: *Roger Malvin's Burial.* In many of his stories Hawthorne uses the forest as a dual symbol—the source of the riches of nature and of spiritual life, and a malignant influence. This story has elements of both. Which do you think predominates? (Reuben's "sin" is not abandoning Roger Malvin, but is rather his concealment of the true facts. The concealment is surrounded by a social situation, and so is his deterioration as his secret sin works on him. It is in the forest that he "expiates" his sin. Comment on these statements.)

IRVING: *The Legend of Sleepy Hollow*. This may be the first literary sketch of note presenting the individual who later became exaggerated into the "backwoods boaster," of which Davy Crockett may be the best known example. Can you think of others? What elements of this character are found in the conventional Western hero? What elements are shown here but absent in the Western hero?

COOPER: *The Death of the Trapper*. Note that Cooper provides for the old trapper two spiritual sons who are both aristocrats of sorts. Do you think Cooper is merely following earlier literary models, or is there deeper meaning to the aristocratic symbols? What "heroic" qualities do you see in this dying old man? Which elements of the scene follow older tradition, and which foreshadow the emerging literature of the frontier? Discuss the elements that are blended in the trapper—individual independence and obedience to higher laws. Are they essential to survival on the frontier? What other qualities are essential? This famous scene still has both starkness and impact. How do you account for this, in view of Cooper's ponderous verbiage?

RICHTER: *It Came a Tuesday*. Note that the "hero" here is female. Is Sayward a symbol of "Momism"? something else? List the actions that indicate Sayward's strength to meet the challenge of the frontier. Will Portius' best qualities emerge before civilization has overtaken the area? How does the author avoid making Portius a purely comic character? How does he avoid making Sayward overwhelmingly virtuous and dominating? This is the first passage in this anthology in which some of the dialogue is in dialect. Does dialect help in some ways and hinder in others?

ROBERTS: *Diony's Vision*. Like the previous selection, this narrative is from a woman's point of view. Compare Diony to Sayward— how are they alike and how are they different? How does the narration differ? What admirable female characters can you think of in other frontier literature? How do they resemble Diony? How do they differ from her?

3. THE MIDWESTERN FRONTIER

MASTERS: *Harry Wilmans* and *John Wasson*. Contemplate the quiet acceptance of John Wasson and compare it to the outrage and disgust of Harry Wilmans. Is there greater tragedy in a mature man separated from his family and enduring hardships for years, or in the disgust of a young man at physical conditions and the loss of his idealism? What significant differences may be found in the identification of the two wars involved? Wasson is obviously a pioneer, but to what extent is Wilmans a pioneer? Comment on the values of "flag" in both poems.

GARLAND: *Under the Lion's Paw.* Remembering that the money-lender is a local citizen, how do you account for his difference from the men who remain farmers, who seem universally kind and generous? Is Garland stereotyping both, or only presenting varieties of men from a similar background? Does Garland make you feel a terrible tragedy is occurring, or only that Council and Haskins should have foreseen that Butler would act precisely as he did? Does Garland's style get in the way of his story, or does it add to the background? What is the role of dialect, in conversation or narration, in stories about people who do not, in fact, use standard speech? When is it valuable and when merely cumbersome?

MORRIS: *Scanlon.* Does the reader feel the past was more admirable than the present, when the description involves a senile man, and the fragments of the past do not seem remarkable? What effect is created by the fact that representatives of the modern generation seem lacking in identity of any sort, whereas the old man, senile or not, seems to be "a character"? Is the clarity of each single fragment responsible for the total impact of the passage? How are seemingly unconnected memories related?

CATHER: *My Ántonia.* "We agreed that no one who had not grown up in a little prairie town could know anything about it." To what extent do you accept this statement? In these selections and in the one by Wright Morris, what dominates your recognition—space? sensations? abstract ideas? growing awareness common to most children?

ANDERSON: *Departure from Winesburg.* Though George travels toward the West, he is moving from rural to urban surroundings. Does this still involve a "frontier" decision—acceptance of the unknown? optimism in the face of challenge? Was there a time when going west to Chicago was really going to the East? Notice that, though others speak, George says nothing. Is that because the author wants to give the feeling that George is waiting for the life ahead? Is George primarily a character or a technical device? George seems to have no emotional tie to the town or the people—perhaps only to the open land along Trunion Pike, where he goes for his last walk. What is the effect on the story of this emotional flatness? Is the focus on the future typical of frontier motivation?

4. THE MOUNTAINS

FISHER: *The Grizzly and the Buffalo.* What other stories can you think of concerning a man attacked by a grizzly or endangered by stampeding buffalo? Where are they exaggerated? Is this? What can be deduced about the character of a man valorous enough to stand up to a grizzly, but willing to remain among sights and sounds evidently disgusting to him? Is it rare to encounter writing that is both of strong sensory impact and truthful to fact, as is the work of this writer? In reading stories with a strong tang of adventure, is the reader apt to be concerned with fact? Are you personally aware of and disturbed by distortions of fact in stories you read for recreation?

MANFRED: *Survival.* In a way, this is the same old story of heroism —a man bears unbearable pain; a man performs an impossible feat. How is this story different from a romantic adventure? Though the story is told in the third person, we are actually given only the thoughts and sensations of Hugh Glass—it is very close to being a first-person narrative. What would the story gain or lose if this story were told from a third-person-omniscient point of view? From the standard first-person point of view? Though the treatment here is fiction, the story is based on fact. Does this knowledge add to your enjoyment, or is it mere background information?

GUTHRIE: *The Way West.* Fort Laramie has a different impact upon Dick Summers, Lije Evans, and Rebecca Evans. What does this difference have to do with the past, present, and future? To what extent are the attitudes involved simply male and female attitudes toward change and danger? How much of Rebecca's attitude is due to simple fatigue and discomfort? Might a man, town-bred or lacking full health, share most of her reactions?

FERGUSSON: *Virgin Earth.* Did the "peace" of nature play an important part in shaping frontier attitudes, or did exploitation and conflict always dominate frontier society?

WHEELER: *Calamity Jane.* List the elements of character attributed to Calamity Jane. Which elements represent sacred femininity? rough efficiency of the frontier? shock value? This story is an excellent example of "popular literature." Define popular literature. What makes it popular? Identify its reading public. Do readers of popular literature also read "serious" literature? to what extent and why? Does popular literature have any historical, sociological, or political value?

5. THE OLD SOUTHWEST

BIRD: *The Jibbenainosay.* Many frontier stories have characters like Nick of the Woods (the Jibbenainosay). Because of some terrible tragedy they are excused from many social requirements; they are allowed to commit atrocities in revenge; and they are frequently given supernatural or myth-like qualities. Does one atrocity excuse another, morally? Is violence more acceptable on the frontier than elsewhere? more understandable? more forgivable? Describe Roaring Ralph. Compare him with the backwoodsmen in Irving, Richter, Roberts, Longstreet, Thorpe, Twain, and Davis.

LONGSTREET: *The Fight.* Compare the characteristics of the fighters of this selection with those of Brom Bones in Irving's story and with such traditional frontier heroes as Davy Crocket and Mike Fink. How are they alike? How do they differ? Does Longstreet's condemnation of such fights seem sincere, when the story lavishes great detail on physical violence? Does the statement tacked on at the end appear to represent a genuine, if contradictory, afterthought by the author, or could there be another reason for it?

THORPE: *The Big Bear of the Arkansas.* Notice that more than half of this selection is background preparation before the bear is even mentioned. Would the story about the bear be as impressive if told without this framework? What is meant by "he was a creation bar," and "that bar was an unhuntable bar, and he died when his time come"?

TWAIN: *Life on the Mississippi.* Choose a half dozen of the more effective phrases in the story and decide whether they are overstatements or understatements. Would it be possible to tell this "story" in anything but first person? There is really no story, only a series of incidents and impressions. Could it be told from an objective point of view? Does this narrator have more in common with sharpster Tom Sawyer or with naive Huck Finn?

6. THE FAR WEST

LONDON: *All Gold Canyon.* Are you disturbed by "chance"—the finding of the location in the first place? and the murderer's missing a sure shot at the climax? the murderer's falling for such a simple ruse as having the protagonist feign death? the murderer's putting himself in a position to be reversed, when all he need do was shoot the protagonist again to make sure he was dead? Is "adventure" literature always full of chance? How does this story resemble and in what ways is it different from Clark's "The Indian Well"?

CLARK: *The Indian Well.* Discuss the role "Nature" plays in this story—character or setting. What is the effect of describing in low key the arrival of man and burro almost dying for lack of water? Though the story takes place in 1940, is there anything in it which could not have occurred at any other time during the last hundred years? If one goes far enough into nature, might time become time-less? What work or works have you read in which the author tried to obliterate time? In what ways is Jim Suttler sensitive or insensi-tive? What characteristics does he have which are common to all frontier heroes? Define *devotion* and *obsession*. Which does Suttler have?

DAVIS: *Honey in the Horn*. Compare this story with "The Jump-ing Frog" by considering humor, narrative method, point of view, elements of violence beneath the surface, and treatment of detail. Would you agree, from this passage, that the book deserved the Pul-itzer Prize? Discuss what qualities a work of fiction should have to be eligible for a major prize. Do you find elements in this passage that peg the story to the twentieth century, rather than to what we usually consider the pioneer period of the nineteenth century?

TWAIN: *The Jumping Frog*. Compare Simon Wheeler's way of talking with that of Old Man Simmons in *Honey in the Horn*. What similarities and differences do you find in the *content* of the two narratives? Consider whether each narrative would be as effec-tive if delivered in a different style—if Simmons' story were told deadpan, and Wheeler's story were acted out. Define *deadpan* deliv-ery. Is it defined in the story itself? Why is this story a classic?

HARTE: *The Outcasts of Poker Flat*. Twain and Harte knew each other, wrote of the same scenes, and employed humor. Compare this story to the two selections of Twain you read earlier. How do the two authors vary in craftsmanship, over- and under-statement, and sentimentality? Which today seems fresh and which riddled with cliche and stereotype? Discuss Harte's ability to depict scene and scen-ery, and to establish unique characters. How does the author's sen-timentality affect the story he tells of an ill-prepared party destroyed by a winter storm? Do you find Oakhurst a "real" character, as a professional gambler who must have been a sort of parasite on the community? Would the pioneer mining community of the day in which this story was written "believe" this story or not? What does your answer tell you about these frontier people?

NORRIS: *Wheat*. Without knowing what has occurred earlier in the story, do you have sympathy for Behrman in his death scene? Why or why not? Is not his attempt to keep his control and find a way out admirable? How then does the author project his own satis-faction at this fitting end, in such a way that sympathy is, at least in part, denied to a man dying a particularly horrible death? Behrman has been the symbol of capital exploiting the farmers but is now "the biter, bit." Knowing this, do you approve of his suffocation, suspend judgment, or pity him?

WHITMAN: *Facing West from California's Shores*. How do you account for the absence here of the optimism you saw in "Pioneers! O Pioneers"? Is the varying tone accounted for by the fact that in this work the poet's horizons take in the entire globe, whereas in the other the poet's vision was limited in time and space? How else do you account for the differences in the two poems? Why does he say, "I, a child, very old"? Compare this poem to Steinbeck's "The Leader of the People," wherein another old man has reached the shores of California and has asked a similarly unanswerable question. What differences and similarities do you find in the two pieces? To what extent is the poet "pleas'd and joyous"?

7. THE CATTLEMAN'S FRONTIER

JOHNSON: *A Girl Called Bluejay*. To what extent do these three persons reflect their own cultures? To what extent does Sarah Harris span both? Does the ending (suddenly shifting to a point fifty years in the future) lend a special poignancy to this scene, or do you find it distracting? Defend your answer. Does the acute consciousness of a time that is gone lend particular charm to stories of the frontier—or does this device detract from the immediacy, hence the impact and value, of the work? In this case, the reminder of perspective comes at the very end of the story; what would be the effect if it preceded the story? How much stark realism and how much sentimentality or idealism do you find here?

CRANE: *The Blue Hotel*. Does the author shock you at the end of the story with the revelation that Johnny had been cheating at cards? How does the revelation affect your re-appraisal of the Swede? How would it affect each of the remaining characters in the story? Which characters are developed and which are stereotypes? Why does the author prefer stereotypes for certain roles? Crane leaves the impression that he doesn't think too highly of men's actions. Do you think this comes entirely from his feelings about people, or is the attitude influenced by the characters having to act in front of the great Western backdrop?

WISTER: *The Virginian*. Assuming that the Virginian is the prototype of all cowboy heroes, describe the hero by including his physical characteristics, his actions, and his adherence to the Western code. What qualities are, or later become. mainly stereotyped? What individual qualities does the Virginian have? How does the cowboy hero differ from other frontier heroes? When the Virginian first pulls his gun on Trampas, how is this different from the stereotyped confrontation? Is that because the event occurs near the beginning of the story, and the author does not want a real showdown? Discuss elements of realism and of romance in Wister's writing, as shown in this passage. Discuss his style. Would you call him a "quality" or "popular" writer? (Keep in mind the standards of the period in which he wrote, rather than those of the present.) Are Wister's basic premises about the West and the cowboy valid? romantically slanted but basically valid? or pure romance?

SCHAEFER: *Shane.* The first-person point of view generally gives immediacy, but a child's point of view usually ignores motivation and other elements. Why do you think Schaefer decided to tell this story from the point of view of a boy, when so few Western writers do this? Judging from this brief passage, was he successful? A child is often an "unreliable narrator." To what extent do you feel this story is going to be realistic, sentimental, or stereotyped? Do you have any impression of the looming of something symbolic or supernatural? If so, is it due to the boy's point of view?

CUNNINGHAM: *The Tin Star.* The motion picture *High Noon* was based on this story, but the picture had many changes. Discuss whether this story as is would make a good movie in 1947, or in 1969. *High Noon* has become known the world over. A Swedish critic, for example, says this film is the clearest statement of the United States' foreign policy. Are you able to infer political, social, economic, or religious meanings from Western stories and films? Is this story realistic or sentimental? Are the characters stereotypes or originals?

FISHER: *The Trap.* Compare this story with "Incident at Owl Creek Bridge" by Ambrose Bierce. In the latter, the story is almost all fantasy with a brief realistic frame. Here almost all the story is realistic, and the fantasy portion is very short. Which method is more effective? Can you defend the statement that, in spite of Canady's death, this story has a happy ending? Can such a statement be defended except in terms of sentimentality and romanticism? Is Canady a hero, non-hero, or protagonist? Do you want him to get away? Should you be pulling for a cold-blooded murderer? Do you always go with the underdog who is greatly out-numbered?

HAYCOX: *A Day in Town.* Does the low-key narration enhance or diminish the desperation of the antagonist? In spite of terrible external pressures, the individual members of this family show no conflicts involving one another. Is that sentimental or romantic oversimplification? Did you recognize the protagonist's gesture—reaching for tobacco he no longer could afford to carry—before the banker's analysis made it clear to you? Did you analyze this and other subtle clues to character, which made you care intensely what happened to this man, or did you find the story lacking adventure and therefore dull? This story contains no villain, no gunplay, and no Indians. Without any of these, can it be called a "Western"? Explain.

8. MEMORY

BENÉT: *The Ballad of William Sycamore (1790–1871)*. The meter and visual images are notable—what else can be readily extracted from this poem? To what extent does it deal in stereotypes, such as the Alamo and Custer, which even a child should grasp immediately, and to what extent does it deal with something more subtle? If the poem gives you a feeling of pleasure, is it because it triggers recognition and nostalgia? Could someone in Europe unacquainted with the frontier make much out of the poem? Are words like *scion, puncheon,* and *flagons* disconcerting, when otherwise the vocabulary is extremely simple?

STEINBECK: *The Leader of the People*. Does the frame setting—an undramatic farm—provide special poignancy in the view of the past? Do you think Carl Tiflin's aggressive manner reflects disappointment that there was no "great thing" for him to do in his lifetime? Does his apology to the old man reflect recognition of the great thing the old man had done, or is his apology merely attempted recovery of a social and personal blunder? Notice that no "story" of crossing the plains is given, only unrelated details, and even they are few. The image of the old man as leader of a westward movement is given indirectly by the comments of others, and some of the comments are disparaging. Do you think Steinbeck did this to reinforce the idea of the past being already irretrievably lost, or for some other reason? Why do you suppose Steinbeck avoided the obvious device of having the old man relate in dramatic monologue an incident in which he figured heroically?

BRANDON: *The Buffalo Singer*. Is this story a fantasy? If a story is told well enough, can you, for a period of time, accept fantasy as reality? Is there a single character in this story you could call a stereotype? Is the story dominated by the white man's culture, or by Indian values? What are the seven directions? What do you think Brandon's "message" is? What elements of character or culture do you think he is endorsing? At the beginning of the story, the family is about to move from the area, but it is noted that this would be harmful to Wully. Is any change of plans made overtly? Implicitly? Explain the apparent calmness among the people: a willingness to accept; to wait with patience, with understanding.

Suggestions for Further Reading

There was but very little belletristic writing about the frontier by people living on it, for mere survival and existence took most of the hours of a day. Yet wherever and whenever man finds a few minutes, he is apt to spend it in creating an expression of beauty or a definition of living.

Thus Anne Bradstreet came to Massachusetts Bay with the Puritans in 1630 where she was the mother of eight children born on the frontier. She found time to write poetry, some of which described life in those early days, particularly "Some Verses upon the Burning of Our House, July 10th, 1666" (1678). Another housewife, Mary Rowlandson, created an account of her capture by the Indians: *A True History of the Captivity and Restoration of Mrs. Mary Rowlandson* (1682). The most significant nineteenth-century writer of life in the Massachusetts Bay Colony was, of course, Nathaniel Hawthorne. He wrote many relevant short stories like "Young Goodman Brown" (1835), but the importance of his major work, *The Scarlet Letter* (1850), cannot be overestimated. It covers the activities of the Puritans from 1642 to 1649. Interesting twentieth-century works of seventeenth-century life are Ernest Gébler, *The Plymouth Adventure: A Chronicle Novel of the Voyage of the Mayflower* (1950), and Ester Forbes, *Paradise* (1937), a fictional account of life in the colony at Canaan.

James Fenimore Cooper told the story of the westward-moving frontier in the five novels of the Leatherstocking Tales, in the following order: *The Deerslayer* (1841), *The Last of the Mohicans* (1826), *The Pathfinder* (1840), *The Pioneers* (1823), and *The Prairie* (1827). The subtitles of a selected list of novels of William Gilmore Simms indicate the localities: *Guys Rivers, A Tale of Georgia* (1834), *Border Beagles: a Tale of Mississippi* (1840), *Beauchampe: or the Ken-*

384

tucky Tragedy (1842), and *Charlemont: or the Pride of the Village, A Tale of Kentucky* (1856). Other novels of the era are James Boyd, *Drums* (1925)—North Carolina in pioneer days; Walter D. Edmonds, *Drums Along the Mohawk* (1936)—life in upper New York State; Kenneth Roberts, *Northwest Passage* (1937)—life with Rogers' Rangers; and two novels by Hervey Allen—the people and the forests of Pennsylvania in the eighteenth century: *The Forest and the Fort* (1943) and *Bedford Village* (1944).

The frontier from the Atlantic to the Mississippi was described in part by Henry Wadsworth Longfellow in his famous poem *Evangeline* (1847); Mark Twain's *Huckleberry Finn* (1884) is the supreme work of life on the Mississippi; Edna Ferber wrote of the wild time of the opening of the Oklahoma Strip, *Cimarron* (1930); one of Zane Grey's popular novels, The *U. P. Trail*, dealt with the first transcontinental railway.

The supreme novelist of the nineteenth-century Midwest and Southwest was Willa Cather, whose beautifully written work includes the following: *O Pioneers* (1913), *The Song of The Lark* (1915), *My Antonia* (1918), *The Lost Lady* (1923), *The Professor's House* (1925), and *Death Comes for the Archbishop* (1927). Life among the Navajo Indians is classically presented in *Laughing Boy* (1929) by Oliver La Farge (Hazard Perry); for a fictional treatment of the Pueblo Indians, one could hardly find a more charming work than Frank Waters, *The Man Who Killed the Deer* (1942). Perhaps today's best fiction writer concerned with the influence of the frontier on modern life is Wright Morris; for him the character of the plains frontier conditions what he sees and writes about in such novels as *Ceremony in Lone Tree* (1960).

For popular fictional accounts of the frontier, one can turn to the hundreds of dime novelists of the nineteenth century; names that come readily to mind are Edward S. Ellis, Edward L. Wheeler, T. C. Harbaugh, Prentiss Ingraham, Ned Buntline (E. C. Z. Judson), A. J. Duganne, and Philip S. Warne. The twentieth century has produced thousands of Western novels and stories by such popular writers as Owen Wister, Zane Grey, Max Brand (Frederick Faust), and Ernest Haycox.

The principal frontier historians have been Frederick Jackson Turner, "The Significance of the Frontier in American History" (1893); Walter Prescott Webb, *The American Frontier Concept* (1952); and Ray Allen Billington, *America's Frontier Heritage* (1966). Two prominent critics of the literature of the frontier are Henry Nash Smith, *Virgin Land* (1950), and Leslie Fiedler, *The Return of the Vanishing American* (1968).

Notes on the Authors

SHERWOOD ANDERSON (1876–1941): After spending much of his life as a businessman, Sherwood Anderson fought his way out of a little Ohio town into the big city where he could become a writer. With a limited amount of formal education, but with an almost perverse determination, he turned his struggles and yearnings—which he had experienced in the late-nineteeth-century frontier of the Middle West—into art. *Windy McPherson's Son* (1916) and *Marching Men* (1917) were sprawling novels that did not sustain the original excitement they created. In *Winesburg, Ohio* (1919), however, Anderson captured the bitterness, loneliness, and longing which had been the core of his life until middle age.

STEPHEN VINCENT BENÉT (1898–1943): A winner of a Pulitzer Prize in 1929, Stephen Vincent Benét is best known for his epic poem *John Brown's Body* (1928). Benét wrote poems, novels, short stories, and librettos for folk opera; but the work that captured the spirit of a great American struggle appealed to a popular audience.

ROBERT MONTGOMERY BIRD (1806–1854): In addition to being a novelist and dramatist, Robert Montgomery Bird was also a doctor who once taught at the Pennsylvania Medical College. *The Gladiator* (1831) was his most popular play, and *Nick of the Woods; or, The Jibbenainosay* (1837) was his best novel.

WILLIAM BRADFORD (1590–1657): After coming to America on the *Mayflower* in 1620, William Bradford was elected governor of the Plymouth Colony in 1621. Thereafter he served as governor or assistant governor until 1656, the year before his death. He began writing his history of the Plymouth Plantation in about 1630, and added to it as late as 1651. Although perhaps it was never intended for publication, both its content and its style have assured it a secure place in American history and literature.

WILLIAM BRANDON (1914–   ): A novelist and historian, William Brandon is also the author of some 300 short stories. His *The American Heritage*

Book of Indians (1961) is unquestionably the most complete story told of the American Indians. In its "Introduction," President John F. Kennedy wrote, "Before we can set out on the road to success, we have to know where we are going, and before we can know that we must determine where we have been in the past."

CHARLES BROCKDEN BROWN (1771–1810): A Philadelphia lawyer and New York businessman, Charles Brockden Brown introducted a new note into American literature. Though his writing was derivative, heavily influenced by the work of William Godwin and the horror stories of Mrs. Radcliffe, it was original in giving Gothic romances American settings. In novels like *Edgar Huntly* (1799), Brown moved the brooding horror of the Gothic novel to the darkness of an American forest menaced by fierce panthers and even fiercer savages.

WILLA CATHER (1873–1947): A distinguished American novelist, Willa Cather wrote some of the most beautiful prose any American has produced. Her first novel, *Alexander's Bridge* (1912), was in the Henry James tradition. With *O Pioneers!* (1913) and *The Song of the Lark* (1915) she began to write about the plains country she knew so well.

WALTER VAN TILBURG CLARK: (1909–) One of America's most challenging writers, Walter Van Tilburg Clark moved from Maine to Nevada, where he grew up and went to the University. His life has been divided between teaching and writing, and he is best known to the public by such works as *The Ox-Bow Incident* (1940) and *The Track of the Cat* (1949). Few contemporary writers are his equal in vividly and artistically portraying the West.

JAMES FENIMORE COOPER (1787–1851): Although James Fenimore Cooper was well known in his own time as a social critic, he achieved lasting worldwide fame as the author of a series of novels called "Leather-Stocking Tales." He was prolific, writing not only frontier sagas but also sea stories, histories, and books of social criticism. Cooper's most famous creation was the hero of the Leather-Stocking Tales, known in different novels as Natty Bumppo, Deerslayer, Hawkeye, Pathfinder, Leather-Stocking, or simply "the trapper." Beginning his career as a young woodsman during the French and Indian wars, this hero is the archetypal frontier and "Western" hero, possessed of special skills and simple moral qualities that have characterized thousands of successors.

STEPHEN CRANE (1871–1900): An Eastern writer who went West for some of his material, Stephen Crane produced memorable literary works. *Maggie: A Girl of the Streets* (1893) was one of America's first truly naturalistic novels, and *The Red Badge of Courage* (1895)—a study of the fine line between heroism and cowardice—has become a minor classic.

Michel-Guillaume Jean de Crèvecoeur (1735–1813):   A French traveler, diplomat, and writer, Crèvecoeur journeyed extensively in Canada and the other English colonies, and he explored much of the Great Lakes region. He married and settled in America until the Revolution, when he returned to France. He later served as French consul to New York from 1782 to 1790. His *Letters from an American Farmer* (1782) was written before the Revolution, and the government he praised was British (Crèvecoeur was a Loyalist).

John M. Cunningham (1915–   ):   A man who has written some excellent Western novels—*Starfall* (1960), for example—John Cunningham is best known as the author of the short story "The Tin Star" (first published in Collier's) because it was made into the famous film *High Noon*.

H. L. Davis (1896–   ):   A Pulitzer Prize winner who wrote in the Mark Twain tradition, H. L. Davis is best known for his novel *Honey in the Horn* (1935). The novel deals with a special survival of the frontier in Oregon in the twentieth century.

Harvey Fergusson (1890–   ):   A veteran writer, Harvey Fergusson has written many fine novels laid on America's frontiers. *Blood of the Conquerors* (1921) dealt with original Spanish landowners, and *Wolf Song* (1927) treated the period of Anglo-Saxon settlement in the Southwest.

Clay Fisher (1912–   ):   A "master" of the Western, Clay Fisher (Henry W. Allen) has written such excellent novels as *From Where the Sun Now Stands* (1959), *The Gates of the Mountains* (1962), and *Mackenna's Gold* (1963). From the Western Writers of America, he has won four Spur Awards and the Levi Strauss Golden Saddleman Award. His recent novel *One More River to Cross* (1967) is a fictional account of a famous Negro cowboy, Isom Dart of Brown's Hole.

Vardis Fisher (1895–   ):   An Idaho author, Vardis Fisher has spent forty years writing novels of man's development and his dramatic conflicts with various aspects of nature. He was learning his trade of writing as early as the 1920's while teaching English at the University of Utah. His subjects include western farmers, mountain men, Mormons, and other frontiersmen. *Mountain Man* (1965) is one of his recent novels.

Robert Frost (1874–1963):   Born in San Francisco, Robert Frost went as a boy with his parents to the New England of his ancestors. As a young man he married and settled on a farm in West Derry, New Hampshire. Most of the poems in his first volume, *A Boy's Will* (1913), were written there. The farm became an extended metaphor for many of his poems, and he became known as a New England poet. By January 20, 1961, when he read his poem "The Gift Outright" at the inauguration of John F. Kennedy as President of the United States, he had become a poet of all America.

HAMLIN GARLAND (1860–1940): While growing up in Wisconsin, Hamlin Garland saw his mother and father age under the hardship of Midwestern frontier life. While his father followed an illusory frontier dream that led him westward to Iowa and then to South Dakota, Garland went east to Boston. But he returned again and again to the Middle West, and it was the hardships suffered by the farmers that he chose to write about. In the autobiographical *A Son of the Middle Border* (1917) and *A Daughter of the Middle Border* (1921), which won a Pulitzer Prize, he told how the frontier had worn down his father and mother.

A. B. GUTHRIE (1901–): After setting out in *The Big Sky* (1947) to cover in fiction the westward movement during the nineteenth century, A. B. Guthrie continued with *The Way West* (1949) and *These Thousand Hills* (1956).

BRET HARTE (1836–1902): A writer who went from New York to California during the time of the Mother Lode, Bret Harte settled in San Francisco, eventually to found and edit *Overland Monthly*. Under Harte's guidance and with his contributions, the *Overland Monthly* soon became famous throughout the country for its stories of local color and Western sentimentality.

NATHANIEL HAWTHORNE (1804–1864): One of America's great prose artists, Nathaniel Hawthorne served a long self-imposed apprenticeship. After the failure of his youthful novel *Fanshawe* (1828), he set about to learn his trade by working with the short story. He continued in this genre, experimenting with a great variety of fictional techniques, for more than twenty years. The result of his efforts was evident in his second novel, *The Scarlet Letter* (1850).

ERNEST HAYCOX (1899–1950): One of the most talented of all Western story writers, Ernest Haycox began with *Free Grass* (1929). That story of the Texas country, a cowboy, and a herd of cattle set the tone for the many Westerns that were to follow. Along the way there were but few aficionados who missed such novels as *Alder Gulch* (1942), *Bugles in the Afternoon* (1944), and *Canyon Passage* (1945).

WASHINGTON IRVING (1783–1859): The first American to be recognized in Europe as a man of letters, Washington Irving was born in New York City, where he grew up and where he soon began to enjoy society. Although he was known as a young-man-about-town, he took several long trips up the Hudson River, going as far as Montreal and Quebec. Irving preferred the past, which he generally found in Europe and wrote about in such works as *Conquest of Granada* (1829) and *The Alhambra* (1832). When he dealt with the American scene he also used the past, as in *Knickerbocker's History* (1809), in which he described the founding of New York.

DOROTHY JOHNSON (1905–): One whose writing has shown much concern for the struggle for land between the Indian and the white settler, Dorothy Johnson is thought by many to be one of the finest writers of the West. She has consistently proved that the frontier involved real women, women as strong as the men. From her home in Montana she wrote, "Man's efforts—and sometimes his failure—to adapt to his environment fascinate me. I have a theory that most of the white men who peopled the frontier West went there because they did not quite fit back home. They were too rash or violent or ambitious or lazy or poor; they did not match the pattern. But the nineteenth century was a time of freedom for those who did not fit. They could always move westward."

JACK LONDON (1876–1916): Born in San Francisco, Jack London grew up on the Oakland waterfront; he made a precarious living as an oyster pirate, sealer, and vagabond. When he became a writer, at the turn of the century, his work showed the influence of his youthful struggles. London's characters and animals are invariably divided between the weak and the strong. His first collection of stories, *The Son of the Wolf* (1900), shows his concern with violence, brutality, and survival as they are manifested in nature on the frontier.

AUGUSTUS BALDWIN LONGSTREET (1790–1870): A jurist and writer, Augustus Baldwin Longstreet was also the president of four Southern colleges and universities: Emory, Centenary, Mississippi, and South Carolina. His best-known book was *Georgia Scenes, Characters and Incidents* (1835). It contained humorous sketches of the time when the area from Georgia to Mississippi was still a frontier.

FREDERICK F. MANFRED (1912–): One of the best known writers describing the Western frontier, Frederick F. Manfred wrote from 1944 through 1951 under the name of Feike Feikema. But as either Manfred or Feikema, he is now an author to be reckoned with. *Lord Grizzly* (1954) is one of his best books, and it has made a dramatic impression on many thousands of readers who are fascinated by the history of the West.

EDGAR LEE MASTERS (1869–1950): One of the bitterest critics of the unequal struggle between man and his social environment on the Midwestern frontier, Edgar Lee Masters is best remembered for his *Spoon River Anthology* (1915). It includes 246 poems, each an epitaph written in free verse. As people speak from the grave we learn their secrets, secrets they could not express, of course, while alive.

WRIGHT MORRIS (1910–): One of America's foremost novelists, Wright Morris was born in Central City, Nebraska, and writes about the Middle West he inherited. His art is in part his ability to "catch time"—to start it, stop it, reverse it, or slow it down—as if he had his finger on the button of a movie projector. In *The Inhabitants*, he literally matched texts with photographs. Although there are no people in the photographs, one can easily see them as he reads the text: "He was lyin' there. Willie, I said, why the hell ain't you up loafin?"

FRANK NORRIS (1870–1902): The writer who was concerned with man's struggle to stand up against the "Force" of society, Frank Norris began a trilogy which was to tell the story of "Wheat." *The Octopus* (1901), the growing of wheat in California, was the first novel. It was followed by *The Pit* (1903), the manipulation on the exchange in Chicago. The third, which he did not live to write, was to be called *The Wolf*, and he planned to take the wheat, as bread, into European villages where bread was life.

CONRAD RICHTER (1890–1968): After years of careful research into the history of life on the frontier, Conrad Richter wrote several fine novels about the struggles and joys of the pioneers, and his efforts were recognized when his novel *The Town* won the Pulitzer Prize in 1951.

ELIZABETH MADOX ROBERTS (1886–1941): A descendant of pioneers, Elizabeth Madox Roberts was born and reared in the Kentucky about which she wrote with strength and affection. Her first novel, *The Time of Man* (1926), which has since become her most famous, dealt with Kentucky hill dwellers.

JACK SCHAEFER (1907–): A newspaper man who became famous for his novel *Shane* (1949), Jack Schaefer has become one of the foremost writers of Westerns. He once wrote to a friend in Laramie, Wyoming: "Probably if I had been really aware of the constant flood of westerns drugging the market, I would have shied away from that field. But I had for many years been collecting and reading all authentic material on western history I could find."

JOHN STEINBECK (1902–1968): One of America's great writers, John Stein-

beck was awarded the Nobel Prize for literature in 1962. His early stories
of the California farmers were slow in catching attention, and for some
years his first three novels were neglected. With *Tortilla Flat* (1935), however, Steinbeck's *paisanos* brought him into prominence. From then on
throughout the 1930's he published memorable novels: *In Dubious Battle*
(1936), *Of Mice and Men* (1937), and *The Grapes of Wrath* (1939). It
was the latter novel, a Pulitzer Prize winner, which best caught the spirit
of the depression years and showed compassion for the suffering of "little"
people.

THOMAS BANGS THORPE (1815–1878): After coming to Louisiana from
Massachusetts, Thomas Bangs Thorpe became one of the best-known hum-
orists of the Old Southwest. He was a master of the art of telling tall tales;
his "The Big Bear of Arkansas" was first published in *The Spirit of
the Times* in 1841. He later published many collections of humorous tales
and army reminiscences. He was also an editor, artist, and illustrator.

FREDERICK JACKSON TURNER (1861–1932): A Wisconsin-born historian
who taught at the University of Wisconsin and Harvard University, Frederick Jackson Turner was also associated for several years with the Hunt-
ington Library. Although he was never a prolific author, his theories and
interpretations of the American historical experience profoundly influenced
generations of historians.

MARK TWAIN (Samuel Langhorne Clemens) (1835–1910): Born in Florida, Missouri, and reared in Hannibal, Samuel Clemens became a printer,
a steamboat pilot, and a journalist. After he adopted the pseudonym Mark
Twain in 1862, he began writing a series of books that have become classics
of American literature. According to Ernest Hemingway, *The Adventures
of Huckleberry Finn* (1884) is the source of all modern American fiction;
other critics have considered the book the greatest social document this
country has produced. Yet this one masterpiece is only a small part of the
rich and variegated work of a resourceful and inventive genius.

WALTER PRESCOTT WEBB (1888–1963): A Texas-born author who was
professor of history at the University of Texas, Walter Prescott Webb once
served as president of the American Historical Association. He was a
pioneer in writing the history of the American West, and his books *The
Great Plains* (1931) and *The Great Frontier* (1952) have become classics.

EDWARD L WHEELER (ca. 1854–1885): One of the most popular and prolific of all authors of dime novels, Edward L. Wheeler advertised himself
as a "sensational novelist." He created the character of Deadwood Dick
as well as less well-known heroes like Rosebud Rob and Sierra Sam. Of

the 3,158 dime novels published by Beadle and Adams between 1860 and the end of the nineteenth century, 33 were Deadwood Dick novels. Though Wheeler created one of the most famous of Western heroes, he himself never traveled west of Pennsylvania.

WALT WHITMAN (1819–1892) : America's foremost poet, Walt Whitman spent his first thirty-six years enjoying only indifferent success as a journalist. At the age of thirty-seven he published his now famous *Leaves of Grass* (1855). The first edition of only twelve poems grew eventually into an edition of more than 400. In the first edition, the poet celebrated himself as a unique individual; in later editions, he also celebrated national unity and identity in such poems as "Pioneers! O Pioneers!"

OWEN WISTER (1860–1938): A Pennsylvania lawyer and writer, Owen Wister created the archetypal Western story. His *The Virginian* (1902) has been the inspiration for thousands of "Westerns," some published on pulp paper or smooth, some filmed for motion picture or television audiences. Wister was a Harvard classmate and lifelong friend of Theodore Roosevelt, himself a one-time cattleman, and they shared a great love for the West.